AFTER IMPERIALISM

*The Search for a New Order
in the Far East*
1921–1931

Akira Iriye

Imprint Publications

Chicago

Published by Imprint Publications, Inc., Chicago, Illinois.
Copyright © 1990 by Akira Iriye. All rights reserved.
Printed in the United States of America.

Library of Congress Catalog Number: 90-084056
ISBN 1-879176-00-9

Original edition published in 1965 by Harvard University Press.

PREFACE TO THE NEW EDITION

This book was first published in 1965. At that time few studies of Asian international affairs during the 1920s existed, and, moreover, the decade had not yet been fully explored by historians of American foreign relations. Scattered monographs had been published on Japan's China policy, but hardly any had appeared on Chinese foreign affairs. Students of interwar European diplomacy had been more productive, but few of them, if any, had made use of documents in Asian languages or in Russian.

What I tried to do, then, was to remedy these gaps in the scholarly literature and to contribute to an understanding of the 1920s. Fortunately, archival documents were just then becoming available in the United States and in Japan, and I was also able to obtain access to Chinese material in Taiwan, at least through 1927. For German documents I had to turn to the microfilms of captured archives, and for Russian sources to published collections. Perhaps the most serious gap was in British material, as I was unable to consult documents at the Public Record Office. Even so, I felt I had gained access to a sufficient amount of primary material to enable me to undertake the project. Since then, much more has become available, and various writers have produced impressive studies, some of which will be noted below. But the book shows what was possible even twenty-five years ago, and therefore may be worth republishing as an example of multiarchival history.

There is nothing new, of course, about multiarchival history in Asian, let alone European, historiography. Even before the war Chinese and Japanese diplomatic historians had published works using many languages, and after the war a new generation continued the work. I was especially fortunate in that both from my father (who in 1935 published what may still be a useful study of Chinese-British-Russian relations in the nineteenth century) and my father-in-law (who was a founder of the study of comparative literature in Japan) and from my American mentors (John K. Fairbank and Ernest R. May) I was taught to make use of as many languages as possible as tools of research.

Multiarchivality, however, would mean little unless it produced a significant reinterpretation of the past. What I sought to do in this book was to trace the dynamic of Asian affairs during 1921–1931 as a distinctive aspect of interwar international relations. That is to say, I wanted to treat the 1920s not merely as a prelude to the disasters of the 1930s but in their own terms. The interwar period seemed to me to consist of two more or less distinct phases, separated by the events of 1929–1931, so that it would be wrong to talk of weaknesses and contradictions within the postwar international system encompassing both decades indiscriminately. Whatever validity there might be about treating the "twenty years' crisis" as a whole for European affairs, the situation in Asia, it seemed to me, warranted a different perspective. American diplomacy, too, appeared to have been characterized by contrasting forces before and after the Depression. The book in a sense was intended to demonstrate these points. It developed the notion of "the Washington Conference system," the structure of peace for the Asian-Pacific region defined at the Washington Conference (1921–1922), and analyzed how various countries—the United States, the Soviet Union, Japan, China, and others—related themselves to it, in the process challenging, fortifying, or undermining the system. Neither the concept of the Washington system nor the story of its eventual collapse was original, but the book, I believe, was the first systematic analysis of Asian international affairs in that framework.

In the last twenty-odd years both these perspectives—the distinctiveness of the 1920s and the Washington Conference order—have been subjected to much scholarly debate. In the literature of recent international history, nothing is more striking than the outpouring of impressive monographs on the 1920s. The new generation of historians, writing in the

1970s and the 1980s, has transformed our understanding of that decade so that today few would view it merely as a prelude to the tragic developments of the 1930s. Instead, as Charles Maier notes in *Recasting Bourgeois Europe* (1975), some trends that became noticeable in the 1920s—economic interdependence among capitalist states, the close connection between international economic order and domestic political order, the corporatist approach to problems of industrial and consumer society—would reassert themselves after the Second World War. Without the Depression, these trends might have perpetuated themselves. Few historians would be willing to accept all the implications of such a perspective, but there is little question that recent monographs on European affairs during the 1920s—for example, Walter McDougall, *France's Rhineland Diplomacy* (1978), Steven Shuker, *The End of French Predominance in Europe* (1976), and Jon Jacobson, *Locarno Diplomacy* (1972)—document serious attempts on the part of France, Germany, and Britain to redefine and, to the extent possible, to restabilize international affairs in the wake of the calamitous war.

The role of the United States becomes extremely important in this context, for it was undisputably the principal economic power after 1918. Economic historians (e.g., C. P. Kindleberger, *The World in Depression*, 1973) have for some time been stressing the theme of Britain's decline as the economic hegemon and its replacement by the United States. Paul Kennedy, in *The Rise and Decline of the Great Powers* (1987), notes how the latter, despite its emergence as the new dominant power, failed to play a requisite role in maintaining international order. This is an old view, and while most students of American foreign relations would agree with the broad picture, they have sought to move away from the conventional picture of interwar American isolationism. As Warren Cohen notes in *Empire without Tears* (1987), the United States played crucial roles throughout the 1920s in such issues as disarmament and economic reconstruction, while Emily Rosenberg, in her *Spreading the American Dream* (1982), has had little difficulty in applying her argument about the spread of American liberal developmentalism to the 1920s. The decade, she and others have pointed out, saw a tremendous expansion of American economic and cultural influence abroad, which amounted to the Americanization of the world. The theme is developed with respect to Europe in an admirable study by Frank Costigliola, *Awkward Dominion* (1984). Because America's economic role was of fundamental importance, both in the prosperity decade of the 1920s and in the world economic crisis that came after 1929, it is not surprising that some of the best monographs have analyzed the economic aspects of American foreign relations. Following the pioneering work by Joan Hoff Wilson, *American Business and Foreign Policy* (1973), others have sought to reexamine the relationship between business and government, and in the process developed the concept of corporatism. Michael Hogan's *Informal Entente* (1977) and Burton Kaufman's *Efficiency and Expansion* (1974) are examples. Melvin Leffler's *The Elusive Quest* (1979), while chronicling the often frustrating story of American-European economic cooperation, broadens our understanding considerably by focusing on activities by bankers and investors who stood somewhere between government officials and private citizens of the countries involved. All these works present the picture of the 1920s as one of active American involvement in international affairs, not so much in the military or political sphere but in all other respects. Thus in a way they are reconfirming Herbert Hoover's perception, as expressed in *American Individualism* (1922), that Americans could best serve themselves, their country, and the world through private initiatives.

What do these reinterpretations mean in terms of post-1918 world history? They would seem to add up to an emphasis on peaceful international relations, or rather on serious attempts that were made to restabilize international order. The 1920s made a significant contribution to man's long quest for peace by emphasizing themes such as economic interdependence, international cooperation, and cultural diffusion. Just because the attempts did not succeed, and were followed by a decade and more of war, aggression, and atrocities, it would be wrong to attribute these crimes to the efforts made in the opposite direction during the preceding decade. In this sense, numerous monographs that have been published on peace movements are particularly important. Books like Charles Chatfield, *For Peace and Justice* (1971) and Charles DeBenedetti, *Origins of the Modern American Peace Movement* (1978) have done much to rescue interwar peace movements from a minor footnote which they tended to occupy in the literature. In the same way, recent studies on the relationship between advanced and dependent areas of the world have contributed to elucidating the nature of international order after the First World War. Earlier the story had tended to be treated as a chapter in the history of imperialism, but that framework has been refined by works like Robert Freeman Smith's *The United States and Revolutionary Nationalism in Mexico* (1972) and William Kamman, *A Search for Stability* (1968), which have traced United States-Latin American relations during the 1920s and stressed the theme of accommodation between the two on the basis of American support for economic development in the Western Hemisphere. The story thus fits into the integrationist view of the decade with an emphasis on interdependence and interpenetration, rather than disorder and conflict.

All these historiographical trends serve to put Asian international affairs in perspective. Books such as Warren Cohen's *The Chinese Connection* (1978) and Russell Buhite's *Nelson T. Johnson and American Policy toward China* (1968) have examined individual Americans who played pivotal roles in Chinese-American relations, while Roger Dingman's *Power in the Pacific* (1976) and Thomas Buckley's *The United States and the Washington Conference* (1970) point to the origins of the relatively stable relationship between the two naval powers across the Pacific. Aspects of British-Japanese relations are studied in some of the essays contained in Ian Nish, ed., *Anglo-Japanese Alienation* (1982), and additional monographs dealing with Japanese-American relations appear in a Japanese volume:

Hosoya Chihiro and Saito Makoto, eds., *Washington taisei to Nichi-Bei kankei* (The Washington Conference system and Japanese-American relations, 1978).

On the whole, these studies serve to integrate Asian affairs into the overall trends in postwar international history. In *After Imperialism,* I developed the theme that the Far East became separated from the rest of the world as an arena in international relations. In view of the literature cited above, I would modify this perspective a little, were I writing the book today. At the same time, I believe the concept of the Washington Conference system will take on fresh importance when it is integrated into our understanding of global developments. For it seems to me that the Washington formula represented an approach to international affairs that was typical of the period; its emphasis on disarmament, international cooperation, economic interdependence, etc., provided a model for other parts of the world in order to reduce tension and eliminate chances of war. In this book I trace how "the spirit of the Washington Conference" ultimately disappeared because of the Soviet challenge, radical Chinese nationalism, and Japanese unilateralism. But the ultimate failure should not, perhaps, lead us to dismiss the attempt itself, for the same ideas and features that informed the Washington system would return after the Second World War. In this sense, as is the case with the study of interwar European affairs, it would seem to be as important today as it was thirty years ago to go back to the 1920s and reappreciate the heroic efforts made in many parts of the world for international order.

I am indebted to Anthony Cheung who almost single-handedly undertook the task of preparing this edition. Without his encouragement, and without the support I have received from my professional colleagues over the last twenty-five years, I would not have felt justified in having my first book reprinted.

Chicago
August 1990   Akira Iriye

PREFACE

The study of diplomatic history in the Far East has reached a stage where meaningful and fresh interpretation can be attempted. Monographs by pioneering scholars and the availability of published and unpublished documents in English, Japanese, German, and to a lesser extent in Chinese and Russian, enable the researcher to develop a framework within which the complex of international relations may be comprehended.

This monograph is an attempt to develop such a framework for the 1920's. I have tried to see in the decade something more than a respite in Japanese aggression, the emergence of Chinese nationalism, or a period of international cooperation, which are themes usually presented by historians. My research has led me to the view that the collapse of the diplomacy of imperialism as a mechanism of power politics, and the consequent search for a new order provide a meaningful context in which the various countries' foreign policies can be analyzed. Since the main purpose of this study is to develop this theme, I have not felt it necessary to recount in detail well known data and episodes. For the sake of clarity and economy of space, I have emphasized Japan and, to a secondary degree, the United States.

John K. Fairbank and Ernest R. May have given their most generous assistance through each stage of the manuscript's preparation. I could not have ventured on such an ambitious topic without their encouragement. James W. Morley has been a constantly inspiring critic of my ideas. Albert M. Craig, Donald H. Fleming, and Benjamin I. Schwartz have read the entire manuscript and given me stylistic and other useful suggestions. Oscar Handlin showed me the way when I was a first-year graduate student, just as Wallace T. MacCaffrey showed me the way when I was a freshman. The Committee on American Far Eastern Policy Studies at Harvard University has generously made time and funds available for me to do research on this book. Officers of the Japanese Foreign Ministry Archives, the Academia Sinica, the National Archives, the Library of Congress, the Harvard, Yale, and Cornell University Libraries, the War History Division of the Japanese Defense Agency, and the Tokyo Institute for Municipal Research have extended their invaluable help as I attacked mountains of unpublished material. Rolland Henderson, Lauro Halstead, and Miss Catharine W. Pierce have given me and my wife what we most needed as we worked on the manuscript: constant and friendly encouragement. Finally, the editorial staffs of the Harvard University Press and the East Asian Research Center have been extremely helpful and efficient during the last stages before the book's publication.

Spring 1965

A. I.

CONTENTS

INTRODUCTION: THE AMERICAN INITIATIVE

The decade of the 1920's has been one of the most difficult periods to evaluate in the history of international relations in the Far East. There are certain signposts: China's unification by the Nationalists; their attack on foreign rights and privileges; the Kuomintang-Communist alliance and rupture; the Nanking incident; and the assassination of Chang Tso-lin. These episodes have been subjects of extensive study, and excellent monographs deal with them. Most often, however, diplomatic historians have interested themselves in uncovering data rather than proposing a systematic method of analysis. When interpretation is attempted, it has often been in terms of relations between two countries, as between China and the Soviet Union, between China and the United States, or between China and Japan. While there are general treatments of the multinational relations in the Far East, no systematic work has been devoted solely to the period between World War I and the Manchurian incident.

One reason for this lack is that there are still thousands of pages of archival materials which remain to be studied. Published documentary collections have tended to neglect the 1920's, often skipping from 1919 to 1931. While State Department documents and private collections of American policy makers have been utilized by historians for over a decade, the rich sources of the Japanese and German foreign ministries have been consulted only sporadically. With these basic data unstudied, historians have hesitated to draw conclusions on the prehistory of the Far Eastern crisis.

Another, even more important, reason is that the 1920's have been overshadowed by the turbulent decades which flanked them. These years have been given meaning only as a transition period. Questions on the 1920's are conditioned by the events of the 1910's

and the 1930's. Since Japanese expansionism reached its climax
in 1918 and then came to a rather abrupt halt, only to be revived
in 1931, historians have sought factors in the twenties which prepared for this revival. Since, in the thirties, neither China nor the
Western powers could effectively combat Japanese aggression, the
questions often asked are: What went wrong in the previous
decade? What might have prevented the crisis in the Far East?

These are legitimate questions; but they are inadequate because they assume that foreign policies are autonomous and con-
tinuous. Japanese expansionism, for instance, is taken as a given
factor, expressing the country's fixed interests and causing other
nations to respond in ways dictated by their own considerations.
Such a view tends to isolate individual nations. International relations are seen simply as a mechanical sum total of isolated national policies. At the same time, it is obvious that no nation has
complete freedom of action. It has only a given number of alternatives, and this range of possible action is often determined by
extranational factors, such as considerations of alliances and ententes, as well as of what are generally regarded as legitimate and
plausible goals of foreign policy. Japanese expansionism, even if
it did exist in the abstract, would take different forms as conditions change in the concepts, practices, and patterns of international relations. Changes in these variables, which constitute
what one may term the framework or system of diplomacy, will
often modify the content and expression of a policy. A country's
foreign policy will be fully understood only when it is related to
such external factors. Only then will it become possible to examine its role in creating an environment, the way its freedom
of action is in turn limited, and its decision whether to continue
to observe the existing rules of the game or to seek an alternative
scheme of international affairs.

This study tries to take these matters into consideration to fill
the gap in our understanding of the 1920's. A radical transformation in the framework of Far Eastern diplomacy took place during World War I. The Washington Conference (1921–1922) was
an expression of the powers' interest in redefining their mutual
relations. Under the American initiative, they took cognizance
of the passing of the old order and tried to bring about a new

era of "economic foreign policy" as a basis of reconciling and promoting their interests. Their attempt was frustrated from the beginning by an active anti-imperialist campaign of Soviet diplomacy, trying to define yet another alternative system of Sino-foreign relations. This is the story of Part One. Between 1922 and 1927 the Soviet Union was the most active agent of change in the Far East, and the Russian-inspired Nationalists successfully conquered half of China. The Peking Tariff Conference, meeting between 1925 and 1926, was the last occasion where the "Washington powers" tried, unsuccessfully, to give concrete content to their definition of a new order. By the time the conference was suspended and the Nationalist Northern Expedition begun, in the summer of 1926, the United States, Britain, and Japan had come to realize the futility of basing their policies on the framework of the Washington Conference.

Japan, in particular, took the boldest steps during the years of the Northern Expedition. Impressed with Soviet initiative and believing the Washington powers uninterested in challenging it in unity, Japan adopted its own policy of unilateral action. It sought a new era of Sino-Japanese coprosperity as a guarantee for protecting Japanese interests in China and Manchuria. The Japanese initiative, treated in Part Two, was frustrated not only because the Nationalists did not share the Japanese view of a new order, but also because of Japan's lack of a clearly defined chain of command. By the end of 1928, when all of China was unified, at least nominally, it had become evident that the Japanese initiative had only encouraged China to turn to other countries, especially the United States, for support.

Part Three carries the story from 1928 to the eve of the Manchurian crisis in 1931. Here the unifying factor was Nationalist China's initiative in bringing treaty-revision negotiations to a successful consummation so that an entirely new order of international relations would arise in the Far East. All countries willingly or unwillingly hastened to reorient their policies to respond favorably to the Chinese challenge. Unfortunately, such reorientation served to widen further the already deep chasm between Japan's foreign policy and its military thinking. The military, committed to their own idea of national security, resolved to resort to force to retain Manchuria as part of the Japanese defense system. The world economic crisis added an air of legitimacy to Japanese military aspirations, since the basic structure of Japan's economic relations with China and the United States had been destroyed.

Such an analysis in terms of initiatives, expressing various countries' interest in creating a new international order after the passing of the "diplomacy of imperialism," provides one method of correlating many complicated episodes of the 1920's. In this study the emphasis will be on Japan, not only because of the country's crucial role in the prelude to the Far Eastern crisis but also because there exists no satisfactory analysis of Japanese foreign policy in the decade. The basic aim is to use Japan as an example, in order to examine various systems of international relations and their impact on foreign policy.

THE STRUCTURE OF INTERNATIONAL ACTION IN THE FAR EAST

Until after World War II the Far East had been a land of empires, not of nation-states. This is perhaps the most important fact in the diplomatic history of the Far East. It may be said that multinational relations such as those developed in Europe after the sixteenth century were unknown in an area where one empire, China, presided over the scene and defined its external relations as tributary relations. No debate on national interest — such as those which added color to European diplomacy in the seventeenth and the eighteenth centuries — took place in the Chinese empire; navigation laws, carrying trade and territorial expansion as instruments of foreign policy, the balance of power, and national security were concepts alien to this land. Before the 1840's the only exception to this rule was Sino-Russian relations. They had signed various treaties regulating land trade. But Russia, too, was an empire, expanding eastward and southward both geographically and commercially after the sixteenth century. The beginnings of official Sino-Russian contact in the late seventeenth century meant that the two empires had met and defined the way in which they would confront each other.

The Opium War and the treaties of the 1840's marked the

effort of the Western nations to change the situation and bring China into the "society of nations." But China did not become an equal member of the community. In the Far East the "society of nations" meant a meeting place of empires — the Russian in the north, the Chinese in the middle, and the European colonies in the south whose affairs were directed from the West. Western countries participated equally in the new arrangements, based on the principle of "most-favored-nation treatment," and China accepted treaty tariffs and consular jurisdiction as the basic framework of contact with the West. This was certainly an "unequal" relationship, but it was a relationship not just between two governments but between two systems of empire. In this sense the treaty system served to provide an order in the Far East when the Chinese empire was for the first time confronted with a group of differently oriented countries.[1]

After the 1880's and in particular following the Sino-Japanese War of 1894–1895 the new "diplomacy of imperialism" was superimposed on the treaty system. The "diplomacy of imperialism" must be distinguished from "imperialism" as such, which has been traced back to antiquity. What characterized the decades after the 1880's was a new conception of national security. Colonies, overseas naval bases, spheres of influence, and particularistic concessions began to play vital roles in a country's defense system. They, as well as rapid industrialization and armament at home, were indexes of power; their retention and extension were considered to contribute to the security and strengthening of the mother country. It was no accident that during this period foreign policy was strongly determined by, if not identical with, military policy. Civilian and military officials worked closely to safeguard national security.

The Far East, like other parts of the globe, was divided between those countries which expanded and those which were victims of expansion. Japan, successfully negotiating the termination of unequal treaties with the West and snatching Korea away from the Chinese imperial sphere, now joined the ranks of imperial powers. Together these powers obtained exclusive rights and particularistic arrangements from the decaying Chinese empire. At the same time, the very multiplicity of imperial powers with global interests tended to create a subtle equilibrium in the Far East. A *status quo* was constantly redefined, and there was always the possibility of war when an imperialist seemed to alter it to the detriment of other powers' interests. But there was also a mechanism for preventing a radical upset in the *status quo:* the imperial powers tried to maintain an equilibrium by means of a series of alliances, ententes, and agreements designed to affirm their mutual spheres of influence and to harmonize the interests of as many imperialists as possible.[2]

World War I did irreparable damage to such a structure of imperialist diplomacy. This fact sets the stage for a discussion of the 1920's. The undermining of the old order came about in two ways. On the one hand, Japanese expansion on the continent, coupled with the temporary distress of the European powers, destroyed the balance in the Far East which, though always precarious, the imperialists had managed to maintain. On the other hand, there were new forces undermining the very foundation of the old diplomacy — the "new diplomacy" of the United States and the Soviet Union, and the self-conscious assertion of nationalism in China.

Available evidence and recent scholarship make it amply clear that at least until 1910 Japan had acted in a cautious and "realistic" manner to emerge as a respectable member of the Western imperialist community. This policy, consistently pursued by Meiji leaders, had reflected the realization that Japan's existence as an independent power depended on continued understanding with and economic assistance of as many Western nations as possible. It is also true, however, that the success of this policy had not totally destroyed the fear of a complete Western domination of Asia. In fact, the stronger Japan became the greater the apprehension grew that eventually the West would reject Japan's bid as its equal. Some influential Japanese had for some time been calling for the solidarity of all Asian peoples under Japanese leadership as an inevitable choice forced on Japan because of its anomalous position between East and West.[3]

Under the circumstances it is not surprising that the outbreak of war in Europe meant the disappearance of the existing frame of reference for the conduct of Japanese policy. As a result, these two views of Japan's national interest began to be reflected in its wartime foreign policy. On the one hand, Japan continued to act within the framework of the diplomacy of imperialism, seeking understanding with Western powers wherever possible; agreements were signed with Britain, France, Russia, and the United States through which Japan sought their explicit or implicit recognition of its special interests in the Far East. Even with regard to the Twenty-one Demands of 1915, it is possible to argue that their primary objective was the perpetuation of Japan's existing rights in south Manchuria and eastern Inner Mongolia, and that the Tokyo government did its best to assure the powers that it was acting according to the prescribed rules of the game and was not impinging on their vested rights in China. At the same time, there were certain areas where Japan definitely did depart from the principle of understanding with the Western imperialists. Japanese policy toward Yüan Shih-k'ai and Tuan Ch'i-jui and toward the Bolsheviks revealed willingness to act independently of other powers, in fact to take advantage of their distress, and to establish Japanese hegemony in China, Manchuria, and eastern Siberia. These steps reflected the belief, commonly held by the military, that Japan should forestall the probable postwar resurgence of Western domination in Asia by cementing close ties among Japanese, Chinese, and non-Bolshevik Russians.[4]

The mention of the military raises an important point about the conduct of Japanese foreign policy. The tug of war between the two ideas of national interest was often acrimonious because it also reflected the uncertainty in the decision-making process. A handful of influential elder statesmen who had controlled foreign policy had begun to disappear from the scene, and even the authority of the still active *genro*, such as Yamagata Aritomo, had been challenged by second-generation leaders who had had no part in the internal turmoil of the middle nineteenth century. The country's political unification and world status had been achieved not by them but for them. It was to be expected, then, that they would have a far greater diversity of views as to the future of Japan, both as to its external affairs and as to its development at home. This dual phenomenon — the challenge of the first by the second generation, and the internal disunity within the latter group — explains much of the "Taisho democracy." It also sheds light on the way foreign policy was made and carried out at this time.

The Foreign Ministry, representing second-generation civilian bureaucrats, formulated and executed most foreign policy decisions, but first-generation leaders and second-generation non-bureaucrats (or former bureaucrats) such as military officers, businessmen, and party politicians also participated in the work. The Foreign Ministry had grown in self-confidence and *esprit de corps* after the diplomatic successes of the early twentieth century. Its bureaus of commerce, Asian affairs, and Euro-American affairs boasted trained experts in Japan's relations with the world. They and their representatives abroad had been picked from a much greater number of candidates for foreign service and were almost invariably graduates of the Tokyo Imperial University. They had traveled widely and looked to the West as a model for Japanese diplomacy. They had grown up in the age of imperialist politics, and they were accustomed to ententes and alliances as means of safeguarding national interests. For this reason almost without exception they had opposed Japanese wartime expansion in Manchuria, Shantung, and Siberia without prior understanding with one or more Western powers. They were wary of violating too radically the existing rules of the game. In this sense these bureaucrats were all imperialists.[5]

Pitted against them were *genro*, army and navy officials, and others in business and in politics. A handful of their most influential members were active in the "foreign affairs council" established during the war to supervise Japanese foreign policy. It did not function as a group, however, since its members represented diverse interests. Among them the military were most important. Like civilian bureaucrats, they had gained in the sense of their own importance after the successful wars against China and Russia. By the 1910's the Meiji constitution had been so interpreted as to give them the exclusive "right of supreme command"; in matters of military tactics and operations they were not controlled by the cabinet and they had the right to report directly to the Emperor, circumventing the civilian authorities. Their tendency to act independently of civilian officials had become especially pronounced after the overthrow of the Manchu dynasty in 1912. Unmindful of the repercussions of their action on Japanese-Western relations, army officers attempted various plots and coups in Manchuria and Inner Mongolia to detach them from China proper. After the Bolshevik revolution the supreme command in Tokyo actively interested itself in creating buffer zones in eastern Siberia. Naval planners, in the meantime, worked out fleet construction programs and strategic schemes, assuming that the expanded empire would clash with American policy and might lead to war.[6]

The military extremism and disregard of the principle of imperialist collaboration collided with civilian bureaucratic thinking. Prime Minister Hara Kei, coming to power just prior to the armistice day in 1918, did his best to reassert the policy of understanding with Western powers. It may be said that when the war ended the Japanese government was willing to cut back its wartime excesses and once again act as a respectable imperialist. Economic considerations did much to encourage such orientation. During the war Japanese export trade more than tripled, bringing in a surplus of over a billion yen. This and revenues outside of trade enabled the country to emerge as a creditor nation at the end of the war. Only the United States reaped such benefits from the European conflict. Both countries expanded their trade with China at the expense of Britain, Germany, and other belligerents. Japanese-American economic ties were also strengthened; during the war Japanese exports to the United States almost tripled, and American exports to Japan increased by more than 500 percent. When the war ended Japanese officials realized that the country's postwar economic growth depended to a large extent on further expanding trade with the United States and at the same time minimizing the effects of the expected European comeback to China trade. Such considerations dictated a policy of understanding with Western countries.[7]

Finally, mention must be made of nonmilitary outsiders — intellectuals, party politicians, businessmen, journalists, and others who were excluded from the government and who felt more and more alienated from the bureaucratic elite. It seemed anachronistic, in that period of Taisho democracy, that a handful of experts should control Japan's external affairs. It is at this time that the slogan, "people's diplomacy," began to be mouthed by these outsiders. The extent of the outsiders' influence upon foreign policy remained to be seen; but they could pose a serious threat to Foreign Ministry control over policy, for they were far less committed than the bureaucrats to the idea of understanding with the West as a basic orientation of Japan's foreign relations.[8]

In this way, Japanese military expansion during World War I not only destroyed the power equilibrium in the Far East, but it also increased the tension between decision-making groups in Japan. Foreign policy, which had earlier sought specific and well-defined objectives within the framework of collaboration with Western powers, had become divorced from military policy. The military developed their own definition of national goals and the means of achieving them, whereas civilian leaders continued to emphasize the need to maintain close political understanding and economic relations with various Western countries. In so doing, however, the civilian officials had no idea that the imperialist diplomacy which they sought to restore had been undermined by the United States, the Soviet Union, and China. Here lay the basic problem for postwar Japanese diplomacy.

There is no question that the United States had fully participated in the diplomacy of imperialism. It had not only acquired territories in the Pacific but had also entered into various arrangements with China, Japan, and Western powers to respect the *status quo* in the Far East and extend political and economic influence there. The United States was different from other imperial powers before the war only insofar as it actively interested itself in forming close ties with China as a means of influencing power politics in Asia. Such an attempt had not meant a radical departure from the existing system of diplomacy. The United States continued to recognize, explicitly or implicitly, the rights of other powers to special interests.[9]

During the war, however, President Woodrow Wilson and the American government came out definitely against the practices and concepts of the "old diplomacy." Not that the United States turned against the existing treaty structure itself. Concepts such as "national sovereignty" and the "self-determination of peoples" applied primarily to Europe and were not to be taken literally elsewhere on the globe. The United States was not yet ready to endorse China's national sovereignty immediately and unconditionally. But it resolutely opposed particularistic policies and power rivalries in the Far East at the expense of China. It would define a new *status quo*, not based on a temporary balance of power among the imperialists but on their pledge to refrain from military and political expansion and assist weaker peoples to "walk in the difficult paths of independence and right." [10]

The United States, it is true, was not always consistent. The so-called Bryan message of March 1915, and the Lansing-Ishii agreement of 1917 gave rise to the suspicion, justifiably or not, that the United States government recognized Japan's special interests in Manchuria. At the Paris Peace Conference, President Wilson had to be satisfied with Japan's pledge that it would restore Shantung to China in due course, despite his initial determination to dislodge Japan from the peninsula. What is important is that American officials themselves regretted having had to take these steps as contrary to their principles. Moreover, the "nonrecognition doctrine" of 1915, the new consortium scheme, and steps leading to the Siberian expedition all indicated America's interest in seeking an alternative to the existing practices of diplomacy in the Far East.

The American attack on the existing framework of Far Eastern diplomacy was matched by that by the Soviet Union. Combining the Marxist theory of history with his own interpretation of colonialism, Lenin defined the situation in Asia as an integral part of the world-wide struggle against imperialism. Russia was to lead that struggle, and immediately after the October revolution it took steps to repudiate all the secret and open agreements the Tsarist regime had entered into with the powers at the expense of China. In China, in particular, foreign powers and their Chinese allies — warlords, "comprador capitalists," and big landlords — were pictured as seeking the domination of international monopoly capital. Now that Russia had become anti-imperialist, revolutionaries in China and elsewhere could follow its lead and work together to overthrow imperialism. Thus from the beginning Soviet policy consciously sought to emphasize its opposition to the existing system of Sino-foreign relations. In July 1918, Georgi Chicherin declared, in his capacity as people's commissar for foreign affairs, that Russia was willing to renounce the "conquests of the Tsarist government in Manchuria" and restore the Chinese Eastern Railway to China. The proposal was followed up by the Karakhan manifestoes of 1919 and 1920. They reaffirmed nullification of the old treaties and offered negotiation for new. Such a policy directly undercut the existing structure of power politics in the Far East.[11]

The Wilsonian and Leninist attacks on the diplomacy of imperialism found receptive soil in China. Though the World War had invited further Japanese encroachments and the Peking government's decision to enter the war on the side of the allies had only precipitated another civil war, China had the historic experience of terminating the extraterritorial privileges of Germans and their allies. The European conflict had resulted in the disappearance of a foremost imperial power in the Far East. Perhaps more important, the war had coincided with the emergence of new groups of leaders — foreign-educated diplomats, intellectuals, and *bourgeoisie* — who rose to the defense of their country's rights, even while political disunity and warlord regionalism plagued China. Mostly in their twenties and thirties, these men represented the voice of "young China." While they disagreed among themselves as to the intrinsic value of Western civilization and differed in the intensity of their hatred of Japan, they agreed that China must be reborn and chart a new course of progress and freedom. The voices of young China erupted into impassioned clamor after the signing of the Versailles Peace Treaty, which had failed to restore Shantung immediately to China. The Chinese delegates refused to sign the treaty, and at home the violent May Fourth incident developed into an intellectual revolution.[12]

To Chinese officials and intellectuals, whose confidence in the Wilsonian new diplomacy had been shattered at Versailles, the Soviet offer of equality had obvious implications. While there was skepticism as to the authenticity and practical value of the Karakhan manifestoes, the fact remained that here was a government, at last, which was willing to renounce explicitly the existing system of relations with China and enter into new arrangements as between equals. Because of political instability in Russia, however, no such arrangements were formulated until well into the 1920's. Consequently, the first country which offered more than verbal assurances of equality was Germany. Resigned to the dictated peace settlement and expulsion from Shantung, but eager to restore commercial relations with China, German officials extended overtures for a new treaty in the fall of 1920. They were willing to agree to the abrogation of extraterritoriality and restoration of tariff autonomy to China, if the latter should accord Germany a most-favored-nation treatment with respect to commerce and also cease liquidating German property in China. The Waichiaopu (Foreign Ministry) in Peking in time agreed to these terms, and a new agreement was signed in May 1921. By this time China had also gained similar victories from lesser nations, but the defection of one of the foremost imperial powers from the old system signaled another step in its disintegration.[13]

THE AMERICAN INITIATIVE

The postwar Far East was thus a witness to a variety of forces. The diplomacy of imperialism had been seriously undermined, but a new order was yet to emerge. Whether and in what shape it would emerge depended on the initiative taken by a power sufficiently interested in undertaking the task.

The postwar American initiative, culminating in the Washington Conference of 1921–1922, makes sense in such a context. It was an attempt to re-establish order and stability in the Far East, now that the old framework had been altered beyond recognition. That it was the United States which took the lead was due to the role it played during the war as the conscious antagonist of Japanese expansion, to the Chinese expectation that the United States carry out the Wilsonian principles, to the increasing share of American capital and trade in the Japanese and Chinese economies, and to America's newly acquired sense of power, backed by a spectacular naval construction program.[14] The architects of postwar American policy believed that, first of all, Japan would have to be dispossessed of its wartime fruits and, eventually, a new international order would have to be created in the Far East.

The first policy was defined by John V. A. MacMurray, chief of the Far Eastern division of the State Department, as "restoring the equilibrium in the Far East which has been so dangerously upset by Japan's process of aggrandizement." In his view the Japanese government was "an oligarchy of military clansmen and their adherents, all alike imbued with the same materialistic political philosophy, differing among themselves only in the degree to which their nationalistic aspirations are tempered by considerations of prudence in dealing with the rest of the world." Given such an image of Japan, it became imperative for the United States to roll back the tide of Japanese expansion to restore the *status quo* in the Far East. To this end the United States proposed the internationalization of the formerly German island of Yap, which had been turned over to Japan as a mandate island, and withdrew American troops from Siberia in 1920 as a token of disapproval of Japanese policy there. When, in the middle of the year, Japanese forces occupied North Sakhalin in retaliation against the killing of Japanese residents in the town of Nikolaievsk, the United States protested, declaring that it would not recognize any action undertaken by Japan in contravention of the existing treaties concerning Russia and impairing the latter's territorial and political sovereignty.[15]

The United States was not satisfied simply with restoring the equilibrium in the Far East. It would go a step further and demolish the existing system of imperialist diplomacy. This effort was most clearly visible in the American scheme for a new international banking consortium and attack on the Anglo-Japanese alliance, and it was a basic philosophy behind the calling of the Washington Conference. In order to oppose the exclusive concessions and political privileges China had granted to third powers in return for financial assistance, the United States proposed, in 1918, that a new consortium be organized by American, British, French, and Japanese bankers. The new consortium was to be given a retroactive and current option on all loans to China. By this means a new system of international cooperation to assist China would replace competitive, disorderly arrangements. Characteristically, Japan under Prime Minister Hara responded favorably to this proposal. Trying to restore understanding with the

United States but still acting under the assumption of imperialist collaboration, Japanese leaders believed that here was a good opportunity to exhibit eagerness to restore the principle of joint action in the Far East. They expected that in return the United States would agree to the exclusion of Manchuria and Inner Mongolia from the sphere of operation of the new consortium. Such an attitude revealed that the Japanese policy makers still regarded their country and the United States as imperialists who might cooperate to safeguard mutual interests. In this instance they were not entirely disappointed, as the United States, after long-drawn-out negotiations, consented to the exclusion of certain specific railways in Manchuria and eastern Inner Mongolia from consortium activity and assured Japan that its rights in these regions would not be jeopardized by the new arrangement.[16]

No such compromise was offered by Washington on the issue of the Anglo-Japanese alliance. American policy toward the renewal of the alliance, last concluded in 1911 for a term of ten years, best exemplified the new approach to Far Eastern problems. The alliance, in the opinion of American officials, had not only given Japan a free hand during the war to pursue a "particularistic and aggressive policy," but more fundamentally it epitomized the old type of power relations which the United States was trying to destroy. It had been an instrument through which Japan had been able to have its spheres of influence recognized by Britain. The State Department began its campaign against the renewal of the alliance in the existing form as early as the spring of 1920, and very soon it became opposed to renewal in any form. Here again Japanese officials at first tried to apply their familiar imperialist tactic and persuade the United States to join a tripartite agreement which would approve of the renewal of the Anglo-Japanese alliance but would also enunciate basic principles of peace and harmony among the three nations. These steps would, it was expected, materially contribute to "peaceful cooperation in the Far East" among Japan, Britain, the United States, and China. Anglo-Japanese-American friendship would be re-established, a staff paper noted, just when the Bolsheviks threatened China and Germany seemed to have designs on Central Asia.[17] Such an approach was perfectly in line with the thinking that Japan's rights and interests in the Far East would best be protected and promoted through alliances and agreements with influential powers. It showed no deep appreciation of the developing American policy against the practices of imperialist diplomacy.

It was only during the Washington Conference, meeting between November 1921, and February 1922, that the Japanese government became aware of the need to reconsider its fundamental assumptions concerning the conduct of foreign policy. The background of the conference has been well studied and need not be repeated here. The essential factor to remember, apart from the Congressional movement for naval disarmament, is the American initiative to put an end to the diplomacy of imperialism. This involved the annulment of all deals and agreements among the powers and the enunciation of new principles to govern their conduct in the Far East. The former led to the abrogation of the Anglo-Japanese alliance and its replacement by the Four-Power Treaty, while the latter objective was embodied in the Nine-Power Treaty and other agreements.

The abrogation of the Anglo-Japanese alliance was achieved without much fanfare. Britain and Japan, it is true, did not wish an unequivocal abrogation with no substitute. In London it was felt that if Japan were let loose from the alliance it might either pursue an independent course of action in China or seek an understanding with Germany and the Soviet Union. Since America's strong opposition to the continuation of the alliance was also well recognized, the British government decided to invite the United States to join a modified alliance between Great Britain and Japan. During the Washington Conference, Arthur Balfour, one of Britain's delegates, conveyed to Secretary of State Charles Evans Hughes his personal and informal suggestion that a new "tripartite agreement" replace the existing alliance between Britain and Japan. In Balfour's conception such an agreement was designed to protect the signatories' existing territorial rights. It envisaged the possibility of recourse to force, inasmuch as the proposed agreement stipulated that "If in the future the territorial rights . . . of any of the High Contracting Parties are threatened by any other Power or combination of Powers, any two of the High Contracting Parties shall be at liberty to protect themselves by entering into a military alliance provided (a) this alliance is purely defensive in character and (b) that it is communicated to the other High Contracting Power." This did not explicitly cancel the Anglo-Japanese alliance nor provide against the resumption of the alliance. Balfour sought to supplement this agreement with another defining basic principles concerning China.[18]

Such a policy was similar to Japan's. As noted above, Tokyo's officials had advocated *rapprochement* with the United States and redefinition of relations between Japan, Britain, and the United States. The instructions drafted for the guidance of the Japanese delegation called for "a Japanese-British-American entente aimed primarily at the establishment of permanent peace in the Pacific and the Far East." But Shidehara Kijūrō, the principal Japanese negotiator on the subject, felt that the Balfour draft on a Japanese-British-American agreement would be unacceptable to the United States and decided to change it into a consultative pact. Instead of envisioning a military alliance, the Shidehara draft called for mutual consultation in case "the territorial rights or vital interests" of a signatory power "in the regions of the Pacific Ocean and of the Far East" was threatened.[19]

The United States was not interested in substituting a triple agreement for the existing alliance. Its main concern was with demolishing the old structure of power diplomacy, and there was no thought of establishing particular political ties with Japan and Britain. However, Secretary Hughes was agreeable to a consultative pact if it included France and if it explicitly replaced the Anglo-Japanese alliance. He may have reasoned that in this way the pact would not give the impression of a revived imperialist arrangement and that the Senate and the American public could be persuaded more easily to approve of it. There is some evidence that Hughes lived to regret the decision to invite France to join, but in 1921–1922 this was perhaps inevitable, given the fundamental drive to demolish the basis of the old diplomacy.[20] Strikingly enough, neither Japan nor Britain offered much opposition to France's participation. In the light of America's objection to a political agreement, they perhaps felt that it made little difference whether another power joined the new undertaking. At any rate, the Shidehara draft was compared with Hughes's own draft, and in the middle of December 1921, the Four-Power Treaty was drawn up to the satisfaction of the parties involved. It had no military connotation and simply stipulated that the signatories confer with each other should any threat arise to their rights in relation to their "insular possessions and insular dominions" in the Pacific. What thus emerged was only a "general and harmless international agreement," in the words of Chandler P. Anderson who had helped prepare the American draft.[21]

By this time there is reason to believe that Japanese officials had definitely become aware of the passing of the familiar concepts of international relations. The failure of their scheme for a Japanese-British-American alliance revealed beyond doubt that the old framework of imperialist diplomacy was no longer adequate for reconciling Japanese interests and those of other countries. It is impossible to determine precisely when the realization of this change caused a shift in Japanese policy. Neither would it be accurate to say that the old attitude disappeared completely. Japanese participation in the Nine-Power Treaty and other agreements indicates that a shift in thinking did take place among Japan's policy makers and that, while the old habit of thought died hard with some of them, they were willing to work together with other countries to develop new rules of the game.

The Nine-Power Treaty was a product of America's effort to have the powers enunciate new principles to guide their conduct in China. The signatories, including the United States, Britain, and Japan, condemned spheres of influence, upheld the principle of equal opportunity, and solemnly confirmed the "sovereignty, the independence, and the territorial and administrative integrity of China." In themselves these were abstract principles, and the powers were by no means committed to uphold China's diplomatic independence. What is more striking is that the Nine-Power Treaty was meant to be "a substitute for all prior statements and agreements" concerning China, to use Secretary Hughes's expression.[22] In other words, the treaty characterized the new approach to Far Eastern diplomacy; it would operate, not within the framework of particularistic arrangements, but on the basis of an over-all international agreement participated in by all the major countries, including China.

Japan's participation in these two arrangements — the Four-Power and the Nine-Power treaties — indicated that it, too, had been persuaded to recognize the passing of the diplomacy of imperialism. It is true that some Japanese leaders, for whom the old system was the only frame of reference, accepted the new treaties only after they were assured that they did not repudiate Japan's vested interests in the Far East. The "security clause" in the Nine-Power Treaty, for example, enjoining the signatories to refrain from infringing upon each other's rights in China, was interpreted as having tacitly recognized Japanese influence in Manchuria.[23] The fact that Japanese leaders chose to be satisfied with such implicit assurances was important, however. This fact alone indicates their decision, willing or reluctant, to reformulate the basis of their foreign policy.

Other agreements concluded at the Washington Conference revealed that Japan was ready to go along with the United States in an attempt to found a new basis of international relations in the Far East. In the Five-Power Treaty, Japan was willing to accept the inferior ratio of five to three with respect to capital ship tonnage vis-à-vis the United States and Britain in return for maintenance of the *status quo* with regard to the fortification of the Pacific islands. The basic assumption was that Japan would not wage an offensive war against either of the two and that for defensive purposes the five-to-three ratio plus the nonfortification agreement would sufficiently guarantee Japan's security in its home waters.[24]

Other arrangements in which Japan participated can be summarized briefly. Reversing the position held at the Paris Peace Conference, Japan showed readiness to modify certain provisions of the treaties with China which had grown out of the Twenty-one Demands. Shidehara explicitly stated that Japan was ready to withdraw Group V of the demands, about which no agreement had been reached with China, and to decline its preferential rights concerning the engagement by China of Japanese political, financial, military, and police instructors in south Manchuria. Furthermore, Japan renounced the railway reservations in the new consortium and was ready to "throw open" to consortium activities its options on railway loans in Manchuria and eastern Inner

Mongolia as well as loans secured on taxes in these regions. The knotty question of former German rights in Shantung was solved by Japanese and Chinese delegates meeting outside of the conference. Japan agreed to restore the Kiaochow leased territory and to withdraw troops "as soon as possible." The Tsingtao-Tsinan Railway was also to be transferred to China. Regarding the Siberian expedition, the Japanese delegation promised withdrawal of troops from the Maritime Province and North Sakhalin, pending satisfactory arrangements with Soviet authorities. Finally, Japan agreed to accord specific rights to American nationals on the island of Yap, in return for America's recognition of Japan's administrative authority over the Japanese-mandated islands.[25]

The Washington Conference had signalized the end of an era in Far Eastern politics. If it had merely resulted in Japan's retreat from its wartime expansionism, it would have meant the return of the prewar equilibrium within the framework of the old diplomacy. But now the mechanism of maintaining balance among the big powers was destroyed and replaced by multinational agreements repudiating expansionism.

This did not mean that imperialism as such was gone. It simply meant that the old concepts and practices defining relations between empires had now been discarded. Here lay the crucial weakness of the "Washington system." Germany and Russia, which had taken unilateral steps to renounce the old treaties, were not signatories of the Washington treaties. Their exclusion meant the parallel existence of a second pattern of international relations in the Far East. More fundamentally, China did not emerge as a nation with all the attributes of sovereignty. To the delegates of the Washington Conference the country seemed to lack essential characteristics of a modern state. The authority of the central government in Peking extended only to those provinces which happened to be under control of the warlords in support of the government. At the time of the Washington Conference the Canton regime under the leadership of Sun Yat-sen desperately sought to be recognized as a distinct government and, when this failed, it chose to ignore the conference and declared beforehand that it would not recognize any decisions of the conference dealing with China. Apart from the absence of central authority commanding the loyalty of all citizens, China seemed to lack even those elements of a sovereign power which, as Sun Yat-sen was wont to point out, characterized the Western nations and Japan: rapidly increasing population, national sentiment, technological progress, and extensive transportation networks.[26]

Unlike Germany and Russia, the Washington powers were hesitant to accord a full sovereign status to China. When Chinese delegates put forth the famous ten-point program for restoration of equality and independence to China, the other delegates countered by adopting the "Root resolution" pledging themselves "to provide the fullest and most unembarrassed opportunity to China to develop and maintain for herself an effective and stable government." To put this principle into effect, a resolution was adopted to convene a tariff revision commission to revise the rates of import duties to an effective 5 percent, and to hold a special tariff conference to consider granting interim surtaxes to China. Another resolution provided for a fact-finding commission on extraterritoriality with a view to recommending measures "to assist and further the efforts of the Chinese Government to effect such legislation and judicial reforms as would warrant the several Powers in relinquishing, either progressively or otherwise, their respective rights of extraterritoriality." [27]

These were significant steps toward modifying and ultimately abolishing the treaty system. Coupled with other measures, such as Japan's agreement to restore Kiaochow to China, Britain's promise to follow this up by restoring Weihaiwei, and abolition of foreign postal agencies, political control of the powers over China was definitely curtailed. Nevertheless, China was denied an immediate restoration of tariff and jurisdictional autonomy. The United States, the one power which might have taken the initiative in this direction, was satisfied that unstable and disturbed conditions in China were such that any radical change in the status of foreigners and their activities there was undesirable. The internal problems of China were in fact only a minor part of the Washington Conference. The basic objective, as it related to the Far East, was to redefine relations among Japan, the United States, Britain, and other powers. China entered the picture only insofar as these powers agreed to limit their expansion and renounce particularistic agreements.[28]

The old order was gone, and the Washington Conference had set up the framework for a new. It remained to be seen whether the Washington treaties in fact provided a workable alternative to the diplomacy of imperialism as a mechanism to harmonize the divergent interests of the powers. Much depended on the degree to which the principal participants in the Washington treaty structure would continue to work together to solidify the emerging new order, and to meet in cooperation the challenges presented by Soviet Russia and Germany and by Chinese nationalism.

Part One

· THE SOVIET INITIATIVE

I · THE LOST OPPORTUNITY,
1922–1925

For some time after the Washington Conference the powers self-consciously talked of a "new epoch" in the Pacific. A decade of naval competition and power politics seemed to have been replaced by another era of equilibrium, based on the principles of peace, harmony, and orderly change. "Economic diplomacy" became a keynote of the Far Eastern policies of the powers. In Japan succeeding cabinets publicly declared their adherence to the "spirit of the Washington Conference." They expressed confidence that the nation's interests would best be served through a policy of "international cooperation." To prove its faith in the new order of things Japan withdrew its forces from Shantung, north Manchuria, and Siberia, and agreed to the abrogation of the Lansing-Ishii agreement.

The years immediately following the Washington Conference were to show, however, that conflicts of interests and policies among the nations had not been eradicated by the demolition of the old order. The new system of international relations, based on the Washington treaties, could have been solidified only if the Washington powers had been willing to cooperate actively in the Far East. They would have done so only if they had reaped tangible benefits from the new order. This was not the case. In retrospect the inability of the principal governments to subordinate their individual interests to a higher goal of cooperation was a crucial factor, setting the stage for the Soviet initiative.

"THE SPIRIT OF THE WASHINGTON CONFERENCE"

The destruction of the old diplomacy brought about an improvement in official Japanese-American relations. The governments in Tokyo and Washington were soon describing in glowing terms the coming of a new era of peace in the Pacific. John V. A. MacMurray, who had been a strong exponent of resistance to wartime Japanese expansionism, was referring, in 1924, to "a friendly people who have shown themselves disposed to put aside mutual distrust and rivalry and to cooperate loyally with us in our traditional Far Eastern policies." [1] The disparity between the two countries' close economic ties and political animosity, which had characterized the 1910's, was disappearing. During the 1920's the United States continued to be Japan's biggest customer, annually taking at least 40 percent of total Japanese exports. Japan, in return, bought more from America than from any other country, and its share in the American cotton export increased steadily. More important, the decade saw a phenomenal expansion in America's capital export to Japan. Private Japanese firms as well as the national and municipal governments turned to the United States for assistance, and at the end of the decade nearly 40 percent of the total foreign loans outstanding in Japan were held by Americans. Debentures floated abroad, which increased from 13 million to 253 million dollars between 1922 and 1931, were mostly issued in the United States. The dependence on American financial resources was particularly noticeable after the great earthquake of 1923 which resulted in an estimated property damage of five billion dollars. [2]

If the Washington Conference promoted further economic interdependence between the United States and Japan, it is equally evident that the new order in the Far East did not result in a marked expansion of American and Japanese economic interests in China. The China market expanded by only 50 percent between 1919 and 1924, and both the United States and Japan faced keen competition of European countries, now that the latter were making determined efforts to re-enter the arena. Britain and Hongkong quickly regained some of the losses incurred during the war; as a result Japan's share in the China market dropped from 40 percent in 1917 to 23 percent in 1924, while America's share fluctuated between 16 and 18 percent. Japanese-British competition was especially acute because both countries exported large quantities of cotton goods to China, whereas the United States had begun concentrating on the export of tobacco, petroleum, raw cotton, and machines. For the major Washington powers the immediate prospect for economic expansion in China was not bright. Since the Washington Conference presumably had ushered in an era of economic diplomacy and harmonious relations, the stagnation of the China market could threaten to undermine one rationale for the new order. The story of the Washington powers' policies during the first half of the 1920's is in effect a story of their unsuccessful effort to bridge this gap between expectation and reality.[3]

For one thing, the continued civil war in China made it impossible for the powers to implement further their idea of a new order so as to maximize their economic benefits. During the first half of the year 1922 war between the Fengtien clique led by Chang Tso-lin and the Chihli clique controlled by Wu P'ei-fu plagued north China, and the situation was repeated in the summer and fall of 1924. This time Feng Yü-hsiang's revolt against Wu precipitated the latter's temporary eclipse from the Chinese military scene. The two years between 1922 and 1924 were characterized by infinitely complex personal-political issues involving the constitution and the office of the president. In the south there were constant skirmishes between Sun Yat-sen and his erstwhile supporter, General Ch'en Chiung-ming, and in the major cities communists and labor leaders were gaining strength following the second congress of the Communist Party in 1922.[4]

The Washington powers had pledged not to interfere in China's internal affairs and to refrain from taking advantage of China's troubles for their own selfish ends. Adhering to this principle, not only Britain and the United States but Japan, which had openly assisted one faction against another during the 1910's, remained neutral and passive. It is true that Japan was often suspected of standing behind Chang Tso-lin, and that some Japanese believed Wu P'ei-fu was supported by Britain and the United States. Such allegations were not entirely without foundation. American, British, and Japanese military advisers were found in various warlords' headquarters. During the second Fengtien-Chihli war some Japanese officials in China advocated strong measures to preserve the *status quo,* with a view to safeguarding the treaty rights in Manchuria. Furthermore, a few Japanese military acted as middle-

men between the anti-Chihli forces and Feng Yü-hsiang, leading
to the latter's betrayal of Wu P'ei-fu. What was remarkable at this
time was that the governments in Tokyo, London, and Washington disavowed any such action and forbade their nationals to involve themselves in the Chinese civil war. The Japanese government, in particular, took steps to disband or reprimand those reserve officers and idlers in Manchuria who had joined the Fengtien
army in private capacity.[5]

The adherence to the "spirit of the Washington Conference"
meant that the foreign governments stood by passively while
Chinese factions continued their struggle for power. As Mac-
Murray put it, "We have no favorites in the present dog fight in
China; they all look alike to us . . . our various instructions to
Peking have all been drafted with the idea that we should keep
out of the mess and merely pray that somebody, whoever it may
be, may lick his rivals completely enough to make possible the establishment of some Government which would have to be recognized by the various rival factions — in other words, that they
fight it out to a conclusion." [6] Such an attitude spelled inaction for
the Washington powers, even while they bemoaned the absence
of peace and order in China, a condition essential for the pursuit
of their economic foreign policy. They failed to implement actively the programs outlined at the Washington Conference. This
failure needs to be further examined, since it was in sharp contrast to the vigorous Soviet policy in China.

The Washington signatories tried to justify their inaction by
pointing out the continued danger to foreign lives and property in
China. The Washington formula for a new order in the Far East,
they maintained, had been dependent on China's meeting its part
of the obligations. Since this condition was apparently not being
met, the powers came to take the view that they could not further
assist China.

The increasing sense of irritation the foreign countries felt with
the situation in China can best be seen in the attitude of the
United States government, which had taken the initiative in demolishing the old order. When, in December 1922, an American
merchant was cavalierly shot to death by Chinese soldiers at
Kalgan, Secretary of State Hughes immediately telegraphed Min-

ister Jacob Gould Schurman, "Should the [Chinese] Government fail to deal with the case energetically and promptly, without quibbling but with manifest sincerity, you may indicate that this Government regards the matter as a test of the degree of confidence which may be placed by it in the Government of China." Perhaps the best expression of the changed American attitude was Hughes's memorandum of May 1923, at the time of the Lincheng incident, involving the kidnapping of several foreigners by Chinese bandits. Hughes wrote:

The course of political development in China since the Washington Conference has thus far . . . been a disappointment to those who had hoped that a fuller measure of opportunity for independent development would hasten the evolution of a more normal and orderly internal administration of the country and make possible the establishment of a governmental entity capable of fulfilling the international obligations correlative to the rights of sovereignty which the Conference had recognized and sought to safeguard for China. The recent bandit outrage at Lincheng affords evidence such as cannot be ignored, that the present unfortunate political disintegration in China involves a failure of appreciation, on the part of the Chinese officials, of their definite responsibilities with respect to the safety and the interests of those sojourning in China under the protection of the Treaties.[7]

These and other incidents strengthened the impression that China was far from being unified and that there was no authority to check lawless attacks on the legitimate interests of foreigners guaranteed by existing treaties. The "rights of sovereignty" which the treaty powers had conceded in principle to China had been conditional upon the latter's honoring "international obligations." Now that the Chinese authorities seemed incapable of protecting foreign lives and interests, the signatories of the Washington treaties and resolutions appeared to be absolved from carrying out their promises. They continued to disappoint the Chinese who requested time and again that the meeting of the extraterritoriality commission be expedited.[8]

The powers' apparent inaction and failure to implement the Washington program did not imply their lack of interest in seeking ways to stabilize political and economic conditions in China. In fact there were various suggestions designed to bring about such a situation and thereby to promote foreign economic interests in China. None of these suggestions, however, resulted in concrete action because the Washington powers failed to cooperate. There was no realization of the need to develop a cooperative framework of international relations in the Far East, if this meant sacrificing what each country considered its essential national interests.

Given political and economic instability in China, it was natural that suggestions should have been made for financial assistance to the Peking government, either through an outright loan or by convening a tariff conference which might grant additional customs rates to Peking. Such assistance might have stabilized the economic base of the central government and contributed to its extension of authority over the rest of the country. China's foreign trade might then have been expanded. That such a program of financial aid would have been a formidable assignment for the powers to carry out became clear as soon as a first proposal was made.

In July 1922, the representatives of France, Britain, Japan, and the United States in Peking proposed to their governments that the consortium banks be authorized to make advances to the Peking government under Li Yüan-hung so that it might strengthen its foundation and carry out a program of reconstruction. The Chinese government was to pledge, in return, "to negotiate with the consortium the consolidation of the internal and external floating debt." The loan, in the ministers' suggestion, could be secured on an anticipated 2.5 percent customs surtax as authorized by the Washington Conference.[9]

These suggestions raised many complicated questions. The Peking government obviously could not carry on without money. But any loan would be wasted unless the government in power had some promise of stability to begin with. Moreover, China was already heavily in debt, and unsecured and insufficiently secured obligations had accumulated over the years. Any further loan would be hard to obtain unless China's credit was somehow improved by redeeming these debts. Finally, until additional customs duties were granted it was difficult to find any new security on the basis of which loans could be extended.

The United States and Japan were very much concerned with

the problem of consolidation of existing foreign debts of China. American bankers had bought millions of dollars of Chinese government bonds since 1912, which were either unsecured or only inadequately secured. As a result, it was estimated that in 1922 the Chinese government's obligations to American bankers had exceeded fifty million dollars. Furthermore, certain American firms had supplied railway and other materials to the Chinese government, which remained unpaid for. These business interests regarded payment of the existing debt as a precondition for discussion of any further loan.[10] The State Department well understood their views, but it was unwilling to countenance the advance commitment of the anticipated customs surtax for consolidation of existing debts, as this would not leave much for the real needs of the Peking government, such as administrative and fiscal reforms. In the American government's opinion, the consortium members should take the opportunity to cooperate and extend assistance to Peking without dictating in advance how it should consolidate its debts.[11]

This was also the position taken by the British government. Having extended credit to China on very cautious terms, British financiers held a negligible amount of defaulted and unsecured Chinese obligations. The Foreign Office would, therefore, object to a loan secured on the basis of the anticipated customs surtax, but it would endorse consortium action in otherwise extending financial assistance to the Chinese government. As a result both Washington and London decided, in early November, to seek cooperation of the other consortium powers, France and Japan, and consider loan arrangements with China.[12]

Thus there was a possibility that the consortium members, coinciding with the signatories of the Four-Power Treaty, might cooperate in China in assisting its central government to stabilize political and economic conditions. This might have provided a workable precedent for Sino-foreign cooperation and opened the way for further implementing the provisions of the Washington Conference. All powers concerned might have drawn economic benefits from such an arrangement. But this emerging opportunity was wrecked by Japan.

In August, October, and December, the Tokyo government re-

peatedly expressed its view that any loan to the Chinese government would be premature. The stated reason for this attitude was
that such a loan would in effect be tantamount to assisting those
Chinese who happened to be in control of Peking. This was a
justifiable argument. As the Japanese government maintained, "to
extend financial aid to the Government at Peking solely because
it is the recognized government would . . . end in benefiting
only a small group of individuals who have no interest in common
with the general public of China." [13]

The fundamental reason for Japan's lack of enthusiasm was,
however, derived from considerations of debt consolidation. Given
the enormous amount of unsecured and inadequately secured
securities owed by the Chinese government and private concerns
to Japanese creditors, Japan was unwilling to underwrite any
further loan until a clear formula was devised for "stabilizing
Chinese national credit" and "establishing a sound financial system for the future." Japan's policy makers were especially worried
about the "Nishihara loans," extended to the Communications
Ministry during the war. The loans, totaling nearly 90 million
dollars, had been unsecured and, together with the Siberian expedition, greatly reduced wartime Japanese surpluses. Until the
Chinese government could be induced to consider redeeming
these loans, Japan was not to advance further credit. Because of
postwar trade deficits the matter of debt consolidation assumed
importance which no Japanese cabinet could ignore. Pressed by
the United States, the Tokyo government at one time half-
heartedly expressed readiness to consider a small loan to Peking,
but it equivocated on concrete details.[14] The State Department
in time gave up its effort, and thus died the first and in fact last
opportunity for the major Washington powers to assist China
financially in cooperation through the consortium.

Convening a tariff conference, as stipulated in a Washington
Conference resolution, would have been another means of assisting the Chinese government, but there would have existed the
same difficulties as with a loan proposal. The London Foreign
Office, aware of these difficulties and desirous of regaining for
British commerce a position of supremacy in Chinese trade,
sought to obtain American support of its position at an anticipated

tariff conference. Objecting to the Japanese emphasis on debt consolidation, which in the British view would make the tariff conference merely a "foreign debt collecting commission," London officials were inclined toward the idea that the proceeds from additional duties, to be granted at the tariff conference, might be distributed among provincial governments in China in return for their abolition of the likin transit tax. Strategic cooperation with the United States was considered essential in these matters, and early in 1923 Victor A. A. H. Wellesley, chief of the department of Far Eastern affairs of the Foreign Office, was sent to Washington to initiate discussion on the tariff question. A year later the Foreign Office suggested that the State Department, in its turn, send MacMurray to London to hold confidential conversations with his counterpart so that they might agree on common strategy at a tariff conference. Interestingly enough, the American government was reluctant at this time to engage in such conversations as it might give Japan an impression of Anglo-American collusion. As MacMurray reasoned, it "would defeat the very purposes we have in view if we and the British, while getting closer cooperation among ourselves, should definitely alienate the possibility of Japanese cooperation. It would take us back to such a situation as existed before the Washington Conference, and establish a new cleavage of interests among the treaty powers." [15] Here was another instance in which the "spirit of the Washington Conference" precluded cooperation.

Cooperation between the United States and Britain, or even between these two and Japan, would have meant little if a tariff conference had not been convened. As it turned out, a petty squabble over the Boxer indemnity issue prevented France from speedily ratifying the Washington customs treaty, which stipulated the calling of such a conference three months after the treaty was ratified by all the nine signatories. The Banque Industrielle de Chine had failed in June 1921, and the French government had decided to rehabilitate it by diverting to it the major portion of the Boxer indemnity funds. Chinese payments of the indemnity had been suspended after 1917 because of the war, but China was expected to resume payment in December 1922. At this juncture France insisted that the payments be made in "gold francs" at the prewar rate of exchange between the franc and the silver *tael*, rather than in "francs" which had been divorced from a gold standard. This was in contrast to the Chinese view that the "debt in gold" stipulated in the Boxer protocol simply referred to the payment of the indemnity in the currency of each country concerned, rather than in the Chinese silver currency. In France the paper franc had depreciated to such an extent that, in the event of the Chinese construction being accepted, its share of the indemnity would decrease to about three-eighths of the amount realizable if it were paid in "gold francs."

Irked by Chinese persistence, France, along with Belgium and Italy, decided to force the issue by intimating that it would not ratify the customs treaty unless the Chinese accepted the French interpretation of the Boxer question. It was only in early 1925 that the Peking government under General Tuan Ch'i-jui decided to grant the French request, primarily because of the need to relieve the financial distress of the warlord regime after the Maritime Customs administration had decided to set aside the customs and salt revenue surpluses to cover the indemnity payments.[16]

It was not until July 1925, that France ratified all the Washington treaties and resolutions, thus in effect delaying the convening of the tariff conference which might have served to consolidate a central government in Peking. Throughout the episode the powers endorsed the French stand without much enthusiasm. At times Great Britain and the United States openly opposed some courses of action suggested by France and Belgium.[17] As MacMurray reflected somewhat later, the French attitude did irreparable damage to the emerging understanding between China and the foreign nations. It is difficult to say what would have happened if France had promptly ratified the Washington treaties and a tariff conference had been convened in 1923 or even in 1924, instead of late in 1925. One could probably agree with MacMurray that the powers could have extended their goodwill to China before the latter's nationalism took a decisive turn toward radicalism. Differences of policy on such matters as debt consolidation and tariff rates would have remained, but the powers' gesture of helpfulness toward Peking might have brought about an improvement in relations among the signatories of the Washington Conference treaties. That this step was never taken until it was too late attested to the lack of real interest in cooperation as a means for implementing the new order in the Far East.[18]

The absence of genuine understanding was not limited to the situation in China. American-Japanese relations were dealt a hard blow by the immigration dispute, and naval planning on both sides of the Pacific belied governmental professions of friendship. The long drama of the immigration episode came to a climax after the war as Congress became more receptive to California's plea for total Japanese exclusion. A bill introduced by Representative Albert Johnson, coupling a quota system with a Japanese exclusion provision, passed the House and the Senate in the spring of 1924.

From the point of view of State Department officials the Congressional action came at a most unfortunate moment for it marred the developing friendship between the two countries. MacMurray warned that the Johnson bill, if enacted in entirety, would "make difficult, if not impossible, that sympathetic and whole-hearted cooperation, in the area of the Pacific Ocean, which the results of the Washington Conference have brought within the range of practical realization." Secretary Hughes was even more distressed. He wrote to Senator Henry Cabot Lodge five days after the passage of the bill in the House,

I am deeply concerned. It seems to me that an irreparable injury has been done, not to Japan but to ourselves, and, as I think, most unnecessarily. It is a dangerous thing to plant a deep feeling of resentment in the Japanese people, not that we have need to apprehend, much less to fear, war, but that we shall have hereafter in the East to count upon a sense of injury and antagonism instead of friendship and cooperation. I dislike to think what the reaping will be after the sowing of this seed. I fear that our labors to create a better feeling in the East, which have thus far been notably successful, are now largely undone.[19]

The impact of the exclusion act was felt strongly in Japan. Saburi Sadao, counselor of the Japanese embassy in Washington, had warned MacMurray that an exclusionist legislation in the United States would spell death to the "conciliatory party" in Japan and depreciate American moral force in the Far East. He was afraid that this would result in a revival of spheres of interest in China. For Shidehara, who became foreign minister a month after the passage of the immigration law, it was useless to protest strongly to the American government as the latter could do nothing against state and federal legislatures. He would not sacrifice the basic framework of understanding with the United States for the sake of vindicating the national honor. Such a stand, as Saburi had predicted, alienated many Japanese who now attacked America's "white imperialism." Many right-wing societies mushroomed around this time, and mass meetings were organized in protest against Japanese discrimination in the United States. More important, there was agitation in the streets and in the press for an independent policy in the Far East, instead of following the lead of the West. In time this mass agitation would pose a serious threat not only to the idea of a cooperative international order but to the civilian leadership in Japan.[20]

In fact the Japanese military had never given up the idea of future conflict with the United States. Despite the Tokyo government's adherence to the Washington system, both army and navy supreme headquarters had continued to regard conflict with the United States as likely and made this the basic assumption in their defense policies. After 1917 the navy had regarded the United States as the most probable enemy, and the idea was reaffirmed in the war plan of February 1923. Even the army was now willing to take this view, since the immediate danger from the Soviet Union seemed unlikely. Such thinking was now potentially more dangerous than earlier in that it was confined to the military and a few civilian leaders. Before World War I, an imperialistic conflict with the United States was visualized by the Japanese government as well as by the navy whenever the subtle balance of power was broken in Asia; but such a conflict was considered totally out of the question by the postwar exponents of economic foreign policy. The military, on the other hand, insisted that considerations of cooperation or of friendship should not be allowed to interfere with the basic task of preparing the nation for future warfare with a Western power.[21]

Strikingly enough, such bifurcation of foreign policy and military thinking was not confined to Japan. It was also true of the

United States. Naval planners in Washington had also developed war strategy against Japan after the Russo-Japanese War. They continued their planning in the 1920's, and in 1924 they drew up a revised "orange plan," which remained the basic strategy till 1938. Here the principle of establishing naval superiority over Japan in the western Pacific in case of war was emphasized, and the idea that the Philippine islands could not be defended was explicitly repudiated. Since the Five-Power Naval Treaty had not limited the construction of auxiliary craft, the United States and Japan stepped up the building of cruisers, destroyers, and submarines.[22]

In both Tokyo and Washington, to be sure, the primacy of economic over military policy was clearly asserted during the first half of the 1920's. Because of this very fact, however, the distance grew steadily between the professed policy of friendship and cooperation on the one hand and the military strategy of eventual warfare on the other. At a time when the immigration dispute and the unstable situation in China discouraged genuine cooperation between the United States and Japan, the divorce of military from foreign policy threatened to nullify the basic framework of the Washington treaties.

THE SOVIET INITIATIVE IN CHINA

The greatest threat to the consolidation of the Washington treaty structure came from Russia. The story of Soviet diplomacy and Comintern activities in China, culminating in the dual achievement of 1924 — the conclusion of a new agreement with Peking and the consummation of the Kuomintang-Communist alliance at Canton — has been well recounted by historians. Here a bare outline will suffice to indicate the way in which Sino-Soviet relations contradicted the efforts of the Washington powers to establish new principles of international action.

In retrospect, Soviet diplomacy in north and south China had the effect of nullifying what little effort the powers were making to implement the Washington Conference order. With regard to the Peking government, Moscow's chief objective was to establish normal diplomatic relations, in such a way as to advertise

Russia's initiative in bringing about a new situation in Sino-foreign relations, and to protect its essential interests in connection with the Chinese Eastern Railway, Outer Mongolia, and other matters. These were the guidelines as Adolf Joffe, representing the Narkomindel (People's Commissariat for Foreign Affairs), began informal discussions with the Waichiaopu in the summer of 1922. Negotiations lasted nearly two years, the Chinese refusing to accept the Soviet contention that despite the earlier Chicherin and Karakhan declarations the Chinese Eastern Railway was still Russian property and that troops must remain in Outer Mongolia where they had been sent in 1920, following its declaration of independence.[23]

The challenge to the Washington powers, which was latent in such official Soviet moves, became unequivocal when Comintern agents met Chinese revolutionaries. The former's task was to disseminate propaganda and organize opposition to the Washington powers and their alleged allies in China, such as warlords, "comprador capitalists," and big landowners. While native Chinese revolutionaries might have been just as active even without direct Comintern assistance, it is likely that they would then have been more concerned with social reform at home, such as trade unionism and land redistribution, than with anti-imperialist campaigns. It was the Comintern which consistently pointed to anti-imperialism as the immediate goal for the Chinese. This view was behind the Comintern's strategy of uniting all anti-imperialist forces in China, including the "national bourgeoisie," "petty bourgeoisie," middle and poor peasants, and proletariat. The consummation of such a union was tantamount to creating a great movement against the treaty powers in China, just as the latter had defined their new approach to the Far Eastern situation.[24]

The anti-imperialist initiative undertaken by the Soviet Union was given a tremendous boost when the Kuomintang decided to join forces with the communists and the Comintern. The alliance, consistent with Comintern strategy, was by no means foreordained. Official Russian policy was to deal with the Peking government in order to realize the Soviet conception of a new order, and the Narkomindel was initially hesitant to commit Russia explicitly to the support of a minority faction in south

China. Sun Yat-sen, too, was at first eager to turn in any direction in order to obtain foreign assistance. He had a long record of fund-raising in Europe and America, and he had close associates in Japan. In the early 1920's he sent a letter to President Harding soliciting American support, contracted a loan with the Anglo-French China Corporation of London, toyed with the idea of Sino-German cooperation for industrial development of China, and talked of allying China with Japan, Russia, and Germany against other powers.[25]

It was due to Russia's adroit diplomacy and the Washington powers' passivity that Sun finally turned to the former. In June 1922, Sun Yat-sen's headquarters in Canton were attacked by soldiers belonging to General Ch'en Chiung-ming, who had hitherto given his support to the revolutionary leader. Faced with this betrayal, Sun barely escaped Canton with his life and fled to Shanghai. Just then Joffe was carrying on his talks with the Waichiaopu, and he decided to take advantage of Sun's exile in Shanghai and approach him. Perhaps Joffe felt that there was a chance the Kuomintang might become stronger and once again coordinate anti-establishment forces in China, eventually forming a strong government. If so, it was best to exploit any opportunity for cultivating Sun's friendship.[26]

Sun eagerly responded to Joffe's overtures, and in January 1923, the two issued the celebrated joint manifesto. The document shows Sun's desperate need for a foreign ally. As Joffe expressed the Russian people's sympathy and willingness to lend support toward China's national unification and independence, Sun reciprocated by accepting a *modus vivendi* to reorganize the management of the Chinese Eastern Railway under joint Sino-Russian arrangements. He further went on record as refusing to "view an immediate evacuation of Russian troops from Outer Mongolia as either imperative or in the real interest of China." It should be noted that Sun Yat-sen was making these concessions even while his enemies in Peking, Waichiaopu officials, were steadfastly refusing to accommodate Joffe's demands.[27]

Sun now returned to Canton, as General Ch'en, who had driven him out of the city, had in turn been defeated by a combination of the Yunnan and Kwangsi armies. Back in his revolutionary stronghold, Sun resumed his scheme for overthrowing the northern regime. He was as yet by no means convinced of the absolute need of a Soviet alliance. But he needed substantial support from his potential allies, which was not forthcoming except from Russia. In the fall of 1923 the Canton government's money shortage was acute. Sun could not impose more taxes on the merchants, who had not concealed their resentment of the Kuomintang government's exactions. Out of desperation Sun and his government resorted to planning the seizure of customs surpluses. On September 5, 1923, the Canton government presented a note to the diplomatic body, containing "the claim of the Southwestern provinces for their share of the customs surplus." The note emphasized that foreign obligations charged on the customs revenues would be paid but that part of the remainder collected in the southwestern provinces should be turned over for "constructive purposes" such as currency reform and river conservation. There was a possibility that the southern government might declare Canton a free port if the request was denied.[28]

The powers responded coolly to the request. The diplomats at Peking decided to dispatch war vessels to Canton with a view to impressing the determination of the powers to prevent seizure of customs funds by the Canton government, which was considered a direct contravention of the existing system of Sino-foreign relations. On December 20, Sun Yat-sen finally issued an order to the commissioner of customs at Canton to hold in custody all customs revenues collected within its jurisdiction after deducting the sums payable to foreign obligations. Francis Aglen, inspector general of the Customs administration, stood firm and refused the request. The matter was allowed to remain at this stage until the naval demonstration was called off in the middle of 1924.[29]

The Canton customs episode convinced Sun Yat-sen of the futility of counting on the support of the Washington powers. He had already despatched Chiang Kai-shek and others to Russia to explore further the possibility of Russian assistance. Upon their return, Sun decided to give Chiang a free hand in reorganizing military institutions of the southern regime after the model of Soviet discipline. Also at this time Leo Karakhan arrived in Peking, to succeed Joffe as negotiator with Peking, and Michael

Borodin reached Canton with an introduction from Karakhan. Events moved rapidly as Karakhan, through Borodin, worked to consummate a Soviet-Kuomintang alliance primarily, it appears, because he feared lest the Kuomintang should turn to other countries for assistance unless the Soviet Union showed some positive interest in its scheme.[30]

Upon his arrival at Canton, Borodin began reorganizing the Kuomintang. Strengthened by Chiang Kai-shek's favorable report of the Soviet system, Sun agreed to accept the new party constitution and a political program which had been drawn up by Borodin. The first Kuomintang congress of January 1924 formally launched an alliance between the Kuomintang and the Chinese communists, who now were to form a "bloc within" the former party. The declaration of the congress boldly proclaimed the principle of "the liberation of China by the Chinese people." It was categorically stated that "All unequal treaties are to be abolished: foreigners' leased territories, consular jurisdiction, foreigners' management of customs duties, all political power exercised by foreigners in China at the cost of Chinese sovereignty. New treaties are to be concluded based on recognition of China as an equal and sovereign nation." Regarding foreign loans, China was not to repay those loans which "were contracted by an irresponsible government, such as the Peking government, to maintain the power of the war lords." On the other hand, any nation which would voluntarily relinquish unequal treaties and privileges in China would be accorded the status of "most favored nation." [31]

Soviet diplomacy also scored a triumph in Peking. The menacing spectacle of relations between Moscow and Canton finally drove Peking officials to come to a hasty agreement with the Russian representative on various issues which they had discussed for six months. The result was the Wang-Karakhan agreement of March 1924, setting forth general principles which should govern the formal negotiations at a forthcoming conference. In the agreement the Chinese government extended *de jure* recognition to the Soviet government, withdrawal of Russian troops from Outer Mongolia was stipulated to be effected as soon as certain conditions were agreed upon, and it was decided that the Chinese

Eastern Railway should be redeemed by China and its future "be determined by the Republic of China and the USSR to the exclusion of any third Party or Parties." Finally, as Germany had done three years before, Soviet Russia renounced extraterritoriality and special rights and privileges in China. More than two months were to elapse before the agreement, in a somewhat modified form, was ratified by the Peking government. Wellington Koo replaced C. T. Wang as Chinese negotiator after a furor was created over the Wang-Karakhan agreement. The rigid stand of Karakhan in the end brought the Chinese to recognition of the new agreement on May 31, 1924. The "agreement for the provisional management of the Chinese Eastern Railway," signed on the same day, provided for a joint management of the railway under a Russian manager, five Chinese and five Russian directors.[32]

The Russian initiative definitely had borne fruit. The Soviet Union was now recognized by the Peking government. Russian advisers actively engaged in assisting the rebel movement in the south; they and Chinese communists occupied important positions within the Kuomintang and the military academy newly established at Whampoa with Chiang Kai-shek as its first principal. Some Nationalists, such as Chiang himself and Hu Han-min, did not abandon their suspicion of Soviet designs, apart from their admiration of the Soviet system, and others were openly critical of the alliance with the communists. But Russians enjoyed the complete confidence of Sun Yat-sen. Their influence was visible in Sun's lectures on the "three people's principles," delivered to Party members and students in Canton between March and August 1924. In this Kuomintang canon the principle of nationalism was equated to anti-imperialism, and it was unequivocally asserted that China should demand nothing less than total revision of the existing treaty structure.[33]

The second Chihli-Fengtien war, which broke out in the middle of September 1924, did not nullify these achievements by the Russians, north and south. To be sure, the war was just another struggle for power among warlords. But Sun Yat-sen decided to take advantage of it to extend Kuomintang influence in the north. He entered into an alliance with Chang Tso-lin and Tuan

Ch'i-jui against Wu P'ei-fu, and he launched a northern expedition in late September, using the troops of certain southern warlords. Moreover, Feng Yü-hsiang, whose revolt against Wu caused the latter's defeat in the war, was known to be an admirer of Sun Yat-sen. Huang Fu whom Feng picked as temporary premier was also favorably inclined toward the Kuomintang.[34]

Toward the end of November, Feng Yü-hsiang and other victorious generals decided to ask Tuan Ch'i-jui to assume the office of "provisional chief executive." As the Provisional government had no constitutional or legal basis, Tuan, Feng, and others felt the need to summon a national assembly to organize a formal government. Toward the end of the year Tuan sent telegrams inviting over one hundred and twenty prominent leaders, including Sun Yat-sen, to attend a reconstruction conference as a step toward a national assembly.

Sun had already left Canton in mid-November to travel northward and meet the new leaders. Before his departure he issued a declaration calling for an end to imperialist domination and for the convening of a conference representing industrial associations, universities, chambers of commerce, educational associations, provincial student associations, labor unions, peasant associations, political parties, and all armies opposed to Wu P'ei-fu. In Peking, C. T. Wang, appointed temporary foreign minister, declared that "we wish to remind the friendly powers that China has a right to her own existence. Any conditions derogatory to her rights to exist as a free and independent nation must by necessity be rectified by mutual arrangement as quickly as the exigency of circumstances requires." All this was interpreted by at least one foreign diplomat as a sign of growing Soviet influence in Chinese politics. Ferdinand Mayer, the American chargé in Peking, opined that "In the present Peking Government the Soviet influence is very strong if not dominant. It is working chiefly through the Kuomintang Party."[35] The small beginnings of 1923 had grown into impressive proportions, and the Soviet Union had become definitely the most important outside factor in the Chinese scene.

THE PARTING OF THE WAY

The Soviet initiative came before other powers had time to put into effect the new ideas of international relations which they had formulated as an alternative to imperialist power politics. They had failed to make good their promises to assist China to emerge as a sovereign nation, nor had they given a substantial content to the "spirit of the Washington Conference." The Soviet successes in north and south China were a challenge to the Washington powers precisely because they were successful; Soviet policy had achieved what they had visualized but not implemented — a new order of Sino-foreign relations. The Sino-Russian *rapprochement* could mean the emergence of a parallel system of international relations in the Far East, challenging the structure of the Washington treaties. Although the powers had hoped to have enunciated universal principles and prescribed new rules for the conduct of all countries, the Soviet initiative and the Chinese response seemed to reduce them to the status of partial doctrines and particularistic rules.

Such a trend is clear now, but to the policy makers of the 1920's the basic nature of the Soviet initiative was only dimly discernible. The result was that the Washington powers failed to work out a systematic joint strategy to cope with the challenge. Because this side cf the problem has not been sufficiently explored by historians, it seems worthwhile to investigate in some detail the reaction of the powers to the emerging ties between China and Russia.

Two important problems confronted the Washington powers. One was the question of policy toward the Tuan government in Peking, which had the support of anti-Chihli factions and generals, including Chang Tso-lin, Feng Yü-hsiang, and Sun Yat-sen. The other problem was closely related to it; in defining their attitude toward the new regime, the powers would have to formulate their strategy on the issue of treaty revision. Spokesmen for the new government were loudly proclaiming the necessity to change the existing system of treaty relations, while the Kuomintang had consistently spoken of a complete overhaul of the treaty arrangements. The powers, therefore, would ultimately have to clarify their stand on the Nationalists' revolutionary nationalism.

On both counts the powers exhibited a striking lack of imagination. They neither took determined steps to check revolutionary influence in China, nor yielded to the Chinese demand for immediate treaty revision. They were still guided by the framework of the Washington Conference treaties, in which all would participate and contribute to China's gradual and peaceful emergence as an independent nation. But this principle was not translated into specific action to encourage the Chinese to proceed along evolutionary lines.

The point can be seen in the powers' attitude toward the Tuan Ch'i-jui government. To begin with, the foreign governments readily accepted their legations' recommendation that they extend recognition to the new regime only on condition that it undertake to observe the existing treaties and seek their modification only with the consent of the powers. A joint note to that effect was sent to and duly acknowledged by the Waichiaopu in December. The latter, while giving assurances that the existing treaties would be fully respected, reiterated the wish that the "well-known national aspirations of the Chinese people" be given prompt and sympathetic consideration by the powers.[36]

There was nothing striking about these exchanges. The powers had always coupled their recognition of a new Chinese regime with similar conditions. The latter, desirous of obtaining recognition, had given required assurances. This time some foreign officials did propose that the Tuan government be given substantial assistance in order to encourage mild, as opposed to radical, nationalism in China. Japanese officials in Peking and Tokyo believed that by such action the powers could undermine revolutionary radicalism and assist in the establishment of a responsible government in China. The American legation in Peking likewise suggested that treaty revision might be negotiated with the Tuan regime to undercut Soviet and Kuomintang influence.[37]

The subsequent course of Chinese history might well have been different if these proposals had been accepted. To be sure it cannot be proved that Tuan Ch'i-jui, if given a chance, would have become the focal point of mild nationalism in China, leading the nation in the task of regeneration. His deals with the Japanese in 1918 were too recent to be forgotten. In 1924–1925, however, he showed an unusual enthusiasm to restore order in the country on the basis of an alliance between Chang Tso-lin, Feng Yü-hsiang, and the Nationalists. He recognized the extreme importance of reducing the size of the warlords' armies and prepared a concrete plan for their demobilization. It should also be noted that not only Japanese but American and British officials in Peking were inclined to regard Tuan Ch'i-jui as the best safeguard against radicalism. With men like Huang Fu and C. T. Wang working for the government, there was a chance that the new regime might be enticed away from Soviet influence and persuaded to establish its authority on the basis of understanding with and support of the Washington powers.

Here again the opportunity was lost because of the powers' failure to agree on joint action. The Japanese minister in Peking, Yoshizawa Kenkichi, was so convinced of the need to give support and encouragement to the Peking government that he even suggested unilateral action — Japanese loans to help China stabilize its financial base. This counsel was rejected by Foreign Minister Shidehara on the ground that cooperation with the powers should not be given up. Instead, Shidehara sought to persuade the powers jointly to extend financial assistance to the Tuan government and buttress its position by raising the legations in Peking to the rank of embassies, as the Soviet Union had already done so, thereby creating an anomalous situation of the Russian representative's functioning as dean of the diplomatic body. Neither the United States nor the British government was favorably disposed to these schemes. Britain was disturbed that the Tuan government, despite its apparent stability, did not rest on a constitutional basis. The still prevailing uncertainties as to the nature and future of the government did not seem to justify the raising of the legations to embassies. The State Department was also skeptical of the durability of Tuan's alliance with Chang Tso-lin and Sun Yat-sen. As a staff memorandum put it, China's "incapacity for self government has now become obvious and [its] impending collapse in the face of the impact of the modern world threatens to be as complete as that of the Roman Empire." While it was the United States that had suggested financial help to Peking only two years earlier, conditions in China in the winter of 1924–1925 were considered less promising. American bankers, too, continued to oppose loan arrangements until there was a government in Peking with some promise of stability.[38]

For these reasons, no step was taken to encourage the allegedly moderate regime of Tuan Ch'i-jui. This raises a question about the powers' attitudes toward revolutionary nationalism in China. What knowledge did they have of the Kuomintang-Communist entente? How did they relate their attitude toward this entente to their over-all policies in China and the Far East?

Of the major powers the United States remained most passive toward the Kuomintang and its relations with the Soviet Union. The official American attitude toward Sun Yat-sen before his entente with Russia had been cool and indifferent. The legation in Peking and the State Department had taken the view that the Canton regime was a rebel government and Sun an impractical dreamer. There were exceptions; Vice Consul Ernest B. Price at Canton warmly supported Ch'en Chiung-ming and Sun Yat-sen before their open break in 1922 as "enlightened men" and the best hope for the future of China. His views were not shared by Minister Charles R. Crane. Neither was the State Department receptive. When, in May 1921, Price forwarded a personal appeal of Sun Yat-sen to President Harding, he was reprimanded for functioning as "a vehicle of official communication for an organization in revolt against a Government with which the United States is in friendly relations." The State Department's injunctions against interference with China's internal affairs were such that in August 1922, Sun was refused use of an American naval vessel to transport him, after his defeat by General Ch'en, to Shanghai.[39]

The United States had at most only second-hand information about the developing Kuomintang-Soviet ties. Neither Edwin S. Cunningham nor Raymond P. Tenney, American consuls general at Shanghai and Canton during the crucial months of late 1922 and early 1923, had any inkling of Sun's initial ties with the Soviets. About the activities of Borodin's group in Canton in late 1923 Consul General Douglas Jenkins had only hazy notions. His despatches to the State Department were filled with his confession of inability to discover Borodin's and Sun Yat-sen's true intentions. Nelson T. Johnson, on a tour of inspection of Far Eastern consular posts, was another official who had the opportunity to observe the Canton scene at this time, but he was not overly impressed with the evidence of Russian activities there. He felt that there were so many divisions within the Kuomintang that it would be difficult to evolve a tight revolutionary organization of the Russian type. In Peking, Minister Schurman remained skeptical of China's ever turning to communism. As he commented on one occasion, "Communism is wholly alien to Chinese life and sentiment and institutions, and the dictatorship of the proletariat is in complete contradiction with the democracy of the self-governing (or non-governed) patriarchal family communities which cover like clusters of bees the entire country." [40]

State Department policy toward the Kuomintang reflected these views which were at best complacent and even ignorant. As Hughes instructed the legation on one occasion, the "question of dangerous Bolshevik activities in China primarily is one of domestic Chinese administration" and "the American Government cannot concern itself with the matter except in case American interests are directly involved." While some officials suggested that the United States might enter into negotiation for treaty revision with Peking in order to undermine radical strength, the Department at this time was reluctant to take the initiative; it was extremely unwilling to give the impression of interfering in Chinese domestic affairs. Unilateral action was likewise shunned by the State Department. It still wished to act cautiously within the framework of the Washington treaties. Coupled with France's failure to ratify the Washington customs treaty, such an attitude spelled inaction.[41]

In this way the United States, which as the originator of the Washington system might have been most concerned with the Soviet initiative in China, allowed the situation to drift without attempting to reverse or channel the tide. There was no realization of an urgent need to redefine the basis of the Washington powers' diplomacy in the Far East.

Great Britain was more outspokenly hostile to the Kuomintang than perhaps any other power, but the hostility did not result in any positive action. This was primarily because of reluctance to act alone, another expression of the "spirit of the Washington Conference." All the same, British policy contributed nothing to the clarification of the powers' stand on the Kuomintang question.

After Sun Yat-sen's return to Canton early in 1923 British officials in Hongkong and Canton had temporarily changed their attitude and warmly approached the Nationalists. It was felt that Sun might be assisted financially so as to prevent another seamen's strike, which had severely affected Hongkong's trade in 1922.[42] The Nationalists, however, did not abandon their suspicion of Britain, especially as they feared that the British fleet was in a position to blockade the revolutionary center.[43] Antagonism flared up again during the merchants association incident in the summer and fall of 1924. Canton's merchants, who for over a decade had organized themselves into an armed association for self-protection, had become steadily alienated from Sun Yat-sen by his excessive demands for money and support of labor activities. In the summer of 1924 they purchased 1129 cases of arms from Denmark through a German agent. They were shipped to Canton on a Norwegian ship. The British were involved insofar as the customs authorities at Canton authorized the import of these arms and the payment for them was made through the Hongkong and Shanghai Banking Corporation. The Nationalists, moreover, suspected that the British in Hongkong were actively in collusion with the antirevolutionary merchants. Sun Yat-sen ordered seizure of the weapons. A period of tension followed, lasting from August to October 1924. Toward the end of August the British consul general at Canton warned that the government forces would be attacked by the British navy if they started shooting in the city against the merchant militia. Sun Yat-sen responded by publicly denouncing the merchants as agents of British imperialism and protesting to Prime Minister J. Ramsay MacDonald against interference with China's internal affairs. At the same time, menaced by the spectacle of British intervention, Sun proposed moving revolutionary headquarters northward, even abandoning the Whampoa Military Academy. He wanted to take advantage of the Fengtien-Chihli war in the north and extend Nationalist influence in central China. Chiang Kai-shek opposed this,

and in the end the militia of the merchants' association was surrounded and disarmed by government troops, including cadets
of the military academy.[44]

The Nationalists were further embittered toward Britain because of the cool reception of Sun Yat-sen by British officials in
the north. The consul general at Shanghai unsuccessfully sought
to obtain approval of his colleagues to the suggestion that Sun
not be permitted to enter the international settlement. The British minister in Peking also suggested, in December, that the
Washington powers issue a joint statement saying that they would
not "recognize or have truck with any administration which might
be set up in Peking by those Peking leaders in China who in the
present as in the past have been and are seeking to incite the
Chinese people against the friendly attitude [of the] powers."
While nothing came of it, owing to the opposition of other ministers, this and other acts by British officials in north and south
China revealed their hostility to the Kuomintang regime. But this
was not the kind of hostility which could lead to positive action.
Lacking international cooperation, Britain bided its time, without defining a clear policy.[45]

Finally, Japanese policy was no more calculated to bring about
meaningful cooperation by the powers concerning revolutionary
nationalism in China. This was primarily because the Japanese
government at this time did not take the alleged communist
menace seriously enough to propose action, and also because
Japan sought to avoid friction with the Soviet Union while it
negotiated the restoration of diplomatic relations with Russia
after the Siberian fiasco.

Foreign Ministry officials in Tokyo had more information on
Soviet activities in China than their counterparts elsewhere,
thanks to their extensive intelligence network. But the civilian
officials were not prone to be overly alarmed by the reported
Soviet activities. They noted that the growing anti-imperialist
agitation was not specifically directed against Japan and that
there was more division than unity among Kuomintang leaders
now that Sun had approached Soviet Russia. The consul general
at Canton reasoned that much talk of a national assembly and
anti-imperialism was meant to increase the influence of the Kuo-

mintang, rather than to enunciate serious policies which its leaders believed could be achieved in the near future. In this way Japanese officials tended to minimize the danger of Bolshevism in China and regard the Kuomintang-Soviet alliance as a tactical maneuver by the former. Basic to these attitudes was the belief that China could never become a communist country. Shidehara told the American ambassador, Edgar A. Bancroft, that "he did not think Sovietism would take any hold on the Chinese: the Chinaman loves money and has his little property and is the greatest individualist and it is wholly unlikely that he would accept communism; while Dr. Sun was a radical idealist and for this reason his political career had been a failure, he did not think Sun was favorable to communism." [46]

Such an assumption was in contrast to military thinking in Japan. Army and navy strategists in the early twenties had come to visualize the United States as the foremost enemy. This did not mean that they envisioned friendly relations with Russia. The army continued to play up the fear of Russian domination of the Far East. This was partly mere propaganda, calculated to justify their demand for a larger defense budget. But there was also genuine concern with Soviet influence in China. War Minister Ugaki Kazushige's diary is a record of his indignation at the failure of his civilian colleagues to appreciate the scale of the communist danger in China.[47] At this time, however, the cabinet of Katō Takaaki had firm control over China policy, and the civilian estimate of the Chinese situation was accepted as the basis for policy.

An equally important reason for Japanese inaction was the fact that negotiations had been opened between Tokyo and Moscow for the restoration of normal diplomatic relations. There were a number of factors behind Russo-Japanese *rapprochement*. The Soviet government wanted recognition by one of the major powers, which would add tremendously to its prestige. As an independent country, Russia could not long tolerate the presence of Japanese troops in its territory of North Sakhalin. On the Japanese side the picture was more complex. The War and Foreign ministries were initially not very enthusiastic about resuming diplomatic relations with Russia; ideologically, both were strongly anti-communist, and professional bureaucrats did not wish to depart from the framework of American-British-Japanese cooperation. On the other hand, the Navy Ministry vigorously advocated Russo-Japanese *rapprochement* in order to stabilize conditions in northeast Asia and to secure for Japan the rich oil resources of Sakhalin. There was also an influential group of statesmen, headed by Viscount Gotō Shimpei, who pressed the government to settle outstanding disputes with the Soviet Union. For Gotō nothing could be more harmful than Russia and China coming together without Japanese participation. Japan's solid understanding with the Soviet Union was the best protection of the rights and interests in China and the strongest check on American influence in Asia. He completely agreed with the critics of Japan's official policy who did not believe that American and Japanese policies in the Far East could be harmonized. Gotō was a strong advocate of the need to maintain a balance between the "new continent" represented by the United States and the "old continent" in which Japan, Russia, and China should develop close ties.[48]

In order to push ahead with these views, Gotō invited Joffe to Japan early in 1923, shortly after the latter had concluded a series of talks with Sun Yat-sen. The presence of Joffe forced the Foreign Ministry to agree to open exploratory talks on the pending issues between the two governments. There is no evidence that the Foreign Ministry was won over by Gotō's views. Rather, it was felt that informal negotiations would do no harm to the basic solidarity of the Washington powers and could probably lead to a solution of various complicated problems which had arisen as a result of the Siberian expedition. During June and July 1923, Joffe talked with Kawakami Toshitsune, the appointed Japanese negotiator. Discussion ranged over all possible sources of conflict between the two countries, such as the settlement of the Nikolaievsk incident, the disposition of Sakhalin Island, and treaty obligations of the Soviet Union. The conferees reached general agreement on the sale of North Sakhalin to Japan or, if the price could not be agreed upon, Japanese lease of natural resources and various concessions on a long-term basis. Furthermore, Joffe consented to granting Japanese mining and timber concessions in the "Far Eastern territory" of Russia. Joffe and Kawakami also successfully brought the two nations' views together on such matters as the prohibition of "harmful propaganda" and the guarantee of Japanese business activities in Russia. On two issues the negotiators failed to agree. Concerning the Nikolaievsk incident, Japan wanted a straightforward statement of regret by Russia, whereas the latter insisted on including a passage pointing out the inevitability of some military action by the Soviets to defend their own revolution. Japan had at first insisted on reparations but later waived the demand, and agreement on the incident did not seem impossible. The Narkomindel representative stood firm, however, on the issue of existing treaties. Japan insisted that the new regime in Russia had the obligation to honor all outstanding treaties concluded between Japan and Tsarist Russia, although Japan expressed willingness to consent to the abrogation of these treaties following formal negotiation of new treaties guaranteeing existing Japanese rights. On this issue Joffe was adamant, maintaining that the war had necessitated change in old treaties. Moreover, the Russian representative refused to accede to the Japanese demand that Soviet Russia recognize existing debts contracted by the previous regime. He was particularly firm on insisting that Russia had the right to refuse to pay wartime debts as the war had brought no benefit to the Russian people.[49]

Throughout these exploratory talks the Japanese government remained inflexible on what it considered essential conditions for the restoration of diplomatic relations. It was not convinced of the urgency of the problem. Japanese policy makers feared the implications of any recognition of the Russian contention for Japan's still more important relations with China. With an ever-growing movement in China for national independence and equality, Japan had to be doubly cautious lest its new relations with Russia be interpreted as weakness on its part with regard to existing treaties.[50]

Less than a year later, Moscow and Tokyo once again tried, this time successfully, to normalize their relations. Japan was now willing to compromise on issues on which it had stood adamant a year earlier. It was solicitous of good understanding with the Soviet Union. In part, cabinet changes in Japan may have accounted for this development. The short-lived cabinet of Admiral

Yamamoto Gombei (September 1923–January 1924) included Gotō Shimpei as home minister. There is reason to believe that this cabinet took the first step in changing Japan's Soviet policy. Yamamoto was succeeded as prime minister first by Kiyoura Keigo and then by Katō Takaaki, the latter assuming the office in June 1924. This period of frequent cabinet changes coincided with the recognition of the Soviet Union by Britain, Italy, Austria, and other countries, and Japan could follow their lead. Perhaps even more important was the unmistakable spectacle of Sino-Soviet *rapprochement,* also taking place at this time. While the Foreign Ministry remained skeptical of the possibility of a communist China, special arrangements between China and Russia could evoke memories of imperialist diplomacy. Gotō's fear of Japanese isolation in the face of Sino-Russian entente came to be shared by Foreign Ministry officials, especially since the Washington powers seemed incapable of meeting the challenge in unity.[51]

Negotiations this time were carried out in Peking, between Ambassador Karakhan and Minister Yoshizawa. Talks dragged on for eight months, but both sides showed enough patience and compromising spirit to save the negotiations from another deadlock. The issue of recognition of the Soviet regime was readily agreed to, as Karakhan acknowledged the validity of the Treaty of Portsmouth and the general principle that other treaties and agreements should be modified or abrogated at a conference to be convened in the future. The one issue which threatened to break up the talks was the problem of economic concessions in North Sakhalin. To the Japanese, Russo-Japanese *rapprochement* seemed barren of any content without such concessions. In return for withdrawing the troops from North Sakhalin, Japan demanded oil, coal, and timber concessions rather than indemnities for the Nikolaievsk incident, in addition to an apology from the Soviet government. Even then, the original Japanese demand for a monopolistic right was steadily compromised, so that in the end Japan was satisfied with the concession to develop 50 percent of the oil fields in North Sakhalin. In addition Japan was granted coal mining and timber concessions in specified areas of the island. In return, Japan promised to withdraw its troops completely from

North Sakhalin by May 15, 1925. Karakhan's written expression of regret solved the Nikolaievsk incident. Russia also pledged to forbid subversive activities in Japanese territory in return for Japan's promise not to recognize anti-Bolshevik organizations in Japan.[52]

The subsequent history of Russo-Japanese relations indicates that the Japanese government never gave up its suspicion and distrust of Soviet motives and policies. Nevertheless, in the context of the Soviet initiative in China, the new treaty with Russia was another piece of evidence that Japan could not ignore the trend toward yet another new order in the Far East, prompted by the Russo-Chinese entente. Japan sought to mitigate its effects, and it was willing to offer inducements to Russia to achieve this end. Because Japan still operated within the framework of the Washington Conference treaties, however, there was no thought of forming a close partnership with the Soviet Union.

The three years following the Washington Conference saw many changes in the Far Eastern scene, not of the powers' making but due largely to the Soviet initiative. The Washington signatories had failed to respond constructively to the continuing civil war and spreading disorder in China, while Russian officials and Comintern agitators worked assiduously to enter the vacuum and create a new order at the expense of the Washington powers. Though the latter had defined their own new order, they had failed to implement it. This was a period when the powers failed to cooperate in China to realize their vision of a new order or to seek yet another solution to the problem of promoting their interests and maintaining the peace in the Far East.

The picture is that of a lost opportunity. After 1925 it was hopeless to appease Chinese nationalism with programs outlined at the Washington Conference and impossible to counter the tides of antiforeignism and radicalism spread by the Kuomintang and Chinese communists. The Washington powers lost the opportunity to translate their professions of friendship and cooperation into concrete action. While they disagreed over the method and timing of bringing this about, the Chinese were seeking new treaty relations with non-Washington powers patterned after their agreements with Germany and Russia.[53] Statistics showed little increase in Sino-foreign trade after 1921, as if to demonstrate that the restoration of amity among the treaty powers bore no relation to the outcome of their economic activities in China. Meanwhile the gap between foreign policy and military thinking in the United States as well as in Japan continued to widen. All these vectors of policies and attitudes neutralized each other and spelled confusion in the Far Eastern scene. The pattern which had seemed to be emerging in early 1922 had become blurred.

II · COLLAPSE OF THE WASHINGTON
SYSTEM, 1925–1926

The year 1925 was a turning point in the history of the postwar Far East. Now that the cooperative action envisioned in the Washington Conference structure had been powerless to stem the tide of Soviet-inspired radicalism in China, London, Washington, and Tokyo had begun to grope for some alternative. The May 30th incident added urgency to these efforts. In a tariff conference at Peking, the powers cast about for new modes of cooperation. The conference, however, was to prove a failure. It was to mark the end of the fiction of Anglo-American-Japanese cooperation in China.

THE MAY 30TH INCIDENT

Sun Yat-sen entered Peking on the last day of the year 1924. He was seriously ill and exhausted after a long journey from Canton. But he was once again a national figure who might even head a coalition government with northern warlords and politicians. On his way back to north China, Sun had visited Japan and in Kobe had given his now famous lectures. In one he exalted the moral and cultural values of the East and urged Japan to make a choice between the West's "interest- and power-centered" culture and Asia's culture of the "royal way." In the second lecture Sun exhorted Japan, "China's younger brother," to free China from his masters in order to live once again as brothers of the same family. When he entered Peking on December 31 he declared that he would continue to struggle to liberate China from its "colonial status." [1]

It is ironic that while Sun was advocating Sino-Japanese *rapprochement* the movement which he had helped to develop had reached a point at which it would directly challenge Japanese rights in China. For one thing, his apparent readiness to come to terms with Tuan Ch'i-jui precipitated a split within the Kuomintang. Some advocated Nationalist participation in the reconstruction conference, opened in Peking on February 1, while many influential leaders were opposed to it. The former also espoused anticommunism, and in early March it formed a separatist organization. The struggle for power between the right and the left wings of the Kuomintang had begun. Such a struggle had the effect of making the factions all the more anti-imperialist, as they tried to attract mass following by antiforeign propaganda. At this time the leftists, including Chiang Kai-shek, Wang Ching-wei, and Hu Han-min, were in the ascendancy. When Sun Yat-sen died, on March 12, the Kuomintang leaders sent a telegram to Moscow, expressing determination to carry on the task of national liberation. With Sun gone there was no question of the Nationalists' further associating themselves with Tuan Ch'i-jui or seeking *rapprochement* with Japan.[2]

What was equally significant, Sun's last days coincided with an intensified labor agitation in the treaty ports, led by Kuomintang and communist agents. They clandestinely made contact with Chinese workers in foreign-owned factories, organized them, disseminated Marxist propaganda, and directed strikes against such abuses as the beating of laborers, long working hours, employment of children, and poor dormitory conditions.[3]

Of all foreign factories Japanese-owned cotton mills occupied a conspicuous position because of their number and size. Expanded tremendously during the World War, they numbered over forty in 1925, as compared with three British and nearly eighty Chinese factories. In Shanghai, the center of the spinning and weaving industry, more than half the spindles were owned by Japanese mills and more than half the Japanese investment was devoted to the industry. Many of the larger mills were the branches of those in Japan which were owned by the same companies. As the industry was one of the largest in Japan and operated by big concerns, it had not suffered severely from the postwar, post-earthquake depression but on the contrary had expanded its operations enormously in China. Protected by extraterritorial rights and treaty tariffs, Japanese mills competed favorably with native Chinese factories, which had also expanded during and after the war. Since Japanese exports to China had leveled off, it was natural that the Tokyo government should wish to further the interests of these mills as a harbinger of greater economic expansion in China.[4]

Historic factors rooted deeply in the eighty-year-old treaties, peculiar characteristics of the Japanese cotton spinning and weaving industry in China, intensified propaganda work by revolutionary agitators, and the failure of the Tuan Ch'i-jui regime to form a representative government — all these conditions added to specific grievances of Chinese employees at several Japanese mills in the early months of 1925 and produced a highly explosive situation. A strike was declared in Tsingtao in April and in Shanghai once in February and then in May. The strikes were at first aimed at specific ends; at a Japanese mill in Tsingtao the company's refusal to recognize the workers' union was the first step toward the strike, while at Shanghai death of a child laborer brought about a strike.[5] This year, however, labor disputes developed into threatening proportions as Chinese authorities became involved and as Japanese officials became aware of "outside" influences upon the workers.

In mid-February, the Japanese consul general at Shanghai concluded that the strikers were agitated from outside and that the core of the agitators seemed to be members of the Socialist Youth Corps and the Communist Party. From Tsingtao the consul general reported that a search of Chinese laborers' residences had uncovered some communist propaganda material. From these and other reports Foreign Ministry officials in Tokyo concluded that the agitators were playing a crucial role in the strikes and that political action must be taken to safeguard the factories against further attack. In early May, Foreign Minister Shidehara instructed the Japanese official at Tsinan to express to the provincial governor the wish that "efforts may be made to solve the strike by such effective and appropriate means as arresting outside agitators." The assumption here was that the labor movement had become menacing as a result of the activities of a few radicals and outside agitators. Consequently it was believed that once these were removed the movement would subside unless the management drove employees to desperation by refusing to grant reasonable demands. Concurrently with the above instruction, therefore, Foreign Ministry officials tried to persuade the representatives of the Japanese cotton industry to take no harsh measures to cope with the strike but to offer some compromise. Some reform was considered necessary to head off more radical demands.[6]

The Japanese government also desired that Chinese authorities take strict measures to maintain order and stability within the country. Deeply concerned with the stability of the Peking government under Tuan Ch'i-jui, Foreign Minister Shidehara was worried lest the continued labor dispute have an adverse effect upon it. If Chinese authorities were unable to maintain order by suppressing strikers, he reasoned, confidence of the powers in the Peking government would be lost.[7]

In this way Chinese officials, civilian and military, were drawn into the situation created by laborers. They had to step in and do something. Chambers of commerce and other organizations were calling for the solution of each strike, while Japan was constantly pressing them for forceful measures. Both Peking and local officials complied with Japanese request in principle, promising to take effective means of lessening the danger and urging influential merchant and industrial leaders to mediate between factory owners and laborers. In Tsingtao, where strikers occupied factory buildings in defiance of the company managers, the military governor of Shantung finally took the drastic measure, on May 28, of arresting the leaders and disbanding the laborers' organization. The action was understood to have been taken under pressure from the Waichiaopu and Marshal Chang Tso-lin.[8] In Shanghai the concession police and the municipal government, organized by the treaty powers, were the main organs of control. Before native Chinese organizations could take any step toward the solution of a strike in Japanese mills, which had begun early in May, the concession police resorted to force and on May 15 killed one laborer. Eight days later six students were arrested for distributing pamphlets in protest against the killing. The situation grew tense and on May 30, when several hundred demonstrators attacked the Louza police station, the British inspector in charge ordered his men to fire. The result was nine casualties and many injuries. The student demonstrators had borne no arms.[9]

In this way the strikes in the Japanese factories culminated in the May 30th incident and developed into a nation-wide movement of protest against Japanese and British acts. Clashes continued to occur between Chinese on the one hand and British and Japanese residents and officers on the other in Shanghai, Nanking, Wuhu, Kiukiang, Hankow, Changsha, Chungking, and other cities. Boycotts were declared against British and Japanese goods beginning in late June, and a national movement for liberation from foreign control started. In the south, on the Shakee bund opposite the island of Shameen where the British and French concessions in Canton were located, there was firing on both sides, resulting in the "Shameen massacre" of June 23. About one hundred and twenty Chinese were killed or injured. A general strike was immediately declared in Hongkong and a boycott of British goods began in Canton. A military council was organized in early July to map out strategy against imperialists as well as warlords. Chiang Kai-shek declared that there was no room for compromise with Great Britain and that the Chinese revolutionaries must keep in touch and cooperate with world revolutionary forces.[10]

The Chinese government in Peking was placed in a difficult position. It could turn the nation-wide sense of indignation to its advantage by supporting the Chinese people's militant stand; this would perhaps give the Tuan regime moral support of the people. There were already signs, however, that the anti-imperialist movement was also directed against the warlords as "running dogs" of foreign powers. As Kuomintang and communist agents spread northward and intensified their activity following the May 30th incident, their twin opposition to imperialists and warlords came to be accepted by students and laborers involved in anti-British and anti-Japanese boycotts. Peking authorities and the military power behind them could not, as a consequence, condone the nation-wide movement with equanimity. Moreover, they could not seriously entertain the thought of antagonizing the treaty powers as a whole. What was needed was a device by which the government could placate national feeling and at the same time avoid inviting the anger of all the powers.[11]

The Peking government took two major steps. One was to attempt to isolate Britain by approaching Japan. Chinese officials urged that Japan be cool and cautious in this dangerous hour and take no oppressive measure which would further irritate the populace. They hoped that the labor strikes could be solved by the two countries and separated from the nation-wide movement of protest against the shooting of May 30 in which presumably only the British were involved. At the same time, officials in various cities took the initiative in directing and coordinating demonstrations and boycotts, seeking on the whole to turn the movement into an exclusively anti-British affair.[12]

The second and more sensible step taken by Peking was the handing of two notes to the Washington powers on June 24. One note referred specifically to the May 30th incident, presenting thirteen demands for solution of the affair. In addition to demanding the release of the Chinese who had been arrested, indemnity to the "victims," and formal apologies, the note stated that "in order to assure definitely friendly relations between China and the foreign powers and a permanent peace, all the unequal treaties which have been concluded in the past must be revised." This last point was explicitly brought forth in the second note. There the "inequalities and extraordinary privileges" under the old treaties were blamed for having caused the May 30th incident, and it was declared that "there should be a readjustment of China's treaty relations with foreign Powers to bring them more in line with the generally accepted conceptions of international justice and equity and more in conformity with existing conditions in China."[13] Peking officials, in this way, were taking advantage of the incident in Shanghai in order to perpetuate their own power; by taking the initiative in effecting revision of the existing treaties they would be able to pose as champions of Chinese freedom and at the same time undermine radical opposition to their government. But the survival of the Peking government depended on the responses of the powers.

BEYOND THE WASHINGTON FORMULA

Both London and Washington had been reconsidering their China policies even before May 30. Within the British government the realization had grown that the powers had already missed the opportunity to work in cooperation within the framework of the Washington Conference treaties. It was felt that Britain should be prepared to go beyond them if it were to placate Chinese nationalism and protect its own interests in China. Specifically, in 1925 the Foreign Office was considering the grant of a tariff increase up to 12.5 percent at the tariff conference which would be convened as soon as all the powers had ratified the Washington customs treaty. Such a proposal went beyond the provisions of the treaty, which had promised China an immediate increase in the tariff rates of only 2.5 per cent on ordinary imports and 5 percent on luxury items.[14]

Such a policy was maintained even after the outbreak of the anti-British boycott following the May 30th incident. Officially London could not condone the violence of the Chinese or give the impression of capitulation by agreeing to a settlement of the incident on other than its own terms. At one point, indeed, the British government went so far as to invite the cooperation of the powers to cope with "Moscow's plot" which was held to be responsible for conditions in China.[15] But quite apart from the issues directly connected with the incident, Britain was willing to continue exploring various alternatives to the Washington formula, which was "out of date" according to Wellesley, now assistant undersecretary of foreign affairs. Such a policy did not imply support of the Peking government, but revealed Britain's interest in finding a new basis of Sino-foreign relations.[16]

In the United States the new Secretary of State, Frank B. Kellogg, was similarly determined to put an end to the period of indecision in Sino-American relations. Though he had never been in the Far East, Kellogg had observed the Chinese scene in London, where as American ambassador he had carried out Hughes's instructions to cooperate with Britain in Chinese matters. Apparently his experience had convinced him of the futility of cooperation, for as Secretary he proved himself much less interested in maintaining a framework of joint action in the Far East. Kellogg had his own ideas about Sino-American amity as a cornerstone of peace in that part of the world. He was convinced of the need in time to restore essential ingredients of sovereignty to China, particularly tariff and judicial autonomy. It is difficult to say to what extent he was motivated by a desire to counter the Soviet initiative. He did state on several occasions that America's conciliatory policy, extended regardless of the attitudes of other powers if necessary, would help in checking violent antiforeignism in China. There is also evidence that he sought to encourage the impression that the United States was a sympathetic friend of China, since this would presumably exempt it from much of China's antiforeign feeling.[17] If Kellogg had seriously considered a new American initiative, however, the result must have been rather disappointing. Not only did some of his advisers in the State Department disagree with his policy of friendship, but he soon found out that the real situation in China did not correspond to his image. The story of American policy in 1925–1926 is in effect a story of Kellogg's gradual sobering. Still, the implications of his initial policy for Sino-foreign relations were unmistakable.

America's first response to the May 30th incident was to placate Chinese nationalism by taking the initiative to reconsider the existing treaties. The first logical step was the fulfillment of the promises given at the Washington Conference. As the American legation in Peking suggested, the time had come for the powers to carry out these promises in order to come to terms with moderate Chinese nationalism. While Consul General Cunningham at Shanghai strongly upheld the action of the concession police on May 30 and requested the dispatch of additional American war vessels to protect nationals, Ferdinand Mayer, the chargé, believed that "while law and order must be maintained by all necessary force, if conciliatory measures will contribute to bring return to normal conditions I consider these should be used whenever possible." Mayer believed that the time was opportune to expedite the meeting of the tariff conference to stabilize conditions in China and normalize Sino-foreign relations. On June 18 he tried unsuccessfully to persuade his colleagues to issue a joint statement expressing their countries' readiness to meet their obligations under the Washington treaties. Minister John V. A. MacMurray, who arrived in his new post a month after the May 30th outbreak, also favored diverting Chinese nationalism from indiscriminate attack upon foreign rights by carrying out the promises of the Washington Conference. This was "the only safe road." [18]

In Washington officials supported such a policy, especially following the receipt of the Chinese notes of June 24. On July 1, Secretary Kellogg telegraphed Mayer that "the Chinese proposal should be made the occasion of evidencing to the Chinese our willingness to consider sympathetically and helpfully the modification of existing treaties," if authorities in China demonstrated "their willingness and ability to fulfill their obligations." More specifically, Kellogg urged that a tariff conference be convened as soon as possible and that the conference be requested "to make concrete recommendations upon which a program for granting complete tariff autonomy to China may be worked out." In addition, an extraterritoriality commission should be despatched to China without delay with a view to making specific suggestions for a gradual relinquishment of extraterritoriality.[19]

In this manner the May 30th incident served to induce London and Washington to articulate policies which they had already begun to consider. The State Department went further than the Foreign Office in that it was considering discussion of the extraterritorial matter, in addition to tariff revision. All the same, these crucial decisions by Britain and the United States put Japan on the defensive.

Japan's basic policies were outlined in Foreign Minister Shidehara's two instructions to Minister Yoshizawa, dated June 29 and July 3. The minister was to cooperate with his British and American colleagues and seek to mediate between China and the powers for a solution of the May 30th incident. Compensation to Chinese victims and punishment of responsible settlement officials could be offered in return for China's pledge not to condone strikes and antiforeign movements. Japan was also sympathetic toward China's reasonable national aspirations, but treaty revision must be effected only through legitimate means.[20]

Basic to these policies was the Japanese government's interpretation of the May 30th movement and the possible Russian implication. War Ministry and General Staff officials, in possession of intelligence reports on Soviet activities in China, continued to be alarmed by the growth of Russian influence in Manchuria and China proper. It was believed that the Nationalists were deceiving themselves in entering into an alliance with the Soviet Union and that the threat of communism was very real. War Minister Ugaki regarded China's antiforeignism as a result of the postwar decline in prestige of Japan, Britain, the United States, and other countries. Somewhat paradoxically, he thought that America's "hypocritical humanitarianism" had much to do with the general decline in foreign prestige and the corresponding growth of China's contempt of Japan. The more concessions Japan offered to China, Ugaki believed, the more would the latter's arrogance increase. The essential thing was to re-establish the prestige of the empire.[21] Such thinking was in line with the military's assumption in Japan's basic conflict with Russia and America and with their continued habit of looking at international relations in the frame of reference of the old diplomacy.

Civilian officials also were aware of the Soviet background of the May 30th incident. Japanese consuls in China had repeatedly reported to Tokyo the activities of communist agents among the laborers in foreign factories. Some, like Consul General Yada Shichitarō at Shanghai, who had not taken an alarmist view of the situation, now realized the seriousness of the communist menace. Yada had believed at first that the student demonstrators were motivated by patriotism and that labor unions should be recognized as legitimate organs by the foreign capitalists so long as they did not aim at the destruction of the existing industrial system. But after May 30, seeing and talking with Li Li-san, the leader of the Shanghai laborers, the consul general came to feel that Li was an "authentic red" and that communist-based unions should be opposed.[22] Officials in Tokyo did not think the information at their disposal warranted their presupposing that the agitation in China was Soviet inspired. Instead they assumed that the Chinese nationalistic movement could be turned from radicalism if Japan took a calm stand and offered timely concessions. Kimura Eiichi, chief of the Asian affairs bureau, considered it impossible to eradicate the new ideologies in China, which were a "necessary evil" accompanying political changes in that country. He urged that an honest effort be made by Japanese capitalists to settle the outstanding labor disputes in Shanghai, Tsingtao, and elsewhere by extending moderate terms to workers.[23]

Foreign Minister Shidehara agreed with such an approach. In early July, when Britain's representative in Tokyo conveyed his government's proposal that the powers agree upon a common policy to cope with "Moscow's plot," the Foreign Minister replied that he did not "share such pessimistic and alarming views." There was no clear evidence, he said, that Russians were behind the May 30th incident. It was doubtful whether the Kuomintang government had the intention or even the strength to turn China into a communist country. Shidehara said he was firmly opposed to forceful action on the part of the powers as it would only incite further anti-foreign movements throughout China. Instead, he advocated the temporary withdrawal of Japanese nationals from the interior of China to places of safety.[24]

Such a stand did not imply independent action by Japan in China. Consular and legation reports from China had indicated a growing trend on the part of Chinese to distinguish Britain from Japan and concentrate their venom on the former. Some Japanese urged, consequently, that Japan follow its own course of action and ingratiate itself with the Chinese. Shidehara, Kimura, and others in the Foreign Ministry refused to do so. Their policy toward the anti-British agitation in China was to mediate between the two countries, if possible in cooperation with other powers. In Canton, for example, the Japanese consul general gave no encouragement to the Nationalists who sought to isolate Britain by approaching Japan and asked that the latter express sympathy with China's cause. When the governor of Hongkong expressed his wish that Japan follow Britain's example in prohibiting the export of coal to Canton, the Tokyo government was even willing to consider such an embargo, which would be disadvantageous to Japanese exporters, because of its desire to show sympathy with Great Britain.[25] At this time Tokyo officials were cool to the Chinese suggestions for unilateral action as well as to those from some Japanese in China that Japan detach itself from other treaty powers and enter into bilateral relations with China.

Japan could not afford to antagonize the powers, especially Britain and the United States, over the settlement of the May 30th incident, because their cooperation was needed in a much more important matter, treaty revision. Indeed, the Chinese note of June 24 calling for new treaties was not answered by the powers until early September, primarily because Japan sought to press its views on the matter on the other governments.

For Japan the issue of tariff revision was of utmost importance. The initial British draft reply had referred to willingness to make the forthcoming tariff conference "of a more far-reaching and comprehensive nature than was originally contemplated" at the Washington Conference. As noted earlier, Britain was contemplating granting a tariff increase up to 12.5 percent. The American draft reply also stated readiness "either at the tariff conference or at a subsequent time to take up the subject of a comprehensive revision of the treaties, looking toward ultimate tariff autonomy." Japan strenuously objected to these proposals. It dreaded nothing more than having a uniform surtax applied to foreign goods immediately and indiscriminately, with the probable result that Japanese imports to China, especially cotton fabrics, would have to compete with native Chinese products. There was also the fear that China might turn to foreign borrowing on the security of the increased revenue, even before redeeming its existing debts, of which the Nishihara loans were most conspicuous. Japan would consent to a change in the economic order of the Far East only if the change insured against the loss of China as a market for Japanese goods and capital.

These points were spelled out fully in a number of instructions Shidehara sent to the legation in Peking. They are worth recording here, as they reflected Japanese thinking at this time and remained the basic Japanese position during the Peking Tariff Conference. Shidehara said that the most he would agree to would be to put into effect the stipulations of the Washington customs treaty: to grant 2.5 percent surtaxes on ordinary goods and 5 percent on luxury imports. Even this was conditional upon two terms; there must be levied in China "a countervailing excise duty upon native produce" so that the surtaxes would not hamper the growth of foreign trade, and prohibitions and restrictions upon the exportation of Chinese raw materials must be removed. Furthermore, the surplus revenues thus acquired from increased duties should be applied to the consolidation of unsecured internal and foreign debts, as well as to meeting administrative expenditures.[26]

In the months of July and August, Japan made strenuous efforts to convince Washington and London of the inadvisability of mentioning tariff autonomy in their reply to China. As time dragged on while the three governments sought to coordinate their action, the realization grew that they might have to send separate notes to the Chinese government expressing their respective views. Before actual steps were taken in this direction, however, France at last ratified the Washington customs treaty, thus making it mandatory for the Washington powers to agree to the convening of a tariff conference within three months. On August 19 the Waichiaopu seized the initiative and presented to the Washington signatories an invitation to a special tariff conference to meet on October 26, 1925.[27]

The day before the invitation was issued a member of the Chinese Foreign Ministry visited Minister Yoshizawa and conveyed the hope that, in view of the close relations between the two countries, Japan would assist China at the forthcoming tariff conference. It was intimated that China wanted tariff autonomy as a matter of principle but that in actuality it had no intention of hindering foreign trade. The national tariff schedule which a Chinese governmental committee had already drafted ranged from none to 35 percent, the higher rates applying to luxuries. Under the circumstances Shidehara concluded that the time had come for Japan to make some concession in drafting a joint reply to the earlier Chinese note of June 24. In this way the Japanese, American, and British governments finally came to an agreement on the wording of their identic reply to China; the section on the tariff matter was to read, "the Government of the United States [Britain, Japan] is . . . willing, either at [the special tariff] Conference or at a subsequent time, to consider and discuss any reasonable proposal that may be made by the Chinese government for a revision of the treaties on the subject of tariff." The identic notes were issued on September 4.[28]

Despite a propensity toward independent action on the part of the various governments, a degree of unity among the treaty powers had survived the turbulent months of mid-1925. There was thus some possibility that they might yet jointly put forth a bold scheme for a new economic order in the Far East. It is a matter of historic interest that Germany was at this time showing signs of approaching the Washington powers rather than standing with Russia in China. As Soviet activities and intentions in China became known through the internal disturbances of 1925, German officials were confronted with the necessity ot redefining their position in China with regard to Russia and other powers. They felt that Germany should not discredit itself by cooperating with the Soviet Union in China. German interests in the Far East were defined as predominantly economic, and here Germany would have more to gain than lose by standing behind Britain, the United States, and Japan against Russia. When China suggested that Germany send observers to the tariff conference, probably in order to bolster Peking's diplomatic prestige, the latter declined, fearing that its participation might result in Russian participation which the powers would not tolerate; in that case, Germany would be caught between the two camps. On October 1 the United States invited Germany to adhere to the Nine-Power Treaty, and the latter gave a ready assent.[29]

In such a context, the tariff conference, convened in Peking on October 26, 1925, took on symbolic significance. It represented a final attempt by the Washington powers to act in cooperation and redefine the framework of the international order in the Far East. As such, their efforts stood opposed to Russia and its diplomacy. Though Soviet policy had been successful, and Russian-inspired demonstrators, strikers, and students were calling for a revolutionary definition of the new order, the Russian story was not all bright. The more the communists gained in strength by taking advantage of the excitement following the May 30th incident, the more alarmed merchants and noncommunist intellectuals became, and the more serious grew friction within the Kuomintang. Tai

Chi-t'ao openly criticized the communists for subverting Kuomintang principles, and Liao Chung-k'ai, a prominent party official, was murdered by rightists in Canton in collusion with Kwangtung warlords.[30] The tariff conference might have further reversed the tide and brought about a new era in Sino-foreign relations. In fact, it signalized the final demise of the Washington system and witnessed the exit of the Washington powers as a group. They had completely failed to devise a framework of international cooperation in the Far East.

THE PEKING TARIFF CONFERENCE

One obvious factor behind the failure of the Special Tariff Conference was the perennial phenomenon of the Chinese civil war. No sooner had the conferees met than it became evident that the powers were dealing not with China but with a Chinese government. The Tuan regime had been dependent upon the alliance of Chang Tso-lin and Feng Yü-hsiang, but the latter's allegiance was always shaky and his Kuominchun (National Army) had a hand in encouraging the unsuccessful revolt by Kuo Sung-ling against Chang toward the end of 1925. Feng's growth in power brought about a *rapprochement* between Chang Tso-lin and his recent enemy, Wu P'ei-fu, and in April 1926, a *coup d'état* by one of Feng's betraying generals in Peking resulted in the resignation of Tuan Ch'i-jui. During this half year of intense civil strife in north China the cabinet was changed several times: in December 1925, and March, May, and June 1926. Kuomintang and communist agitators were very active during this period. They and Soviet advisers successfully made contact with Feng Yü-hsiang and his army, and they stood behind Kuo Sung-ling when he revolted against Chang Tso-lin. On November 18, 1925, students and workers staged a violent demonstration in Peking against the government.[31]

The Tariff Conference was held during this critical period, when power was divided among several warlords and the Peking government had no assurance of stability and permanence. The anomaly of holding a conference to fulfill China's national aspirations when the country was represented by a shaky cabinet was picturesquely pointed out by Minister MacMurray, who wrote to Nelson T. Johnson in private in November:

> You cannot imagine the curious adaptation of one's mind that is necessary, in order to discuss at one meeting the business of realizing for China its national aspirations towards tariff autonomy and unrestricted sovereignty, and ten minutes later having to discuss whether or not we should telegraph the latest phase of the military situation which seems to make it impossible that the administration with which we are dealing can continue for more than a few weeks or even a few days. . . . It is an unreal world.[32]

Nor was the whole of China united on the tariff issue. Tariff autonomy was on the lip of practically every warlord, politician, and diplomat as well as of every student, merchant, and laborer, but there was a serious division of opinion regarding the Special Tariff Conference. Among the warlords, Feng Yü-hsiang and Chang Tso-lin favored the convening of the conference and supported Tuan Ch'i-jui's effort to complete it. Wu P'ei-fu, on the other hand, in his desire to hamper the Peking government and the generals behind it, declared his opposition even before the conference met. But the most vocal opposition to the Tariff Conference came from the Canton government and its allies. They held that an increased customs revenue would only accrue to the central government and benefit the northern warlords. To them the conference appeared to be a last-ditch effort by the warlords to consolidate their power against the Chinese revolutionaries.[33]

It was all the more remarkable, therefore, that a core of Chinese bureaucrats held steadfastly to their task at the conference and managed to create the impression of consistency in Chinese policy. Despite vicissitudes in domestic warfare and shifts in the administration, these men — officials of the Waichiaopu and such other offices as the Finance Ministry and the Taxation Bureau — had worked hard to prepare a reasonable basis for discussion. Several months before the conference they had drafted a basic plan for tariff revision and a blueprint for subsequent developments of Chinese finance. While aspiring to tariff autonomy in principle, they were ready to put forth some concrete proposals such as a grant of import surtaxes in excess of 2.5 percent as specified by the Washington customs treaty, revision of export dues to an effective 5 percent, imposition of additional export taxes, and abolition of special rates granted to trade across land frontiers. They had also studied various ways of abolishing likin in return for gaining tariff autonomy.[34] Their united effort might have produced results if all the powers had shown cooperation with one another and understanding of the Chinese position.

Events proved otherwise. The three powers upon which the success of the conference depended — Great Britain, the United States, and Japan — once again failed to coordinate their action. Britain and the United States were ready to proceed without regard to the details of the Washington customs treaty, and Japan took steps to approach China unilaterally. The British government had decided to grant full tariff autonomy to China "in stages and in the measure in which the Chinese authorities carry out their part of the programme adopted at the Conference." This last specification applied primarily to the abolition of likin and other internal transit taxes. Given the weakness and instability of the central government, these measures could be carried out only with the consent of provincial authorities. Consequently, Britain proposed that an increase in the tariff rates, up to 12.5 percent, be granted and distributed among provincial governments. The collection and distribution of the surtaxes could be performed by the only nation-wide organization in China, the Maritime Customs. British policy in the mid-1920's was predicated upon an image of China which was federal rather than centralized, in which each province enjoyed fiscal autonomy and was only loosely related with other provinces and with the central government. This realistic image provided the setting in which British officials sought to promote their country's trade with China and maintain the integrity of the still predominantly British-controlled Maritime Customs Administration.[35]

American policy was even more explicit in its departure from the formula of the Washington customs treaty. In his instruction to the American delegation to the Tariff Conference, Secretary of State Kellogg stated that the conference "ought to go beyond the strict scope of its activities as defined in the Customs Treaty and enter into a discussion of the entire subject of the conventional tariff, even including proposals looking toward ultimate tariff autonomy." More specifically, Kellogg insisted that the conference bestow upon China an immediate and unconditional grant of the 2.5 percent surtax promised by the Washington treaty. Furthermore, the United States would agree to an increase in the import duties up to a maximum rate of 12.5 percent in return for some practicable device for an eventual abolition of likin and other restrictions on domestic trade. In that event Kellogg would view favorably the assignment of the increased revenues to local authorities "to such an extent and in such a manner as might be necessary to the practical working out of such a scheme." Finally, the Secretary expressed his desire that, "while exhibiting toward all a most liberal spirit of cooperation, you should retain your complete independence and avoid the possibility of any charge that the American Government is taking sides for or against any other government represented at the Conference." [36]

The basic attitude of the State Department as expressed in these instructions was to be sympathetic toward the "demands of the conservative elements of the Chinese people" and to act independently of other powers if necessary. On this second point Secretary Kellogg indicated his willingness, in his telegram to MacMurray early in October, to see a new tariff treaty between China and the United States restoring tariff autonomy to China, which would then promulgate a general tariff applicable to American goods for a specific period of time but guaranteeing a most-favored-nation treatment to American commerce.[37] In other words, the United States would endeavor to bring about a new order in the Far East based on Sino-American understanding and the new tariff arrangement. Such an order would not be identical with the one envisaged at the Washington Conference, which had been based on the assumed solidarity of the treaty powers.

Japan was also strongly interested in charting an independent course of action. To its policy makers it was evident that the "spirit of the Washington Conference" had brought Japan no visible benefits in its relations with China, and that the renunciation of particularistic diplomacy had served no useful purposes in reconciling Chinese nationalism and Japanese interests. While, during the May 30th episode, effort was made to coordinate action with Britain and the United States, the cooperation apparently had not prevented these powers from devising their own tactics for the tariff question. It was natural that the government in Tokyo should once again have decided to act unilaterally in China and try to enter into bilateral arrangements in order to protect and promote Japanese interests.

This shift in policy at first gave the appearance of retreat. Realizing that sooner or later China would demand, and the powers would consent to, the restoration of tariff autonomy, Tokyo gave up resisting. It was decided instead to agree to tariff autonomy in principle. Japan would thereby ingratiate itself with the Chinese and persuade them to accept certain conditions to go with tariff autonomy. Despite the acclaim of Japanese publicists then and since for the "friendly" attitude thus manifested, it did not amount to much. China would be asked to enter into a special tariff arrangement with Japan even in the event of its acquiring tariff autonomy. Before then, China could be granted interim customs surtaxes on condition that excises on native Chinese goods be levied and the extra revenue from surtaxes be used partly for redemption of the outstanding debts.[38]

Following the opening plenary session of October 26, the delegates to the Special Tariff Conference divided into several committees and subcommittees and altogether had twenty-four formal meetings until the conference was suspended in April 1926. On November 19 the delegates resolved that "The contracting powers other than China hereby recognize China's right to enjoy tariff autonomy, agree to remove the tariff restrictions which are contained in existing treaties between themselves respectively and China, and consent to the going into effect of the Chinese national tariff law on January 1st, 1929." This resolution was to be incorporated in a treaty to be signed at the conclusion of the conference. At the same time, the Chinese government declared that "likin shall be abolished simultaneously with the enforcement of the Chinese national tariff law and . . . that the abolition of likin shall be effectively carried out by [January 1, 1929]."[39]

Thus, within less than a month after the opening of the conference, the representatives of the powers had agreed to the principle of tariff autonomy in return for the abolition of likin, and committed themselves to a specific date upon which China's own tariff law would become effective. Japan, which might have opposed such a step under different circumstances, consented to tariff autonomy in principle once the Chinese delegates made it clear that their government was willing to enter into a reciprocal agreement with any country before or after the enforcement of the national tariff law. The American delegates also considered it best to accept whatever the Chinese offered in return for tariff autonomy rather than risking an outright denunciation of all the treaties. The British and French positions were stiffer at first; they wanted more specific arrangements for the abolition of likin. In the end, all delegates decided to accept the above declaration with the understanding that it would be a part of a larger treaty providing for details of provisional arrangements, to be carried out before China regained complete tariff autonomy.[40]

China's victory proved more ephemeral than real. Obstacles arose when the Tariff Conference proceeded to discuss these interim arrangements. The representatives of the different governments never reached agreement on the important question of the rates of the surtaxes which were to be levied during the interim period. The Chinese wanted much higher rates than those provided for by the Washington customs treaty, whereas the Japanese would never consent to depart from the Washington formula of 2.5 percent on ordinary goods and 5 percent on luxuries. The American and British delegates tried in vain to offer compromise rates.[41] Despite such disagreement, it is evident that all participants recognized the possibility of immediately putting into effect a 2.5 percent surtax as the lowest common denominator of all proposed rates. The fact that this minimal and seemingly simple step was never taken is another indication that there never was a meeting of minds between Chinese and foreigners and among foreigners themselves. For one thing, Chinese delegates at first held out firmly for their own version of interim rates and would not be satisfied with a lower rate. The Japanese tried to persuade them that an increased revenue derived from the imposition of the Washington surtaxes "would be sufficient to enable us to devise a feasible plan for meeting the need of the Chinese

Government and, at the same time, for furthering the general financial rehabilitation of China." The Chinese contended that the extra revenue thus obtained was hardly enough to carry out such projects as the abolition of likin, consolidation of debts, and administrative reforms. Moreover, Peking authorities were unwilling to give the impression to the public that the Tariff Conference only met to endow the central regime with the minimum rates agreed upon four years earlier in Washington.[42]

Foreign representatives, for their part, never applied sufficient pressure on the Chinese to accept the Washington surtaxes. They spent much of their time wrangling over such technical questions as the definition of "luxuries," concrete methods for carrying out the abolition of likin, and the basis of valuation for the calculation of tariff rates. It was taken for granted by all delegates except the Japanese that the minimum rates proposed by the latter were unrealistic and inadequate. The American representatives continued to try to find a workable solution in order to bring the conference to a quick and constructive conclusion. Taking into consideration both Chinese aspirations and the Japanese desire to protect their trade with China, the Americans in time drafted a tariff schedule which was divided into seven grades, rather than two as provided for in the Washington customs treaty or three as proposed by the Chinese delegation. The idea was that the interim customs duties should be graded into several categories in order to take into account the differences in quality and volume of trade among luxury items. The American delegates were willing to see inexpensive Japanese imports go into lower-rate categories. The British also endorsed such a plan in principle. They continued to be most interested in the abolition of likin and proposed an imposition of a likin compensation tax of 2.5 percent, the proceeds to be allocated by the Customs Administration to the provinces in lieu of likin. The tax was to be levied in addition to the customs surtaxes, which the British suggested could range from lower to higher rates as proposed by Americans.[43]

The Japanese held their ground. While American and British delegates busied themselves with devising an adequate tariff schedule, they decided to prepare for bilateral negotiations with Chinese for the conclusion of a reciprocal tariff treaty. It was expected that such a treaty would effectively protect Japanese trade, while it would placate the Chinese by formally restoring tariff autonomy. The bilateral arrangement would also include concrete measures for the consolidation of China's foreign debts, guaranteeing the redemption of Japanese loans which had either been unsecured or inadequately secured. Japan was not insistent on the likin issue, regarding its abolition as purely a theoretical proposition and much less important than debt consolidation.[44]

By the time the Tariff Conference recessed in late December 1925, no agreement had been reached on the surtax problem, owing primarily to the recalcitration of the Japanese who were more interested in concluding a reciprocal tariff treaty than a multinational agreement granting provisional tariff increases to China. During the recess of the conference, Japan formally expressed its desire to enter into discussion of a bilateral tariff treaty. The Waichiaopu responded by alerting its officials in Japan and Korea to commence a careful survey of Chinese trade with Japan in preparation for the negotiation.[45] Unfortunately, the recess period coincided with another outbreak of civil war in north China, following the revolt of Kuo Sung-ling against his Manchurian overlord, Chang Tso-lin. The revolt was eventually put down, but fighting continued between allies and enemies of Feng Yü-hsiang who had supported Kuo. Feng's influence temporarily dominated Peking politics, causing pro-Chang politicians to flee from the capital, but his rise in power had the effect of binding Chang Tso-lin, Wu P'ei-fu, Chang Tsung-ch'ang, and others, forcing the Christian General's abrupt announcement of retirement in January 1926. Feng's generals remained a dominant factor in the metropolitan area, but the anti-Feng coalition encroached steadily upon the Peking-Tientsin region and in the middle of April forced the withdrawal of the Kuominchun.[46]

Throughout this period of renewed civil conflict the security of foreigners was more than once threatened. In mid-December, anti-Feng forces fired upon an international train bound from Peking to Tientsin, as Feng's armored trains were closely behind it. Both sides exchanged fire in the area around the railway station at Yangtsun, in violation of the Boxer protocol to keep open the route between Peking and the sea. Later that month another international train bound for Shanhaikuan was fired upon near Hsinho by Feng's soldiers, who boarded and inspected the train over the protest of its Japanese commander. The train was forced to return to Tientsin.[47]

Under the circumstances, the delegates to the Special Tariff Conference grew reluctant to adopt measures which would authorize an immediate levying of additional customs duties; this would only provide money to the warring factions, in particular the ones which happened to be in control of Peking at a given moment. It could be said in retrospect that the powers should at least have granted the Washington surtaxes at this time to the Peking government. It might then have bolstered the Tuan Ch'i-jui regime, averted a serious civil war, and demonstrated the workability of the Washington Conference formula of cooperative assistance to a nonrevolutionary China. But Japan was the only power then interested in the stability of the particular government in Peking headed by General Tuan, and even the Japanese government failed to work actively toward this end because of its preoccupation with reciprocal arrangements and consolidation of debts. Furthermore, Japanese action during the Kuo Sung-ling revolt was not calculated to endear Japan to the Peking authorities. The supreme command in Tokyo as usual decided on a policy of noninterference and repeatedly telegraphed the Kwantung Army, urging caution in its troop movements. As Kuo's forces defeated Chang Tso-lin's in a series of battles and steadily marched on to Mukden, however, Japanese authorities in Manchuria feared disorder along the South Manchuria Railway and in areas resided by Japanese. As a result warnings were issued to the fighting factions to keep away from the railway, and troops were reinforced from Korea and Japan to carry out the warning. Contrary to the generally accepted view, there was no thought of openly assisting Chang Tso-lin against Kuo Sung-ling. But these moves in effect doomed the success of Kuo's revolt as his troops could not utilize the South Manchuria Railway. The impression was bound to arise that Japan had actually brought about the collapse of the revolt. Chinese opinion, just as it had been favorably impressed by Japan's acceptance of tariff autonomy in principle, turned against Japan.[48]

Japan was not the only country to alienate the Peking government in the winter of 1925–1926. The United States embittered Chinese officials by its invitation to Germany to adhere to the Nine-Power Treaty. From the Chinese point of view the treaty, "relating to principles and policies concerning China," was intended to modify the old treaties and there was no reason why Germany, having discarded the old treaty relations with China, should sign it. Such an act would make Germany a Washington power, a retrogressive step from China's standpoint. Germany, while desirous of remaining in friendly terms with China, welcomed the opportunity to free itself from isolation in the Far East. Despite Chinese and Russian pressure on Germany the latter did not change its attitude, and the United States just as firmly refused to withdraw the invitation.[49]

DEMISE OF THE WASHINGTON SYSTEM

Conditions of Chinese politics and Sino-foreign relations had definitely worsened when the Tariff Conference reconvened in the middle of February 1926. No sooner had the delegates assembled than a new crisis arose between the powers and the Peking government. In early March, as the combined forces of Chang Tso-lin and Wu P'ei-fu steadily encroached upon the Peking-Tientsin area controlled by Feng Yü-hsiang, the latter placed a series of electrically controlled mines in Taku channel and forbade shipping between Tientsin and the gulf of Chihli. Anti-Feng troops were landed at Tangku and engaged in fighting along the Peking-Mukden Railway. Communication between Peking and Tientsin and beyond to the sea was interrupted, contrary to the provisions of the Boxer protocol. Momentarily united as representatives of the protocol powers, the foreign ministers in Peking protested to the fighting factions as well as the Peking government. As the latter failed to respond, the foreign representatives presented an ultimatum, on March 16, that the Chinese military authorities should remove all restrictions upon free navigation. If they failed to comply with the request by March 18, the powers' naval authorities were to take forceful measures to secure free navigation. The ultimatum was given to the press, and agitation started, under Kuomintang and communist auspices, against its acceptance by the Tuan government. The Peking authorities as well as Chinese military factions decided to submit to the ultimatum, thus inviting a mass protest demonstration at the capital on March 18. Government guards fired at them, killing scores of demonstrators.[50]

Chinese action at the resumed Tariff Conference reflected the central government's relative weakness after these incidents. The Chinese delegates now showed readiness to accept the minimum benefits to strengthen the Peking regime. They were eager to obtain the Washington surtaxes which they had originally considered insufficient.[51] But time was against them. Before anything was decided the Tuan regime fell, in April, and, with most Chinese delegates fleeing from the capital, no further meeting of the Tariff Conference was possible.

Even if Tuan Ch'i-jui had managed to stay in power a little longer, it is doubtful that he could have obtained additional tariff increases. As political conditions in China grew worse, the Japanese stand became more rigid than ever. Though the Tokyo government was interested in assisting Tuan, this was going to be done on its own terms. Japanese reasoning was very simple, and shows the fundamental inflexibility of the "Shidehara diplomacy." Given the increasingly unstable conditions in China, the chances appeared slim for a quick conclusion of a reciprocal tariff treaty or of a multilateral tariff agreement. Under the circumstances an immediate and unconditional imposition of the Washington surtaxes, divorced from a general tariff arrangement, would seriously damage Japanese trade with China. Though earlier the Japanese had advocated the imposition cf the minimum Washington surtaxes, they now preferred a graded schedule which would discriminate between cheap Japanese exports and more expensive goods of other countries. They would agree to the grant of the 2.5 percent tax only on condition that its application be limited to a few years and its use specified by the powers. This last condition obviously referred to the debt consolidation question. As the last resort, Japan would concede the Washington surtaxes if the extra revenue were put aside and not used until the conference had agreed upon the aims and terms of the collection. This was Japan's final concession in the spring of 1926.[52]

This stiff attitude had doomed the Tariff Conference even before the fall of Tuan. While agreeing to the need to specify the use of the surtaxes, the American, British, and other delegates were eager to fix a date upon which the collection of the additional duties would begin. This would have been a tangible, though small, achievement of the conference. But the Japanese delegates were under instruction never to agree to such a date unless the use of the new tax could be determined. As they persisted in their opposition to specifying the date when the imposition of the surtaxes would commence, no achievement had been made before the downfall of the Tuan government in April.[53]

For their part, the British and Americans had already lost interest in maintaining the fiction of the conference, primarily because of their disgust with the impermanence of a Peking government. In both nations, crucial policy changes were already germinating by the spring of 1926. Great Britain showed least eagerness to carry forward the discussion of the tariff matter even informally with other countries. The British had always opposed giving debt consolidation priority in the list of purposes for which increased revenues would be used. With Japan insisting on this point, the British government saw no way but to withdraw from further deliberation of the tariff issue. They could attribute the failure of the conference to causes beyond the reach of British capacity to alter. Another reason for British inaction in Peking seems to have been their fear of Nationalist reaction to the powers' undertaking, it might give the impression that they were furnishing the warlord regime with a source of revenue. This might have been all right while the Peking government was stable. But since early in 1926 Britain had become increasingly interested in the attitude of Canton and in affecting *rapprochement* with the Kuomintang regime. In March, Hongkong and Canton officials had approached each other, trying to solve the British-Cantonese dispute following the May 30th incident. The dispute had cost Hongkong 40 percent of its trade, and British exports to China had declined by 25 percent in 1925. An end to the general strike in Hongkong and the anti-British boycott in Canton would naturally be an essential step if British trade were to regain its strength. The Nationalist government, too, was showing interest in settling the dispute as it prepared for a northern expedition. Though the negotiations in March had failed to produce concrete result, the Nationalists continued to express willingness to come to terms with Britain. Under the circumstances it was best for the latter not to irritate Canton which was opposed to the conference in Peking.[54]

Changes in American policy came about more slowly and cautiously. Throughout the informal sessions in the spring and summer of 1926 Minister MacMurray and other delegates continued to press for an immediate granting of the Washington surtaxes. This was the least the powers could do, they felt, to show their sincerity to the Chinese in meeting their national aspirations. Nevertheless, American officials in Peking were beginning to show signs of despair and discouragement with the political conditions they saw around them. In time MacMurray came to doubt the advisability of maintaining even *de facto* relations with the changing cabinets in Peking. At a time when China was so apparently hopelessly divided it seemed unwise for the powers to be dealing with only one faction as the government of China. This belief was strengthened as a result of a tour of the southern provinces conducted by Mayer, counselor of the legation, in June. After talking with United States consuls in the south as well as with Chinese officials, Mayer returned with the recommendation that the United States cease to cherish the myth of China's territorial and administrative integrity and deal individually with the various "semi-autonomous regions" into which the country was divided. MacMurray endorsed this view. He telegraphed Washington early in July that Mayer's "observations tend strongly to increase my doubt whether the Peking regime has not so far dwindled into insignificance and contempt throughout the country as to make our insistence upon dealing with it a positive detriment to our interests and a means of increasing the antagonism of the Chinese people toward us." The mere agreement to release the Washington surtaxes would be tantamount to *de facto* recognition of the government happening to be in control of the capital, and this Minister MacMurray advised his government to avoid in view of the reality of Chinese politics. In the middle of August he urged that the American government declare its intention of withholding recognition of the government in Peking and suspend all efforts to carry out the Washington treaties.[55]

In Washington the evaluation of the existing situation in China was beginning to be equally pessimistic. The head of the Far Eastern division of the State Department, Nelson T. Johnson, wrote in a personal letter to MacMurray in June, "History . . . will record that Chinese would-be nationalists did what the United States tried to prevent, namely, divided China. One looks in vain for Jeffersons and Franklins capable and unselfish enough to bring these people together." When MacMurray's recommendation to cease to deal with the Peking authorities as the central government of China reached Washington, Johnson approved a draft statement to that effect. He believed that the Tuan Ch'i-jui regime had failed to function as a formal government and that thereafter there was no central government in China. He endorsed MacMurray's suggestion that the United States act singly in this matter as it would be impossible, although preferable, to get the cooperation of Great Britain and Japan. Secretary of State Kellogg, on the other hand, was unwilling to make such a pronouncement independently of other nations. To do so would give the impression that the United States was responsible for breaking up the long-suspended Tariff Conference. Since it was the United States that had taken the initiative in trying to fulfill the Washington Conference treaties, Kellogg reasoned, his government should not take the lead in abandoning the effort. He did nothing, however, to encourage resumption of the Tariff Conference.[56]

The defection of Britain and the United States made Japanese policy appear contradictory. Japan was opposed to the termination of the Tariff Conference and at the same time to an immediate grant of the Washington surtaxes. It was believed in Tokyo that the conference, despite obstacles, had in fact taken a step in the right direction. The conferees had discussed the question of debt consolidation and considered an interim, graded tariff schedule. If the conference were terminated, Japan feared that the powers would have to start all over again and probably deal with a more radical regime. For these reasons, Foreign Minister Shidehara instructed his delegates to obtain their colleagues' explicit promise to reconvene the conference in order to work out a satisfactory tariff agreement. But he was unwilling to countenance an immediate grant of the surtaxes as evidence of Japan's interest in the success of the conference. Such an attitude was in direct contradiction to that of Britain and the United States. These countries were always ready to sanction the levying of minimum surtaxes, with due consideration given to their distribution to regional regimes; but they did not want to commit themselves to future eventualities by agreeing to the resumption of the Tariff Conference before they ascertained China's political stability.[57]

The Special Tariff Conference died a natural death. The delegates of the powers found how difficult it was to reconcile their different concepts of national interest and to implement the program for a new order in the Far East which they believed had emerged from the Washington Conference. A minor incident in June 1926 illustrated how an inflexible policy of a country could undermine even a fiction of international cooperation. Members of the Japanese delegation to the Tariff Conference had grown more and more unhappy about their Foreign Ministry's stiff stand on the surtax question. They thought that by not agreeing to the granting of the additional duties Japan was giving the impression that it was responsible for the inaction of the conference. They had moreover been impressed by the sympathetic attitude of their American colleagues, especially when they drafted a graded tariff schedule, and they wished to strengthen the ties of the two countries on the China question. In early June the Japanese delegation sent Tokyo a strongly worded telegram declaring that there could be no solution of the tariff matter except by an immediate grant of the Washington surtaxes and that "it would be extreme foolishness on our part to break cooperation with the United States at least during the duration of the conference." Tokyo officials were unmoved. A staff paper stated that "there has in fact been no specific benefit resulting from American goodwill toward us. It is sentimentalism and not national policy to argue that we should give up our long-held and cardinal principles and agree to the irrational and haphazard device of effecting a 2.5 percent surtax, simply in order to repay American kindness and save the face of the country which had initiated the Washington Conference." Shidehara fully agreed, and in so doing he was mocking his public image as a man who stood for international cooperation.[58]

The Tariff Conference was dead. But it left behind it two distinctive achievements, full of significance for the future. First, before their initial enthusiasm wore off, the delegates had explicitly agreed to restore tariff autonomy to China in 1929. Though they never signed a general treaty in which this point was to have been specifically mentioned, they had in effect left on record their willingness to see the old arrangements terminated in 1929. Second, apart from the surtax question, the delegates had successfully composed a graded tariff schedule. The rationale behind the schedule was the powers' reluctance to see China proclaiming a unilateral national tariff after 1929. The impact of sudden customs increases on foreign imports would be serious, and the trading countries wished to lessen the effect by imposing on China a provisional treaty tariff until the country gained complete autonomy, having successfully abolished likin and otherwise met conditions in return. Toward the end of March 1926, British, American, and Japanese technical experts succeeded in drafting a schedule ranging from 2.5 percent to 22.5 percent. This schedule was expected to yield ninety million dollars (Chinese currency), the amount the Chinese had earlier put forth as the minimum requirement for their needs. The Japanese accepted the program, as 60 percent of Japanese trade items such as cotton goods and shirtings came within the 2.5 percent category. The schedule, it is true, was never formally adopted by the Tariff Conference; but it was to serve useful purposes when China was once again unified.[59]

These were noteworthy achievements, but they do not alter the fact that the Tariff Conference was the last occasion when the Washington powers conferred jointly with China to bring about a constructive order in the Far East. It is significant that the Extraterritoriality Commission, meeting simultaneously with the Tariff Conference in Peking, revealed more unity among the powers but that this unity was achieved primarily because they were agreed on the inadvisability of restoring judicial autonomy to China in the near future. In September 1926, the commissioners drafted a report dealing with their findings and recommendations for reform. The implication was that the powers would consider the abolition of extraterritoriality only after the Chinese government had carried out certain of these recommendations, such as the establishment of a unified system of laws, judicial independence from military authorities and executive branches of government, and extension of the system of modern courts, prisons, and detention houses.[60]

For all practical purposes the Washington powers had ceased to function as a group by the fall of 1926. The vaguely defined "spirit of the Washington Conference" had not been sufficient to ensure coordination of action among the principal powers. Their different interests in China were stronger than their interest in cooperation to found a basis of postwar international relations. They felt that their interests could better be safeguarded and promoted through bilateral arrangements with China rather than through multilateral agreements. They were thus unwittingly putting an end to one act of the Far Eastern drama and ushering in the next.

All this did not result in an immediate antagonism among the Washington powers. Herein lies the essential difference between the prewar diplomacy of imperialism and that of the mid-1920's. Earlier, when international relations were envisioned in terms of the imperialists' struggle for power and a subtle and precarious balance was maintained by means of bilateral arrangements, there was always a possibility of conflict whenever one of the powers appeared to encroach upon the preserved sphere of influence of another. When, for instance, Japan extended its influence in Manchuria and China, its leaders were aware of the need to obtain prior consent of other imperialists, and they knew that even then some of the latter might resent such an upset in the balance of power. In the 1920's, on the other hand, it was not felt that a Washington Conference power's unilateral action in China would necessarily lead to a clash with others; such action was not viewed by civilian officials as affecting that power's relations with other countries. While Japan, the United States, and Britain lost interest in cooperative policy and began looking for separate arrangements with China, these governments continued to view each other in friendly terms. America's and Britain's economic assistance to Japan, and the latter's cooperative diplomacy at the League of Nations are good examples.[61] Such a phenomenon signalized the isolation of the Far East in world politics. It may be said that foreign policies of various governments were polarized; they applied one set of policies to the Far East and another elsewhere. Meanwhile the military in Japan and the United States had not abandoned their mutual suspicions and planning for a probable conflict in the future. The old order was passing with nothing solid to take its place.

III · DIPLOMACY OF THE NORTHERN
EXPEDITION, 1926–1927

The suspension *sine die* of the Peking Tariff Conference coincided with the beginning of the Nationalist Northern Expedition. While one did not necessarily cause the other, it was symbolic that the final period of the Soviet initiative should have coincided with the abandoning of all efforts by the Washington powers to define a new order in the Far East. Committed to their own image of Sino-foreign relations, the Nationalists pushed their military campaigns northward. With them marched the Russians. Determined to establish Soviet-Kuomintang-Communist hegemony in the Yangtze River region, they encouraged anti-imperialist agitation by workers, students, and scholars. More than that, Soviet influence was also visible behind merchants and industrialists of the northern cities who now joined the chorus demanding fundamental revision of all existing treaties.

The Washington powers confronted this grave crisis by clarifying anew their basic interests and strategies in China. Since the wrecks of the Tariff Conference had left them no framework for cooperation, each country devised its own scheme to cope with the situation. Britain, the United States, and Japan all made their policy pronouncements in the winter of 1926–1927, defining their respective positions. Historians have almost invariably referred to them as new policies which these governments adopted in response to the Nationalist challenge. In fact there was nothing new in these policies; the powers had already departed from their previously held positions during the Tariff Conference. It is pertinent to examine how Japan and others tried to respond to the critical situation in the Far East.

ASSAULT ON THE TREATIES

The Nationalist Northern Expedition was formally launched on July 4, 1926. Its military phase was remarkably successful as the Nationalists took advantage of the mutual suspicions and self-interests of the warlords in south and central China and managed to secure the neutrality of some and betrayal by others of their overlords. The Wuhan area, comprised of the three key cities in Hupeh Province — Wuchang, Hankow, and Hanyang — was overcome in September. Next the Nationalists engaged the forces of Sun Ch'uan-fang, the warlord of the "five southeastern provinces," who had initially remained passive, thereby facilitating the northward march of the revolutionary soldiers. After a series of defeats Sun withdrew to north of the Yangtze, leaving most provinces south of the river at the mercy of the Nationalists.[1]

There was at first no unity among the anti-Kuomintang warlords in the north. After the collapse of the Tuan Ch'i-jui regime in Peking, the two warlords behind the move, Wu P'ei-fu and Chang Tso-lin, had met in Tientsin and agreed to support a compromise cabinet headed by Tu Hsi-kuei and to wage a campaign against Feng Yü-hsiang's Kuominchun. The result was that the Manchurian army under Chang Tso-lin extended its influence south of the Great Wall, and Wu P'ei-fu was thereby induced to consolidate his own base in central China just at the moment when the Nationalists launched their expedition. After Sun Ch'uan-fang's defeat the northern warlords belatedly realized the need for unity and organized themselves into an anti-Nationalist army. In December, Chang Tso-lin was appointed commander in chief of the Ankuochun (National Pacification Army). Two months of severe battles in northern Chekiang followed, culminating in a decisive Nationalist victory on February 19, 1927. Revolutionary troops successfully occupied the provincial capital, Hangchow, causing the eclipse of Sun Ch'uan-fang. The Nationalists then prepared for an assault upon their next target, the adjoining province of Kiangsu with its two major cities, Shanghai and Nanking.[2]

Russian, communist, and leftist strength among the revolutionaries reached a peak at this time. At first the Soviet advisers at

Canton had opposed the idea of a northern expedition. When in late January 1926, the Kuomintang political council adopted a resolution that an expedition be launched, to take advantage of the civil war in the north, the Russians and communists opposed, presumably under instruction from the Comintern. They apparently feared that an enlarged military operation would either strengthen Chiang Kai-shek and the right wing or weaken the stronghold in Kwangtung and invite a serious blow to the revolutionary base. They had enough justification to fear Chiang's anticommunist tendencies. He had been instrumental in causing the removal of several Russians from positions of influence, following the "March 20th coup." Borodin now decided to strike a compromise and gave his support for a northern expedition in return for Chiang's promise to purge the party of rightists.[3]

Once the expedition was launched, Russians and communists decided to support it actively and turn it to their own advantage. Comintern agents such as Teruni and Nikitin directed military tactics as advisers to various units of the expeditionary force. Within the Kuomintang, Russians and communists sought to strengthen the left wing and undermine Chiang Kai-shek's authority. In this task they were aided by the undercurrent of anti-Chiang sentiment which had persisted after the March 20th incident. There were men in the party who opposed Chiang Kai-shek because they believed in civilian control over political affairs and were disturbed by Chiang's assumption of dictatorial power as commander in chief of the revolutionary army. There were also mutual suspicions and jealousies between Chiang and fellow-traveling warlords such as Feng Yü-hsiang and T'ang Sheng-chih, and Borodin and the Chinese communists played them against one another to check Chiang's influence. But the most spectacular communist gains were registered in the field of organized mass movements. Some of the party representatives attached to the revolutionary army, youth groups, labor and peasant leaders, and communist agitators actively engaged in organizing the masses and spreading radical slogans.[4]

Wuhan, in which prominent Kuomintang officials and generals gathered in the winter of 1926–1927, became the center of Russian and leftist activities. A "joint council" was established as an interim government, including Borodin, Sun Fo, and Eugene Ch'en, and headed by Hsü Ch'ien. The Wuhan group attacked Chiang Kai-shek as a "new warlord" and looked to Wang Ching-wei, on his way back from Europe, as the rightful leader of the party.[5] In February 1927, it was officially announced that the Nationalist government and party headquarters would move from Canton to Wuhan. Not only in the Wuhan cities but in Changsha mass demonstrations and meetings were held, factories were seized, strikes were declared, and banks went out of business. Foreign trade along the Yangtze declined noticeably in the early months of 1927, and foreign residents evacuated en masse to Shanghai and even back to their own countries. The appearance of radical strength at the Nationalist center was such that a number of foreign observers felt that Borodin and a handful of Russians and Chinese communists had become the masters of half of China.[6]

It was at this point that Chiang Kai-shek decided to show his colors. He had been well aware that the military campaigns could result in a spread of communist influence. To provide against such an eventuality, he had taken steps to curb communist activities within the Kuomintang. He was instrumental in the central executive committee's adoption, in May 1926, of new regulations governing the conduct of communist members within the Nationalist Party. They were forbidden to criticize the "three people's principles" and to organize meetings and groups without the party's authorization. Communist membership in the Kuomintang's important offices was not to exceed one-third of the total. Chiang Kai-shek openly exhorted the communists in the Kuomintang to renounce their communist connections and contribute to the unity of the Chinese revolutionaries. Chiang was still desirous of keeping internal disunity to a minimum, so that the northern warlords and foreign countries would not take advantage of it. But, in January 1927, he was so impressed with Soviet and communist influence at Wuhan that he decided to declare his defiance openly by remaining at Nanchang and gathering his own followers.[7]

The most striking phenomenon of this time was not that Chiang Kai-shek became definitely anti-communist but that the split between right and left among the revolutionaries had few immediate effects on their foreign policy. Paradoxically, they were more united in their attack on foreign rights and privileges in China. Anti-imperialism had been an essential ingredient of revolutionary diplomacy and a necessary tactic to ensure mass following. The Nationalist declaration of July 4, 1926, launching the Northern Expedition, had pointed to the economic invasion and political aggression of the imperialists upon China and their collaboration with the warlords in the exploitation of the masses. "The ultimate cause of all the difficulties and sufferings of the Chinese people," it stated categorically, "lies with the aggression of the imperialists and the cruelty and violence of their tools, the nation-selling warlords." [8] The same refrain was echoed wherever the Nationalists went, whether centers of the left or of the right wing. In places where communists and leftists dominated there was a strong emphasis on friendship with the Soviet Union; in Changsha a mass demonstration in October commemorated the Bolshevik revolution, and pamphlets distributed depicted bright pictures of Russia and the Comintern. At Hankow more than thirty labor unions declared strikes within a month after the entrance of the southern forces, and on the anniversary of October 10 anticapitalist handbills were disseminated. One of the first acts of Ch'en Kung-po, Nationalist commissioner of foreign affairs before Eugene Ch'en arrived, was to put an end to the rule that no Chinese were allowed on the river banks within the British concession in Hankow. Thereafter Chinese freely entered the area and processions were held within the concession until they were proscribed in late November. The climax of antiforeign agitation at Hankow was reached on January 3, 1927, when Chinese demonstrators, sufficiently aroused after two days of anti-imperialist mass rallies, again forcibly entered the British concession. There were fights between Chinese and British, but the latter did not use weapons. As the Chinese police and army guaranteed to control the mob, the British officials, marines, and residents withdrew to warships on the Yangtze. Five days later the concession at Kiukiang was similarly abandoned by the British.[9]

In Shanghai, the center of the rightist Western Hills faction, anti-imperialist propaganda was just as intensive as at Wuhan.

In September 1926, it reiterated the demand for abolition of all unequal treaties and insisted that as first steps in this direction foreign troops and gun-boats should be withdrawn from China.[10]

Chiang Kai-shek and his supporters vied with these groups in denouncing the treaty powers. Chiang shared the widely held suspicion that Japan was behind Chang Tso-lin, Great Britain behind Wu P'ei-fu, and the United States possibly behind Sun Ch'uan-fang. To combat these alleged designs to obstruct the Nationalist expedition, Chiang considered the Soviet alliance still of great importance. On July 9, 1926, when he was formally installed as commander in chief of the revolutionary army, he addressed a message to the officers of the army, reminding them that imperialism was the cardinal target of their campaign. As he left Canton to the front later that month, Chiang said that the most important thing for the success of the revolution was to unify all revolutionary forces and devote their full strength to the eradication of imperialism.[11]

Chiang was not unmindful of the danger of antagonizing all foreigners and the disadvantage of a wholesale attack on the rights of all treaty powers. Unlike the communists he was willing to distinguish between friendly foreigners and imperialist governments. In a declaration to the foreign powers, issued in Changsha on August 20, he said that Wu P'ei-fu was deceiving the foreigners; they should realize that the Nationalists sought not only to unify China and alleviate the people's misery but also to contribute to the peace of the world. They could look upon those who approved of and aided the revolution as friendly nations, and they would protect the lives and property of foreigners who did not interfere with the action of the revolutionary army. In early September, Chiang Kai-shek ordered his troops to respect foreign nationals and forbade them to use foreign churches and schools as camping quarters. To a few foreigners he was even willing to confide his opposition to radicalism.[12]

As the Wuhan-Nanchang rift widened, however, Chiang had to renew anti-imperialist pronouncements in order to secure mass support and vindicate himself against the charge that he was in secret communication with the imperialists. In January and February 1927, he made radical speeches denouncing unequal treaties; on one occasion he said that Sun Yat-sen's basic slogans — overthrow the imperialists, overthrow the warlords, join forces with the Soviet Union, and assist peasants and workers — could never be altered. On March 7 he declared that, so long as the Soviet Union did not abandon the spirit of equality in dealing with China, the latter should not abandon the policy of cooperating with that country.[13] Thus it happened that, the more he disliked the communists, the more loudly he felt it was necessary to denounce foreign rights in China.

In this way all factions within the Kuomintang were united in their attack on the rights and privileges of the treaty powers. What was more, anti-Nationalist warlords and Peking officials also partook in the assault on foreigners and their treaties. In their fight against the revolutionary soldiers, northern warlords took the same measures as their enemies, such as inspecting foreign ships, firing at them, and looting foreign buildings. The warlords had more men than ships and frequently commandeered foreign vessels to transport their troops. Most often foreign captains submitted, but not always. A serious case arose in early September when soldiers belonging to Yang Sen, the Szechwan warlord, seized two British steamers in order to transport his troops. As a British flotilla tried to release the boats, the Chinese responded with machine-gun fire. In retaliation British ships bombarded the city of Wanhsien, killing many civilians. Instantaneously anti-British movements spread to the cities both in Nationalist control and belonging to warlords.[14]

The Peking government, despite its nominal existence, was also active. Though the Tariff Conference had been disappointing, Waichiaopu officials continued their effort to bring about a more equitable tariff schedule. They felt that, with changing prices of commodities, the existing tariff schedule was no longer yielding an effective 5 percent, despite the adjustments effected in 1922. They decided, consequently, to organize a committee to revaluate commodity prices as a basis for import duties, and the committee was formed and sent to Shanghai in July 1926. In early August the Waichiaopu invited interested powers to participate in the work of revising the tariff schedule, and the latter responded by sending commercial attachés and consuls in Shanghai to participate in this task. The "tariff valuations revision commission" thus organized went to work immediately and was to continue its study till the middle of 1928.[15] By this time, however, simply carrying out a minor provision of the Washington Conference treaties had become totally inadequate from the point of view of northern officials and the public. They demanded more drastic revision of the existing treaties. It so happened that the bilateral treaties of commerce and navigation which had been concluded earlier by Ch'ing officials and provided the framework of Sino-foreign commercial relations were all due to terminate in the late 1920's or the early 1930's. Here was an opportunity not to be missed.

The treaty with Japan, signed and ratified in 1896, logically came up for consideration. It was effective for ten years, after which period either of the signatories had the right to propose revision. Thirty years had passed without revision, but a supplementary protocol had been added in 1903. Now in 1926 the time seemed opportune to propose a fundamental revision. Almost daily letters and telegrams poured into the Waichiaopu from merchants, industrialists, and even warlords in the north, who insisted that the government take such a step.[16] Under such pressure the authorities in Peking formally broached the issue to the Japanese government. In a note dated October 20, 1926, the Waichiaopu expressed its wish for a "fundamental revision" of the 1896 treaty "in order to promote the mutual interest of the two nations."

The Chinese government hopes that the Japanese government will adjust itself to the current of recent international progress, satisfy the desires of the Chinese people, and establish a new basis for the diplomatic relations between China and Japan, and for the friendship of the two peoples, based upon the principles of equality and reciprocity. . . . If after the period for treaty revision [i.e. six months] a new treaty has not been established, the Chinese government, since it cannot long delay the issue and will be constrained to decide on and express its attitude regarding the old treaty, wishes to declare that it reserves right regarding this point which naturally accrues to itself.

As if to illustrate what the concluding sentence implied, the Waichiaopu unilaterally declared, on November 6, the abrogation of the Sino-Belgian treaty which had been in effect since

1865. As an indication of what might come in the future, this action was hailed by the Nationalists and by the northern press and was greeted with consternation by the powers.[17]

The Nationalists were not entirely happy about the northern government's negotiations for treaty revision, as they would imply recognition of the Peking regime, controlled by the Chihli-Fengtien coalition. Eugene Ch'en made known his view, in late January 1927, that "negotiations for new treaties between the foreign powers and the Chinese authorities at Peking at this juncture when the wave of nationalism gives promise of shortly spreading over the whole country, would be particularly inadvisable and would adversely affect the interest of foreign [people] and the Chinese alike." Both north and south, however, cavalierly disregarded the deliberations of the Peking Tariff Conference and proceeded to collect customs surtaxes. The Nationalists had opposed the grant of Washington surtaxes by the Tariff Conference as this would merely enrich the northern warlords, but this did not prevent them, after the conference was suspended, from imposing their own surtaxes on goods coming through the treaty ports under their control. The Peking government followed suit. When Francis Aglen, inspector general of the Maritime Customs, refused to allow the use of the customs establishments for collecting the surtaxes, Peking issued a presidential mandate relieving him of his duties.[18]

In this way the winter of 1926–1927 saw a dramatic rise of all China, north and south as well as right and left, to defy the existing framework of treaty relations. What was envisaged was no less than an entirely new order of things based on the principle of absolute equality. Foreigners were put on the defensive.

THE BRITISH AND AMERICAN RESPONSES

The powerful Nationalist expedition, revolutionary diplomacy, intensified struggle within the Kuomintang, and increased danger to the lives and property of foreigners incidental to the chaos and confusion of China all had serious implications for Sino-foreign relations. Most basically there was the question of a new order in the Far East. Should the powers accept the Chinese definition of the situation and agree to a radical alteration of the treaty system? Even if this question were settled, how could they bring about an alternative structure of treaty relations when China was still divided politically and friction was developing within the Kuomintang? These were vexing questions, and London, Washington, and Tokyo felt obliged to clarify their positions publicly.

Great Britain had already seriously reconsidered its policy toward China. It had been the chief target of antiforeignism after the May 30th incident. It served as the symbol of imperialism to the Northern Expeditionary forces. At this time whenever they talked of and attacked "imperialists" they were likely to have British in mind. Their declaration of July 4, 1926, referred to Britain's help to Wu P'ei-fu to crush the national movement for freedom and independence; Chiang Kai-shek mentioned Hongkong as Britain's base for economic invasion of China; in Hunan it was reported that the slogan of revolutionary students in the fall of 1926 was, "fight the British; be friendly to the Americans; and ignore the Japanese." [19]

It is easy to understand why, in the course of the year 1926, Great Britain should have gradually shifted its attention from the government in Peking to the Kuomintang regime in the south. More aware perhaps than any other Washington power of the potential strength and danger of a regime dominated by Nationalists, communists, and Russians, it sought to come to some understanding with them. In the middle of July, following closely the launching of the Northern Expedition, British officials in Hongkong offered a loan to the Nationalists for the development of the port of Whampoa in return for a satisfactory settlement of the year-long dispute, including the complete cessation of the Hongkong strike, the anti-British boycott, and all other unfriendly acts in the Nationalist-controlled provinces. Nothing further came of this proposal, but the Cantonese were sufficiently interested in solving the dispute to agree on instituting a commission of inquiry for the settlement of the anti-Hongkong boycott. They had been forced to recognize the impracticality of spending ten thousand dollars daily to maintain the strikers. For a time there seemed no prospect of Nationalist-Hongkong *rapprochement* as anti-British feeling spread with the northward march of the revolutionary soldiers and as Chinese opinion was exacerbated by the Wanhsien incident of September. But the Northern Expedition in effect strengthened the need for an amicable settlement as the Canton government prepared to move to central China. By an ingenious stroke of policy Nationalist officials decided to put an end to the boycott but also to levy import and export surtaxes at Canton to provide the sinews of war under the pretext that extra revenues were needed to meet the liquidation expenses of the boycott. As a *quid pro quo* for the cessation of the anti-Hongkong boycott, the British government was willing to acquiesce in the imposition of the surtaxes. At Peking the British minister was the only one among the representatives of the treaty powers who did not oppose the new taxes at Canton. He was willing to accept them if they were collected by the Maritime Customs Administration. While finally he agreed to sign a protest sent to the Canton government in late October, the British government in effect offered no actual opposition to the imposition of the surtaxes. Although they were collected outside of the Customs, the latter often assisted Chinese officials in the technical matter of collecting the taxes. Thus Great Britain openly carried to the logical conclusion the policies it had formulated during the Tariff Conference.[20]

The culmination of this line of policy was the memorandum sent from London to Minister Miles Lampson on December 2, the text of which was published on Christmas Day. The memorandum contained a few impressive passages which have led observers to conclude that it was "a sweeping re-examination" of the principles of Sino-foreign trade relations.[21] For example, it stated that the powers "should abandon the idea that the economic and political development of China can only be secured under foreign tutelage" and declared that the "situation which exists in China today is . . . entirely different from that which faced the Powers at the time they framed the Washington treaties." It was proposed that the powers should issue a joint statement to this effect, "declaring their readiness to negotiate on treaty revision and all other outstanding questions as soon as the Chinese themselves have constituted a Government with authority to negotiate; and stating their intentions pending an establishment of such a Government to pursue a constructive policy in harmony with the spirit of the Washington Conference but developed and adapted to meet the altered circumstances of the present time."

The memorandum merely restated the positions which the British government had begun to take during the second half of the Tariff Conference and continued to do so following its collapse. These positions related to the Nationalist regime and the Washington surtaxes. The memorandum stated, as if it were an undisputed fact, that the authority of the Peking government had diminished to a vanishing point while in the south "a powerful Nationalist Government at Canton definitely disputed the right of the Government at Peking to speak on behalf of China or enter into binding engagements in her name." In this way Britain justified its own passive attitude during the last months of the Tariff Conference and at the same time revealed its recognition of the potential strength of the Canton regime. The second point was made unmistakably clear when the memorandum reiterated Britain's insistence on an immediate and unconditional grant of the Washington surtaxes and suggested that "It would in each case be for the competent Chinese authorities to decide all questions as to the disposition and banking of these additional revenues." About half of this memorandum was taken up by an implicit attack on the Japanese position that the purposes and conditions for the surtaxes must first be determined. Here again it was pointed out that "in China today debt consolidation could only enable the faction which happened to be in power in Peking to resort to fresh ruinous and unproductive borrowing." [22]

The so-called "Christmas message" was a forceful restatement of British policy and recognition of the absence of a central government in China. It did not imply sweeping revaluation of the existing treaty system. It was specifically stated that "Protests should be reserved for cases where there is an attempt at wholesale repudiation of treaty obligations or an attack upon the legitimate and vital interests of foreigners in China, and in these cases the protests should be made effective by the united action of the powers." No wonder that the British proposal not only did not evoke any sentiment of gratitude on the part of the Chinese, especially the Nationalists at whom it had been aimed, but it aroused the latter to still further anti-British acts. In Canton the Nationalist press noted that British warships were being dispatched to China even while the memorandum was published, revealing its desire to maintain its rights in China. At Hankow the "anti-British and anti-Fengtien people's assembly" passed a resolution to continue opposing Great Britain, while at Kiukiang, Chiang Kai-shek declared that this leader of all imperialist nations must be by all means overthrown. Even the British offer of the Washington surtaxes to local authorities did not produce the expected result; Eugene Ch'en declared that the real purpose of the offer was to give two-thirds of the extra revenue to the northern warlords, thus prolonging the civil war and delaying the liberation of China from international control.[23]

The possible reason for British miscalculation was that the "Christmas message," meant to appease the Nationalists by conceding what in fact had already been surrendered, had not taken into account the serious rift within the revolutionaries. Such a memorandum might have been welcomed at the inception of the Northern Expedition, when the Canton government conferred with British officials for settling the May 30th affair. After influential Nationalist government and party officials moved to the Yangtze valley, however, the struggle for power among the revolutionaries had grown so intense that they vied with each other in denunciation of foreign rights. Under the circumstances they could not publicly appreciate such mild concessions as the British memorandum offered. On the contrary, Wuhan leaders were eager to enhance their prestige by continuing their antiforeign propaganda and appearing as the center of China's struggle for freedom. The Hankow and Kiukiang incidents were significant victories for them, and Borodin, Ch'en, and others did their best to exploit these achievements in order to consolidate further their power against the rightists.[24]

British policy makers were uninformed of these developments within the Nationalist ranks but continued to be guided by the basic principle of the December memorandum; to acquiesce in minor infringements of treaty rights by Chinese but to protest in case "where vital interests are at stake." The Hankow and

Kiukiang concession incidents were considered to be of the first category, while the threatened Nationalist assault upon Shanghai was judged to be of far greater importance. In the former instances, as Chinese mobs overran the concessions, the British forces did not open fire but quietly withdrew. Talks were held immediately between Eugene Ch'en and Owen O'Malley, sent from the British legation in Peking. O'Malley agreed to Ch'en's view that negotiations should be conducted on the basis of the *fait accompli*, in other words looking to the retrocession of the concessions to the Chinese.[25] It was the view of the British government that a satisfactory settlement of the Hankow and Kiukiang incidents would provide guarantees against similar occurrences elsewhere, especially in Shanghai. It was not considered inconsistent, therefore, that, while Britain offered conciliatory terms at Hankow, outlined by the "seven proposals" on the modifications of treaty rights, it also decided to reinforce troops and ships in the Shanghai area to defend the international settlement from a possible mob attack. Failing to secure cooperation of the United States and Japan in this regard, Britain decided, on January 22, 1927, to dispatch an additional 13,000 marines to Shanghai independently of other nations. It was judged that the cardinal importance of the international settlement to British trade and business activities in China warranted such precautionary measures.[26]

Paradoxically, this last decision strengthened the Wuhan regime. The British expedition, as soon as its plans became known, aroused the resentment not only of Nationalists but also of northern warlords and officials such as Sun Ch'uan-fang and Wellington Koo. Both northern and southern generals were afraid of appearing soft on the British now that the latter had explicitly made clear their intention of defending Shanghai by force. As the seat of the Nationalist foreign ministry, Wuhan commanded support of Chinese opinion in its dealings with Britain through O'Malley. Eugene Ch'en made the gesture of suspending his talks with the British representative, saying that he could not sign the agreements on the concessions which they had just drawn up, as this would imply his capitulation to British intimidation by force.[27] In reality, Ch'en sought a quick settlement on the concession issue to enhance his government's prestige. In the middle of February he eagerly grasped at Foreign Secretary Austen Chamberlain's speech at the House of Commons that most forces being sent to China would be detained in Hongkong if the Hankow agreements were signed. Ch'en assured O'Malley that the Nationalist army did not intend to change the status of the Shanghai settlement by force and confided that he believed the British intention behind the expedition was simply to protect the lives of the nationals. Agreements were signed on February 19 and March 2 on the Hankow and the Kiukiang concessions, respectively. March 15 was set as the date on which the administration of these municipalities would be handed to the Chinese.[28] These were significant achievements which enhanced the prestige of the Wuhan faction and probably induced Chiang Kai-shek and his supporters to hasten their push toward Shanghai and Nanking.

British policy during the first phase of the Northern Expedition was thus guided by the realization of Nationalist strength and need to relinquish significant portions of the treaty rights in order to safeguard fundamental economic interests. There was nothing contradictory between the "soft" stand of December and the "hard" policy of January. Policy makers were looking ahead to the time when the old framework of treaty relations would be replaced by a new one in which Britain's trade and investment would be protected. They were not aware as yet of the Wuhan-Nanchang rift and continued to deal with Eugene Ch'en as the representative of Nationalist diplomacy. All the same, the importance of Britain's clear enunciation of policy was undeniable; by its action during this phase of the Northern Expedition the British government dramatized the lack of interest among the powers to meet the Nationalist challenge in unity.

American policy was less clearly defined but equally predisposed to independent action. Two examples illustrate the way the United States government responded to China's revolutionary diplomacy. These examples — the surtax question and the defense of Shanghai — revealed that Secretary Kellogg continued to entertain his own image of a new era based on Sino-American understanding, in which American interests would be protected but China would also possess self-respect.

On the question of China's unilateral levying of the Washington surtaxes, the United States, unlike Britain, at first hesitated to condone the act. Entertaining the vision of a peaceful and evolutionary transition from the existing treaty system to an era of equal treaties, Secretary Kellogg could not acquiesce in a unilateral action by China. At the same time he was extremely reluctant to employ force to prevent the imposition of the surtaxes; to perpetuate the *status quo* by force would militate against everything for which Kellogg stood. Consequently, he made formal protests against the levying of the taxes but vetoed the suggestion of the legation in Peking for military action in cooperation with other powers.[29]

The second important episode was that of the defense of Shanghai. As the revolutionary army moved northward toward the Yangtze River delta region, the United States had to determine how to protect its nationals and at the same time avoid giving the impression of using force just to maintain existing treaty relations. It is illuminating to note that the withdrawal of all Americans from Shanghai was considered out of the question; as a staff paper put it, this "would, of course, paralyze American business interests there and would be most disastrous." Consequently, the Navy Department ordered Admiral Clarence S. Williams, commander in chief of the American Asiatic fleet, to proceed to Shanghai to ensure the safety of American nationals.[30] As Americans in Shanghai lived with other nationals in the international settlement, a question arose as to whether the United States should employ force to defend the integrity of the settlement, besides protecting its own nationals. Here was a typical problem of cooperation versus independent action. When Secretary Kellogg solicited Minister MacMurray's opinion, the latter emphatically replied that in order to protect American citizens in Shanghai the United States must be prepared to defend the settlement itself and give other powers "a resolute and wholehearted cooperation to make what indeed would be the last ditch stand in China as to foreign rights and foreign interests." Aware of the technical difficulties involved in singling out American residents for protection, the State Department, too, was for once inclined to cooperate with the powers. As soon as it became known, however, that Britain was alone in its determination to defend Shanghai against any form of attack and that Japan had not committed itself to this position, Secretary Kellogg vetoed the suggestion for an international defense of Shanghai. It became necessary to find a formula which would protect Americans in the settlement without having to despatch a large number of troops in cooperation with other powers.

In this situation the Department decided to see if the contending Chinese factions could not be induced to keep away from the international settlement. This would spare the United States an embarrassing decision of whether to join forces with Britain to defend the settlement, a symbol of foreign domination of China. The idea of neutralization was not new, and it had often been put into effect in the early half of the 1920's. But the timing was important. On January 26 the British government communicated a note expressing its intention of sending reinforcements from India and Europe. Fearing that a British-Chinese clash might result, the State Department decided to proceed with the neutralization scheme. The Secretary of State directed the legation in Peking to address a note to Chang Tso-lin and Chiang Kai-shek, inviting them to agree that "the International Settlement at Shanghai be excluded from the area of armed conflict and that the authorities in control of all the armed forces in China shall voluntarily undertake to abstain from all effort to enter the International Settlement by force and even to station military forces in its immediate vicinity." [31]

The note, which was delivered to Chang Tso-lin on February 4 and indirectly to Chiang Kai-shek on the 6th, met the approval of the former but was denounced by all others. Eugene Ch'en regarded it as an offense to "an independent nation with strength to protect foreign lives." He condemned the American proposal as indirect assistance to Sun Ch'uan-fang. Marshal Sun himself expressed his "absolute opposition" to the proposal.[32] Consequently nothing came of the American scheme.

The effort was fruitless, but together with the surtax episode it served to illustrate America's policy on the protection of nationals and treaty rights during a time of chaos in China. The United States would not employ force, either jointly with other powers or singly, in order to safeguard existing treaty relations with China. Neither would it leave American nationals in China entirely to their fate or withdraw them from the country until quiet returned. The shortsightedness of this approach would become apparent when Americans in Nanking were intentionally attacked by Chinese.

For the time being, the severest test that Kellogg's policy faced arose from the question of how the United States was to deal with the contending factions in China. Should it treat with the Kuomintang? If so, with which faction? Or should it wait until China was finally unified by some faction or government? Kellogg himself realized this difficulty and often showed exasperation. When Minister Alfred Sze insisted that the United States should enter into negotiation for treaty revision with delegates representing factions in China, he bluntly replied that "there seemed little to be accomplished in starting negotiations with factions which might disappear over night and leave nothing tangible accomplished." In early January 1927, when the Chinese minister reiterated "the desire of the Chinese Government to enter into negotiations" for treaty revision, the Secretary asked Sze "who the Chinese Government was and who would negotiate." Kellogg stated that "it was almost impossible for him to find out what [the Chinese] wanted; that they were not united and conditions were getting worse; that he was not prepared to negotiate with Canton and Chang Tso-lin and then with some one else who might appear." [33]

Neither was Kellogg prepared to deal with the Kuomintang. While Britain was anxious to define its relations with the Canton authorities, the United States remained cautious. When, in the fall of 1926, London asked Washington "on what footing they [the United States] propose to treat with the Canton Government in the future," the State Department replied that "this Government is not prepared to enter into negotiations with a view to concluding a general tariff agreement with individual provinces or groups of provinces." It was considered unlikely at that time that the Kuomintang would succeed in extending its effective control over the whole of China. The result was a passive attitude of waiting as exemplified by the draft reply to Britain's "Christmas message" that "the Government of the United States awaits anxiously the day when a Government will appear in China which will be prepared to negotiate in China's behalf concerning the many questions outstanding." [34]

Kellogg's China policy was faced with a dilemma; the United States was interested in extending its sympathies to China but was unable to do so because of the absence of a central government in China. How the State Department solved this dilemma provides much of the background of Kellogg's famous statement of January 27, 1927. Historians have been impressed with this document for the wrong reasons. It never amounted to a workable program for Sino-American friendship; but it symbolized intentions and difficulties of American policy at this time.

The main inspiration behind the statement seems to have been public opinion within the United States, calling on the government to enunciate its position in China, now that Britain had declared its policy. The key figures in this connection were A. L. Warnshuis, secretary of the International Missionary Council, and Stephen G. Porter, chairman of the House foreign affairs committee. Warnshuis thought that the Secretary of State should issue a public statement expressing willingness to discuss treaty revision with "the duly accredited representatives of the Chinese Government, authorized to speak for the entire people of China." This formula, Warnshuis believed, would take care of the difficulty arising out of the American government's reluctance to enter into negotiations with regional and not national representatives of China. Probably under this suggestion, Porter introduced a concurrent resolution in the House on January 4, 1927. The Porter Resolution corresponded almost verbatim with the draft which Warnshuis had sent to Johnson. It requested the President to "enter into negotiations with the duly accredited agents of the Republic of China, authorized to speak for the entire people of China, with a view to the negotiation and the drafting of a treaty, or of treaties" between the two countries to replace the existing unequal treaties.[35]

The State Department apparently had no foreknowledge of the Porter Resolution. But Secretary Kellogg concluded that public opinion as represented by the resolution would have to be satisfied. So did the chief of the Far Eastern division. Instead of replying to the British note of December, Nelson T. Johnson suggested that Kellogg might make a statement of facts and policy concerning China; this would enable him to present his ideas to the public and "forestall any action on the Resolution." By January 24 such a statement had been drafted, and, overriding the objection from the legation in Peking that it was hardly realistic, Kellogg issued it on the 27th.[36]

Explicit in the statement were three main ideas. First, the American government expected the Chinese authorities to protect American lives, property, and rights, and American naval forces were to be kept in Chinese waters lest the Chinese be unable to extend the desired protection. Second, American citizens were to be granted "equal opportunity with the citizens of other Powers to reside in China and to pursue their legitimate occupations without special privileges, monopolies or spheres of special interest or influence." Third, in return for this promise for a most-favored-nation treatment, the United States would be "prepared to enter into negotiations with any government or delegates who can represent or speak for China for not only putting the surtaxes of the Washington Treaty into force but entirely releasing tariff control and granting complete tariff autonomy to China." In addition, the American government was ready to "negotiate the release of extraterritoriality as soon as China is prepared to grant protection in her courts to American citizens, their rights and property."

The statement was welcomed by the American public and Congress.[37] Historians have interpreted it as a historic document expressing American friendship with China. It is rather difficult to see what was offered in the Kellogg memorandum which was specifically new and practical. It would seem that America's participation in the Special Tariff Conference and the Extraterritoriality Commission had already indicated its willingness to take up these issues, with a view ultimately to relinquishing special treaty privileges. With respect to American nationals in China, no change was indicated; they were to be protected by all available and practical means. By borrowing the phraseology of the

Porter Resolution and asking China to appoint delegates who could represent the whole of the country, Kellogg merely avoided commitment to any one faction and in fact asked the impossible. On the specific issue of the Washington surtaxes, the granting of which the British memorandum had explicitly proposed, the American stand still held to the position that it must be negotiated with a representative Chinese government.

It is, therefore, easy to see why Minister Sze was disappointed that "the statement was not very clear as to what the United States was prepared to do" and why the "Shanghai associated assembly of all trades" attacked it as vague and inopportune. American consuls in China reported that the Chinese generally gave the statement little comment since they regarded it simply as a reiteration of America's previous policy toward China.[38]

The contrasting reception of the memorandum at home and in China was not surprising. Kellogg directed it at American public opinion, not at the Chinese people. As Nelson T. Johnson recalled nine months later, "at the time the statement was made our eyes were turned more upon the situation here in the United States than our situation in China and I do not know that we gave any particular attention to the question of making any particular appeal to the Chinese."[39] It can be said that the Kellogg statement, like the British memorandum of December, was a restatement of basic positions which the United States government had already formulated.

The historical significance of the January 27th statement has been exaggerated. But it did help to re-emphasize America's interest in forming friendly ties with China, once there was organized a representative body in that country. Soon after he issued the statement, the Secretary instructed the legation in Peking "to study the question of the provisions which should be written into a new treaty to take the place of existing treaties between the United States and China." In Washington the Far Eastern division also began such a study.[40] While the American government believed that actual talks on treaty revision would not open for some time because of the continued civil war in China, these studies could lay a foundation for future negotiations and serve in time to bring about a new era in Sino-American relations.

Like Britain and the United States, Japan continued to pursue goals which it had defined during the Peking Tariff Conference. In the winter of 1926–1927, Japan had further to clarify these objectives, now that the Nationalist advance to north China seemed imminent and confusion could be expected in the areas adjacent to Manchuria. Unlike Britain and America, Japan possessed fairly accurate information on the growing rift within the Kuomintang. It became imperative to fit this phenomenon in the over-all Japanese policy toward China.

In examining Japanese policy at this time, it would be convenient to deal with four major issues confronting the Japanese government — the deterioration in the political and economic situation of Manchuria, Peking's diplomatic offensive, the Nationalist advance northward, and the developing rift within the Kuomintang. All these problems were broadly dealt with by Foreign Minister Shidehara in his speech at the opening session of the fifty-second Diet, on January 18, 1927. This speech has since been celebrated as an epitome of the "Shidehara diplomacy." In it, first, he reiterated the hope that peace and order would be restored in China as soon as possible but declared that the Chinese should work out their own salvation and that foreign powers should never intervene beyond morally supporting China's own efforts to achieve peace. Implicitly referring to the Soviet intervention, Shidehara expressed confidence that the Chinese would never for long acquiesce in and follow the guidance of a foreign power. He predicted that they would ultimately choose a leader who advocated policies fitting the Chinese national character and looking toward internal prosperity and international confidence. Concerning China's national aspirations, he declared that Japan was prepared to consider with sympathy and understanding the "reasonable" demands of the Chinese people. Shidehara also emphasized the need to promote economic cooperation between the two countries on the basis of "coexistence and coprosperity." Finally, he asserted that the Japanese people had a right to have their lives and property protected in China. He said that Japan sought such protection through local leaders who had actual power.[41]

Like the Kellogg statement nine days later, the Shidehara speech expressed an attitude rather than concrete policy. But it summarized the position of the Japanese government on the various specific issues which had arisen since mid-1926. First of all, though the Foreign Minister did not mention Manchuria in his speech, it was implied in his statement that Japan's fundamental rights in China should be maintained regardless of political or social changes in that country. As Chang Tso-lin had extended his influence to north China, in his fight against Feng Yü-hsiang's Kuominchun, and the southern revolutionaries were steadily marching northward, steps must be taken to safeguard these rights and prevent the spread of chaos and confusion north of the Great Wall.

At this point it would be useful to review Japan's attitude toward Manchuria after the Washington Conference. With the diplomacy of imperialism the old practice of recognizing each other's spheres of influence had also gone. Japan had refrained, consequently, from asking for recognition of what it considered its superior rights in Manchuria. But these rights remained, and in Japan at least it was difficult to think of Manchuria except in terms of them. Shidehara himself had often referred to Japan's "visible and invisible rights and interests" in Manchuria and Mongolia. The visible rights were those guaranteed by treaties, including the agreements of 1915. They included the lease of Kwantung Territory, the management of the South Manchuria Railway, the right to station troops along the railway, and various other rights to engage in mining, farming, and business activities in specified areas of Manchuria and eastern Inner Mongolia. There were also "invisible" rights which resulted from Japan's "peculiar relations with Manchuria" — the war against Russia in which "one hundred thousand soldiers' blood" was spilled, the investment of more than one billion dollars to turn Manchuria into an industrially developed region, and Japan's "right of survival" which required that the "untouched treasures" of Manchuria and Mongolia be made available for Japanese use. For the military, Manchuria meant the Kwantung Army and its strategic location facing Soviet Russia, although the United States had replaced Russia as Japan's foremost imaginary enemy in purely military thinking.[42] For all these reasons, Manchuria continued to be regarded by Japan as an area of particular significance. There was not a dissenting voice in the government when it firmly rejected China's request, in 1923, that the Kwantung Leased Territory be restored to it.

Japan's Manchuria policy was reinvigorated in 1926, following Chang's and Wu's fight against Feng. Chang's decision to extend his power into north China had brought about the resignation of one of his ablest civilian advisers, Wang Yung-chiang, who had done much to stabilize financial conditions of Fengtien Province. It could be foreseen that continued campaigns by the Fengtien army would only increase the need for funds, and that Chang Tso-lin would resort to his favorite solution of issuing paper currencies, known as *feng p'iao*. This time he also talked of levying customs surtaxes at the treaty ports in Manchuria, as all other warlords and governments would soon be doing.[43] This boded ill for Japanese interests in the Three Eastern Provinces.

To meet this emergency Japan's military and civilian officials began a serious study of the Manchurian question. In the General Staff, General Matsui Iwane, chief of the second (intelligence) division, wrote a memorandum in early August and advocated certain policies with regard to the continuing war between the Kuominchun on one hand and the armies of Chang Tso-lin and Wu P'ei-fu on the other. First, singly or in cooperation with Britain, the United States, and other powers, Japan should advise the various Chinese military leaders to come to a peaceful settlement of the civil war. Second, Japan should informally warn Chang Tso-lin to desist from attacking the Kuominchun, defend his present sphere in Manchuria and north China, and come to terms with moderate elements within the Kuominchun. Japan could provide him with loans for constructing one or two railways in Manchuria if Chang was willing to devote his efforts to stabilizing internal conditions there. Third, Japan should persuade the powers to assist in the establishment of a firm government in Peking based on an alliance of Chang Tso-lin and Wu P'ei-fu, and to give it moral support by reconvening the Special Tariff

Conference and by other means. Lastly, Japanese and Chinese authorities should together dispatch observers to Kalgan in order to halt or at least curtail Soviet assistance of the Kuominchun.[44]

These views reflected the military's fear of communism and overriding concern with the stability of Manchuria. It was assumed that Japan's interests and rights there could be solidified only if that region was not dragged into war and that only a peaceful Manchuria could withstand the potential threat of the Soviet Union. On the basis of these ideas, in late August definite instructions were sent from the War Ministry to the Japanese advisory corps attached to the Fengtien army. Chang Tso-lin was to be persuaded to come to a compromise with the Kuominchun and devote himself to "pacifying the people." Otherwise, it was pointed out, a continuation of war could lead to the downfall of Marshal Chang. At the same time, Chang Tso-lin was to be persuaded voluntarily to seek Japanese assistance in reforming financial, military, and transportation affairs in Manchuria.[45]

The Foreign Ministry generally concurred in such a policy. The numerous memoranda and instructions drafted in the latter half of 1926 revealed civilian officials' equally strong concern with the stability of the Three Eastern Provinces. Japanese enterprise in Manchuria would never be safe unless economic conditions there were stable. But instability would remain as long as the Manchurian authorities were in need of funds to finance their campaigns. They must therefore be urged to curtail them. Since it might require monetary incentives to induce them to stop their lucrative military exploits, Japan would have to offer them loans in return. Consequently, the Foreign Ministry contacted various Japanese financiers to persuade them to extend loans to Fengtien authorities under the direction of the Tokyo government and in return for certain concessions. More fundamentally, the Foreign Ministry recognized the need to reform radically Manchuria's political and economic institutions, if the area was to be turned into a truly peaceful region where foreign business could prosper. A Foreign Ministry memorandum recommended that Chang Tso-lin be advised to establish a constitution for the Three Eastern Provinces, divide civil from military affairs, organize a systematic budget, convert one of the existing banks into a central bank in order to stabilize the *feng p'iao* currencies, and let Japanese create commercial ports along the railways.[46]

Japanese officials, civilian and military, regarded Manchuria as an area of unique concern, where they believed they were justified in devising special tactics apart from their strategy in China proper. When, in November, Chang Tso-lin organized the Ankuochun and dashed the Japanese hope that he would abstain from the civil war, the Foreign Ministry went as far as to prepare a list of specific Manchurian leaders whom Japan might support instead of the Old Marshal, in case his involvement in the south caused further deterioration of the peace.[47] Foreign Minister Shidehara was in full accord with the views set forth in these memoranda, for the policies which are sometimes attributed to General Tanaka Giichi had germinated under him.

The second important problem facing the Japanese government was Peking's diplomatic offensive. Shidehara's speech of January 18 expressed the hope that Chinese nationalism would be "reasonable" and would not work to the detriment of Japan's "reasonable" interests. Asked what he meant by the term "reasonable," the Foreign Minister replied that it would be reasonable for the Chinese to seek "coexistence and coprosperity" with Japan and that it would be unreasonable for them to threaten Japan's economic existence. Nor would it be reasonable for Japan to employ force to protect the rights and interests in China before peaceful, diplomatic means were tried. Japan would view with sympathy China's reasonable demand for treaty revision, but it would also expect the latter to show equal understanding of Japanese interests.[48]

Such an apparently innocuous formula concealed Shidehara's strong determination to compel China to accept a new order of Sino-Japanese cooperation as defined by Japan. This can be illustrated by Japan's response to Peking's initiative in convening the tariff valuations revision commission and demanding revision of the Sino-Japanese treaty of 1896. On the first issue, Japan's participation in the commission's work was made conditional on the provision that the new schedule be subject to approval at a conference of interested powers and by each power individually and that a certain period of preparation elapse before it would be put into effect. Moreover, the Japanese at first opposed taking the year 1925 as the basis for revaluating the tariff schedule. Instead they proposed taking the first six months of 1926, when commodity prices had fallen below the 1922 level. All these efforts indicated Japan's determination to assert its "reasonable" economic interests in China.[49]

Concerning treaty revision, when the Waichiaopu handed a note in October 1926, proposing negotiations on the subject, Minister Yoshizawa telegraphed Tokyo advising that Shidehara express sympathy with the Chinese people's justifiable and proper demands and state his willingness to start informal discussion on revision of the 1896 and 1903 treaties. But Shidehara hesitated to consent to an over-all revision of the treaties. After unsuccessfully trying to get the Chinese to modify the phraseology of their note, especially the "veiled threat" in its last paragraph, the Foreign Minister decided to give in partially. On November 10 he sent a note to Peking consenting to enter into negotiations for a revision of tariffs and that part of the treaty of 1896 which pertained to commerce.[50]

Negotiations were opened on January 21, 1927. Aware of Kuomintang strength, the Tokyo government did not wish at this stage to commit itself to a definite stand concerning the Peking regime. But the discussions which did go on in the Chinese capital served to illustrate what sort of "reasonableness" the Japanese expected of Chinese. The Peking government was never to see its work completed before it was overthrown by the Nationalists, but it did all it could to devise a treaty which would meet the aspirations of the people. Japan, on the other hand, while conceding the Chinese demand for new treaty status, tried hard to maintain the existing advantages vis-à-vis China and other countries.

The conflicting attitudes of the two governments were revealed when they outlined their respective basic terms of negotiations. For the Japanese Foreign Ministry there were two fundamental principles of treaty revision:

1. to make provisions for quickly realizing China's national aspirations concerning extraterritoriality and tariff autonomy, on the basis of mutuality and equality.
2. in view of the intimate and particular relations between Japan and

China, to provide for adequate, temporary adjustments lest the interests of the two countries be seriously jeopardized by radical changes in treaty relations.

Specifically, the second principle called for granting tariff autonomy to China only in return for a reciprocal tariff agreement, and for a Chinese promise not to discriminate against Japanese nationals in the administration of justice after the abolition of extraterritoriality.[51]

These two principles were inseparable. As the Foreign Ministry expressed it, "it is only because we want to maintain our trade with China, to plan the economic development of our people in China, and to promote economic cooperation between the two countries, that Japan is taking the lead to help China realize its national hopes as quickly as possible." This was the view which the Tokyo officials had taken throughout the Tariff Conference, and their attitude had not changed. When, soon after the Sino-Japanese negotiation opened, Minister Yoshizawa asked authorization to declare Japan's willingness to restore tariff autonomy to China as a gesture of friendship toward its "relatively sound elements," Foreign Minister Shidehara refused to do so unless the Chinese subscribed to the principle of "adequate temporary adjustments." Shidehara was reluctant to isolate an issue, such as tariff autonomy, and wanted to solve all relevant questions simultaneously.[52]

This attitude contrasted sharply with the Chinese position. The Peking authorities had carefully studied tariff autonomy, extraterritoriality, inland navigation, and other issues connected with treaty revision and had apparently drawn up a rough draft of a new treaty of commerce and navigation. Concerning tariff autonomy, for example, the Chinese government believed that it "is an essential sovereign right which is not to be curtailed except by bilateral engagements on the strict basis of mutuality and reciprocity. Its exercise is essential to the promotion of the economic welfare or industrial prosperity of a nation. To place the finances of a state on a sound basis, freedom of action in regulating its customs duties is also necessary." Furthermore, the Chinese reminded the Japanese that during the Peking Tariff Conference the latter had already accepted the principle of restoring tariff autonomy to China. For these reasons, they maintained that the discussion of a reciprocal tariff agreement should be preceded by Japan's explicit recognition of the principle of tariff autonomy.[53] As neither Shidehara nor Wellington Koo would retreat from his position, deadlock was the only outcome.

The same fate met the discussion of another important issue: the most-favored-nation clauses in existing treaties. China was determined not to incorporate such a clause in any of its new treaties, regarding it as an instrument of foreign encroachment upon Chinese sovereignty for over eighty years. From the Japanese point of view, however, a most-favored-nation provision was indispensable. Without it Japan could not safeguard itself against foreign competition in China.[54]

As Shidehara was neither willing to depart from his fundamental principles nor to offer specific alternatives to Chinese proposals concerning tariff, extraterritoriality, and other matters, the three-month period of negotiation, within which time revision must be agreed upon according to the stipulations of the old treaty, passed with little concrete achievement. China proposed to lengthen the period of negotiation and continued to do so every three months, while Japan persisted in employing a delaying tactic, waiting for clarification of the political-military scene in China.[55]

Here again was an illustration of the rigid stand maintained behind the façade of the "Shidehara diplomacy." His policy of "coexistence and coprosperity" was so defined as to leave little room for compromise. In persisting in his stand, he was defeating his basic ideal of a new order based on friendship between China and Japan. In this period he could perhaps have done little else because the government he was dealing with was steadily losing ground. It would not have been expedient to conclude a new treaty with a government which might topple soon afterwards. Thus the question of treaty revision was intimately connected with the third question confronting Japan at this time, the Nationalist Northern Expedition.

Throughout the 1920's Tokyo officials had coupled patience with and noninterference in Chinese internal strife with determination to uphold fundamental treaty rights against radical attack. The attitude was maintained in the period of the Northern

Expedition. When, in the fall of 1926, Sun Ch'uan-fang asked Japan not to support Chiang Kai-shek and to exert moral influence upon Chang Tsung-ch'ang, the Shantung warlord, so that the latter might desist from intruding into the Yangtze River region, Shidehara replied that it was "absolutely imperative for Japan not to incline toward one faction or another in China; to do so may serve temporary interests of Japan, but not the permanent interests of Japan and China." [56] He felt that interference in Chinese internal politics would ultimately damage Japan's economic interests. This attitude of neutrality was necessitated by the extreme unpredictability of events in China; it was imperative to avoid supporting a faction which could at any moment be defeated. For the same reason, Shidehara was practical enough to realize the need to shift Japan's attention from Peking to local provinces, especially the Nationalist-dominated areas. No wonder the Kuomintang leaders favorably received his speech of January 18, in which this policy was implicit, in contrast to the negative response they showed to Kellogg's message nine days later.[57]

Japan was also disinclined to cooperate with the powers to protect nationals in China. During the Wanhsien incident of September 1926, the Foreign Ministry showed no sympathy with Britain's retaliatory policy and bombardment of the city. The only effect of such a policy, said a spokesman for the Foreign Ministry, "would be to strengthen the antiforeign feeling among all groups of Chinese." Even after the Hankow incident of January 3, 1927, Shidehara held to the position of patience. The cabinet decided that, while the dignity of the nation and rights guaranteed by the treaties should not be compromised, Japanese residents in the concession must be evacuated in case a Chinese mob entered it. If the situation developed out of hand, the entire consulate was to be closed and the police and marines withdrawn. Similarly, Japan refused to cooperate with Britain to defend the international settlement in Shanghai. Early in January, the Tokyo government did decide to have 1,500 marines ready to land on the settlement in case of emergency. But when, on January 20, the British ambassador in Tokyo sought the cooperation of Japan in dispatching further marines to defend Shanghai, Shidehara replied that the forces then available appeared sufficient under the conditions obtaining in the Yangtze Valley. The next day he explicitly stated Japan's refusal to act jointly with Britain because of the serious effect of such an action upon Chinese and Japanese public opinion. The result was the British decision to send an additional 13,000 marines singlehandedly. Shidehara thought that all powers might join in such a neutralization scheme as Secretary Kellogg was contemplating in Washington, but the latter went ahead alone, considering that time was an important factor.[58]

Shidehara's disinclination to use force in cooperation with the powers to defend their nationals in China can be explained easily. For him priority had to be given to the search for a new definition of Sino-Japanese "coexistence," and the sending of troops to protect nationals could seriously lessen the prospect for success. Joint action with the powers was out of the question. Shidehara felt that, only by being patient in the midst of confusion in China, could Japan earn the gratitude of the Chinese, who would respond by subscribing to the Japanese conception of a new order.

The best evidence of this line of thought is Shidehara's handling of the surtax question. Despite Washington's and London's acquiescence, the Tokyo government persisted in opposing the Chinese imposition of the Washington surtaxes. Tokyo's uncompromising stand was such that it was willing to consider the use of force to prevent its collection in north China and Manchuria. Forgetting its profession of strict neutrality in the Chinese civil war, the Foreign Ministry toyed with the idea of offering inducements to the northern warlords, primarily in Manchuria and Mongolia, in return for their pledge not to levy the surtaxes.[59]

The fourth problem facing Japan was that of the rift within the Kuomintang ranks. In the preceding chapter it was seen that Foreign Ministry officials doubted that a "red revolution" was imminent or even possible in China. This attitude was maintained after the launching of the Northern Expedition. Despite the radical professions and defiant acts of the Nationalists, Japanese officials were disposed to the belief that at bottom they were mostly reasonable and wished to cooperate with Japan. This, of course, necessitated search for "reasonable" Nationalists who might accept the Japanese definition of a new order. The result was that, at a time when American and British officials were only vaguely aware of the existence of factions within the Kuomintang, Japan was sensitive to any sign of rift between radicals and moderates within the revolutionary party.

In November 1926, Shidehara instructed Saburi Sadao, chief of the commerce bureau and a delegate to the Tariff Conference, to proceed southward and talk with top Kuomintang officials. Saburi met with Eugene Ch'en, Chiang Kai-shek, and other leaders. He noted, as Shidehara had thought he would, that there was a gap between the Nationalists' public professions and their real intentions. They wished, Saburi believed, to effect revision of unequal treaties by "adequate rational means" rather than by total repudiation. Eugene Ch'en, for example, expressed no objection when Saburi insisted that a reciprocal tariff arrangement should be the price for a grant of tariff autonomy. Furthermore, Ch'en said that the Nationalist government well understood the Japanese position in Manchuria. Later in January 1927, the Japanese consul at Kiukiang reported a conversation with Chiang Kai-shek at Lushan. Chiang said that, far from intending to repudiate the unequal treaties, he would respect them as much as possible. He would see to it that foreign loans were honored, foreign enterprises fully protected, and the industrial development of China not impeded.[60]

These were little more than vague promises, and certainly the subsequent acts by the Nationalists belied their soothing words. But to Japanese officials they provided convincing proof that some Nationalists at least were reasonable. The reported rift between Wuhan and Nanchang fitted this image of the Chinese revolutionaries. The right wing of the Kuomintang could be identified as moderates with respect to the treaties and Japanese rights in China. As early as the end of December 1926, a group of Japanese businessmen in Shanghai sent identical letters to the Foreign, Navy, and War ministries in Tokyo stating that "it is urgently needed for the interest of Japan and China to maintain the peace in Kiangsu and Chekiang Provinces and further to cause the Kuomintang left to be replaced by the right which represents China's 'national aspirations.'" The memorialists hoped that the government would take proper steps toward this end. The Japanese military in China, too, began to notice the internal friction of the Nationalists and to approach the rightists. Supporting such a move, Consul General Yada at Shanghai telegraphed early in January that "the opportunity seems approaching when we can approach the rightists (including the elder people and upper-class moderates here), come to some understanding with them, and with our assistance 'eliminate' the communists and Soviet Russia from the revolutionary army." Chang Chi was particularly active as a spokesman for the right-wing Kuomintang, talking with Japanese business groups in Shanghai, and Yada reported that Chang might visit Japan to represent his faction's interests. In February, in fact, Tai Chi-t'ao appeared in Japan as Chiang Kai-shek's delegate, adding to the bitterness of the Wuhan faction. All this served to strengthen Shidehara's optimism. While he avoided taking any overt action to support one faction against others, his awareness of the existence of a core of moderate leaders in China was an important factor pregnant with future significance.[61]

The first phase of the Northern Expedition by the Chinese Nationalists marked the culminating point of the Soviet initiative. As all groups of Chinese accepted most or part of the Soviet program, there was a distinct possibility that they would define their own framework of Sino-foreign relations. Apart from the communists and the majority of the Wuhan faction, it is doubtful if the Chinese would have accepted the idea of close Sino-Soviet partnership. But it is remarkable that even Chiang Kai-shek, despite his open hostility to Wuhan, still saw fit to profess his friendship for the Soviet Union. More than that, that part of the Soviet program designed to destroy the structure of the treaty system was accepted by all factions and governments. The Chinese were struggling to create a new order of their own choice in the Far East, under Soviet inspiration.

In this period of crisis and change, Japan, Britain, and the United States were also eager to clarify their own images of a new order, as a substitute for the Sino-Soviet definition. There was little interest in joint stands because all three governments believed more could be gained by independent action. While they opposed radical change in the basic structure of the existing treaty system, all realized the advantage of forestalling such a change by entering into friendly, bilateral relations with China. Japanese policy, in particular, reflected a feeling that it was urgent to achieve Sino-Japanese cooperation, and, after the winter of 1926–1927, Japan was to take the place of the Soviet Union as the nation whose policies would shape Far Eastern politics.

Part Two

• THE JAPANESE INITIATIVE

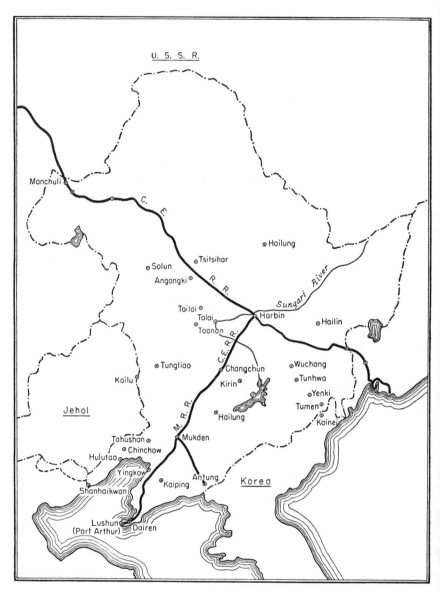

Manchuria

IV · REVOLUTION AND COUNTER-REVOLUTION, 1927

The apparent successes of the Soviet initiative in China, culminating in the Northern Expedition, at last evoked a determined response from Japan. Historians have often spoken of Japan as shifting from the "internationalist" policy of Shidehara to the more nationalistic policy of General Tanaka. Unquestionably there was some shift. Tanaka came to power just when the Nationalists successfully achieved the military unification of China; he came from a military background; he was head of a political party opposed to the government's foreign policy; and his personality was different from Shidehara's. But much of what is usually attributed to Tanaka can be traced to Shidehara; the latter's "friendship" for China had an extremely high price. Both Shidehara and Tanaka were groping for a solution to the same problem — that of protecting Japanese interests in China at a time when the old mechanisms of international relations had broken down. In effect, Tanaka carried on the Shidehara policy, but in circumstances that eventually made it a different policy.

THE NANKING INCIDENT

The simmering antagonism between the Nationalists and foreigners came to a head in March 1927. Revolutionary soldiers neared Shanghai and Nanking after their successful conquest of Chekiang Province in February. An atmosphere of tension and uneasiness prevailed in Shanghai as the General Labor Union called a general strike and mobilized its armed pickets. On March 21, as Nationalist troops arrived outside of the international settlement, the municipal council asked the assistance of foreign naval forces for an "international defense" of Shanghai. Some foreigners had already been evacuated, and American, Japanese, and Dutch forces were landed to maintain order. The workers, under Moscow's direction, opened the city gates to Nationalist troops in the evening of the same day, and the remaining northern soldiers surrendered to foreign troops. General Pai Ch'ung-hsi, commanding the Nationalist force in Shanghai, issued proclamations accepting responsibility for the maintenance of public order. He added that the Nationalists had "no intention [to] recover China's sovereign rights by military force or measures endangering foreign lives and property." The situation was still extremely tense, but there was no serious clash between Chinese and foreigners.[1]

In Nanking the story was very different. Southern soldiers invaded the river-bank suburb of Hsiakwan on the morning of March 24, and within one hour and ten minutes of their entrance their shells had killed a Japanese naval officer. At the University of Nanking, Nationalists in uniform wantonly shot to death an American, Dr. J. E. Williams, vice president of the university. Elsewhere business establishments of foreigners were looted and many lives endangered, including that of the British consul. As many foreigners took refuge in buildings belonging to the Standard Oil Company in Socony Hill, British and American warships on the Yangtze dropped shells around this area to protect them.[2]

Contemporary testimony regarding the incident varied. The entering southern army, under the command of Ch'eng Ch'ien, reported to Wuhan that Dr. Williams had been shot to death by fleeing northern soldiers. On March 25, General Ch'eng reported, "Before order was restored the reactionary elements at Nanking instigated rebels and bandits to plunder foreign property, set fire to houses, and injure lives. This resulted in the firing by British and American ships. . . . At that time our soldiers were engaged in exterminating the remaining rebels and guarding the Yangtze River region. A few soldiers noticed the foreign bombing and, as the truth had not come out, thought the imperialists were aiding the rebels and intentionally challenging us. Our soldiers thus returned fire. [I] saw this and ordered that firing cease." On the basis of these reports Eugene Ch'en at Hankow told the British consul general that "Shantung troops must have committed the outrages because he could not believe that Nationalist troops would be guilty of such conduct." A similar conclusion was reached by several foreign and Chinese eyewitnesses who assembled evidence to show that the demoralized retreating soldiers were the actual perpetrators of the attacks.[3]

Such reports ran counter to the official reports of the American, British, and Japanese consuls on the spot. John Davis, American consul at Nanking, did not doubt that the outrages were committed by southern soldiers. The consulate itself was not attacked before its staff evacuated it, although a Chinese officer passing by told Davis, "you Americans have drunk our blood for years and become rich. We are busy now killing Fengtien soldiers but we will soon be killing all foreigners in Nanking regardless of what country they are from." Following the news of Williams' death and other acts of violence by Chinese, Americans at the consulate left for Socony Hill, overlooking the Yangtze. There they were met by bands of soldiers who threatened them with pistols. As a party of Americans decided to escape beyond the wall to the ships on the river, Consul Davis signaled the ships to commence a barrage to drive off Chinese assailants. As the Americans came to the bank of the river, they were approached by a group of Chinese representing the local red swastika society. They transmitted a message from General Ch'eng Ch'ien saying that the outrages had been committed by "rioters" who had been instigated by the enemies. As he would take the responsibility of suppressing the rowdies and protecting foreign lives and property, his letter said, the powers were implored not to continue the bombardment.[4]

On the question of the identity of the looting and attacking soldiers, Consul Davis reported, "They were of the sixth army and seemed very proud of being General Cheng [sic] Ch'ien's men who they said 'do not care what we do to foreigners'. . . . From my long observation of the soldiers on the Standard Oil hill, from conversations with others at the entrance gate of the Consulate, and from the soldiers whom we met on the way from the latter to the former place, I am convinced beyond the slightest possibility of doubt, that all were regular Kuomintang troops who were operating under orders."[5]

The occupants of the British consulate in Nanking, who suffered even worse treatment, reached the same conclusion as to the identity of the Chinese attackers. Consul General Bertram Giles was shot in the leg, two Britishers were killed by rifle, and the consulate building was completely looted. Chinese soldiers did not cease plundering till the H.M.S. *Emerald* began its barrage in response to the request from the American consul on Socony Hill. Principal British eyewitnesses all believed that the attackers were southern soldiers, since the northerners had completely cleared from the area by midnight of March 23.[6]

The Japanese consul at Nanking, Morioka Shōhei, also ruled out the possibility that the northerners were the culprits since they had disappeared from the area around the consulate by the late afternoon of March 23. Southerners first appeared, according to Consul Morioka, at around half-past five the following morning. In order to avoid inciting the revolutionary soldiers the consul had the Japanese military disarm. At seven o'clock a party of southern soldiers inquired about the presence of northern troops. There was no incident at that time; but a moment later about fifty southern regular troops invaded, fired at, and plundered the consulate building. The invaders carried the revolutionary flags and shouted, "Down with Japanese and British imperialists," "Unity of the Soviet Union and China," and "Japanese have plundered China, so let's take it back." The consul himself was lying ill in bed, but he was twice shot at and was in peril for three hours. At half-past ten in the morning a representative of the second army appeared and stopped the violent acts of the soldiers. He expressed his regrets to the Japanese consul, saying that these unruly soldiers were "rowdies" within the second and sixth armies. He promised to maintain strict vigilance thereafter and to provide whatever food and medical supplies the Japanese might need.[7]

At noon of the following day the Japanese commander of the marine force which had just been landed saw General Ch'eng Ch'ien and strongly urged that he at once take steps to protect Japanese lives. Ch'eng said that the southerners would take responsibility for the outrages. As the British and Americans were expected to renew the bombardment at night, Japanese residents were withdrawn to the destroyers at Hsiakwan. As they were leaving, Yang Chieh, commander of the seventeenth division, came and told Consul Morioka that the violence had been committed by "bad soldiers" instigated by communists in Nanking. On the same day Chiang Kai-shek, who had been at Wuhu when the incident broke out, arrived at Nanking. Though he stayed only a few hours, according to the Japanese consul's account, he "killed whomever he saw plundering and closed the Nanking branch of the Communist Party." [8]

From these pieces of evidence Morioka concluded that the responsibility for the Nanking outrages rested entirely with the revolutionary army. More important was his inference that not the southern army as such but the communist elements were most to blame. In his report to Foreign Minister Shidehara he concluded,

The Nanking incident was a systematic and antiforeign act of violence which had been planned and prepared by party commissars and communist officers of lower grades within the second, sixth, and fortieth armies . . . and members of the Communist Party's Nanking branch. The latter acted as guides, and the violence was particularly aimed at foreign consulates, churches, schools, and foreigners in general. There was practically no damage to the Chinese. Chiang Kai-shek and his subordinates (commanders of the several armies, divisions, etc.) have expressed regrets and have been putting forth effort to maintain security, but it would be the impartial judgment today that the communist ideology has permeated the lower officers and the greater part of the army, and there is nothing which can improve the situation.

This strong conclusion was based on a rather isolated remark by Yang Chieh. As time passed the Nationalists themselves would come to interpret the incident as a communist plot to embarrass Chiang Kai-shek in the eyes of foreigners. In the first few days after the incident Morioka was the only foreign official who identified the instigators of the outrages as communists, and his conclusion did not seem to be founded on substantial evidence. It was this view which ultimately influenced the policies of the powers regarding the Nanking incident.[9]

Judging from the reports of the foreign consuls, it may be tentatively concluded that the Nanking incident was provoked by disorderly soldiers within the Nationalist army, whose superiors immediately disavowed the deeds. The problem of communist implication remains, but it would seem that this aspect of the story was fabricated at first by some Nationalists and finally by all of them in order to escape exposure of their own responsibility.

The relevance of the incident to the discussion of Japanese policy lies in the fact that it made Shidehara more aware of the power struggle within the Kuomintang. He could encourage the antiradical faction in order to bring about his own project of Sino-Japanese coprosperity. Quite opportunely, Chiang Kai-shek's initial reaction to the incident was such as to fit Shidehara's image of a moderate Nationalist. Chiang was at Wuhu when the incident broke out. As soon as he had the report of the happenings at Nanking, he sent a messenger to the Japanese consulate to promise that he would take the responsibility for solving the incident. Chiang also asked the Japanese consul to intercede on his behalf and get in touch with American and British authorities in order to have them cease bombardment. On March 25 he left for Nanking. He stayed there for only a few hours and then slipped away to Shanghai.[10]

Such an attitude, plus Consul Morioka's initial reports, convinced Foreign Minister Shidehara of the correctness of his assumption. He could single out Chiang as the leader of the moderate faction within the Kuomintang and, by showing him sympathy and understanding in this period of trouble, perhaps expect to build a solid foundation for a new order of Sino-Japanese relations. Since British and American naval commanders in China had taken a strong stand, demanding satisfaction over the incident, and since Japanese public opinion was critical of the apparent inaction of their government, the first thing necessary was to persuade Chiang and top Chinese officials to terminate the riots without delay and negotiate for a speedy settlement of the incident.[11]

The Japanese military were in essential agreement with such an approach. They had distinguished communist and noncommunist factions within the Kuomintang and sought to support the latter against the former. For General Matsui of the General Staff the Nanking incident was an opportunity to promote the unity of southern moderates presumably led by Chiang Kai-shek. Matsui advocated that Japanese civilian and military officials informally approach the Kuomintang right wing in order to undermine communist strength. Similarly, War Minister Ugaki felt that the time had come for Japan to supply arms to northern and southern moderates so that they might jointly crush communists. In his policy toward Chiang Kai-shek, Shidehara enjoyed support among all the top policy makers.[12]

On March 26 the Foreign Minister instructed the consul at Wuhu to see Chiang Kai-shek and advise him to proceed in person to Nanking and there negotiate with the American, British, and Japanese representatives. Otherwise, Shidehara pointed out, Great Britain and the United States might resort to drastic measures. As Chiang had arrived at Shanghai when Shidehara's instructions reached Wuhu, Yada, the consul general at Shanghai, immediately contacted Huang Fu, one-time prime minister in Peking but also a close acquaintance of Chiang's. Yada had already warned Huang that the powers would probably demand apology, reparations, punishment, and future guarantees as conditions for the settlement of the incident. The Japanese consul general now admonished Chiang, through Huang, to act on his own initiative and declare that he would take these steps at once. When presented with Shidehara's message Chiang Kai-shek agreed to send a commissioner to the foreign consulates to express regrets and promise punishment, reparations, and other measures, as soon as the facts had been investigated. After learning of this response Shidehara voiced to the American ambassador his belief that Chiang would do his utmost to suppress disorderly elements and maintain order in Nanking. The Foreign Minister also said he believed that "the outrages at Nanking were committed partly by the Cantonese and partly by the Shantung defeated army but insofar as they were due to the Cantonese soldiers they were instigated by the radicals among the Cantonese who are aiming at the destruction of Chiang Kai-shek." [13]

Meanwhile, in Peking, on March 28, the representatives of Japan, Britain, the United States, France, and Italy agreed to recommend a common course of action to their governments. They suggested that their home governments present to Chiang the following terms: first, adequate punishment of the commander of the troops responsible for the outrages and of all persons found to be implicated; second, written apology by Chiang Kai-shek, including a pledge to suppress violence and agitation against foreign lives and property; and third, complete reparation for personal injuries and material damages. The British minister wished to attach a time limit to these demands, but his American and Japanese colleagues thought it would be more advantageous to leave a little leeway, and all three agreed to add the recommendation that Chiang be informed that, "unless he demonstrated to our satisfaction his intention to comply with these terms the interested powers will find themselves compelled to specify a time limit for compliance, failing which they reserve themselves the right to take such measures as they consider appropriate." [14]

With the proposed formula of the ministers Shidehara received Consul Morioka's telegram definitely attributing the Nanking incident to communist instigation and planning. He was also informed of a further interview between Yada and Huang, in which the latter had conveyed Chiang Kai-shek's view that he could not publicly declare his intention of punishing the responsible soldiers and paying indemnities, as the communist faction was endeavoring to undermine his authority.[15] Having these data before him, Shidehara saw it as more imperative than ever that Chiang Kai-shek on his own initiative make positive amends for the outrages. In that way Chiang's position as a moderate would be recognized and the alleged communist plot to discredit him frustrated. Consequently, the Japanese Foreign Minister objected to the time limit proposed by the ministers on the ground that it would embarrass Chiang Kai-shek and play into the hands of the communists. The best policy for the powers, Shidehara said in his telegram of March 30 to Minister Yoshizawa, was to let the Chinese maintain their own order and give "sound elements" among the southerners an opportunity to stabilize the situation. He went on to say,

The policy of encouraging Chiang Kai-shek through the consul general at Shanghai is based on the belief that neither Chiang Kai-shek nor the powers should be drawn into the communist plot but that Chiang Kai-shek and other sound elements should be allowed to solve the present issue and eventually to stabilize conditions throughout the south. To this end it is best for the powers to avoid taking measures which might result in inviting the downfall of Chiang Kai-shek and others. . . . One of the reasons for Japan's participation in joint action with the powers [regarding the settlement of the incident] is that by doing so Japan should be able to soften the stand of other powers in case the latter should propose too harsh demands.[16]

There was definite purpose in Shidehara's handling of the Nanking incident. He meant to achieve understanding with the moderate Nationalists. And Chiang Kai-shek at this time showed real interest in reciprocating. He said, for instance, that Japanese policy differed from the "oppressive" attitudes of Britain and the United States. His fight against the Wuhan faction had just begun. At the same time, until his supremacy was ensured, he could not risk appearing too conciliatory toward any foreign government. He felt that the solution of the Nanking incident should be postponed until the power struggle within the Kuomintang came to a certain conclusion. This decision was unfortunate from the Japanese point of view. Much as Shidehara hoped to see Chiang triumph over his radical opponents, he also felt that time was an important element. Procrastination could only bring about additional pressure from the Western powers, and the Foreign Minister's own position might be jeopardized since Japanese lives had been killed and injured without a settlement having been reached. The opposition party, the Seiyukai, had been denouncing Shidehara's "weak policy," and it was imperative for the Tokyo government to show some proof of its wisdom.[17]

In this way, the Nanking incident became bound up not only with the internal strife within the Kuomintang but also with party politics in Japan. Late March and early April were months of tension in the Far East. What new order might emerge depended on the outcome of the Kuomintang power struggle, the attitudes of the powers toward the situation in China, and the course of party rivalry in Japan.

THE ROLE OF KUOMINTANG "MODERATES"

The story of Chiang Kai-shek's "counterrevolution" has been so often recounted that a bare outline will suffice here. As soon as he entered Shanghai on March 26, Chiang conferred with such anti-Wuhan leaders as Ts'ai Yüan-p'ei, Li Shih-tseng, Wu Chih-hui, and C. C. Wu. He also contacted military leaders including Pai Ch'ung-hsi, Ho Ying-ch'ing, and Li Chi-shen. Chiang began putting his own men in key administrative posts, refused to recognize the provisional municipal government which had been set up under communist leadership, organized an anticommunist labor union, and appointed a commissioner for foreign affairs. Rightwing Nationalists in Shanghai also sought to obtain the support of Wang Ching-wei, who returned to China on April 1 from his European trip through Moscow. Chiang Kai-shek announced that he was ready to submit to Wang's authority in civil matters and that Wang should assume supreme leadership and centralize in himself control over party affairs. Li, Wu, and other supporters of Chiang also tried to convince Wang of the seriousness of communist strength. Wang Ching-wei was well aware of it, perhaps too well aware of the communist threat to break with communists and Russians abruptly. He hoped that some compromise, other than the unilateral solution contemplated by Chiang Kai-shek, would be worked out. With Ch'en Tu-hsiu, the communist leader, Wang issued a manifesto on April 4, strongly denying that communists and Nationalists were about to split. The manifesto said, "We must stand on the common ground of revolution, give up mutual suspicions, reject rumor-mongering, and respect each other." Wang Ching-wei told Kuomintang leaders that he hoped the next plenary session of the central executive committee would be held in Nanking on April 15 and, probably fearing lest he be detained in Shanghai, secretly left for Wuhan on April 5.[18]

Things moved fast not only at Shanghai and Wuhan but also at Peking. In this last city the Chinese metropolitan police conducted a search of the Soviet embassy buildings on April 6, "knowing that these places have been centers of Communist agitators." The diplomatic corps in Peking had given formal approval for the search. The raid was directed as much against the Kuomintang as against the communists, but the documents seized revealed the extent of Soviet activity in China and its connection with Chinese communists. Both Chiang Kai-shek and Eugene Ch'en issued statements denouncing the raid, the former declaring that it was an unprecedented outrage maneuvered by the imperialists to crush the Chinese revolution.[19] Still, Chiang was not deterred from taking the course of action which he and his supporters had already mapped out.

Disappointed that Wang Ching-wei did not share his aims and evaluation of the existing situation, Chiang Kai-shek proceeded to bring about the forceful suppression of the communists. After preparations were made for a radical step against laborers of Shanghai, Chiang departed for Nanking on April 9, leaving Pai Ch'ung-hsi in command. His troops started disarming workers on April 11, and on the following day an assault was made upon the General Labor Union. Assisted by underground terrorist organizations, General Pai's soldiers attacked, disarmed, arrested, and killed labor leaders and pickets. On April 13 an order was issued dissolving the General Labor Union and the provisional municipal government. The white terror spread to other areas in the south; similar coups were effected in Kwangtung under Li Chi-shen, Fukien under Fang Sheng-t'ou, Szechwan under Liu Hsiang, and Kiangsu and Chekiang under the direction of Pai Ch'ung-hsi.[20]

On April 18 a plenary session of the central executive committee and the central supervisory committee of the Kuomintang, meeting in Nanking, resolved to dissolve and transfer the Wuhan government to Nanking. The same day Chiang Kai-shek declared that China must rid itself of communists as well as warlords and imperialists. He accused communists of breaking what he called the Kuomintang principle of dealing with one foreign country at one time and pushing all imperialists to coalesce and fight against China but then throwing the country to the sphere of influence of the Soviet Union. "We must join the world revolution as an independent, free, and equal member; we should not be led into it," Chiang said. In another speech on the same day, he attacked Russia for not having treated China as its equal, as shown by Bordin's domination, and he asked if Russia was not becoming a "red imperialist." In other words, he opposed the Soviet idea of a Far Eastern order based on Sino-Soviet ties but did not go back to the idea that China should cooperate with other powers on their terms. Sensitive to the accusation that he was in collusion with them, Chiang declared that he had never received a single gun, bullet, or penny from imperialists.[21]

As far as the Chiang Kai-shek faction was concerned, the revolutionary system in the Far East pursued by the Soviet Union was at an end. Whether and to what extent this affected China's own search for a new order of complete equality remained to be seen. Anything could happen, and the powers were once again compelled to clarify their policies in China.

On March 28 the five ministers in Peking had recommended to their home governments certain terms for the settlement of the Nanking incident. The Tokyo government approved of the terms except the threatened time limit. The United States also objected to this provision, and the British government insisted that it was not advisable to single out Chiang Kai-shek for responsibility and that the note should also be presented to Eugene Ch'en at Wuhan. On the basis of these recommendations the ministers rewrote their draft note and readied it for presentation to the Chinese.[22]

Action was delayed due to last-minute maneuvers in Tokyo and London. Although he had more than once given such advice to Chiang Kai-shek, Foreign Minister Shidehara decided to urge him again to take the initiative in settling the Nanking incident. The wisdom of Shidehara's policy of patience and encouragement of moderates would be vindicated only if Chiang responded before he was presented with formal demands of the powers. Consequently, the Foreign Minister promised Chiang that, if he would consent to declare his willingness either to punish guilty officers and otherwise settle the Nanking incident, or to join with the powers in an investigation of the incident in order to find a basis for its solution, Japan would see to it that the presentation of the powers' notes would be postponed for several days. Chiang Kai-shek replied that he would agree to the second alternative.[23] Unfortunately, just at this juncture another incident occurred at Hankow, where Japanese sailors clashed with Chinese mobs with casualties on both sides. Shidehara's policy came under fresh attack at home. Realizing the inadvisability of further delay in the Nanking affair, he consented to instantaneous dispatch of the notes to the Chinese.[24]

In London, meanwhile, the Foreign Office was unhappy about the omission of a time limit from the proposed note. It served notice that, while omitting a time limit, the powers should "accept in principle the application of sanctions in the event of the Nationalist Government refusing to give satisfaction to their demands." This effort by the British to get the powers to agree on the principle of applying sanctions was instantly and strongly rebuffed by the American and Japanese governments. Kellogg flatly declared that the United States "does not consider that by sending a demand to the Cantonese military commander it is obligated in any manner to apply sanctions." Shidehara had already tried to impress upon the British government his views regarding the impracticability of imposing sanctions. At Peking, Minister Yoshizawa was alone in refusing to give a prior consent on the matter of sanctions, while the other four ministers insisted that an agreement on this matter was essential. But finally Kellogg's and Shidehara's reasoning prevailed upon Sir Austen Chamberlain, who decided to waive insistence upon the principle of sanctions.[25]

Thus it was not until April 11, the day before the Shanghai coup, that the demands of the powers were presented to Chiang Kai-shek and Eugene Ch'en. The crisis within the Nationalist party was clearly reflected in Wuhan's reaction to the identic notes. Ch'en decided to take advantage of this occasion to bolster up the Wuhan regime as the only Nationalist government. Apparently Wang Ching-wei, who had arrived at Wuhan on April 10, advocated the tactic of relying on Japan for a way out of the impasse. Eugene Ch'en, accordingly, approached Japan and sought to have it recognize Wuhan's authority. He had already prepared a statement for the purpose, to be communicated to Japan. In it he said that Japan's nonparticipation in the Nanking bombardment was in contrast to the "cruelty inherent in the Western civilization" and indicated Japan's friendship for China. The statement declared that the fulfillment of the demands of Nationalist China would not endanger or menace Japan's proper interests and welfare. Therefore the Nationalist government at Wuhan would like to invite Japan to appoint delegates not only to solve the Nanking incident but also to negotiate new treaties. The basic strategy here was to induce Japan to enter into formal negotiations with Wuhan. This would greatly enhance its prestige.[26]

After April 12, with Chiang Kai-shek's "betrayal" and an open split between right and left, the Wuhan regime was more than ever impelled to vindicate its legitimacy. The Kuomintang central executive committee at Hankow retaliated to Chiang's coup by expelling him from the party and issuing an order for his arrest. At the same time efforts were redoubled to obtain diplomatic recognition of the Wuhan regime as the sole representative of the Nationalists. Accordingly, in his replies to the powers, issued on April 14, Ch'en invited them to initiate negotiation not only for a "prompt and friendly settlement" of the Nanking incident but also for "modernizing international intercourse," namely for treaty revision.[27]

The ministers in Peking agreed that Eugene Ch'en's replies were "wholly unsatisfactory and unacceptable." His words attempted to "obscure by irrelevant matters the plain issue of amends for the Nanking outrages." Using unusually strong language, the ministers condemned Ch'en as "an unscrupulous dialectician who does [not] himself possess either the authority or the power actually to conduct these negotiations in good faith, but who is a mere tool of the Soviet influence now dominant at Hankow, and who under such influences has set himself to evade and obscure the one vital issue while making the discussion a means of further anti-foreign propaganda." Consequently, the ministers recommended that their respective home governments authorize them to present identic notes to Ch'en, this time clearly saying that, "unless the Nationalist authorities state unequivocally and without delay that they intend to proceed to the integral fulfillment of the terms presented, the Governments concerned will be obliged to consider such measures as may be necessary to obtain compliance."[28]

Whether such strong action was desirable depended on each power's interpretation of the rightist coup within the Nationalist party. Among American officials, Minister MacMurray remained least convinced of the strength or even the sincerity of the Nationalist "moderates." He believed that the Nanking incident had been "created" by the "Russian advisers." As he considered Chiang Kai-shek also to be under Russian control, he felt that resolute action was called for in order to "avoid an unfortunate new Boxer movement." His policy was therefore punitive and preventive.

He believed that American citizens in Kuomintang territory should be completely withdrawn to Shanghai or other areas where they could reasonably be protected. Then the United States should blockade all Chinese ports south of Shanghai. Recommending these steps to his government, MacMurray concluded, "I believe that action such as I have indicated could yet keep China from becoming a hostile agent of Soviet Russia against western powers, including the United States. If this situation is not resolutely met, it will mean the downfall of western influence and interests in the Orient." On April 9 the American minister reported to Washington that "nobody viewing the situation from the standpoint of China can seriously entertain a doubt that the Russians are now the masters of the whole Nationalist movement which prevails in the South and is sweeping northward like a prairie fire." To MacMurray the only hope for the powers lay in the northern warlord regime. If the Nationalists should persist in refusing to satisfy the demands of the powers on the Nanking incident, then "the Northerners must come into our camp unless we betray ourselves." This conviction was undoubtedly strengthened as Soviet ties with radical Chinese were revealed by the raid of April 6. Even after the April 12 coup MacMurray refused to regard the reported moderate-radical split as fundamental and long-lasting. Available evidence did not warrant the assumption, he advised Washington, that "the moderates are attempting to drive the radicals from control in the so-called Nationalist Government." He even surmised that the appearance of a fundamental split was a result of the tactical maneuver by the Russian advisers to divide responsibility for the Nanking incident, so that the powers would have difficulty in enforcing their demands. With respect to Chiang Kai-shek, MacMurray reported,

There is furthermore reason to believe that Chiang is most untrustworthy and at heart, scarcely if at all, less extreme and antiforeign than his opponents, so that in the event of his prevailing we would find ourselves dealing with a leader whose purposes and methods are scarcely different from those of the Russians. I therefore do not feel that circumstances thus far known would justify us in singling out Chiang to back as our hope for a saner and more moderate nationalism.[29]

Consul General Jenkins at Canton, on the other hand, believed that the moderate-radical strife within the Kuomintang was real. He thought that the powers should encourage the moderates by adroit handling of the Nanking episode. He saw the possibility of placing the blame for the incident squarely on the radical faction at Wuhan and absolving the moderates led by Chiang Kai-shek of all responsibility. On April 17, Jenkins telegraphed Kellogg, urging, "As the Nanking incident was undoubtedly the work of the very elements now being routed out by Chiang and his supporters, it is to be hoped that some means can be found to avoid complications in the matter with the moderates and that responsibility may be placed as far as practicable on the Hankow group, and not on Chiang Kai-shek and the present leaders in the Canton regime." [30]

In Washington there grew awareness, though at first very vague, of the significance of the split within the Nationalists. On April 14 Secretary Kellogg remarked to the British ambassador that "the Cantonese seemed to be divided and seemed to be having more or less difficulty between their two factions, the Conservatives and the extreme Radicals." By April 20 the State Department had become aware of the effort "being made by the moderates to drive the radicals from the control of the Chinese Nationalist Government." It would weaken the moderates if the demands were pressed in the way suggested by the five ministers. Kellogg accordingly did not authorize MacMurray to join in presenting the second identic note suggested by them. Moreover, in early May, MacMurray was instructed to explore the possibilities of negotiating the settlement of the Nanking incident with C. C. Wu, who had been appointed Nanking's foreign minister.[31]

In this way some understanding between Nanking and Washington might have developed. The Nanking incident had come as a rude shock to the government which had publicly professed its sympathy with Chinese nationalism and sought to enter a new era of Sino-American friendship. If the Chiang Kai-shek regime could show real sincerity in atoning for the death of an American and otherwise taking full responsibility for the Nanking incident, the United States might single him out as the object of support. But, to the dismay and disappointment of Kellogg and his staff, the Nanking government never squarely faced the issue of responsibility for the incident, primarily because the civil strife in China engaged its total attention. C. C. Wu continued simply to heap blame on communists. Since the State Department believed that Nationalist soldiers had been involved in the outrages, the attitude could only be considered an excuse. From the American point of view the incident had to be solved satisfactorily before anything could be done to bind Nanking and Washington.[32]

British policy showed a greater degree of flexibility. Britain had initially been determined to exact satisfaction from the Chinese for the Nanking outrages, and British officials had even considered taking such measures as bombarding the Hanyang arsenal or reoccupying the Hankow concession. Developments in China after the Shanghai coup of April 12, however, had necessitated a shift in policy. From the reports of the officials in Hankow the Foreign Office gathered that the Wuhan government was under strong communist influence and was placed "in serious financial difficulties by the defection of Chiang Kai-shek, by the cutting of their communications with Shanghai and Canton and by the cessation of foreign business owing to the disturbed conditions and the lack of security either for life or for property." Chiang Kai-shek, on the other hand, was considered to have the support of the more moderate elements of the Kuomintang as well as of military authorities in the coastal provinces. As the Wuhan government seemed to have dwindled in influence and authority, the British government did not think it wise to continue talking with Eugene Ch'en. On May 9, Foreign Secretary Chamberlain declared that "The Nationalist Government at Hankow has lost its dominating position and is at present little more than the shadow of a name. Mr. Chen's notes have received their answer in the practical disappearance of the power which he affected to represent." Chamberlain subscribed to the communist-conspiracy theory of the Nanking incident and stated that the communist agitators "have been punished by the Chinese Nationalists themselves with a severity and effectiveness of which no foreign Power was capable." Though Britain still had to ask for reparation for the damages done during the incident, no sanction would at present be taken; to do so might embarrass the Nanking government "in their task of introducing order in the territory under their control." Official connections with Wuhan, which had been established when O'Malley was sent to Hankow to confer with Eugene Ch'en, were explicitly severed in the middle of May, when an official who had replaced O'Malley was withdrawn from the city. The reason for his termination of relations with the Wuhan government was that the latter had not exhibited the "responsibility of a civilized government." [33]

In contrast to American and British policies Japan's attitude in April and May 1927 gave the impression of greater consistency and specificity. This is all the more remarkable since Shidehara was replaced by Tanaka as foreign minister in the midst of the Nanking crisis. Shidehara had foreknowledge of the April 12 coup. Chiang Kai-shek had assured him that he would consider solution of the Nanking incident as soon as he carried out a coup against radicals.[34] The Japanese government understood the nature of the Shanghai incident and was encouraged in the hope that moderate Nationalists under Chiang would emerge as leaders of the Kuomintang. Quite opportunely, soon after the April 12 coup, Huang Fu told Japanese officials that the Nanking authorities would be willing to assume all responsibility in order to solve the Nanking incident, once the negotiations between the powers and Wuhan came to a stalemate.[35] Before Shidehara could proceed further with Nanking, however, he was replaced by Tanaka Giichi.

Tanaka's Seiyukai Party had attacked the Wakatsuki cabinet's China policy as conciliatory to Chinese revolutionaries and negligent of Japanese rights. On April 16 Tanaka criticized the government's "policy of nonresistance" and called for "a great renovation of our China policy in order to carry out the defense of our country and the protection of our rights." The next day the cabinet fell as a result of the refusal of the Privy Council to sanction a government plan to save the Bank of Taiwan from financial collapse. It was the obvious intention of some Privy Councilors to use the bank issue in order to force the downfall of a cabinet which was associated with a "weak" China policy.[36]

Tanaka had been a professional soldier and had participated in the wars with China and Russia. During the 1910's he played an active role both in the Siberian Expedition and in various political schemes in China. But he also acquired an interest in politics after he served in Hara's Seiyukai cabinet as war minister. In 1925 Seiyukai politicians, leaderless after Hara's assassination in 1921, decided to rehabilitate the party by conferring its presidency on one of the most prominent generals in the country. As president Tanaka continued to criticize the Kenseikai cabinet's China policy and insist that "something must be done" to keep that country from falling to the grip of communism. In early 1927 he sent members of his party to China to obtain firsthand information of the political changes there. They were impressed by the predominance of Russian influence and the decline in Japanese prestige in China, but they were also assured by Nationalists that they would respect Japan's legitimate treaty rights.[37]

Tanaka's military background, his criticism of the government's China policy, and the fact that, after the furor over universal manhood suffrage had dissipated in 1925, the China question had become one of the most prominent issues dividing the political parties, all pointed to a new course in Japanese foreign policy when Tanaka became prime minister in April 1927. Failing to find a suitable foreign minister from the financial community, he appointed himself for the position and gave the office of parliamentary vice foreign minister to a party politician, Mori Kaku. These facts served further to give the impression that the new government would develop a different approach from that of Shidehara.[38]

Contrary to expectations, during the first few weeks after Tanaka's assumption of office there was no noticeable change in Japan's China policy. He shared his predecessor's distrust of the Wuhan regime and was inclined to discard the possibility of reaching accord with it. He expressed the view that the Wuhan government was little more than "a collection of irresponsible people without real power" and agreed that the Nationalists at Nanking should be the main object of negotiation regarding the Nanking incident and other matters.[39] Fortunately, the Nanking faction of the Kuomintang continued to be interested in an understanding with Japan. In early May, Chiang Kai-shek sent three emissaries to Tokyo to talk with the new prime minister and to ask for assistance from the Japanese government. Tanaka was favorably impressed and told them of his sympathy with Chiang's effort to establish a new order in China.[40]

While they were in Japan, Chiang's emissaries met an envoy sent by Chang Tso-lin. The representatives of north and south China agreed to come to a truce under some conditions and meanwhile carry out the extermination of communists within both camps. Chang and Chiang were informed of this accord. These developments were perfectly in line with the strategy of the Tanaka cabinet. It would encourage the moderate Nationalists to carry out their task, so that together with Japan they might contribute to the peace and order in China. Tanaka strongly hoped that the northern government under Chang Tso-lin would not interfere with Chiang Kai-shek as he tried to deal with communists and overthrow the Wuhan faction. When that was accomplished, he told the British ambassador, although China might still be divided between north and south, the powers would be able to arrive at a solution of the Nanking incident through the Nanking government.[41]

This line of argument was put into the instructions Tanaka sent to Minister Yoshizawa and Consul General Yada on May 20. Here the Prime Minister stated that if Chiang Kai-shek and his faction continued to suppress communists and insured their own internal stability, the Japanese government should give them "moral support" and assist them in attaining their political goals. Consequently, in case they should start war against the Wuhan government, the north should be made to refrain from intervening. If Chang Tso-lin and Chiang Kai-shek should desire to reach a compromise, such a move should be encouraged. At the same time, Tanaka emphasized that all efforts toward compromise should come from the Chinese and that the Japanese government and its officials should refrain from throwing themselves into the situation.[42]

It is evident that for a month after he came to power Tanaka faithfully followed his predecessor's China policy. They shared an image of a new era based on solid understanding between

Japan and China. The existence of Chinese radicals was an obstacle to this scheme, and both Shidehara and Tanaka did all they could to support any movement against them. But even Tanaka could not keep up with the rapidly changing developments of events in China, and these in time caused him to depart in certain respects from the policies formulated by Shidehara.

DECLINE OF SOVIET INFLUENCE

In the early summer of 1927 events in China did not proceed in accordance with hopes and expectations of foreign governments. No compromise was reached between the Nanking generals and northern warlords; not only did the existence of independent powerful warlords like Yen Hsi-shan and Feng Yü-hsiang render the approach of Chiang Kai-shek and Chang Tso-lin difficult, but Marshal Chang also sought to strengthen his own position while the revolutionaries were internally split. Both Nanking and Wuhan forces, the former led by Chiang Kai-shek and the latter by a former warlord, T'ang Sheng-chih, after Chiang's expulsion from the party, were intent upon pushing their campaigns northward to control the Peking-Tientsin region to consolidate and enhance their strength.[43]

There was thus created a feeling of renewed danger among foreigners in such key cities as Peking, Tientsin, Tsinan, and Tsingtao. The protection of nationals again became a matter of cardinal importance in the middle of May. By this time the British and American governments had come to the conclusion that, should an emergency arise in the Peking-Tientsin region similar to the Boxer crisis of 1900, it would be best to evacuate their nationals from these cities instead of risking an all-out war with the Chinese. Another Nanking incident was to be avoided at all cost. The Tanaka cabinet in Tokyo, too, had at first seen no need to increase troops in north China as the preceding cabinet had already doubled the size of the Japanese protocol force at Tientsin. As late as May 23, Tanaka was instructing Minister Yoshizawa not to involve himself in any discussion of joint defense with his colleagues. Although troops might be dispatched from Manchuria should an unexpected incident occur in north China, the

Prime Minister said in the telegram, there was no need nor possibility of making any promise to other countries about future reinforcements.[44]

Then on the following day, in a cabinet meeting, the Minister of War suggested that Japan carefully devise measures for the protection of its nationals in Shantung, as it was likely that the Tsinan-Tsingtao area might be thrown into confusion as a result of a clash between Chiang Kai-shek and Chang Tsung-ch'ang, the Shantung overlord. The War Ministry and the General Staff had made plans to dispatch troops to China to protect over twenty thousand Japanese nationals who were concentrated in such northern cities as Peking, Tientsin, and Tsinan. As head of a political party which had stood for the "protection of nationals on the spot," Tanaka was also obliged to consider reinforcing Japanese troops in north China. He held to the view, which was supported by Foreign Ministry officials, that such additional troops as might be necessary should be sent from Manchuria. This would involve less expense as compared with dispatching troops from Japan proper and would also save time.[45]

The decision for a Shantung expedition, which was quite different from reinforcing the treaty-based protocol force at Tientsin or augmenting marines to defend a settlement such as Shanghai, was reached within a few days. At the cabinet meeting of May 27 it was decided that, as danger to Japanese lives in Shantung seemed to have increased, two thousand troops should be sent from Dairen to Tsingtao. An imperial decree was given on the following day, and the reinforcements arrived at Tsingtao on June 1. They were to be kept there unless a serious situation should develop in Tsinan, in which case they were to be sent inland to the capital of the province. The Foreign Ministry declared that the dispatch of troops from Manchuria "is nothing but an emergency measure forced upon the Japanese Government in self defense and in order to insure the safety of Japanese residents." It promised that, "Immediately the fear of menace against the safety of the Japanese people in [Tsinan] is removed, the whole contingent of these troops will be withdrawn without delay." [46]

The first Shantung expedition was an abrupt departure from

the policy of patience and caution established by Shidehara which Tanaka at first had followed. Contrary to the generally held view, Tanaka did not reach his decision until the very last moment, and there was no thought of interfering with China's internal warfare. It seems that the basic motivating factor was the consideration of party politics. Tanaka had to bow to the argument, put forth by Mori and others, that as head of the Seiyukai he should show that he was different from his weak-kneed predecessor. But the fact remains that here was an important departure from Shidehara's policy against the use of force. This was to prove only the beginning of the troubles the Japanese government was to encounter in its China policy because of Tanaka's tendency to be easily swayed by men around him.

The Chinese government and public, whose initial misgivings about the Seiyukai cabinet's alleged "positive policy" had begun to be replaced by a feeling of relief that Tanaka, like Shidehara, was pursuing a moderate policy in China, felt betrayed. Any such expedition was considered an invasion of Chinese sovereignty, and regrets were expressed by officials and publicists that Tanaka had taken a retrogressive step to hinder the emerging Sino-Japanese friendship. Anti-Japanese boycotts were resumed, and because of Kuomintang influence they were much better organized and more widespread than previous boycotts.[47] And yet, fortunately for Tanaka, Sino-Japanese relations did not immediately worsen. This was due partly to the moderation shown by Japanese officials and soldiers during this episode, but more fundamentally to the complex events within China itself.

The arrival of Japanese troops in Tsingtao coincided with the beginning of the last chapter of the Soviet interlude in the Nationalist revolution. Briefly speaking, the Wuhan Nationalists, led by Wang Ching-wei, chose to side with their military supporters against Soviet advisers and communists when their conflict grew acute in the early summer of 1927. They had been allied against Chiang Kai-shek, but Hunan warlords turned against the alliance as soon as some peasant leaders began carrying out agrarian reforms, going probably beyond the official communist policy of confiscating the lands only of big landlords. Realizing the untenability of their position, the Wuhan Nationalists proceeded to purge the party of communists and seek a new military alliance with warlords. The climax came in July, resulting in an exodus of Russian advisers and Chinese communists from the once powerful revolutionary center.[48]

This might have paved the way for a swift reconciliation between Nanking and Wuhan. It did come about, but only at the expense of Chiang Kai-shek and Wang Ching-wei. In a way so characteristic of the Chinese political scene in the 1920's, Chiang abruptly resigned from his position of command in the middle of August. Ostensibly he was taking the responsibility for the Nationalist defeat at the battle of Hsuchow. In fact, Chiang's position had become untenable. He had antagonized the Wuhan leaders by his unilateral action in April, and his continuance in the highest offices of the party and the government was considered a hindrance to the restoration of Nationalist unity. Furthermore, the Nanking government was suffering from financial distress and its imposition of new taxes had increased its unpopularity. Animosities and suspicions were developing among the generals, many of whom complained about lack of funds and materiel. Chiang's "Chekiang faction" was opposed by the Kwangtung and Kwangsi factions. Wang Ching-wei, too, saw fit to tender his retirement in the middle of September. His resignation had been demanded by the Nanking faction as a condition for *rapprochement* with Wuhan. Some of Wang's staunch supporters remained in Wuhan, but most Nationalist leaders met in Nanking and formed a special committee to conduct the affairs of the united Nationalist government.[49]

How did these developments in China affect the policies of the powers? In London officials were content to deal with local Chinese authorities from time to time as occasion arose and to watch quietly the course of events in China. At the same time, as conditions in central China somewhat improved after the expulsion of Russians and communists from Wuhan, the British government encouraged the resumption of trade and business activities along the Yangtze. British shipping service was restored between Hankow and Changsha, and merchants gradually returned to Ichang, Chungking, and other cities. Britain still held out the promise that it would negotiate new treaties with China whenever there was a government "which can speak in the name of China and can discharge the obligations which it takes upon itself." No such government was in sight as of the end of the year, and, as Chamberlain pointed out, since in China "every Government with which you have not made an agreement resents your having negotiated with the one with which you have made an agreement," the Foreign Office had to be overly cautious in approaching Chinese officials. After the resignation of Chiang Kai-shek there was no thought of singling out an individual or a regime for support.[50]

In the United States the Department of State was kept abreast of developments by constant dispatches and telegrams from China. While there were variations, on the whole these reports painted a pessimistic picture of the Chinese revolutionaries. The Department was, therefore, induced to be ever more cautious in dealing with the Nationalists or the "moderates" among them. For example, there is no evidence that American officials were overly impressed by the expulsion of the Russians and communists from Wuhan in July and August and the resulting *rapprochement* of Wuhan and Nanking. On July 12, Secretary Kellogg advised Minister MacMurray that the State Department was not convinced that the Nanking authorities were in control of China or sufficiently representative of the Chinese people to discuss treaty negotiation with the powers. The retirement of Chiang Kai-shek on August 14 was immediately reported to the Department by the legation in Peking. But Mayer, chargé d'affaires, did not find cause for optimism or hope in this development. Instead, he felt Chiang's collapse was a Russian failure and that China was once more thrown open to activities by the military. The naval attaché was even more outspoken. He wrote to the office of naval intelligence that "the 'nationalism' that the missionaries, idealists, and dreamers built such high hopes upon, when relieved of its only spur and support — bolshevism — has gone the way of all ideals in this country. We are back to the old war among Tuchuns. . . . Chang Tso-lin is, of them all, the only one hope for any order in this chaos." In late October, Mayer summed up the situation in a lengthy telegram:

In the Yangtze Valley and in the South, the cohesive and directive dominant Soviet influence having been removed, the Kuomintang has practically disintegrated into several military factions, whose groupings are characterized by impermanence and complete mutual distrust, and which while temporarily able no doubt to combine for destructive purposes are incapable of cooperation toward constructive establishment of Government. . . . the present struggles have reverted to the character of Chinese civil wars prior to the active Russian intervention in China.

Such pessimism was echoed at home, where Nelson T. Johnson privately confided, "I see little prospect of any change for the better in the near future." The American government and its representatives in China did not recover their confidence in the "moderates" or in the Nationalist movement for the rest of the year. They more or less agreed with the naval attaché's condemnation of the movement as "nothing but a militaristic movement." [51]

Given such pessimistic estimates of conditions in China, the State Department was naturally extremely cautious in its dealings with particular factions in that country. Kellogg's January 27th message was still the basic policy, and it had made it clear that the United States would be willing to discuss treaty matters only with such Chinese delegates as would "represent the authorities or the people of the country." It was judged that no such representatives were discernible. The State Department would not establish formal relations with Nanking or any other contending centers in China. [52]

This attitude of caution, however, could be criticized as a pretext for stalling treaty revision. Minister MacMurray, who was temporarily in the United States in the fall of 1927, then suggested that in order to meet such a criticism he might be authorized to approach several factions in China with a view to persuading them to establish a joint committee of negotiation, with which the American minister would discuss the issue of tariff autonomy, leaving aside extraterritoriality for the time being. Such an approach would have been in agreement with the policy put forth in the January 27th statement. The Chinese were interested in the suggestion, and both Peking and Nanking appeared intent on acting in accordance with such a scheme. In the State

Department both Kellogg and Johnson, who had just been promoted as assistant secretary of state, were favorably inclined toward MacMurray's suggestion. The Secretary accordingly instructed the legation that in the event a joint Chinese commission was formed spontaneously, "an announcement of our willingness to conduct negotiations with it might conceivably lead to a further *rapprochement* between Peking and Nanking, and afford a basis for terminating the civil war, and serve toward mitigating antiforeign feeling in China, as well as give satisfaction to that portion of the American public which insists that every opportunity possible be given the Chinese for achieving their national aspirations." This time MacMurray opposed such a step unless negotiations specifically excluded extraterritorial matters and unless they took place in China rather than in the United States, and here the matter was allowed to rest.[53]

Such was the attitude of the United States government concerning China's factional strife. It is evident that Kellogg and the Department continued to be guided by their objective of finding a new basis for Sino-American friendship. But they were reluctant to commit their support to a faction in China, and they were never impressed, at this time, by the sincerity of the Nanking government. If the Nationalists had sought any moral support from the United States, they would have been very disappointed. Certainly the American government gave them no cause to hope for assistance.

In contrast to the positions taken by Britain and the United States, Japanese policy was more openly sympathetic toward Nanking and in particular Chiang Kai-shek. Despite the minor friction caused by the Shantung expedition, Tanaka carried out a consistent policy toward the Nationalists. The extraordinary interest he showed in the China question can best be seen in his convening of the "Eastern Conference." Since much confusion surrounds historical writing on this conference, it will be well to deal with it in some detail. It reveals what the Japanese officials were thinking about at this time.

Soon after Tanaka succeeded Shidehara, plans were made for a conference of important civilian and military officials to discuss various issues arising out of the Chinese civil war. By the middle

of May officials of the Foreign Ministry had decided on an agenda
for such a conference, including policies toward the southern
government, toward Manchuria and Mongolia, schemes of economic development for the Japanese in China, and relief of the
distressed nationals there.[54] It was felt that, while Tanaka followed Shidehara's policy of encouraging Kuomintang moderates,
in particular Chiang Kai-shek, this broad orientation was not
sufficient to cope with each new development in China. There
was a need for a careful report of the situation by diplomats and
for a frank exchange of ideas between them and the government
personnel at home.

This was the origin of the conference that met in Tokyo between June 27 and July 7. By this time the Shantung expedition
had taken place and Sino-Japanese relations were menaced with
a new crisis. Clarification of Japanese policy was imperative lest
the fruits of the initiative taken by Japanese diplomacy in China
should be lost. The participants in the conference included Minister Yoshizawa, Consuls General Yoshida Shigeru of Mukden,
Yada Shichitarō of Shanghai, and Takao Tōru of Hankow, the
commander of the Kwantung Army, and the governor of Kwantung Leased Territory. They were joined by sixteen officials from
the ministries of Foreign Affairs, War, Navy, and Finance, and
the General Staff.

Given the name of "Eastern Conference," the conference was
publicized as an attempt to formulate a new Japanese policy toward China. It attracted the attention of Chinese and was interpreted as an aspect of Tanaka's "positive policy." This interpretation has been echoed in most historical writings on Tanaka's
China policy. In fact the conference was more a meeting of officials to exchange information than to define a new policy. It did
little more than sanction the existing policies toward the Nationalists and nationalism in China.[55]

Of the topics outlined beforehand by a preparatory committee,
those dealing with the relief of and assistance to Japanese residents in China were mostly disposed of at preliminary meetings
which were held prior to the formal convening of the conference on June 27. During the formal sessions of the conference,
discussions were devoted almost exclusively to China proper and

Manchuria. The participants were asked their views of the Nationalist movement and then their recommendations as to specific steps for Japan to take. Some of the views presented may be summarized here, as they reflected the various attitudes toward the Chinese situation that existed within the Japanese government.

Consul General Yada, back from Shanghai, gave a very favorable view of the Nationalist movement. It had worked a transformation within the lives of the Chinese people, he said, and Sun Yat-sen's "three people's principles" had assumed an aspect of a religion. Consequently, it was impossible to disregard the movement, regardless of its moral right or wrong. Yada then predicted that, since the Nationalist forces stood upon a popular basis, eventually they would dominate the whole of China proper. With regard to the Wuhan government, Yada did not think it was going to last much longer, but he felt the Wuhan faction of the Kuomintang might decide to divorce itself from the communists and Nanking and Wuhan might again be united. Events were to bear out his predictions.

While Consul General Takao, who had observed the Nationalist take-over of Wuhan, generally agreed with Yada's evaluation of the Nationalists, Minister Yoshizawa gave a more pessimistic view. Though he conceded that they might eventually defeat the northern generals, he doubted whether the southern forces could long maintain a unified China or China proper. The Chinese people, Yoshizawa said, were a jealous and suspicious race and quite sensitive to profit opportunities. Therefore, splits and strife within the Kuomintang government and army would not early come to an end. These views probably represented the pessimism shared by the heads of legations in Peking.

Finally, General Matsui, representing the General Staff, revealed the Japanese military's serious concern with Soviet influence in China. Although he had endorsed Shidehara's policy of approaching Kuomintang moderates, he now indicated his skepticism about the allegedly moderate intentions of the Nationalists. He said that the Nanking group included young power aspirants who could espouse the cause of radicalism, while the Wuhan faction obviously contained communists and could not entirely divorce itself from the Comintern. Nor was accord likely between these two groups so long as the Wuhan faction retained its communistic policy and entente with the Soviet Union.

Such varied interpretations on conditions in China produced equally divergent recommendations. Consul General Yada strongly pleaded for support of the Nanking government. To employ force to suppress communists when they seemed to be rooted in the mass of people, to let Chinese politics disintegrate when the result might be to Japan's disadvantage, to pick up an individual warlord and assist him with money and arms, to put pressure on various factions to come to a compromise when no such arrangement had the possibility of durability, all these policies were mistaken. Yada concluded his statement with a classic expression of Japan's real interests in China as civilian bureaucrats saw them.

Japan's main object lies in seeing to it that its trade and investment in China are impartially and justly protected. To ensure this goal, there must be found a government which will maintain peace and order necessary for this end. Such a government must have political, economic, and social organizations similar to those in Japan, and it must have a certain durability.

Yada insisted that the Nanking government met these criteria. Japan, therefore, should at least give it *de facto* recognition and explicitly refute the suspicion, deeply rooted in the Chinese people, that it was assisting the northern regime. Finally, Japan should assist the Kuomintang by announcing its sympathetic attitude toward the goals of China's nationalistic movement.

Minister Yoshizawa showed a more moderate interest in assisting the Nationalists. He recognized, he said, the need to come to a full understanding with the Chinese people, as the Japanese economy made necessary the use of the rich natural resources of China. With the nationalistic movement of the Chinese, therefore, the Japanese should deal in a spirit of sympathy, as one would deal with a ward. But Yoshizawa emphasized that Japan must follow a specific order and method in restoring China's national rights and avoid giving cause to the Chinese to become "arrogant." Concerning the civil war, the minister said Japan should aid no faction and desist from any kind of intervention beyond rendering certain moral assistance to end or ease the civil strife in China.

Navy and army officials also presented divergent views. A Navy Ministry representative seconded Yoshizawa's view that the nation's fundamental aim in China was seeing to it that it was guaranteed the use of its neighbor's rich natural resources in peace and war and having the Chinese cooperate in developing their resources under the principle of "coexistence and coprosperity." To achieve this end China must be impressed by Japan's sincere intentions, and Japan must refrain from intervening in the civil war or from going beyond treaty rights to protect the lives and property of nationals. General Matsui, on the other hand, insisted that the coalescence of all southern factions was impossible unless Nanking and Wuhan came closer in their attitudes toward communism. Should such a coalition take place, the Nationalists would have become "pink," and Japan should do its utmost to prevent the color from turning to red.

These were interesting views, but they had, after all, been expressed from time to time by these officials, and there is no evidence that any of them changed his views after the Eastern Conference. Nevertheless, it is significant that the conference adopted the more moderate suggestions represented by Consul General Yada.

Just before the conference closed, the consul general at Tsinan telegraphed Tokyo and requested the sending of Japanese troops at Tsingtao to the provincial capital, as the area around Tsinan seemed about to be thrown into confusion as a result of fighting among the northern forces in Shantung. On July 6, Tanaka made the decision to grant the request, and two days later the cabinet further decided to dispatch additional troops from Manchuria and Japan proper. Shortly afterward the probability of an immediate Nationalist onslaught upon the Tsinan area lessened, and plans were expedited for withdrawing the Japanese troops. The final decision was made at the cabinet meeting of August 27, and all Japanese expeditionary forces were evacuated by early September.[56]

The cabinet decision on the "second Shantung expedition" coincided with the conclusion of the Eastern Conference. On July 7, the last day of the conference, Prime Minister Tanaka gave a "statement of China policy" as a synthesis of the ten-day-long discussion. It reiterated the policies which the Japanese government had repeatedly announced — noninterference with the Chinese civil war, respect for the "popular will," sympathy with the "proper national demands based on the self-awareness of the moderate people," the need to establish *de facto* relations with moderate regimes locally, moral encouragement of any tendency on the part of various regions or factions to come together, and determination to protect the lives and property of Japanese nationals. Parliamentary Vice Foreign Minister Mori's supplementary remarks explicitly recognized Japan's support of Kuomintang moderates. He explained that the "popular will" in the Prime Minister's statement did not specifically refer to the support of any groups or individuals but simply to the fact that the "three people's principles" now permeated Chinese society. Therefore, the consensus obtained at a national congress which the Kuomintang leaders were hoping to convene could be taken as the popular will. Mori also said that Japan should sympathize with and assist the efforts of the moderates within the Nationalist party if their principles and assertions did not clash with Japanese interests economically and socially, and if their methods were not overly radical. With respect to the encouragement of a tendency toward a coalition regime, Mori explained that Japan should welcome any such government, whether based at Peking or Nanking, regardless of its outward format.[57]

The celebrated Eastern Conference thus officially recognized the strength of the Nationalist movement and re-endorsed the policy of assistance of Kuomintang moderates. Both these points had characterized Shidehara's policy. The conference did not evolve any new "positive" policy toward China.

For the next two months and a half, as the Wuhan government expelled its Russian advisers and divorced itself from communists, Japanese policy makers could find much cause for optimism. Despite the temporary worsening of Sino-Japanese relations due to the Shantung expedition, the Japanese government could point out its record of consistently standing behind Chiang Kai-shek's group in China's domestic struggle.

On his way back from the Eastern Conference, Minister Yoshi-zawa visited Nanking on August 9 and 10, before he proceeded to Peking. He was given an overwhelming reception. Parties given by the Nationalist Foreign Ministry and the General Staff commenced with the singing of the Japanese anthem. Yoshizawa was the first foreign minister ever to visit Nanking after it was taken over by the Nationalists. Hu Han-min, in his speech welcoming the minister, said he was pleased with the reported decision of the Eastern Conference to express sympathy with the Nationalist government. Chiang Kai-shek called Yoshizawa his "dear friend" and expressed his confidence that Japan would assist in the Nationalist revolution, as manifested by the visit.[58]

The retirement of Chiang Kai-shek within five days after this manifestation of Sino-Japanese friendship was a puzzling blow to many a well-wisher in Japan. Tanaka chose to believe that Chiang's political eclipse was temporary and that he would certainly stage a comeback in the future.[59] Toward the end of September, Chiang sailed for Japan, ostensibly to see the mother of Sung Mei-ling, whom he was courting for marriage. From Kobe he went to Tokyo, where he was given a rousing welcome by the press and his former classmates of the Military Academy. On November 5 he visited Tanaka's residence and talked with him for two hours.

Tanaka commended Chiang Kai-shek's retirement as most timely, saying that he must have taken this action in order to serve his country in the future. Although Chiang said that all his attempts and plans had proved futile and asked how he should conduct himself thereafter, Tanaka told Chiang that he and no one else could save the Chinese revolution. He said that Chiang should first of all try to consolidate gains south of the Yangtze. Only then could communism be thoroughly eradicated and the Nationalists spared entanglement in the warlord politics of the north. Tanaka added,

Of all the powers, Japan has the closest interest-relations with China. Japan will not interfere with your domestic strife, but it can never allow the spread of communism in China. Therefore, since you are anti-communistic, Japan strongly desires that you consolidate your strength in the south. Japan will not hesitate to assist your efforts, so long as international considerations permit it and so long as its own interests are not sacrificed.

Chiang Kai-shek replied that he agreed that this was the only feasible course of action but that he would have to push the expedition farther northward in order to prevent a split within the revolutionary army. The conversation ended with Chiang's appeal for Japanese assistance in the revolution. Only by aiding the Nationalists, he said, could Japan wipe out the impression that it was aiding Chang Tso-lin. Only thereby could it ensure the safety of Japanese nationals in China.[60]

There is no evidence that Chiang and Tanaka reached any agreement on Manchuria, and this was to become the sorest spot in Tanaka's policy. In the fall of 1927, however, it was enough that Chiang Kai-shek reciprocated Japan's interest. The Japanese policy of independent action seemed to have borne fruit.

As the Soviet offensive in China came to a halt, the major Washington powers responded to the situation according to their different evaluations of the phenomenon. Japan was most active and managed to stand with the winning side within the Kuomintang; despite the senseless expeditions to Shantung, Japanese officials could boast of their foresight in recognizing the potential strength and antiradical nature of the Chiang Kai-shek group. Britain hesitated between action and inaction, and the United States continued its policy of caution and watchfulness. All were interested in defining a new framework of relationship with China, but they pursued this end individually and not collectively. Contrary to the usual Soviet or Chinese interpretation, none of the major powers had played an active role in bringing about Chiang Kai-shek's "counterrevolution." British and American officials were uninformed until the April 12 coup. And even then the United States did not recover from the shock of the Nanking incident. Japanese officials had a better knowledge of the rift within the Kuomintang, and both Shidehara and Tanaka encouraged the trend away from radicalism. Even they did not foresee the rapidity with which Russians would be ousted from Wuhan and the Kuomintang. Nevertheless, because of its role during the Nanking incident episode, Japan succeeded in winning the gratitude of the Chiang Kai-shek faction. It did not seem entirely unlikely that Japan might manage to create a new order of Sino-Japanese relations based on a workable compromise between Chinese nationalism and Japanese interests. Any such compromise would require basic understanding on the crucial question of Manchuria.

V · COPROSPERITY IN
MANCHURIA, 1927

The role of Manchuria in Sino-Japanese relations has given rise to various interpretations. It is tempting to see, as some historians do, in Japan's Manchuria policy after 1905 a fixed, given element in the complexities of Far Eastern international relations. There is no question that in the long run the Manchurian question doomed any attempt by Japan to create a new order of Sino-Japanese understanding by other than forceful means. Given the self-image of an overcrowded empire poorly endowed with natural resources, it was natural that the Japanese would include their rights in Manchuria as an essential part of any bargain with the Chinese. The latter, on the other hand, had their own idea of a new order, based on complete diplomatic equality. Whether one took the Japanese or Chinese side, conflict would be inevitable.

All this is clear enough in outline. But it should be realized that we cannot really speak of "China" or "Japan" when we come to Manchuria, at least not until 1929. As of 1927 Manchuria was politically identifiable with China proper only insofar as its overlord, Chang Tso-lin, was also commander-in-chief of the anti-Kuomintang coalition controlling Peking. But Chang's economic and military base in the Three Eastern Provinces was entirely distinct from China, and in the past he had occasionally proclaimed Manchuria's independence. This is not to say that he and his subordinates did not share the vision of a freer Manchuria, more independent of foreign control. He had consistently refused to be bound by the Sino-Japanese treaty of 1915, pertaining to Manchuria and Inner Mongolia, which provided for the "opening" of these regions to Japanese residence and business activity. Chang Tso-lin had also approved of a plan to build railways in Manchuria with Chinese money, and beginnings had been made to construct lines between Hailung and Kirin and between Tahushan and Tungliao. Japanese regarded them as violations of the "Peking agreement" of 1905, which had presumably forbidden the building of railways parallel to the South Manchuria Railway. Despite all these developments, Manchuria under Chang Tso-lin was administratively distinct from the Peking government, not to speak of the Nanking government. When considering Sino-Japanese relations in Manchuria, therefore, it is extremely important to keep in mind Chang's political interests as well as the general nationalistic movement attacking Japanese rights.

It is equally pertinent to note the breakdown of a uniform line of command in Japanese policy once it was applied to Manchuria. Theoretically all agencies — the consulates, the Kwantung territorial government, the South Manchuria Railway, and the Kwantung Army — were subordinated to the government in Tokyo, and they worked together from time to time to devise common strategy. But such uniformity and cooperation did not always exist. All were agreed on the imperative need of including Japan's rights in Manchuria in any Sino-Japanese settlement, but what these rights were and how they should be protected were questions which produced differing solutions. This was because by the mid-1920's the twenty-year-old Kwantung Army, South Manchuria Railway, and Kwantung territorial government had developed their own philosophies and trained their own personnel. They could easily influence public opinion at home by employing emotional symbols such as the glory of the victory over Russia and Japan's "life line." When talking of Japanese policy in Manchuria, it is essential to understand who is carrying out what policy.

Finally, Sino-Japanese relations in Manchuria would be grossly oversimplified if they were treated in isolation. Manchuria was once a focus of imperialist rivalry in Asia, and it was to become a "cradle of conflict" in the early 1930's. To establish a logical connection between the two, however, would be to ignore the vast changes in the nature of international relations in the Far East after World War I. As had not been true earlier, Japan now devised its own plans of action in China without necessarily presupposing that conflict with a Western nation would result. This was another reflection of the trend after the Washington Conference, when the Far Eastern policies of various governments tended to be divorced from global considerations. Japan's policy in Manchuria was an aspect of the Japanese initiative in this period when, after the demise of the old order, no clearly definable framework for diplomacy existed.

THE EASTERN CONFERENCE

Chapter III mentioned the intensified activities of Tokyo officials to devise basic plans to cope with the new developments in Manchuria. The search for a policy continued during the early months of 1927, now that the Kuomintang was definitely establishing its control in central China and Japan had taken the initiative in coming to terms with moderate nationalism. In January the consul general at Mukden, the commander of the Kwantung Army, and the governor of Kwantung Leased Territory discussed the existing situation and agreed to adhere to the principle of maintaining the *status quo* in Manchuria in order "to protect and ensure Japan's particularly predominant position and rights in Manchuria and Mongolia." In other words, they would still consider protection of Japanese rights in these areas a basic part of Sino-Japanese understanding. Yoshida, consul general at Mukden, devoted himself to the study of how best to achieve such an objective. In April he wrote a letter to Kimura, chief of the Asian bureau of the Foreign Ministry, and explained that Japan should do its utmost to maintain order in Manchuria, not only along the South Manchuria Railway but also along the railways that had been constructed by Japanese capital. Strikes of Manchurian laborers, likely to be agitated by Russians or by southerners, must be "rigorously suppressed by Japanese authorities." Japanese, Chinese, and Russian railways should somehow be connected, and devices should be worked out for a sound monetary system. It was only through railway and monetary reforms that Yoshida felt Japanese interests in Manchuria could be permanently safeguarded. The success of these reforms would, of course, depend on the cooperation of Chang Tso-lin. Since he had already disregarded several provisions of the treaties, he would naturally have to be pressured into changing his fundamental attitude toward Japanese rights.[1]

The military in Manchuria advocated similar objectives but not necessarily identical means of achieving them. Typical of military thinking at this time was a memorandum written in June 1927 by Major General Saitō Tsune, the Kwantung Army chief of staff. Starting from the premise that Japan's basic problems — population increase and inadequate natural resources — must be solved by expansion abroad, Saitō insisted that Japan should base its China policy on the need to strengthen its position in Manchuria and eastern Inner Mongolia. More specifically, Japan should demand the autonomy of these regions under a Chinese governor, the employment of Japanese financial and military advisers, and a new agreement on railway construction and agriculture based on the principle of "coexistence and coprosperity." If China should oppose these schemes, Japan should be resolute and prepared to use force to realize its goal. Furthermore, Saitō touched on an important problem by suggesting that diplomatic and administrative affairs in Manchuria should be unified so that different agencies would not pursue different policies. Finally, on the issue of the Kuomintang rift, he stated that Chinese moderates should be encouraged if they proved to be truly against communism and the Soviet Union. The Kwantung Army was advocating its own method of bringing about a new order in Manchuria.[2]

It was at this juncture that Tanaka came to power. The timing is important; he replaced Shidehara at a moment when Japanese officials, civilian and military, had begun a serious re-examination of the Manchurian question. Such revaluation, it is true, had been started under and with the blessing of Shidehara, but Japanese officials in Manchuria welcomed the advent of the Tanaka cabinet, in April 1927, because he was known to be an advocate of "positive" policy toward Manchuria. General Tanaka had once declared, when he was in that area in 1913, that the "management of the continent" was an inevitable necessity for the survival of Japan and the progress of the race. During the World War, Tanaka, as assistant chief of the General Staff, directed schemes for Manchurian and Mongolian independence. After becoming president of the Seiyukai, he repeatedly had stressed the unique relations between Manchuria and Japan and insisted that it be kept from the effects of the civil war in China and that Japan's particular position be defended and guaranteed.[3]

With such a record Prime (and Foreign) Minister Tanaka was expected to initiate a strong policy of defending Japanese rights and interests in Manchuria. His appointment of Mori Kaku as parliamentary vice foreign minister and Yamamoto Jōtarō as president of the South Manchuria Railway seemed to confirm this belief. Both were businessmen turned politicians. Mori was still in his forties but had worked in China as a clerk and dreamed of himself as becoming a Japanese Cecil Rhodes. He had sought to direct Japan's "management of the continent" by entering politics. He rose rapidly within the Seiyukai by clever political maneuvering and personal connections and was head councilor of the party when Tanaka was made prime minister.[4] Yamamoto, who was chief secretary of the Seiyukai before being appointed president of the South Manchuria Railway, had been actively engaged in all branches of business, both in Japan and in China, in connection with the Mitsui complex. Like Mori he had spent his boyhood as a clerk in China. He was reportedly the first Japanese ever to do business in Manchuria; around 1891 he entered Ying-kow and began exporting soybeans. He was convinced of the economic and political benefits Japan had brought to Manchuria after the Russo-Japanese War. His tour of China and Manchuria in early 1927 had made him pessimistic about the ability of Chang Tso-lin to maintain his position and to keep Manchuria from coming to some compromise with the south. Witnessing communist and Russian activities in the south, Yamamoto was persuaded anew that only by some active policy could Japanese interests in Manchuria be fully safeguarded.[5]

These were the hopes and expectations entertained at the inception of the Tanaka cabinet by the exponents of a strong policy toward Manchuria. But the new foreign minister did not immediately define a fresh approach to the problem. The only policy statement of a sort that he made during the first month in office seems to have been his instruction of May 20 to Minister Yoshizawa and Consul General Yoshida. They were virtually ordered to continue Shidehara's policy: they were to induce Chang Tso-lin to concentrate on problems inside Manchuria and stabilize conditions there. Preoccupied with the Nanking incident settlement, Tanaka saw no need for making a hasty departure from the existing Manchurian policy.[6]

Then came June 1927, and Tanaka began actively interesting himself in the Manchurian question. The reasons for this are not hard to find. He had earlier delineated his policy of giving moral support to moderate Nationalists, and the break between Russians and Nationalists at Wuhan must have given him cause for satisfaction. At the same time, with the prospect looming larger that the Chiang Kai-shek Nationalists would consolidate their authority, the possibility of compromise between northern warlords and the Nationalists was also disappearing. This would mean a probable conflict between these two, and the outcome would naturally affect Chang Tso-lin and Manchuria. That Tanaka was genuinely worried about these questions can be seen in a long telegram he sent on June 2 to Yoshida and Yoshizawa. In it the Prime Minister mentioned the possibility of fighting between Chang Tso-lin and the Nationalists and solicited these officials' views on the attitudes Japan should take in all imaginable cases. First of all, Chang might be defeated and seek asylum in the Japanese concession in Tientsin or in Japan. Then order in Manchuria would be maintained by men with some understanding of "new ideas," willing to compromise with the southern regime. What should Japan's attitude be in a situation like this? Second, if Chang were to return to Manchuria safely with his army, he might again seek to fight the southern army at the Manchurian border, or the southerners might try to undermine order in Manchuria by means of propaganda and terrorism. Were there any methods to prevent such a disruption of order or to intercede between north and south in order to prevent such an eventuality? Third, if Chang carried out an offensive against the southerners and lost, Manchuria would be thrown into chaos by rebel armies. What should Japan's attitude be then?[7]

Replies from Yoshizawa and Yoshida arrived within a week. They are of considerable interest, showing that there was no complete agreement as to what to do, although all entertained similar objectives of Japanese policy and understood the need for formulating a clear approach. Minister Yoshizawa at Peking stressed that Chang Tso-lin was still the best choice for Japan and that it would be unwise to think of an alternative even if he should be defeated and withdraw to Manchuria. If the Fengtien forces should retreat without fighting and Chang Tso-lin were to concentrate on the reform of government in the Three Eastern Provinces, Japan should put pressure on the southern army to desist from attacking him. Southern propagandists and terrorists should be severely dealt with by the Japanese forces stationed along the South Manchuria Railway. Yoshizawa said in this connection, "As Japan can never tolerate the existence of unstable political conditions in Manchuria, which has such close relations with Japan, it should have every right to warn the southerners to desist from resorting to irrational means to disturb the order in Manchuria." Japan should also give strict warning to the Nationalists, in case they defeated the Fengtien army and pursued it into Manchuria, not to infringe upon Japanese rights and interests. In other words, Yoshizawa was wary of the Nationalist attitude toward Japan's vested interests and treaty rights and thought their first defense lay in standing behind Chang Tso-lin under the existing circumstances. The Japanese minister had some reservations about the "moderate" intentions of the Nationalists and foresaw the time when Japan's special privileges in Manchuria would be subjected to severe attack by the Kuomintang government. Until it could definitely be shown that the Nationalists would respect Japanese interests in Manchuria, therefore, Yoshizawa thought Japan should endeavor to protect these through the existing government of the Three Eastern Provinces.[8] In a way this telegram typified Japanese thinking, shared by civilian and military officials alike, that Manchuria was different from China proper because of its historical ties to and economic importance for Japan. It was taken for granted that Japan had the right to take appropriate measures of its own to uphold this unique position. At the same time, Yoshizawa was by no means advocating a unanimous view when he said that Japanese interests should be protected through Chang Tso-lin.

This point, which proved of momentous importance in 1928, becomes clearer if Yoshida's views are contrasted with those of Yoshizawa. In his telegram replying to Tanaka's query, the consul general pointed out that the spread of war to Manchuria would mean a severe blow to Japan's economic development there. To this extent, he agreed with Minister Yoshizawa and with every Japanese official. Yoshida then went further and advocated certain steps to prevent such an eventuality. He advocated, for example, that Japan refuse the use of the Peking-Mukden Railway to the Chinese military, forbid the stationing of Chinese soldiers within twenty li of Tientsin, and even show its determination by temporarily occupying main spots along the Chinese railways in Manchuria and forbidding their use to Chinese armies, in case invading or native Manchurian soldiers attempted to disrupt the peace. But Yoshida made one point which showed a basic philosophy different from that implied in Yoshizawa's telegram. The consul general was opposed to tinkering with the petty project of deposing or establishing rulers in Manchuria. "Regardless of who is in power in Manchuria," he insisted, "Japanese developments there should be planned by the people's own efforts, based on the superior and particular position of Japan and not by reliance on a Chang or a Wu." The implication was that Yoshida would not have been averse to see Manchuria come under any regime, even Nationalist, provided that it brought stability to the land and guaranteed the protection of Japanese rights.[9]

The complexity of the Manchurian question is illustrated by the fact that two foremost civilian experts should have developed different attitudes toward the problem of Manchuria's political future. Basically the difference was whether Japanese rights should be considered genuine economic rights, without political implications, or whether they should be linked with China's civil war so as to induce Chang Tso-lin to accept them in return for certain Japanese favors.

Japanese policy makers had not had to face this question squarely before this time, since the unification of China was at best an academic proposition. But the possible Kuomintang conquest of all of China could no longer be regarded as illusory, and Manchuria's political future had to be seriously considered. In the spring of 1927, given the Foreign Ministry's effort at creating a new order of Sino-Japanese understanding, it is likely that the majority of its officials would have sided with Yoshida. A memorandum written at this time by the chief of the Asian affairs bureau supports this conjecture. The essence of the Manchurian-Mongolian problem, Kimura said, lay not in obtaining minor concessions by taking advantage of the civil war in China but in securing a solid extension of Japan's interests, which were primarily economic. This would be predicated upon the stability of political conditions for some duration of time in Manchuria and Inner Mongolia. But political stability need not be dependent on Chang Tso-lin, as Yoshizawa was saying. Kimura would rather clearly distinguish between Chang's personal vicissitudes and the protection of Japan's special position in Manchuria and Mongolia. This last should be carried out no matter who ruled in these areas. Should Japan's special position and interests be subjected to attack, be it from any faction or any foreign country, Japan should stand up resolutely and stop it. But this should have nothing to do with Chang's person. In view of Chang's unpopularity in China and throughout the world, Japan should be prepared not only not to give him any assistance whatsoever but even to put considerable pressure on him to cause his downfall. "To take advantage of Chang's plight today and expect to acquire great privileges by giving him positive assistance is a shortsighted, suicidal policy which ignores the current of the times and will do great damage to the future of our Manchurian-Mongolian policy."

How this key official in the Foreign Ministry envisaged the new order in Manchuria and the Far East can also be seen in this memorandum. He suggested that once Chang Tso-lin was out of the picture, Japan should encourage his successor to propose a truce with the south, and express approval of the "three people's principles" and the Nationalist revolutionary movement. Second, in case the Nationalist army moved beyond the Wall, Japan should take measures to protect its special interests by forbidding fighting in the Japanese-controlled areas. But somehow Kimura expected that a stable government would ultimately emerge in Manchuria. In that event Japan should encourage convening of a national congress in China, to be attended by both Kuomintang and Manchurian representatives, and should welcome the establishment of a central regime at Nanking. Manchuria would then become a province of unified China, but a frontier province, and the extension of Japanese interests would proceed smoothly and relatively unnoticed.[10]

These were clearly defined policy statements. Coupled with Yoshida's, they may be taken as an enunciation of the view held by a majority of the Foreign Ministry officials. Minister Yoshizawa's memorandum indicated that for some the political question of Chang Tso-lin's and Manchuria's ties with China proper could never be ignored. Prime Minister Tanaka himself must have been interested in the question because it was he who solicited his subordinates' views to begin with. Moreover, regardless of the relevance of the political question to Japan's economic rights and interests in Manchuria, there remained the problem of specifically how to promote them. Should Japan build more railways? If so, which lines? Should the "opening" of the interior of Manchuria and Inner Mongolia to Japanese residents be pushed with vigor? All these questions must have bothered Tanaka as he came to power, pledged to pursue a vigorous policy in Manchuria. He wanted to discuss them fully with his civilian and military advisers, and this was one major reason for the convening of the Eastern Conference.

It is not necessary to reproduce the various evaluations of the Manchurian situation which the participants made at the conference.[11] They simply repeated their own previously held ideas. As was the case with the interpretation of the Nationalist movement, these verbal pronouncements at the conference did not lead to concrete action. Despite the general impression to the contrary, the conference decided nothing positive and very little that could at once be put into effect. Before the formal opening of the conference on June 27, special committees had been organized to study specific problems such as the relief of Japanese residents along the Yangtze. One committee discussed Manchurian and Mongolian issues and was attended by Foreign Ministry officials. Here were presented proposals for stabilizing Manchuria's political and economic conditions and realizing Japan's treaty rights, most of which had been formulated by the Asian bureau of the Foreign Ministry in 1926. They envisaged Japan's financial and technical assistance to Manchurian authorities in return for a promise that Japan's treaty rights would be honored. Japan was also to promote the completion of railways which had been planned and financed by Japanese capital.

The committee and the conference did little more than listen to the proposals put forth by the Foreign Ministry. In fact the conferees, who devoted the fourth day of the meeting almost entirely to the discussion of Manchuria, adopted fewer than half of the ideas presented by the Foreign Ministry. On the issue of railway construction in Manchuria, the proposal had been that six railways be built in order to facilitate Japanese economic development. The participants agreed on the desirability of constructing five of these: the Kirin-Kainei (in Korea) line first, then the Changchun-Talai, Angangki-Tsitsihar, and Tungliao-Kailu (in Jehol) lines, and a line to the Hsinchiu mines. The army spokesmen urged the construction of a railway between Taonan and Solun as a preparatory measure against Soviet Russia, but the Foreign Ministry thought it would be inadvisable to build a railway so close to the Russian border and antagonize the Soviet Union. The latter view prevailed at the conference. The proposed railways were to be built by loans or by concessions leased out to Japanese. Negotiations were to be carried out at the Mukden consulate general, and the tactics left to the judgment of the Foreign Ministry and its representatives in Manchuria. In case Chang Tso-lin failed to respond favorably to Japanese demands on railway construction, it was agreed that the Japanese government would "have to exert considerable pressure."

With regard to the plans for stabilizing the financial conditions in Manchuria, the second item in the Foreign Ministry's policy proposals, the conference decided to separate it from the railway issue, since any scheme for financial reform would be difficult to realize as long as Chang Tso-lin was engaged in war. The same fate befell the third project conceived by the Foreign Ministry, the solution of the land-ownership problem. No decision was reached as to its recommendation that the lands along the South Manchuria Railway be opened up for Japanese occupancy as "commercial ports."

Not only did the Eastern Conference not result in any sweeping change of existing policies toward Manchuria, contrary to rumors in and out of Japan, but it even failed to institute some of the recommendations of the Foreign Ministry for strengthening the basis of Japanese economic activities in Manchuria. The statement by Prime Minister Tanaka on the last day of the conference, which attracted much attention as indicative of his "positive policy" toward Manchuria, contained nothing suggestive of a new departure in Japanese policy. After repeating the platitude that Japan had a particular concern with the peace and order of Manchuria, Tanaka stated that the protection of Japanese treaty rights should be worked out under the principles of the open door and equal opportunity and that in case these rights and interests were threatened as a result of the spread of war to Manchuria and Mongolia, Japan should be "prepared to take proper measures" to defend them against any attack. In elaborating on these points, Parliamentary Vice Foreign Minister Mori pointed out, first, that "the open door and equal opportunity" in Manchuria and Mongolia should apply to foreigners, not excluding Russians. Second, "any attack" in the Prime Minister's statement referred to any threat to Japan's special position, be it caused by Nationalists, Russians, or other nations or by internal causes.

The one item in Tanaka's statement which was not made public stated that "the stabilization of Manchuria's political conditions should best be left to the efforts of the Manchurian people. If an influential Manchurian should respect our special position in Manchuria and Mongolia and sincerely devise means to stabilize political conditions there, the Japanese government would support him as it considers proper." In the light of subsequent developments, it seems clear that this "influential Manchurian" was Chang Tso-lin. It may be that, having studied the suggestions by Yoshizawa, Yoshida, Kimura, and others, the Prime Minister decided to take Yoshizawa's view that Chang ought to be supported by Japan. He probably felt that the Manchurian warlord was genuinely interested in consolidating his position with Japanese assistance, and from this time on support of Chang Tso-lin was a fixed point in Tanaka's policy. The basic idea was that Japanese rights in Manchuria would best be protected through Chang. Tanaka, however, hesitated to enunciate this as a basic policy for his staff to follow. He did not contradict Mori when the latter explained that Tanaka's statement did not imply support or rejection of Chang Tso-lin but the support of any ruler who would "plan economic development, maintain order, stabilize political conditions, and practice the principle of equal opportunity." [12] In leaving this matter ambiguous, Tanaka was to invite a serious crisis in Japanese policy.

Apart from Tanaka's implicit support of Chang Tso-lin, the Eastern Conference followed and re-endorsed the line which civilian officials, in contrast to military and other exponents of strong policy, had advocated. Where is the evidence, then, to support the usual interpretation that the conference enunciated the policy of giving priority to the protection of Japanese rights in Manchuria and Mongolia? [13] Tanaka and the participants in the conference did indeed distinguish Japan's policies toward these regions from those of China proper. Their agenda indicated this. It was also generally agreed that the spread of the Chinese civil war beyond the Wall should be prevented and that efforts should be redoubled to promote economic expansion in Manchuria. These points, however, had long been made during the Shidehara period, and it would be more correct to say that the conference reiterated old policies rather than marking any departure in Japan's policy toward Manchuria.

It was for this very reason that much confusion resulted in Japan's subsequent dealings with Manchurian authorities. The Eastern Conference had not satisfied the aspirations of more militant exponents of positive policy, nor had it put down in specific terms the means by which to achieve economic development in Manchuria. Consul General Yoshida of Mukden, Minister Yoshizawa at Peking, and the new president of the South Manchuria Railway, Yamamoto, all drew differing conclusions from the conference and set out to carry out their assignments without basic understanding in methods to be employed.[14]

BACKDOOR NEGOTIATIONS

Yoshida was the first negotiator to approach Manchurian authorities after the Eastern Conference. On July 20 he received an instruction from Tanaka giving him an outline of new negotiations to be carried out at Mukden. The consul general was to protest against various cases of treaty violation, threatening to withhold supplies from Chang Tso-lin and to deny his forces the facilities of the South Manchuria Railway. In case Manchurian authorities remained adamant, Yoshida was authorized to intimate that Japan might acquiesce in the imposition of a 2.5 percent customs surtax in the Three Eastern Provinces — a departure from Shidehara's rigid stand on the matter. The consul general could also disclose Japanese plans for railroad construction in Manchuria and offer a bargain that would permit Chinese construction of the Hailung-Kirin and Tahushan-Tungliao lines, which Japanese had protested as running "parallel" to the South Manchuria Railway, in return for consent to Japanese construction of the Kirin-Kainei, Changchun-Talai, and Hsinchiu coal mine lines.[15]

These terms demonstrated Japan's determination to have the Chinese honor their treaty obligations in Manchuria, coupled with willingness to accept *faits accomplis* and use their acceptance as a bargaining point for acquiring further rights. According to these instructions, Consul General Yoshida visited Civil Governor Mo Te-hui of Fengtien Province on July 23 and presented him with a memorandum reminding him of the seriousness of treaty violations and urging him to make Manchuria a place of safety for natives and foreigners alike. Subsequently, he hinted at some of the measures Japan might take if the Fengtien authorities failed to give a prompt reply. When Governor Mo made no response, Yoshida guardedly warned the chief of staff of the provincial army that Japan might take steps to safeguard its treaty rights. He asked Tokyo for permission to threaten the stopping of Manchurian military trains in Mukden and its adjoining areas. Without waiting for a reply, he hinted to Governor Mo that such action might be taken.[16]

Such a strong stand, which Yoshida took in accordance with

what he thought had been agreed upon at the Eastern Conference, ran into immediate opposition on the part of other Japanese officials — a clear indication that the conference had not
really drawn up a "positive" policy. Representatives of the Kwantung Army, the Kwantung territorial government, and the South
Manchuria Railway felt that Yoshida was going too far and in any
event should wait to learn the opinion of the president of the
railway, who was at that time in Tokyo. They saw administrative
and technical obstacles to Yoshida's plan and thought specific
instructions from the home government would be needed before
the police force and the army could be employed for the purpose.[17]

Meanwhile Chang Tso-lin had contacted the Japanese attaché
at Peking and expressed his wish that Tanaka be moderate in
dealing with Manchuria. Honjō Shigeru, the attaché, sympathized
with Chang and telegraphed the General Staff criticizing Yoshida's
highhanded approach. The attaché was afraid that a threat of
force might remind the Chinese of the Twenty-one Demands and
not only might jeopardize the success of other negotiations in
progress but might also tend to undermine what he regarded as
Japan's basic policy — separating anticommunist moderates in
China from the communists. Hori Yoshiatsu, the chargé d'affaires
at Peking, agreed. But Yoshida persisted in his belief that only
strong pressure could induce Chang Tso-lin and others to respect
Japanese rights and to seek "true cooperation and understanding."
This was in perfect agreement with his view that Japanese treaty
rights should come before the vicissitudes of individual warlords.[18]

Prime Minister Tanaka showed the indecision which was to
characterize his China policy. On August 5 he instructed Yoshida
that he might continue to hint at forceful measures but that he
should not act. Completely disregarding his initial instruction to
the consul general that the latter open talks at Mukden, Tanaka
now said that Peking would be a better place for negotiation.
Minister Yoshizawa would there talk with Chang Tso-lin and
others, said the Prime Minister, while Yoshida should help him
by giving intimations of Japanese railway construction plans,
thus creating an atmosphere favorable for harmonious compromise. In the meantime, military and railway officials in Man-

churia would consult on the steps to be taken if Yoshizawa was unsuccessful.[19]

Before this telegram reached Yoshida, he had, on August 4, formally warned Governor Mo that military trains might be prohibited to pass through areas around Mukden belonging to the South Manchuria Railway. This measure, the consul general pointed out, was in retaliation for the Chinese construction of railways parallel to the South Manchuria Railway and for other cases of treaty violation. Yoshida intimated to the Kwantung territorial government that he would carry out this measure on August 7 unless he received satisfactory answers from Mukden authorities. He reasoned that the timing was just right, since the Fengtien army was so engrossed in preparation for war with the south that it could not afford to disregard the Japanese threat.[20]

Immediately following the notification from Yoshida, Governor Mo sent a messenger to the consul general with a letter expressing his willingness to come to some understanding. Yoshida found the wording of the letter unsatisfactory. He concluded that his threat would have to be made good at least once, and he notified the Kwantung government that the South Manchuria Railway would be asked to stop the passage of military cars through the zone belonging to it at Mukden. In case the Chinese did not stop, Yoshida suggested, it would constitute an invasion and be dealt with accordingly.[21]

The threatened action was never taken, as Tanaka's telegram of August 5 reached Yoshida in time to avert the crisis. But this episode revealed the lack of consensus among Japanese officials. They had drawn differing conclusions from the Eastern Conference and tended to work at cross purposes. Far more important, the incident once again brought to the surface the fundamental difficulty in Japan's Manchuria policy: whether to negotiate locally or at Peking. So long as the same warlord, Chang Tso-lin, was in control both of Mukden and Peking, the difficulty might not be serious. But once another warlord or faction came to power in China proper, Japan would have to make a really crucial decision. In this sense the Yoshida episode foreshadowed what was to plague Japanese policy later in the decade. In the summer of

1927 the problem was simpler since Chang Tso-lin still presumably represented the Peking government. Despite Yoshida's protest that it would be ineffective and disadvantageous to carry on negotiation at Peking, as this would attract world attention and make the issue one of "face" for Fengtien authorities, it was decided, at a meeting of Japanese officials at Dairen on August 14, to transfer current negotiations to the legation in Peking.[22]

The Peking phase of the negotiation fared no better. There the work of Minister Yoshizawa and the staff of the legation was complicated by the presence of President Yamamoto of the South Manchuria Railway. The result was further chaos.

Yamamoto had been appointed to the office in July. From the sketch, already drawn, of his life and relationship with Tanaka, it may be surmised that the latter hoped to use him as an extra-diplomatic channel through which to solve the Manchurian railway question. It is characteristic of Tanaka's method of conducting diplomacy that even while new instructions were being drafted after the Eastern Conference for the guidance of Consul General Yoshida, Prime Minister Tanaka had begun a series of conversations with Yamamoto. The two worked out a plan by which everything could be kept entirely secret, even from the Foreign Ministry, while Yamamoto proceeded to negotiate on railway construction directly with Chang Tso-lin.[23]

In early August, just as uproar was created in Chinese government circles by the action of Consul General Yoshida, Yamamoto saw Etō Toyoji, a director of the Sino-Japanese Corporation and an acquaintance of Chang Tso-lin, and asked him to return to Peking and start preliminary negotiations with the Old Marshal. Upon his return to China Etō accordingly approached Chang and endeavored to win his consent to Japanese construction of seven railways. Of these seven, two (the Kirin-Kainei and Changchun-Talai lines) were ones which the Tokyo government had decided were of urgent importance. The rest were not identical with those discussed at the Eastern Conference.[24] This further shows that the conference had not satisfied many exponents of positive policy, including Yamamoto. He would pursue one set of goals in a private and secret negotiation while simultaneously Japanese diplomats pursued others in a different way in Peking and Mukden.

The bureaucratic rivalry which Yamamoto's plan was sure to evoke in the Foreign Ministry was revealed when Yamamoto, before his departure for Manchuria, talked with Debuchi Katsuji, permanent vice foreign minister, in the presence of the Prime Minister. Having in mind the debate in Mukden, Yamamoto at the outset expressed his hope that the government would not take an overly stiff attitude toward the Chinese regarding insignificant cases of treaty violation; this might prejudice his own effort to solve the railway question. Debuchi disagreed and said that the important thing was whether the Chinese showed sincerity in negotiating with the Japanese. "If Chang Tso-lin and Fengtien officials should ignore treaty obligations or slight Japan's position in Manchuria and Mongolia, it would be of little significance to humiliate ourselves and obtain one railway concession," he asserted. As the Foreign Ministry had already decided to concede minor treaty violations, however, Debuchi's protestation was obviously aimed at the South Manchuria Railway's usurpation of political and diplomatic functions. Thus, when Yamamoto asked that henceforth the president of the railway be permitted to participate in discussions of Manchurian-Mongolian issues, Debuchi refused to set this down as a specific rule, though he said he agreed with it in principle. Tanaka expressed his agreement with Debuchi's ideas. The Prime Minister was in a difficult position, as he was also head of the Foreign Ministry which was jealous of intervention by military and business officials. While Tanaka was willing to give Yamamoto authority to circumvent the existing bureaucratic structure, he was not prepared to ignore the latter entirely.[25]

Before Yamamoto could try his hand at personal diplomacy, the Japanese legation in Peking had begun a series of talks with Chang Tso-lin. Minister Yoshizawa had been instructed to carry on negotiations, while Tanaka also authorized Yamamoto to do the same. Unfortunately for the speedy success of the legation's effort, the Yoshizawa-Chang talks were interrupted by a new anti-Japanese movement in Manchuria.

In Fengtien Province the spectacle of the Eastern Conference had produced much talk of a Japanese invasion of Manchuria. On August 2 the "association for backing diplomacy in Manchuria" was organized within the provincial assembly. Eight days later the General Chamber of Commerce of Mukden formed a similar body, and these groups started disseminating propaganda concerning Japan's "policy of invasion" of Manchuria and Mongolia. On September 4 a gigantic mass demonstration took place in Mukden calling for the downfall of the Tanaka cabinet and the overthrow of imperialism.[26]

This outburst of anti-Japanese sentiment coincided with various manifestations of Japanese-Nationalist friendship. It is possible, therefore, that the northern generals encouraged the anti-Japanese movement in the hope of embarrassing the Tanaka government and forestalling any further *rapprochement* between Nanking and Tokyo. Tanaka ultimately came to accept the opposite interpretation, namely that some Nationalist radicals disseminated anti-Japanese propaganda in Manchuria in order to forestall a Japanese-Manchurian agreement. In view of his pro-Chang policy, it is easy to see why Tanaka should have readily accepted such a theory. Initially, however, he was genuinely angered at Chang Tso-lin, especially as rumors circulated that the latter gave his blessings to the anti-Japanese movement and since the Tanaka cabinet came under attack at home for its mishandling of the Manchurian issue. He sent a strongly worded message to Marshal Chang, complaining of the specific attack on the cabinet of a friendly nation, not just on Japan. Tanaka threatened that, unless Chang clarified his stand, Japan would be forced to take a firm attitude toward him.[27]

It would have been embarrassing for Tanaka if he had had to take such a firm stand. As it turned out, Chang strongly denied that he had had any part in the movement and promised prompt investigations and suppression of future mass demonstrations. Even if Chang had prevaricated, it is doubtful if Tanaka really would have taken a drastic measure against him. When Consul General Yoshida advised that only the Japanese police and army could control future demonstrations and that they should be used, Tanaka replied that no action should be taken unless Japanese lives were involved. The truth is that the Prime Minister was averse to forcing an issue at this time, since this was the time when Yamamoto, under Tanaka's secret endorsement, was to have commenced talks with Chang Tso-lin. In order not to embarrass Yamamoto's efforts and at the same time to appear firm, Tanaka decided to instruct Minister Yoshizawa to discontinue all talks on railway and related matters until the "sincerity" of the Fengtien officials had been proved. This was an ingenious way of settling the matter. Tanaka was taking advantage of the anti-Japanese riots to open the way for Yamamoto's negotiations with Chang Tso-lin.[28]

Yamamoto had left Tokyo for Dairen in late August. During the first half of September he and his staff made a tour of Manchuria. Everywhere he went he declared to Chinese officials and to anti-Japanese organizations that Manchuria's peace and economic prosperity depended on Japan's strength and goodwill. Early in October, Yamamoto concluded that the time was ripe for his departure for Peking. Preliminary talks conducted through Etō had been promising and Machino Takema, an adviser to Chang Tso-lin, had telegraphed Yamamoto to come to Peking and see Chang in person. Yamamoto had formulated his general line of approach. It was to offer to Chang Tso-lin Japan's positive assistance in maintaining peace and order in Manchuria, in effect confirming Chang in his position of predominance, in return for the latter's consent to the Japanese plan of railway construction.[29]

On October 10, Yamamoto arrived at Peking, and on the following day he visited the Old Marshal. The latter had already been apprised of Yamamoto's scheme for railroad construction in the Three Eastern Provinces. According to Etō and Machino, who were with Yamamoto when he saw Chang, the latter was irritated by Yamamoto's bluntness but did not strongly object to the railway scheme. The railway president then proceeded to work out a detailed agreement with Yang Yü-t'ing.[30]

The agreement on railways was not formally ratified at this time, but its content reveals how far Yamamoto, and through him Tanaka, was willing to ignore the plans worked out by the Foreign Ministry. The Chang-Yamamoto agreement constituted a contract between the Peking government and the South Manchuria Railway for the construction of five railways. These were: Taonan to Solun, Tunhwa to Tumen, Changchun to Talai, Kirin to Wuchang, and Yenki to Hailin. The second of these was a section of the Kirin-Kainei line which the Foreign Ministry had most wanted built. The third had also been on Tokyo's priority list. The fourth and the fifth had not been contemplated either by the Foreign Ministry or at the Eastern Conference, and the first was the very line the Foreign Ministry had strongly opposed as unduly irritating to the Soviet Union because of its proximity to the Siberian border. Yamamoto had thus caused Chang Tso-lin to make a contract which was out of accord with the policies and directives carefully framed by officials of the Tokyo government.[31]

Yamamoto was not satisfied with this agreement alone. Probably with Tanaka's approval he went a step further and sought to extend Japan's influence in Manchuria through Chang Tso-lin. This was to be carried out by means of a political agreement and a treaty between Chang and Japan. With respect to the political agreement Yamamoto proposed that Chang address the following letter to the Japanese government.

It is our understanding that Japan, in view of the fact that the maintenance of security in the Three Eastern Provinces closely affects the peace and economic interest of its territory, will take necessary measures to maintain order in the said provinces, in case order there be disrupted or likely to be disrupted by agents either within or outside China. I consider that such measures as stated above will be taken in order to maintain order in Japan's territory and protect its special economic interests in the Three Eastern Provinces, and should therefore not only be taken solely for self-defense and in case of absolute necessity, but also upon consultation with appropriate Chinese officials. I would therefore like to be apprised of the views of the Japanese government on these points.

While the phrasing of this letter allows different interpretations, and although the maintenance of order in Manchuria had been one of the basic policies even under Shidehara, there is no doubt that such an agreement could have justified extensive Japanese military action in the Three Eastern Provinces.

The second document Yamamoto presented to Chang was a draft treaty. In the preamble the Japanese and Chinese governments were to express their desire "to open the resources of north and south Manchuria and eastern Inner Mongolia equally to all nations, and to facilitate their nationals' economic activities in these areas as much as possible." Consequently, the Chinese government under Chang Tso-lin was to promise to open all these regions to all foreigners under certain rules and conditions. First, all foreigners were to enjoy the right to reside, own property, and engage in all legitimate activities, according to the laws of the Chinese state. Second, all goods produced or manufactured in these regions would be freely exportable. Third, the arrangement was not to alter the existing conditions in the areas already owned by the South Manchuria Railway. Fourth, the Sino-Japanese treaty of 1915 on south Manchuria and eastern Inner Mongolia (originally a part of the Twenty-one Demands) was to be abrogated except for Article I, which extended the lease of Port Arthur, Dairen, and the South Manchuria Railway for ninety-nine years. Finally, all other treaties between China and Japan relating to Manchuria were to remain effective. Here was a far-reaching scheme for opening up Manchuria and Inner Mongolia in return for the relinquishment of extraterritoriality. This ambitious proposal foreshadowed some of the policies the Japanese government was to follow on the extraterritoriality question. The basic idea was to make Manchuria and Inner Mongolia more subservient to the needs of the Japanese economy.[32]

These devices, if put into effect, would have integrated Manchuria more closely with Japan. They would have brought about a new order in the Far East and for that very reason it might have precipitated a Sino-Japanese crisis. There is no question that even Shidehara would have welcomed such a scheme if conflict with China could somehow be avoided. Tanaka, in explicitly or implicitly authorizing Yamamoto to carry on these negotiations, must not have thought that such a conflict would arise. He had made up his mind to support the Nationalists in China proper and was hopeful that they would understand the Japanese position in Manchuria. The Japanese military, too, would have readily agreed to these devices.

The project fell through because of opposition on the part of Minister Yoshizawa and other diplomats. They opposed it not because it was inherently bad, but because they resented Yamamoto's entire disregard of formal diplomatic procedure. All professional bureaucrats rose in indignation, and, to the disgust of Yamamoto, Prime Minister Tanaka failed to support him against their criticism. Apparently Tanaka did not wish to seem to have condoned a complete breach of discipline, although it was he who had originated the idea. He now decided to plead innocence. In a telegram to Minister Yoshizawa he asserted that he had never been informed of the negotiation between Yamamoto and Chang Tso-lin. He declared, "I am at a loss to understand how such things have happened. I consider it lacking in politeness that President Yamamoto should have attempted important negotiations with Chang Tso-lin without first notifying you." Tanaka promised that he would investigate the matter and order Yamamoto in the future to avoid acts which might give the impression of interfering with the diplomatic process.[33]

The incident once again revealed Tanaka's lack of determination and served to highlight the existence of a strong sense of *esprit de corps* among professional diplomats. What is most remarkable is that Tanaka and Yoshizawa soon decided to forget the ill feelings generated by Yamamoto's action and instead to utilize his negotiations with Chang Tso-lin. There is no better proof of the essential unanimity of views held by Tanaka, Yoshizawa, and others in the Foreign Ministry concerning Japanese rights in Manchuria. To be sure the professional diplomats were opposed to the political agreement Yamamoto had proposed to Chang, believing that they would forever commit Japan to the support of the Manchurian warlord. Tanaka, accordingly, had ordered Yamamoto to take back the draft agreements from Chang. On the railway agreement, however, Yoshizawa felt that the Chang-Yamamoto agreement might as well be utilized for future negotiations, once the president of the railway expressed his regrets for his action. Tanaka eagerly agreed, and on November 7 he instructed the minister to induce Chang to write a letter to Yoshizawa, expressing his decision to accept the Chang-Yamamoto agreement as the basis for a new Sino-Japanese accord on railway construction in Manchuria.[34]

This was not an easy assignment, since Chang Tso-lin had become aware of Japanese designs as well as lack of unity. In time he was persuaded to write a personal letter to Tanaka, instead of Yoshizawa, saying that Chang intended in sincerity to settle the issue which he had discussed with Yamamoto and that he would instruct the proper officials to work out the details. In return Tanaka asked Yoshizawa to transmit to Chang his reply, which said that he had no objection to Chang's endeavoring to solve the railway issue according to the agreement between him and Yamamoto. The episode had come to a happy end.[35]

In this way, at the close of the year 1927, there was a faint feeling of achievement on the part of the Japanese negotiators. What they had obtained was a scrap of paper outlining railway construction in Manchuria, but at least a specific blueprint had been produced instead of broad generalities which had surrounded Japan's treaty rights. But it does not follow that Tanaka's Manchuria policy was a success. It is obvious, first of all, that the Chang-Yamamoto agreement was about the only tangible fruit of the so-called "positive policy" which was in effect no different from the one pursued under Shidehara. The railway agreement was made in spite of, not because of, the Eastern Conference. The one positive element in Tanaka's policy, the support of Chang Tso-lin, had not yet materialized. It would be more correct to say that Tanaka introduced new elements in Sino-Japanese relations not in the field of policy but of policy execution. His idea of a new order in the Far East was basically the same as Shidehara's; but in trying to bring it about he tended to bypass regular diplomatic channels and delegate policy-making functions to such men as the military attaché in Peking and the president of the South Manchuria Railway. The jealously guarded supremacy of the Foreign Ministry bureaucrats was challenged, and a precedent had been set for direct action by extradiplomatic personnel. At a time when Japan's systematic and concerted efforts were needed to realize the vision of a new order of coprosperity in China and Manchuria, the Tanaka cabinet's handling of the Manchurian question only exposed the confusion in policy execution. Because he failed to define a uniform chain of command, Tanaka caused Japan's Manchuria policy to seem ambitious, devious, and sinister. While Japan's initiative vis-à-vis the Nationalists had been favorably responded to by them, its uncoordinated and highhanded action in Manchuria contributed to ill feelings between the two countries. This was the legacy of his "positive policy."

As Japan under Shidehara and Tanaka sought to pursue a vigorous policy in Manchuria, some Japanese officials were aware that they might provoke suspicion on the part of the powers. Actually, for some in the military, this was a wrong way of putting the equation. For them it was because of the very inevitability of Japanese-American conflict that Japan should have a predominant position in Manchuria. Some civilians agreed with such a view, especially after the immigration dispute of 1924. For Shidehara and Tanaka, however, the possibility of American-Japanese conflict in the Far East must have seemed very remote. Both were intent on positive action to work out a new system in the Far East, but they did not believe that this undertaking would necessarily antagonize the United States or any other power. They tended to isolate Japan's China policy and deal with it irrespective of Japan's relations with other countries. This is another way of saying that their new order was an *ad hoc* response to the absence of a system in the Far East after the failure of the Washington Conference framework.

In retrospect it might seem that, in seeing a link between Japan's policy in the Far East and its relations with other countries, the military strategists of Japan were far more realistic than their civilian counterparts. Strikingly enough, the Japanese government was not the only one isolating its policy toward China. In the middle-to-late 1920's all the major powers revealed similar characteristics in their Far Eastern policies. Despite the disturbing news from Manchuria, they did not relate it to their over-all policies toward Japan. During the latter half of 1927, Britain acted in cooperation with Japan in the settlement of minor incidents in China, and the Foreign Office maintained official silence about Japanese activities in Manchuria. Germany signed a new treaty of commerce with Japan and hoped to promote trade between the two countries. Even the Soviet Union, pursuing certain definite policies in China proper, considered it expedient to keep on good terms with Japan. Overtures for Soviet-Japanese cooperation in Manchuria, for example by coordinating the traffic schedules of the Chinese Eastern Railway and the South Manchuria Railway, were made, and Moscow was even desirous of concluding a nonaggression pact with Japan.[36]

The United States, too, had managed to keep its policies toward China and Japan separate. American policy makers were aware of the continued economic interdependence between Japan and the United States; Japan was still buying more from America than from any other country, and the United States continued to be Japan's biggest customer. Millions of dollars were being loaned to Japanese municipal governments and private concerns, and firms totally financed by American capital were being established. Official American-Japanese relations were still definable as economic, and civilian officials in Washington believed in the basic framework of amity with Japan.[37] Such an attitude, however, did not prevent the United States from pursuing certain policies in China irrespective of its relation with Japan. This trend was particularly noticeable in Manchuria. The United States continued to profess adherence to the principle of equal commercial opportunity, and suspicions of Japanese designs in Manchuria had not abated completely. The State Department still discouraged American bankers from lending to certain Japanese firms doing business in Manchuria, lest the money be used to the detriment of the open door. As late as March 1927, the cabinet in Washington passed unfavorably upon a proposed loan to the South Manchuria Railway by the National City Bank of New York. While President Calvin Coolidge was "very favorably disposed to the Japanese and therefore to loans to Japan at this time," a loan to the South Manchuria Railway was a different matter since it "might carry with it the implication that we endorsed what might be called the Japanese special position" in Manchuria.[38]

The attitude of adhering to the principle of the open door but at the same time maintaining cordial relations with Japan could be put to a test when China and Japan either collided or simultaneously sought American support for their policies in Manchuria. The United States would then be caught in the middle, and would be compelled to redefine its policy priorities in the Far East. Such a situation arose in the fall of 1927, but quite characteristically the State Department at this time took refuge in a tactic of silence rather than developing a comprehensive foreign policy.

The first forecast of trouble for American policy was made by Consul General Myrl S. Myers at Mukden. He noted that the coming into power of General Tanaka in Tokyo was welcomed by Japanese in Manchuria as offering greater support of their interests than under Shidehara. After the Eastern Conference, Myers became steadily more suspicious of Japanese intentions in Manchuria, which he thought were ultimately to separate it from the rest of China as a region where Japan's economic interests would predominate. In a dispatch of November 23 he predicted,

the ultimate object of a "positive policy" of economic aggrandizement under the peculiar conditions existing in this region — control of principal arteries of communication, presence of military forces at important centers along Japanese owned railways, existence of numerous Japanese settlements along these lines, etc. etc., — would seem logically to be political absorption. The taking of such a step, if not defeated by unforeseen events, will probably be determined by circumstances, fortuitous or devised.

Given such an interpretation of Japanese policy in Manchuria, the conclusion readily followed that the United States should make clear whether it meant to acquiesce in the trend in order not to jeopardize its economic relations with Japan or to protest it in order to further America's ties with China.[39]

These alarmist views were not at first shared by Myers' colleagues. In Peking a legation staff concluded that the new cabinet in Tokyo simply followed the previously adopted policy of slow economic penetration of Manchuria, "combined with a steady and quiet preparation for the impending conflict" with the Soviet Union. From Dairen, Consul Leo D. Sturgeon reported that despite exaggerated accounts of a new, vigorous policy said to be pursued by the new president and vice president of the South Manchuria Railway, Japan's and the railway's basic aims remained the same as before — to monopolize as far as possible the Three Eastern Provinces "as a source of raw materials for home indus-

tries, and as a market for the products of home manufactures."
In Tokyo the American embassy accepted the repeated assurances
of the Foreign Ministry that the change of top personnel would
not result in any drastic alteration of Japan's policy. The military
attaché reported in September that the "positive policy" of the
Tanaka cabinet could mean "nothing more than the construction
of a few well known feeding lines to the South Manchuria Railroad, the practical establishment of the right to lease land in
Manchuria which was included in the so-called twenty-one demands, and the objection to the construction of certain Chinese
railways that would parallel the South Manchurian Railway." In
Washington, the State Department recognized that "a stiffening
of Japanese attitude toward the Chinese situation" had resulted
from Tanaka's assumption of office, but it did not seem to require
re-examination of American policy.[40]

Developments in the Far East in the fall of 1927 temporarily
alerted American officials, who recognized the need for fresh
thinking. One such development was the Mukden demonstration
of September 4 and other outbursts of anti-Japanese feeling, in-
cited by Japanese-Fengtien railway negotiations. Another was a
proposed loan of thirty million dollars by the J. P. Morgan Company to the South Manchuria Railway, for the purpose of refund-
ing the bonded debt outstanding in Japan, replacing rails and
rolling stock, and carrying out productive works in subsidiary
concerns of the railway. Though no formal contract was ever
signed, rumors of the negotiation in Tokyo between Thomas W.
Lamont of the Morgan firm and Inoue Junnosuke of the Bank
of Japan quickly circulated and evoked immediate reaction in
China. Both Nationalist and northern officials denounced the
proposed loan arrangement as evidence not only of Japanese expansionism but also of tacit American approval of it.[41]

These incidents compelled the American government to clarify
its policies toward China, Japan, and Manchuria. Some officials
recommended a clear-cut decision. Consul General Myers in
Mukden felt that the State Department should give priority to
America's economic interests in China and therefore to do nothing which would weaken Sino-American ties. Chargé Mayer in
Peking, on the other hand, believed that the time had come to

adopt a joint stand with Japan for economic development in China. Such a policy would not only prevent the spread of radicalism in China, but it would also ensure the protection of American interests against Japanese discrimination. When anti-Japanese riots broke out in September, Mayer telegraphed Washington, "should this agitation be continued and in this event should Japan not take decisive steps at once to conclude it I am apprehensive that conditions may afford [a] rallying cry for radical elements in China including Soviets with [the] result that [the] situation might get out of hand with [a] similar effect in Chihli and Shantung." The time seemed opportune to devise means to cope with the threatening situation. Mayer's fears proved premature, as steps were taken by Chang Tso-lin to prevent further agitation. Two months later, however, when he heard rumors of a loan negotiation between Lamont and Japanese concerns, he once again tendered the opinion that, since China was in a state of anarchy, the United States should be financially associated with Japan in order to "control the situation and canalize it to our best interests and China's." Charles MacVeagh, American ambassador in Tokyo, went even further. Telegraphing Washington, he said that Japan was only interested in developing Manchuria in such a way as to make it a safe place for the nationals of all countries. Therefore, "we should make use of the first opportunity to convince the Japanese that we have an honest desire to help them in reaching a solution of their difficulties when we can legitimately do so." MacVeagh openly told Prime Minister Tanaka that he sincerely hoped for a successful consummation of the Morgan loan contract. Such an arrangement, he said, would have the effect of further interesting the American public in Manchuria, and there would be others willing to offer similar loans. In this way financial ties between the United States and Japan would be strengthened still more.[42]

In Washington opinion was equally divided. Until November there was general agreement that the United States should continue its professed policies in Manchuria irrespective of American-Japanese relations elsewhere. When he read newspaper accounts of the Lamont negotiation in Tokyo, Secretary Kellogg saw no need to modify the established rule that an American loan to the

South Manchuria Railway should be discouraged. The situation changed when Lamont returned to the United States and, on November 10, inquired of the State Department whether it would object to the thirty-million-dollar-loan proposal, which would be guaranteed by the Japanese government. Lamont forced an issue by affirming that "Japan has definitely abandoned whatever old theories she might have had as to the value of force measures on the Continent of Asia." As he saw no evidence that Japanese were violating the open door in Manchuria, he felt that the United States should respond favorably to their offer of "friendship and cooperation with America." He pointed out that Manchuria was "about the only stable region in all China and that with the Japanese there it is likely to be more of a stabilizing force in Chinese affairs than it is to be a disturbing element." [43]

The State Department found itself compelled to review its Far Eastern policy. Some of its officials, including Under Secretary Robert E. Olds, saw much in Lamont's reasoning. At a time when they were aware of no case of discrimination against American interests by Japanese, it was difficult to refuse to pass the proposed loan. American officials in Washington, however, were not prepared to go a step further, as urged by Lamont and MacVeagh, and to endorse openly the idea of financial cooperation between the two countries. To do so would add fuel to the already aroused Chinese suspicions and impair the framework of Sino-American understanding. Unwilling to develop afresh a comprehensive Far Eastern policy, clearly defining priorities, the State Department simply decided to maintain official silence. It neither endorsed the loan publicly nor refused to pass it. As Nolan T. Johnson put it,

to object to the loan on any ground other than the ground that the railway itself is actively discriminating against American commerce will readily involve us definitely in the Manchurian situation on the side of whatever Chinese situation there is, while the negative action on our part in making no objection will leave us where we stand today with our policy in regard to Manchuria undisturbed.

As this quotation shows, there was no interest in altering "our policy in regard to Manchuria" nor in taking sides in the Sino-Japanese dispute. Johnson kept emphasizing to Chinese and

Japanese officials that, while the Department regarded the loan as a private matter in which it was not interested, the question of policy was in no way involved and that the loan, if made, "could not possibly be interpreted as indicating that the policy of the United States in China had been in any respect altered." [44]

The American government was spared embarrassment, which the policy of silence would have brought, by editorial comments within the United States. They became more and more critical of the loan proposal, echoing the Chinese protestation that America's tacit approval of the loan endangered its friendship with China. The State Department, as a result, started dropping hints that the publicity over the matter had adversely affected the investment market and therefore that the bankers would decide to postpone the negotiation. The Morgan Company accordingly decided to let the matter rest a while until the clamor quieted down. [45]

American policy on the South Manchuria Railway episode does not prove, as some have argued, that the United States and Japan were at that time in basic conflict in China. Neither does it reveal any alteration in American policy toward the Far East. The need for a re-evaluation was felt by a number of officials, but the top leadership in Washington resorted to equivocation rather than facing the issue squarely and trying to resolve the dilemma implicit in applying separate policies to China and Japan. In persisting in its position, the American government may have further convinced the Japanese military of the inevitability of conflict. At the same time, Washington's failure to oppose Japan explicitly contributed to widening the gap between America's foreign policy and military thinking. As revealed at the Geneva naval conference, convened in June 1927, to limit the construction of cruisers, destroyers, and submarines, American navalists continued to consider Japanese aspirations in Asia incompatible with United States policy. The inevitability of war in the Western Pacific was still a basic assumption in naval thinking. Certainly the South Manchuria Railway episode and the State Department's handling of it did nothing to put an end to the existing bifurcation between economic policy and military policy, a prominent feature of Japanese-American relations during the 1920's. [46]

Japan's initiative in Manchuria was an essential part of its search for a realm of coexistence and coprosperity in the Far East. There was more continuity than change between Shidehara's and Tanaka's policies. The difference between the two lay primarily in policy execution and not in policy itself. Both exhibited a remarkable naiveté in believing that Japanese rights in Manchuria could somehow be treated separately from Japanese policy in China proper, and that Japan's program in Manchuria would not arouse opposition from other powers, in particular the United States. On both these counts the Japanese initiative in Manchuria was a failure. At a time when Japanese policy toward the Nationalists had shown some signs of success, the offensive in Manchuria served to forfeit their goodwill. As C. C. Wu protested in October, Japan seemed to have embarked on an "imperialistic new policy" toward China and Manchuria, aimed at depriving China of its sovereignty over the Three Eastern Provinces and practically converting the area to Japan's territory. The Chinese people, he said, would never recognize the treaties which might be agreed upon between Japan and the Peking government under Chang Tso-lin, which controlled at best only six provinces.[47]

The belief that Japan could pursue its independent policy and still be friendly with the powers was not totally illusory. They were at this time not interested in colliding with Japan in Manchuria. But beyond such negative acquiescence they would not go. The United States, whose financial assistance was considered necessary for the economic development of Manchuria, failed to come out in active support of the Japanese program. The United States had its own plans in China, different from Japan's, and there was no serious effort, either in Tokyo or in Washington, to coordinate action and develop a comprehensive strategy for Far Eastern peace.

VI · MILITARY INSUBORDINATION,
1928

Japan's bid for a new order temporarily came to an ignominious end in 1928. While Japanese policy stumbled and its execution was muddled because of military· insubordination, the Chinese Nationalists successfully unified the country and began imposing their own image of a new order. With the United States in the lead, other countries one by one recognized the Nationalist regime and restored tariff autonomy to China. The Japanese initiative had resulted in Tokyo's standing far behind Washington and London in relation to Nanking.

The year 1928 is often taken as a point of departure for Japanese aggression which began in 1931. It was in 1928 that the Tsinan incident put an end to the brief period of Sino-Japanese amity and Chang Tso-lin was murdered by Kwantung Army officers, foreshadowing their independent acts during the 1930's. It was in this year that the Kwantung Army formally began preparations for a possible conflict with the Chinese and that Lieutenant Colonel Ishihara Kanji was detailed to the Army, there to stay until his work was carried out in September 1931. Looking back, one sees a direct line stretching from 1928 to 1931.

Such an interpretation, of course, fails to answer certain significant questions. Why was there no "Manchurian incident" until 1931, and then when Shidehara was once again foreign minister? Why did Tanaka, who had so painfully labored for understanding with the Nationalists, precipitate a crisis with them? Why was there no overt hostility between Japan and the United States, when the Japanese military, taking unilateral action in China, were convinced of basic conflict with the United States? These and other questions cannot be fully answered until certain episodes in Sino-Japanese and Sino-foreign relations during the first half of 1928 are considered. It is worthwhile examining them in some detail since some fresh evidence has only recently become available.

THE TSINAN INCIDENT

Chiang Kai-shek returned to Shanghai from Japan on December 1, 1927. After his marriage to Sung Mei-ling a conference of Nationalist leaders was held at his residence. There it was decided to restore Chiang as commander in chief of the Nationalist army and to carry on the Northern Expedition. Early in January 1928, Chiang returned to Nanking and officially resumed control over the revolutionary army. The confusion and chaos which for several months had plagued the Kuomintang outwardly came to an end.[1]

The second phase of the Northern Expedition, which was formally launched on April 7, 1928, was different from the earlier phase in two respects. The revolutionaries were now allied with warlords such as Feng Yü-hsiang and Yen Hsi-shan. They had joined the Kuomintang, and their forces were incorporated in those of Nationalist generals. Secondly, communists and radicals were absent. The fourth plenary session of the central executive committee of the Kuomintang, convening between February 2 and February 7, ruled that the promotion of mass movements would thenceforth be a minor activity of the reorganized party and that they were to be strictly regulated. All connections with the communists were to be severed.[2]

These changes had immediate implications in Nationalist China's foreign relations. For one thing the anti-Soviet trend of the Nanking regime was confirmed. In December 1927, the government severed relations with Soviet consular officials and trade organizations in Kuomintang territory, following the "Canton commune" of December 11–14.[3] Secondly, new emphasis was put on the avoidance of trouble with the treaty powers. The basic policy of complete national independence never changed; as Chiang Kai-shek declared in late January 1928, in case a foreign country did not consent to enter into negotiation to revise its treaties with China or in case such negotiations proved unsatisfactory, China should abrogate these treaties. But Chiang and other leaders were determined not to precipitate another crisis in

Sino-foreign relations like the Nanking incident. Chiang made several statements expressing readiness to respect the lives and property of foreigners. He guaranteed that he would not tolerate antiforeign outbursts by his troops. Huang Fu, succeeding C. C. Wu as foreign minister, declared that the Nationalists were prepared "to protect to their fullest ability the lives and property of foreigners in China in accordance with international law and usage." [4]

An important corollary of this line of approach was the avoidance of friction with Japan. Sino-Japanese relations had been strained the previous fall by the Manchurian question, and the Nationalists were aware that as they marched northward they might come into conflict with Japanese interests in north China and Manchuria. But before China's unification was completed, they were determined not to provoke a crisis with Japan. There is some evidence that Chiang Kai-shek believed he had obtained Prime Minister Tanaka's tacit endorsement of Nationalist military action in north China, when they conferred in Tokyo the previous November. Since then Chiang had on several occasions expressed willingness to respect Japan's rights in Manchuria. He told Japanese correspondents in March that, since Japan was China's best friend, he hoped the Japanese would not interfere with the revolution but hope for its early completion. He was fully aware of the possibility that relations with Japan might further be complicated and definitely worsen if an untoward incident should occur between Chinese soldiers and Japanese residents in Shantung Peninsula, or if Japan should resort to reckless measures. [5]

Chiang's fears were fully justified, as subsequent events were to show. But it must be emphasized that the Sino-Japanese clash of 1928 was not necessarily unavoidable. In fact, a new era of Nationalist-Japanese understanding might have dawned if the Japanese government had adhered to its basic policies and reached agreement with the Nationalists on that basis. The trouble was, as in the past, Tokyo's inability to prevent the military from trying to implement these policies in their own way. Consequently, despite the residue of good feeling both in Nanking and Tokyo, relations between the two countries steadily worsened throughout the first half of 1928.

There had always been two basic Japanese policies vis-à-vis the civil war in China. One was to protect somehow the lives and property of Japanese nationals in places of danger, and the other was to prevent the spread of chaos to Manchuria and keep it as a stable and peaceful region. While the Japanese government had already taken certain steps to ensure these ends, it was only in late 1927 that policy makers began a serious study of how best to implement them, now that the Nationalist soldiers were about to resume their northward expedition.

Regarding the policy of protecting Japanese nationals in China, Shidehara had been willing at times to evacuate them from places of danger rather than risk a crisis by defending them. Tanaka, on the other hand, had undertaken an expedition to Shantung primarily because his party stood for "protection of nationals on the spot." Due to internal dissension, the Nationalists had temporarily halted their march, and at that time there was no clash. But, when Chiang Kai-shek was restored as commander of the Nationalist army in December 1927, the Tanaka cabinet was obliged once again to consider specific means of protecting Japanese residents in north China. The simplest method was, of course, to carry out another expedition. In the middle of December, the War Minister recommended that Japan should be ready to do so if and when the Tsining-Kunchow area fell to the southerners. The protocol force in Tientsin was engaged in detailed planning for such an expedition, and the War Ministry generally supported this move.[6]

Prime Minister Tanaka was aware that the use of force was not necessarily the best means of protecting Japanese in Shantung; there was always the danger of a clash between Japanese and Chinese soldiers. The General Staff, too, was opposed to an expedition; its principal officials believed that Chiang Kai-shek and moderate Nationalists should be given a chance to protect Japanese interests, cementing the ties between Nationalists and Japanese. This was also Tanaka's idea. On December 23 he instructed Consul General Yada at Shanghai to assure Chiang

Kai-shek and Feng Yü-hsiang that, though Japan might be forced to send troops to the Tsinan area if the safety of nationals was endangered, the government wished to avoid such an expedition if possible. The best solution, Tanaka suggested, would be for southern troops to avoid battle in the Tsinan area and proceed northward without going through the provincial capital. In other words, Tanaka hoped that the Nationalists would so steer their northward march as to enable Japan to refrain from sending troops.[7]

Yada saw Chiang Kai-shek and C. T. Wang on December 26. The latter telegraphed Tanaka's message to Feng Yü-hsiang at Kaifeng. Chiang said that, upon his return to office, he would do his utmost to have Japanese residents in Shantung protected and, therefore, hoped the Japanese government would not carry out an expedition. He expressed confidence that the Nationalist generals, including Feng, would do their best to protect Japanese.[8]

Though there is no evidence that Chiang Kai-shek explicitly promised Tanaka not to attack Tsinan, the Prime Minister apparently decided to be satisfied with Chiang's assurances and watch the course of events. Soon after the resumption of the Northern Expedition in early April 1928, however, it began to appear that the Nationalist troops would quickly sweep through southern Shantung and march toward the Tsinan region and beyond. Japanese officials reported that the combined forces of Chiang Kai-shek, Feng Yü-hsiang, and Yen Hsi-shan were defeating the northern armies led by Chang Tsung-ch'ang and Sun Ch'uan-fang and that Tsinan, with two thousand Japanese residents, was expected to be attacked any day. There is some reason to believe that Chiang Kai-shek really did not intend to go through Tsinan, but this was unknown to the Japanese. Already on April 16 the Foreign Ministry was in receipt of telegrams from its representatives in Tsingtao and Tsinan urging an expedition as an unavoidable necessity to protect Japanese residents.[9]

Prime Minister Tanaka was by no means persuaded that the time had come for action. He was aware of the opposition in financial and industrial circles to a policy which might damage Japan's trade with China. The Nationalists had declared their intention of protecting Japanese lives and property within areas under their control. Some of Tanaka's military advisers, especially in the General Staff, continued to argue that Chiang Kai-shek should be trusted to protect Japanese and should not be obstructed by a Japanese expedition, particularly since Tanaka had expressed his support of Chiang in the previous fall. Others, on the contrary, insisted that neither northern nor southern soldiers could be trusted, that the Japanese government had made it clear that it would take proper measures in case the safety of Japanese lives was threatened anew, that Japanese residents in Tsinan were themselves expecting an expedition, and that in the parliamentary election of the previous February, the first under the universal manhood suffrage law, the Seiyukai had again pledged to stand for the principle of "protecting nationals on the spot." [10]

Pressure from the War Ministry and considerations of party politics seem to have been the two main factors which led Tanaka to sanction another Shantung expedition. On April 18, Tanaka and the War and Navy ministers made the final decision, and the cabinet agreed to the dispatching of five thousand troops of the sixth division in Kumamoto. The announcement by the government on the following day twice repeated the assurance that Japan had no intention of intervening in the actual course of the civil war in China. The statement promised that the troops would be withdrawn as soon as their presence was no longer needed to protect Japanese nationals in Shantung. Prime Minister Tanaka may have hoped to withdraw the troops as speedily as he had in 1927, once the presence of five thousand soldiers at Tsingtao had sufficiently exhibited Japan's determination to protect its nationals.[11]

The protocol force in Tientsin was meanwhile ordered to divert three companies to Tsinan. In transmitting this order the General Staff in Tokyo took care to remind the commander in Tientsin that the troops should avoid all interference with the Chinese civil war. "The southern faction," it said, "has often viewed the action of the Imperial army with suspicion and spread the groundless rumors of Japan's assistance to the northern faction, etc. In consequence of this, you should strictly order your men, in dispatching them to Tsinan, never to act or talk in a manner which may give the impression of leaning toward the north. Also, you should take care that the action of the contending armies be not interfered with by our troops, unless to do so is necessary in order to protect our residents around Tsinan." The General Staff, which had long opposed the Shantung expedition, desired to minimize its hazards.[12]

The Peking and the Nanking governments immediately protested the expedition, terming it a violation of China's sovereignty and saying that it was unnecessary since the Chinese authorities had already expressed willingness to protect foreign lives. At the same time, for obvious reasons, they were determined to avoid unnecessary conflict with the Japanese. The central executive committee of the Kuomintang warned its members, at the front and behind as well, to obey orders and to be wary of communist agitation. Though anti-Japanese posters were pasted and speeches made by Nationalist soldiers who retained their radical nationalism long after the purge of communists, Chinese officers prohibited anti-Japanese agitation where there were Japanese residents.[13]

Thus, despite the ill will generated by Japan's announcement, a clash between Chinese and Japanese soldiers might have been avoided if both had stayed away from Tsinan. But, General Fukuda Hikosuke, commanding the sixth division which landed on Tsingtao between April 25 and 27, decided not to await instruction to proceed farther to Tsinan. This decision seems primarily to have been due to his desire to enhance the prestige of his division, but it was nevertheless a fatal decision, the first serious case of unilateral action by the Japanese military. To make the matter worse, a Nationalist commander also decided to enter the city, following the withdrawal of northern troops under Chang Tsung-ch'ang on April 30. Perhaps this was against the initial orders from Chiang Kai-shek to stay away from Tsinan, but Chiang himself had no choice but to follow them and move his headquarters to the city. This occurred on May 2.[14]

Even then, disaster was by no means predictable. Though there were a few cases of disturbances in which some casualties ensued, on the whole order and discipline were preserved by the incoming southerners and the patrolling Japanese. The Nationalist officials in Tsinan promised to assume responsibility for maintaining order within its sphere of dominance. Japanese authorities believed that the southerners were better disciplined than the northerners. Nationalist soldiers seemed to refrain from occupying private houses in the foreign community and to pay for their purchases.[15]

On May 2 Chiang Kai-shek sent a message to General Fukuda, requesting that the Japanese troops withdraw immediately and remove defense barricades as his army would definitely maintain order and peace in the city. Favorably impressed by Chinese discipline, the Japanese decided to grant the request. The troops that had been sent from Tientsin were ordered to return there on May 4, and throughout the night of May 2 barricades were demolished one by one by Japanese soldiers. It looked as though there might be a peaceful transition from northern to Japanese to southern rule of Tsinan.[16]

The Japanese troops prepared for evacuation on the morning of May 3. At nine o'clock that morning, Nishida Kōichi, the acting consul general, and several Japanese officers visited Chiang Kai-shek at his headquarters. Talking with Chiang, Huang Fu, and other leaders of the expedition, Nishida remarked that he was impressed with the good discipline of the revolutionary army and felt the Japanese forces could at any moment be withdrawn. As the visitors explained their troops' whereabouts, Chiang Kai-shek said that the Northern Expedition would be continued but that he hoped Sino-Japanese ties would become closer. Around nine-thirty, on his way back from the interview, Nishida learned that fighting had broken out between Chinese and Japanese soldiers around the house of a Japanese family within the commercial port of Tsinan.[17]

Concerning the origin of the fight, Japan and China later presented different accounts, and to this day there is no satisfactory explanation. The Japanese version, based on a report prepared by an officer sent from Tokyo to investigate the incident, as well as reports submitted by Nishida, stated that about thirty southern soldiers entered the premises of a Japanese resident and started looting. The soldiers were men of General Ho Yao-tsu, the officer to whom some had attributed the Nanking incident. The resident was reportedly beaten as he tried to escape, but he managed to report to the consular police. Two policemen came to the house but were insulted and threatened by the remaining Chinese soldiers. A few minutes later a group of thirty Japanese soldiers arrived and chased the Chinese soldiers, who fled to a military barracks two hundred yards away. Then shooting started between Japanese and Chinese soldiers, and they could not be stopped even by a Japanese officer who was sent by General Fukuda to stop the fighting. From then on fighting spread throughout the rest of the city.[18]

The Chinese account, prepared by the "association for backing diplomacy in the Tsinan tragedy" and published in the next month, reported that public relations officers of the fourth army were pasting some posters up around the house in question, when they were interfered with by Japanese, and fighting broke out. At the same time, a Chinese barracks was attacked by Japanese soldiers but, under orders, the Chinese did not resist.[19]

While it is impossible to evaluate these reports, there is no question that the simultaneous presence of a large number of Chinese and Japanese troops had provided a setting where small incidents could easily lead to large-scale fighting. Both camps did try at first to prevent the spread of hostilities. As soon as he knew of the incident, the Japanese consul asked General Fukuda to stop the fighting. Nishida also telephoned Chinese leaders and asked them to do likewise. Chiang Kai-shek had already ordered his troops to avoid clashing with the Japanese and dispatched a messenger to Fukuda asking him to follow his example. Despite the confusion in the city and disruption of the regular means of communication, the leaders of both camps managed to get in touch with each other and agree upon a truce. Before noon, both Chiang Kai-shek and Fukuda had issued appropriate orders. But fighting continued, probably because communication facilities had been disrupted and neither commander's orders could be quickly transmitted.[20]

Both sides continued to try to bring about a cease-fire. In the middle of the night Chinese and Japanese representatives met and agreed that the Chinese would immediately withdraw beyond the city walls and that the Japanese in the meantime would not fire upon them. While sporadic fighting continued, a truce agreement was concluded between the Japanese and Chinese commanders on May 5. On that day, Chiang Kai-shek notified the Japanese that his troops had been ordered to leave the areas under Japanese control and that only a few thousands remained behind to maintain order within Tsinan. By May 7 the only Chinese forces that had not left were two companies, amounting perhaps to five thousand men. Obviously, the Nationalists did not want to be hampered in their northward expedition and were willing to suffer temporary humiliation to achieve the ultimate goal.[21]

The truce agreement was destined to be short-lived. Since the Chinese, and above all Chiang Kai-shek, were determined to avoid conflict and proceed northward speedily, the resumption of hostilities must be blamed on the Japanese side. Available documents clearly indicate that the Japanese consul general and residents in Tsinan as a whole definitely wanted a permanent ceasefire, but that the military commanders decided on war. Some have argued that the army was thinking in terms of a semipermanent occupation of the area in order to interfere with the Nationalist expedition and prevent the spread of revolutionary ideas and practices to north China where Japanese interests predominated. While this is a plausible argument, especially in the light of subsequent events, there is little evidence that the commanders in the field had such far-reaching ideas. It is more likely that desire for action and glory motivated Fukuda and other generals, now that they had an apparently legitimate excuse for using force. They explained later that the incident of May 3 had impressed them as evidence of a deep-seated anti-Japanese feeling on the part of Nationalist troops, and they felt that the prestige of the Imperial army would be at stake if the Chinese "insult" were allowed to go unrebuked. This was an emotional response of prestige-conscious generals, not a coldly calculated policy.[22]

The decision to fight to the finish in Tsinan had been made even before the truce agreement of May 3. In fact all evidence indicates that Fukuda's acceptance of truce on the night of that day was designed simply to gain time. The supply of food and munitions had been dwindling, and communication between companies of the Japanese army was entirely cut off. Consequently, the military leaders felt that they should consent to a truce in order to improve the conditions of the army and devise a systematic plan for resumption of fighting.[23]

The supreme command in Tokyo gave Fukuda and his men what encouragement they needed. It seems that the General Staff, despite its original opposition to the Shantung expedition, this time began actively calling for troop re-enforcements. Here again its main purpose was to reassert Japanese military prestige. Stiff opposition came from the Foreign Ministry, which feared that re-enforcements would only worsen Sino-Japanese relations, but Prime Minister Tanaka succumbed to the military's reasoning and the cabinet decided, on May 4, to send additional troops from Manchuria and Korea.[24]

By May 7 the Japanese commanders felt the time was ripe for drastic action. They decided to present an ultimatum to the Chinese, which should serve as a pretext for resuming hostilities. They would make the specifications of the ultimatum so hard that the Chinese would not accept it, which would justify further Japanese military action.[25]

The ultimatum was presented at four o'clock in the afternoon of May 7 to the Chinese commissioner of foreign affairs ad interim, who had remained in Tsinan under order of Chiang Kai-shek. The ultimatum had a time limit of twelve hours and demanded five things: punishment of responsible high officers; disarmament in front of the Japanese army of the troops who were responsible for the outrages; evacuation of two military barracks in the vicinity of Tsinan; prohibition of all anti-Japanese propaganda; and withdrawal of troops beyond twenty li on both sides of the Tsinan-Kiaochow Railway. As the Japanese reported several months later, the ultimatum was meant to exalt the spirit of the Japanese soldiers, shock the Chinese, and impress foreigners with the determination of the Japanese army. The military naturally expected that the Chinese would not be able to answer the ultimatum in time.[26]

The attitude of the Japanese military was in marked contrast to the patience and moderation shown by Chinese leaders. In the train used as headquarters in Taian, Chiang Kai-shek and his aides conferred on the night of May 7 and drew up replies to the Japanese. First, Chiang promised to punish guilty soldiers after an investigation, asking that the Japanese do likewise. Second, he said that anti-Japanese propaganda was already proscribed. Third, he declared that the Chinese troops along the Tsinan-Kiaochow Railway had been ordered to leave it to proceed northward; he asked only that an appropriate number of men be allowed to remain in and around the city of Tsinan, along the railway, and at the stations of the Tientsin-Pukow Railway, in order to maintain order. Fourth, he said that the barracks mentioned in the ultimatum would be evacuated. Finally, Chiang Kai-shek expressed hope that the Japanese would return Chinese prisoners and their arms. Having written the reply, Chiang ordered two messengers to go to Tsinan and present it to General Fukuda.[27]

When they saw him Fukuda stubbornly insisted that the troops which had had a part in the Tsinan incident be disarmed in front of the Japanese army. The Chinese delegates persisted in their refusal, and Fukuda would not back down. The Chinese then receded a step and asked him to write down his demands so that they could return and ask for new instructions. As one of them recalled later, they thought they could capitalize on the written demands by revealing them to the world. Thereupon Fukuda wrote that, as he had not received a reply within twelve hours after the ultimatum was issued, he considered Chiang Kai-shek to be lacking in sincerity. Therefore, Fukuda wrote, he would be forced to take resolute action in order to have the terms of the ultimatum fulfilled, as it was a matter of prestige of the Japanese army.[28]

At four o'clock in the afternoon on May 8 fighting was resumed. The Chinese within the city gates offered stubborn resistance but were finally expelled from the city on May 11, by which time the Japanese had cleared the entire area between the Yellow River and Tangchiachuang. From this time on the city of Tsinan came to be governed by an organization of Chinese citizens under Japanese direction. Until the end of the Japanese rule in early 1929, the Chinese lived under a reign of terror where freedom of the press and meeting was proscribed, the mail periodically censored, and citizens indiscriminately killed for being southern sympathizers.[29]

There is no question that the Tsinan incident frustrated all attempts at further Sino-Japanese *rapprochement*. What had initially been a justifiable though costly and ill-timed effort to protect lives and property had led to a serious crisis from which the two countries were not really to recover. The incident revealed once again how weak was the Japanese chain of command and how powerless were civilian officials in the face of the impetuous acts of the military.

It is not necessary to follow in detail the policies of the Japanese government after the resumption of fighting on May 7. The cabinet in Tokyo, succumbing to promptings by the General Staff, early decided to dispatch another division from Japan, but Prime Minister Tanaka desired to seek a diplomatic solution of the incident. Apparently he let the impression reach the Nationalists, by a secret telegram to Chang Ch'ün, Chiang Kai-shek's aide, that he did not intend to intervene in the Northern Expedition itself but merely wished to have Japanese rights respected by Nationalists. Foreign Ministry and War Ministry officials likewise desired a diplomatic settlement of the dispute. The General Staff, however, was determined to treat it as a military affair and control any truce agreement that might be concluded with the Chinese. On May 15 the Chief of Staff telegraphed to the commander in Tsinan a new set of peace terms, including a demand for a personal apology by Chiang Kai-shek. These terms went beyond those in Fukuda's ultimatum of May 7. In all probability, the General Staff was not deliberately seeking to obstruct the Nationalists' northward march; the military simply felt that, once the Chinese had betrayed their inability to protect Japanese lives, it was necessary to take resolute action to prevent similar incidents. But the General Staff was acting without regard for the views of the Foreign Ministry, the Prime Minister, or even the War Ministry. And neither Tanaka nor anyone else seemed able to remedy the state of affairs. Instead of attempting to impose some control on the General Staff, the Prime Minister chose one of its officers, General Matsui, as the man who should go to China and seek a solution.[30]

What was the attitude of the Nationalists at this time? Briefly speaking, their response to the Tsinan incident was twofold. The Kuomintang and the Nanking government made every effort to gain sympathy abroad. At the same time, they did all they could to avoid further complications with Japan in order to concentrate on their immediate objective, the conquest of north China. On May 7 the Kuomintang central executive committee declared that the action of the Japanese military was unprincipled and contrary to international law. It accused the Japanese government of disregarding Chinese sovereignty and obstructing the unification of China. The Nationalist government requested the League of Nations to investigate the matter and reprimand the Japanese, and it telegraphed President Coolidge, asking "what attitude you and your people would take regarding the grave situation which has been created by the Japanese." [31]

Meanwhile the Nationalists sought to prevent the situation from becoming more complicated. They were determined to maintain order in Nanking and protect the Japanese consulate there. All meetings and demonstrations were proscribed and anti-Japanese posters ordered removed. The Nanking government directed the local governments and the military council to concentrate on the Northern Expedition, guard against communist agitators who might take advantage of the incident, and let the Tsinan incident be solved through diplomatic channels.[32]

There was thus some willingness on both sides to settle the affair through diplomacy. If the incident had been an isolated occurrence, a solution still might not have been out of the question. But May 1928 saw further complications develop, for Japan began then to take steps in preparation for the Nationalist invasion of north China.

THE LAST DAYS OF CHANG TSO-LIN

Throughout the early months of 1928 Japan's policy makers had been engaged in devising plans to cope with the possibility that north China and then Manchuria might be invaded by the Nationalists. The protection of Japanese rights in Manchuria commanded the immediate attention of officials. Unfortunately, they were still divided as to the specific means of protecting the nation's interests in the Three Eastern Provinces.

In the last chapter mention was made of Kwantung Army officers who were thinking of turning Manchuria into Japan's protectorate. Major Ishihara Kanji, who was to join the staff of the Army in August 1928, had already worked out his war philosophy and strategy. For him the world was destined to witness a really global and total war in the future, and such a war was bound to be fought between Japan and the United States. Why? Because these two countries were preparing for such an eventuality. Unaware of the naive circularity of this reasoning, Ishihara put forth the argument that Japan, in order to be ready for such an inevitable war, should utilize the rich resources of Manchuria and Mongolia. Direct control over these regions was a *sine qua non* for Japan. Generals Muraoka Chōtarō and Saitō Tsune, commander in chief and chief of staff of the Kwantung Army respectively, and other staff officers of the Army did not have even this degree of sophistication, but they all agreed that strong action in Manchuria, leading ultimately to its autonomy under Japanese suzerainty, was most desirable.[33]

These extreme views were at this time confined to a handful of Kwantung Army officers. Responsible officials in Tokyo still believed that forceful measures should be taken only as a last resort and then only to protect Japan's rights in Manchuria and not to bring about a drastic change in its political status. As Arita Hachirō, who had succeeded Kimura as chief of the Foreign Ministry's Asian affairs bureau, stated at this time, "even if we gain one thing in Manchuria and Mongolia the loss would equal the profit if our interests were damaged along the Yangtze and in other areas of China and if our relations with the powers worsened." He maintained that the degree of force used and pressure employed to solve the Manchurian question should be determined only after considering these factors. Agreeing with such a view, Sakonji Seizō, chief of the naval affairs bureau of the Navy Ministry, wrote that the expansion of Japanese influence in Manchuria should be based upon treaty rights and not be carried out by military and other radical means. Force was to be employed only as a last resort.[34]

From this viewpoint, the only question for Japan was whether to safeguard its interests through the Fengtien or through the Nationalist government. Both possibilities were explored simultaneously in the spring of 1928. On the one hand, renewed pressure was put on Chang Tso-lin to honor the existing treaties, including the railway agreement he had concluded with Yamamoto in the previous fall. The Foreign Ministry was considering such measures as the withdrawal of the Japanese legation from Peking and the occupation of the Mukden arsenal, hoping to force the Fengtien authorities to respect Japanese rights in Manchuria. Consul General Yoshida at Mukden, who was soon to be appointed permanent vice foreign minister, was advocating pressure for changes in the transportation and financial systems that would give Japan a status in Manchuria comparable to Britain's in Egypt.[35] Although none of these steps were taken at the time, Chang was persuaded to sanction formally the railway agreement with Yamamoto, and in the middle of May tentative contracts were signed for the Kirin-Kainei, Changchun-Talai, Taonan-Solun, and Yenki-Hailin lines. The contracts were to be announced three months later, and construction was to be started within a year.[36]

On the other hand, the Japanese government was simultaneously keeping in view the possibility of an understanding with the Nationalists. Warning that, if fighting extended to Manchuria, chaos would result, Japan asked that the revolutionary soldiers not pursue northern troops beyond the Great Wall. In return, Japan would guarantee the swift withdrawal of Chang Tso-lin from Peking to Mukden. In January, Prime Minister Tanaka and Chang Ch'ün, Chiang Kai-shek's special envoy then in Tokyo, had reached a tacit agreement on these points. In March the Foreign Ministry sharpened these ideas and tentatively decided that, in order to avoid giving the impression that Japan was behind Chang Tso-lin, it should make the truce agreement conditional upon the retirement of the Old Marshal.[37]

These ideas were developed in late April into a draft memorandum to be communicated to the contending factions in China. After reviewing the progress of the civil war since 1912, the memorandum stated, "It has been the settled policy of Japan, which has a particular interest-relationship with Manchuria, to make the area a place of peace for Japanese and foreigners, and to cooperate in the exploitation of its economic resources for the benefit of all." Therefore, the Japanese government could not tolerate the emergence of a situation which directly or indirectly disrupted order within Manchuria. Such would be the case if, after the war had extended to the Peking-Tientsin area, armed soldiers of north and south should enter the Three Eastern Provinces. Under these circumstances Japan would have to take proper and effective measures to prevent the infiltration of armed Chinese soldiers into Manchuria. This draft declaration concluded by saying that Japan would persist in holding an impartial attitude toward both combatants.[38] This was in effect a warning to north and south to arrange a truce so that fighting would not be extended to Manchuria.

Whether such a policy necessitated Japan's use of force turned on the developments in China. The Chinese themselves might work out a cease-fire. This was in fact the situation in late April. General Li Tsung-jen and other southern generals were reported as saying that whether southerners would extend military action into Jehol and Manchuria depended on the attitude of Fengtien authorities. Li told a Japanese official that if, after withdrawing beyond the Wall, Chang Tso-lin should resign and be replaced by others willing to submit to the Nationalist government, the Nationalists would not need to seek total victory but could terminate military action and start toward the task of reconstruction with such Manchurian leaders as Yang Yü-t'ing and Chang Hsüeh-liang. There was a mounting pressure from influential bodies of Chinese citizens for a north-south compromise, and it appeared that Chang Tso-lin might be persuaded to avoid war and withdraw beyond the Wall or come to some peace arrangements with the southern leaders.[39]

It is very likely that the unexpected incident at Tsinan in early May frustrated the Japanese efforts at a peaceful solution of the Manchurian question. The Sino-Japanese clash in Shantung apparently convinced Chang Tso-lin and his subordinates that withdrawal from Peking was premature. They believed that the northward thrust of the Nationalists would be halted for the time being; consequently they could afford to wait and observe the course of events a little longer. Chang Tso-lin's circular telegram of May 9, in which he urged the Chinese people to come to the support of his effort to exterminate communism, revealed his determination to continue the war until his less radical opponents came to terms with him.[40]

With a renewed possibility of fighting at the Manchurian border the Tokyo government decided to have recourse to force in order to preserve order in Manchuria. Overriding the objections of some officials, the Foreign Ministry drew up a final text of the warning in the middle of May. The draft memorandum of late April was shortened and somewhat modified, and it was decided to communicate it to Chang Tso-lin, Chiang Kai-shek, and other southern generals at the earliest appropriate time. In handing out the memorandum, it was to be explicitly stated that Japan was determined to prevent the entrance of armed soldiers into Manchuria, once the war had spread to the Peking-Tientsin area. Such a measure would be carried out by the Kwantung Army in cooperation with the protocol force in Tientsin. Chang Tso-lin was to be informally advised to retire. If he refused Japan would consider taking further measures.[41]

The draft memorandum and these plans were discussed at the cabinet meeting of May 16, and last-minute changes were made with respect to the crucial issue of Chang Tso-lin's future. Prime Minister Tanaka had continued to entertain the belief that Manchuria's peace could best be maintained and Japanese rights best be safeguarded under the rule of the Old Marshal. Once he was gone there was no assurance that Kuomintang influence would not extend itself into the Three Eastern Provinces and undermine Japanese interests. This view prevailed at the cabinet meeting, and the Foreign Ministry recommendation with regard to Chang's retirement was not accepted.[42]

Though at first this change might appear minor and insignificant, it involved a momentous shift of policy. The cabinet endorsed Tanaka's cherished project of basing Japanese-Manchurian relations on a solid understanding with Chang Tso-lin. The Nationalists were to rule south of the Wall, but Manchuria was to be governed by Chang, with whom Japan would have advantageous agreements. Tanaka believed that Chiang Kai-shek had agreed to some such scheme in the previous fall, and reports from diplomatic representatives in China indicated that such an arrangement might be acceptable to war-weary Nationalists.[43]

Specific instructions were sent to officials in China to communicate the memorandum to Chinese leaders on May 18. These instructions and the cabinet discussion of May 18 clearly revealed the methods to be employed to realize Tanaka's scheme. First of all, he instructed Minister Yoshizawa to urge Chang Tso-lin to lose no time in withdrawing beyond the Wall; at the same time, the consul general at Shanghai was ordered to let the Nationalists understand that, once Chang returned to Manchuria, Japan would never tolerate his meddling in Chinese affairs south of the Wall. Tanaka was trying to divide China through persuasion. If the Chinese factions refused to heed his advice and fighting continued, the warning contained in the memorandum would have to be made good to bring about the desired result. The cabinet meeting of May 18, discussing various problems in connection with the disarming of Chinese soldiers at the Manchurian border, openly endorsed the idea of supporting Chang Tso-lin in Manchuria. The "directives and principles to disarm Chinese soldiers," adopted by the cabinet, stated:

It is necessary to retain the northern forces to some extent. Therefore, while on the surface Japan is to be absolutely impartial toward the northern and southern armies, in practice the military commanders in the field must be counted upon to use discretion and subtle hints.

There is a rather strong anti-Chang Tso-lin atmosphere in Manchuria. Therefore we cannot be sure that the anti-Chang elements might not start rioting and disrupt order. To cope with this situation, it is necessary to retain Fengtien strength. Therefore, it is desirable that the northern army withdraw safely [into Manchuria].

The War Minister telegraphed the Japanese military commanders in China, Korea, and Formosa and explained the content of the May 18 memorandum. He said that Chang Tso-lin would not be advised to retire and that Fengtien soldiers need not be disarmed if they should return to Manchuria in an orderly fashion and keep some distance from the southern army. But the Japanese army was absolutely to refuse the passage of the southerners beyond the Wall. Again on May 18, the Chief of Staff instructed the commander of the Kwantung Army to gather all Japanese forces to Mukden, transfer the Army headquarters also to that city, and wait for orders from Tokyo to have the troops moved to the Chinchow area in order to carry out the disarmament program.[44]

These instructions were put into effect immediately. Within a few days the bulk of Kwantung Army forces and its headquarters were moved to Mukden, ready for action in case Chinese soldiers were to be disarmed. Meanwhile, on the night of May 17–18, Minister Yoshizawa handed the Japanese memorandum to Chang Tso-lin. Yoshizawa bluntly told Chang that everyone agreed that the northern army was going to lose the war to the south and that it was obvious that not only Chang Tso-lin but the entire Fengtien army would be doomed to destruction as a result of the defeat. Therefore, Yoshizawa continued, the Japanese government was out to save Chang and his army, and for him to refuse to accept its advice to return to Manchuria would be a great act of folly. Chang was preoccupied with the question of the future of the Peking government. Saying that the fortunes of war lay in heaven, he refused to take the Japanese minister's advice. In Yoshizawa's opinion, Chang maintained his stubborn opposition because he had expected to be given assistance from Japan without having to forego his authority at Peking. The Marshal must have been disappointed to find in the Japanese memorandum little room for hope.[45]

At Shanghai, in the meantime, Consul General Yada communicated the memorandum to Huang Fu on the morning of May 18. Huang said that the Nationalists had already established the principle of not disregarding Japan in dealing with Manchuria and that the Nationalist government had no intention of moving revolutionary forces beyond Shanhaikwan. On the whole, Yada telegraphed, Huang Fu appeared secretly pleased with his explanation of the memorandum. The Japanese official then delivered the note to C. T. Wang, soon to succeed Huang as Nationalist foreign minister. Wang said, "While this is a very serious matter, it does not seem that the Japanese government's idea is too bad." [46]

By the last week of May the Nationalists seem to have decided not to pursue northern soldiers into Manchuria but instead seek some compromise agreement with them. A Nationalist official told Consul General Yada on May 26, "While our government intends to unify China by military force, we will stop the march of our Nationalist troops at a certain point, if the Fengtien army should realize its own situation." Questioned by Yada about the precise meaning of this message, the Chinese official made it clear in English that the southern army had almost reached its "final destination," and would not take further "military operations" if the Fengtien army should "come to [its] senses." [47] At the same time, the Nationalists approached the northern authorities informally to sound out possibilities for truce arrangements. Southern delegates appeared in Peking toward the end of May and proposed some conditions of peace to Fengtien representatives. The Nationalists were anxious that the northerners agree to Chang Tso-lin's retirement and the withdrawal of the army from the Peking-Tientsin area as conditions for a truce. Beyond these terms, the Nationalists seemed to insist upon the raising of the revolutionary flag in Manchuria and the establishment of a Manchurian political council as an equivalent to the several political councils which had been set up in the areas under Nationalist hegemony. In other words, the Nationalists wanted to see the Three Eastern Provinces fully incorporated into the Kuomintang scheme of government in China. As of the end of May, the Fengtien negotiators seemed to have explicitly accepted only two of the conditions, the retirement of Chang Tso-lin and the withdrawal of his forces beyond the Wall. [48]

The last days of the Manchurian warlord at Peking gave an impression of melancholy inevitability. His position had become impossible. The Fengtien forces had been pushed to the Liuli River line by the Nationalists; his lieutenants, such as Yang Yü-t'ing and Chang Hsüeh-liang, were definitely inclined toward retreat if the Nationalists agreed not to pursue them into Manchuria; and the Japanese had relayed the information that the southerners would not do so. After a series of conferences, the

Manchurian leaders decided to depart from Peking late on the night of June 2. Before departure Chang Tso-lin sent a circular telegram to the Chinese people declaring that, despite his life-long devotion to the service of his people, he could not bring the anti-Red campaign to a successful end and was obliged to leave Peking in order to spare further spilling of blood.[49]

The path appeared to have been opened for a new era of Sino-Japanese relations. The Nationalists as well as Fengtien leaders were apparently content to keep within their bounds and refrain from further hostility and to work out a solution of existing problems with Japanese assistance. The Japanese, on the other hand, were willing to see the Nationalists rule in the south so long as their own predominant interests in Manchuria were left un-attacked. For once Tanaka's policy seemed to be working.

Obstacles immediately arose, however, to the Prime Minister's scheme for a new order. While he went much further than Foreign Ministry officials in explicitly assisting Chang Tso-lin in Manchuria, his plans were not completely satisfactory from the point of view of Kwantung Army extremists who wanted virtual control over the Three Eastern Provinces. In late April they had advised Tokyo of the desirability of disarming Chinese soldiers at Shanhaikwan. This was in line with their desire to extend their influence to the Manchurian border and eventually bring about Japanese hegemony over the region. The May 18 memorandum had given these schemers a long-awaited opportunity. Commander Muraoka of the Army had immediately prepared to dispatch troops to Shanhaikwan.[50]

The disarming of Chinese soldiers at the Manchurian border would have been in accord with the cabinet decision of May 18. For reasons already mentioned, however, Tanaka and the Foreign Ministry hesitated to take this extreme measure. Since the Nationalists hinted that they would not pursue northerners beyond the Wall, it did not seem necessary to take the legally dubious measure of disarming Fengtien soldiers as they entered Manchuria. Though the General Staff in Tokyo supported the Kwantung Army, Tanaka decided, on May 31, against an immediate dispatch of its troops to Shanhaikwan.[51]

When their contemplated action was frustrated, it was natural that some of the Kwantung Army officers should have decided to act alone. General Fukuda had already set a precedent for unilateral action at Tsinan. Exasperated by what they took to be Tanaka's indecision, Colonel Kōmoto Daisaku and several others decided to assassinate Chang Tso-lin on his way back from Peking. The assassination itself was not the ultimate end; Kōmoto's idea was to throw Manchuria into confusion, which would provide a pretext for military action.[52]

The assassination attempt worked according to schedule. With the cooperation of a few officers, Kōmoto obtained a detailed description and schedule of Chang Tso-lin's train. Explosives were hidden on the iron land-bridge outside of Mukden, beneath which the Peking-Mukden Railway passed. On the morning of June 4, as the train of political exiles passed the section crossing the South Manchuria Railway beneath the land-bridge, the explosives were ignited, and Chang Tso-lin's car was blown up with a tremendous roar. Chang died soon afterward.[53]

The assassins' hope that Chang's death would lead to military action was doomed to disappointment. Higher authorities both in Japan and China were determined not to precipitate a crisis. It would be another three years before the Kwantung Army felt ready for another attempt, this time with much stronger determination to carry through their project. Nevertheless, the assassination of Chang Tso-lin, coming on the heels of the Tsinan incident, served to demonstrate the instability and confusion in Japan's decision making and policy executing organs. Lacking strong leadership in Tokyo, Japanese relations with China steadily worsened, while the other powers sat by and by their very caution were laying the ground for understanding with Nationalist China.

AMERICA AND BRITAIN BETWEEN CHINA AND JAPAN

In view of the scarcity of available sources, it is difficult to discuss British policy toward China at this time in sufficient depth. All evidence indicates that the London government neither abandoned nor strongly promoted the policy of Sino-British understanding which had been formulated in 1925. After the Nanking incident Britain had temporarily relinquished its prominent position in China, due primarily to the uncertainty of political and military developments there. The Foreign Office in London as well as its representatives in China were skeptical of the renewed Nationalist bid for mastery of the country in the spring of 1928. They did not believe that the Chinese revolutionaries were united, any more than they had been in the previous year. At the same time, it was necessary to be prepared for an eventual unification of China, and the British government repeatedly assured the Chinese that it would negotiate a treaty of commerce, even restoring tariff autonomy to China, as soon as there was a government which could speak for the entire population and did not discriminate against British interests. As the unsettled Nanking incident was the greatest obstacle in the path of possible *rapprochement* between Nationalists and Britishers, Minister Lampson was instructed in March to broach the subject to Nanking officials. No agreement was reached at this time, however, even though the British terms for a settlement were similar to those offered by the United States, which successfully solved the incident in late March. This may have reflected the Nationalists' desire first of all to obtain American friendship.[54]

In the month of May, as tension mounted between China and Japan, some members of the Parliament expressed concern that Japan was intervening in internal affairs of China, and that Japanese action in Manchuria virtually contemplated turning this region into its protectorate. Foreign Secretary Chamberlain, however, chose to be satisfied by Japanese assurances that all their measures were taken simply in order to protect the nationals and to keep Manchuria from being involved in the civil war. But he also made it amply clear that the British government considered Manchuria part of China and did not recognize Japan's special interests in that territory other than those sanctioned by treaties. As Chamberlain remarked in July, "our interest is a united China under one Government, which can take obligations and keep obligations, and with which we can negotiate a friendly settlement and maintain friendly relations." These verbal professions remained the only positive gestures shown by Britain to the Nationalists during the first half of the year; its principal efforts were devoted to maintaining the safety of its nationals in China.[55]

The United States at first adopted a policy of patient watchfulness. It could not have done otherwise, given the pessimistic view of the Chinese internal conditions entertained by the State Department and the legation in Peking. After he came back from the United States, Minister MacMurray saw little change for the better. In middle February 1928 he wrote a sixteen-page report on the expansion of Kuomintang influence and its effects upon the Chinese people. He felt that the old framework of government had definitely been destroyed but that nothing workable had been substituted. The net result, he wrote, had been "the substitution of a new lot of militarists for the old crowd and the disappointment and disillusionment of the common people who had fatuously believed that the sweeping promise of the Kuomintang propagandists presaged an order of things in which they would enjoy a new freedom and an era of unprecedented prosperity." [56]

During the latter part of February and March, the American minister made a tour of the Yangtze valley region, and succeeded quite rapidly in obtaining satisfaction for the Nanking incident. The Nationalists had apparently decided to effect a *rapprochement* with the United States, and accepted the American terms for settlement in return for MacMurray's expression of regrets over the bombardment of the city of Nanking.[57] Even then, the American minister was not persuaded that the time had come to put into effect the programs for Sino-American friendship which his government had visualized. After concluding the Nanking incident talks, MacMurray planned to proceed to Nanking to reopen the American consulate, with proper ceremonies incident to the raising of the flag. Foreign Minister Huang Fu tried to arrange this, but was unsuccessful because Chiang Kai-shek had departed for the front, and no arrangement could be made for the raising of the American flag with full military honors. Huang had to confess to MacMurray that "having no troops of his own he could not arrange anything satisfactory with the military . . . and that if he were to get a guard of honor for the purpose he could not [be] sure that they would not commit some new act of affront to [the American] flag." [58]

On April 7, MacMurray sent a lengthy telegram to Washington,

setting forth the conclusions he had reached. Weakness, inco-
herence, and futility were the words he used to describe the
Nationalist government. He said,

I had hoped and expected to find even amid the known confusion
definite elements of purpose and of patriotic idealism. I was disappointed to find then [sic] practically negligible degree of any such men
in the vast complex of self-seeking jealousy and intrigue into which
the movement has disintegrated. . . . Among the leaders in the South
as in the North there is today no guiding purpose or principle outside
of the self-interest of certain militarists who have grouped themselves
together for their own common profit though with no faith in each
other's loyalty. . . . One who is sympathetic with the temper of the
Chinese and has a certain acquaintance with them cannot escape the
feeling that here is China at its worst — its old traditions fallen into
disrespect, its new sophomoric ideals curdled with cynicism — the
whole thing turned into a derisive scramble for territories and taxes
with no rules for the game.

Regarding the resumption of the Northern Expedition, the American official reported, "nobody really wants the Northern Expedition but . . . they find themselves in a position in which
they cannot abandon it without loss of face. They have only a
praying hope of its success and a dread of the added confusion
and disorganization that would result from its failure." After the
launching of the expedition in April, MacMurray was certain that
the danger of outrages against foreigners in the path of the revolutionary forces would be real.[59]

In Washington private expressions by policy makers revealed
similar attitudes in eary 1928. In March, Assistant Secretary Johnson wrote to a friend that he found "little to choose between the
military men of Hunan and the one who is the top dog in Manchuria." The American government did what it could to be in
a state of preparedness in order to protect its nationals during the
period of the resumed Northern Expedition. The basic attitude
of the State Department was similar to that taken by the Foreign
Office in London, namely to evacuate nationals in China from
areas of danger, but to keep armed forces in readiness to be employed in case of emergency. As of January 1928, there were over
four thousand American troops, comprised of marines and in-
fantry, in the Peking-Tientsin region and twelve hundred marines

in Shanghai, and nearly eight thousand British marines in these regions. These were the largest foreign contingents in China, excluding over ten thousand Japanese troops in Manchuria. When Admiral Mark L. Bristol, succeeding Clarence S. Williams as commander in chief of the American Asiatic fleet, recommended a reduction in size of American marines at Tientsin, as such a step would create goodwill throughout China, the State Department overrode the suggestion. Given its image of the critical situation in China, it did not agree that the time was opportune to reduce American forces. Until the outcome of the second Northern Expedition became clearer, friendship with China was an academic question with no practical implications.[60]

The Sino-Japanese clash in the spring of 1928 was not entirely unexpected by American officials. In January, Minister Mac-Murray had written, "I am beginning to doubt whether the Powers concerned are going to be able to sit by quietly until the Chinese themselves bring order out of the present chaos." He added that the Japanese "are coming more and more to feel, possibly more subconsciously than otherwise, the inevitable cogency of this." In view of the prevailing concern with the safety of Americans in China it is perhaps not surprising that American officials there generally welcomed Japan's new Shantung expedition. The consul at Tsingtao reported that the arrival of Japanese troops "has brought a feeling of relief as it did last year, and this even among Chinese, especially those of the substantial class, notwithstanding the pro forma protests of the officials." The American consuls at Tsinan made similar observations, and they readily agreed to the Japanese defense plan for the city. After the outbreak of the Tsinan incident on May 3, American officials in China were initially sympathetic with the Japanese action. For the American minister in Peking, the incident was an inevitable result of "the gross failure of the so-called Nationalist leaders to face realities and exercise their authority to avert the possibility of a clash with the Japanese." He strongly opposed mediation by the United States as it would be construed as "an effort to champion Chinese 'nationalism' against Japanese 'aggression.'" At Tsinan, Consul Price blamed the poor discipline of Chinese troops for the outbreak of the incident. He felt that the Japanese ultimatum of May 7 was not without justification in view of the "presence of numerous bodies of Chinese troops in the immediate environs of the foreign settlement." He was impressed by the fact that the Japanese forces had not caused much damage to the Chinese civilian population.[61]

In Washington, the American government likewise sought to avoid involvement in the Sino-Japanese conflict. When the Nanking government cabled President Coolidge, asking his opinion about the Japanese action in Shantung, the State Department decided not to express any views as "it did not know all the facts." The United States chose to believe officially that the Japanese troops in Shantung were there solely for the purpose of protecting their nationals and that they would be withdrawn as soon as military protection was no longer necessary. When the Swedish minister suggested to Assistant Secretary Johnson that the Japanese action was contrary to the Nine-Power Treaty, the latter replied that "in view of the status upon which the troops were sent in, it did not seem to us at the present time that the treaty was in any way involved." [62]

If the United States did not champion China's cause, it consciously tried to avoid giving the impression of endorsing Japanese action. This was evidenced, for example, when around this time the military commanders of the powers in Tientsin discussed measures to protect their nationals in the city. On May 11 the Japanese general urged that Chinese troops be excluded from the twenty-li zone around Tientsin, according to the provisions of the 1902 treaties between China and the powers (not including the United States). He further proposed that this zone be cleared of northern troops before the arrival of the Nationalists. General Smedley Butler, commanding the American marine force, proved the obstacle to this scheme. Following the position Admiral Bristol was taking, General Butler took an independent position in these discussions, considering it best "to attend to our own 'knitting' and not become involved in any dark and devious intrigues." The American brigade devised its own plan for the defense of nationals.[63]

The Japanese note of May 18 presented a greater problem to the American government because it obviously represented interference in the Chinese civil war. At Peking, Minister MacMurray accurately analyzed the situation and said the Japanese "definitely sought to bring about elimination of Chang from Peking, possibly with a view to bringing into power here, even if only temporarily, some regime with which Japan would be able to deal successfully." The American minister suggested that the Japanese government had tried to ingratiate itself with the Nationalists by indirectly aiding their conquest of Peking. In Washington, the response to the May 18 memorandum was more cautious and couched in legal phraseology. When the content of the memorandum was relayed to Washington on May 17, Stanley K. Hornbeck, the new chief of the Far Eastern division, analyzed it. He correctly judged that "Japan evidently intends to draw a dividing line in China with Manchuria on one side and the middle kingdom on the other." But Hornbeck's response to the move remained technical and legal. He noted that the Japanese government had not sought the assent or approval of the United States in its action. Nor, his comment continued, had there been any communication between the United States and the other powers regarding joint intervention or intervention by one power with the consent of others. Hornbeck then reiterated the stand taken by his government regarding the Chinese situation: "The American government has maintained a position of absolute neutrality as among the Chinese contending factions and has at all times abstained from any action which would place an obstacle in the way of their carrying their conflicts to a definite conclusion. [It] has always stood for the maintenance of the territorial and administrative integrity of China, envisaging thereby a unitary as distinguished from a partitioned and divided China." He concluded that the United States had not been asked "to modify its views or to participate in any action looking toward the amending, modification or disregard of any of the provisions of the Nine Powers Treaty." While Hornbeck saw dangerous implications in Japan's May 18 warning, he found little that the United States could or should do since it had not been explicitly invited to approve or disprove of the warning.[64]

Kellogg, on the other hand, was disturbed that Tanaka, when announcing his action to the foreign representatives in Tokyo, had remarked that "the Japanese Government were prepared fully to fulfill their obligations in any joint measures which may be taken for the protection of foreign lives and property in Tientsin." On May 18 the Secretary telegraphed MacMurray, "I am not aware of any obligations under the protocol to participate in any joint measures for the protection of foreign lives in Peking or Tientsin. . . . There will be no participation by the United States in joint action with the Japanese Government or any other power to prevent the extension of Chinese hostilities to Manchuria or to interfere with the controlled military operation of Chinese armies, but solely for the protection of American citizens." Kellogg was cautious not to make any public pronouncement which might betray his suspicion of the Japanese motives. At press conferences he stated that he had no comments to make and only confirmed the stand of the United States that Manchuria was a part of China. When the reports of these press conferences were printed in an exaggerated fashion in Japan, they gave the impression that the Secretary was somewhat disturbed by the action on the part of Japan. When Tanaka instructed the Japanese ambassador in Washington to make inquiries, Kellogg strongly denied that he had made any such statement.[65]

Thus there is no substance to the view sometimes presented that Kellogg's strong comments so alarmed Tanaka that he decided to call off his plan of dispatching troops to Shanhaikwan. Nor does it seem that at this time the possibility of American-Japanese conflict was contemplated by any responsible civilian official of the United States. Few would have agreed with Ambassador MacVeagh that the action taken by Japan with regard to the retreat of northern troops to Manchuria was "entirely consistent with the maintenance of the rights of China and the principle of the Open Door." Official and private expressions of views by the State Department demonstrate, however, that the American government remained convinced that there should and could be no real conflict between Japan and the United States. As Johnson wrote in early June, "All of the evidence seems to point to the friendliest of feelings between us and the Japanese which should continue more or less indefinitely. I find it difficult to see where Japanese and American interests can come into conflict in the Far East to such an extent as to make for hostilities." [66] Even while the United States held to the principle of understanding with China, it continued to profess friendship with Japan. It was as if American policy toward China were undisturbed by and unrelated to what was happening between Japan and China. This attitude was in sharp contrast to naval thinking; navy planners in Washington continued to study strategy for an eventual "Orange War," and in 1928 the principle of "strategic offensive" in the western Pacific was reaffirmed.[67] The bifurcation between foreign policy and military thinking was still very much in evidence, as was the unrelatedness between American policy toward China and toward Japan. Such trends in American policy, which were also clearly discernible in Japanese policy, were a necessary sequel to the collapse of the Washington system of international relations. They were in effect an expression of the failure of these powers to define a workable system comparable to that of the diplomacy of imperialism.

By June 1928, it was evident that Japan's initiative in China, aimed at creating a new order of peace and coprosperity, had ended in dismal failure. Several factors were responsible for this outcome. The basic vision of a new order was not one acceptable to the Chinese. They could not long have tolerated a system of Sino-Japanese cooperation in which Japanese economic interests, especially trade with China and investment in Manchuria, were strictly safeguarded. Under Tanaka, moreover, the line of command of policy execution broke down, and the military were allowed to play increasingly important roles. There was as yet no "Manchurian incident." The Tanaka cabinet still retained some control over the Kwantung Army, and the Army had as yet no pretext for military action. Finally, both Shidehara and Tanaka tended to isolate their policies toward China; there was no thought of developing an over-all, well-integrated policy encompassing all aspects of foreign relations. They did not think it was necessary to seek American or British support of Japanese claims in China; neither were they antagonized by these countries' indifference during the Sino-Japanese dispute. Japanese officials continued to stress economic ties with Britain and the United States, but they saw nothing contradictory between these ties and pursuing an independent course of action in China. The result was the isolation of China and Japan in Far Eastern affairs. This, coupled with the divorce of economic policy and military policy in Japan, would have serious repercussions on Japanese diplomacy when China was once again unified and started actively pursuing its own objectives in foreign affairs.

Part Three

• THE CHINESE INITIATIVE

VII · CHINA BECOMES A POWER, 1928-1929

After the middle of 1928, with the Nationalist unification of China at least nominally completed, Chinese diplomacy became the most decisive factor in international relations in the Far East. The Nationalists, who had rejected the Russian bid for a new order and who had just witnessed what the Japanese new order would entail, were determined to inject their own vision of a new era in the Far East.

In this quest for a new order the Nationalists could easily take advantage of the well-demonstrated desires of the powers for cooperation with China. First the United States and then other powers, including Japan, recognized the Nationalist government and entered into negotiation for new treaties. The general outline of these negotiations has been well drawn by historians. Our primary concern will be with the way China's conception of the new order affected the policies of other countries, in particular Japan.

THE AMERICAN LEAD IN CHINA

Four days after the assassination of Chang Tso-lin, the vanguard of the Nationalist revolutionary forces entered Peking. A month later, on July 6, 1928, the four principal generals of the second Northern Expedition — Chiang Kai-shek, Feng Yü-hsiang, Yen Hsi-shan, and Li Tsung-jen — visited the Piyun Temple at Western Hills near Peking, where Sun Yat-sen's remains had temporarily lain. In an atmosphere charged with emotions they reported to the "father of the nation" the consummation of his dreams. The Nationalist unification of the country, which Sun and his followers had outlined in 1905 and which had entered its final stage in 1926, now seemed accomplished.

One of the first goals of the Nationalists after their military victory at home was to obtain recognition abroad. They were particularly solicitous of American goodwill as the solution of the Nanking incident had cleared the way for *rapprochement* between the two countries, while Britain, Russia, and Japan had successively alienated Nationalist opinion in recent months. At the same time, desiring to revise treaty relations with all countries, the Nanking government issued a mandate, on July 7, declaring its intention of replacing all unequal treaties with new arrangements. It declared that all treaties which had already expired were *ipso facto* abrogated, and those that had not would be terminated "in accordance with proper procedure." New treaties would in time be concluded, but in the meantime interim regulations would be promulgated by the Nationalist government.[1]

The United States was the first to respond favorably to these moves. Sino-American *rapprochement* had been delayed due to the instability in China. In fact, even as late as June 4 Assistant Secretary Johnson was writing that the "taking of Peking will merely bring into prominence once more the fact that there are within the Nationalist forces certain elements which are at odds with each other. I think most of us hope that these elements will be able to work out some kind of a method of cooperation among themselves, but we will have to wait and see." Secretary of State Kellogg, however, was desirous of taking the first opportunity to express America's friendship with China, once the Nationalists displayed some promise of stability and permanence. In early July he decided that the time had come for action. On July 11, Kellogg explicitly stated, in his telegraphic instruction to Minister MacMurray, that "It is the opinion here that in the near future understandings should be effected with the Government at Nanking, which apparently is demonstrating a capacity to establish itself in China as the accepted government." [2]

The reasoning behind this decision was simple. By agreeing to deal with the Nanking government, the United States would at last be contributing to improvement in Sino-American relations and to the peace in the Far East. As Kellogg told MacMurray, only a strong, centralized government could check chaos and disorder in China and contribute to peaceful conditions in that part of the world. According to Johnson, "conditions had proceeded to such a point in China where anything that we could do to give encouragement to those interested in setting up a stable government should be given." [3]

The upshot of this policy was the signing of a new tariff treaty on July 25. It provided for the nullification of existing treaties relating to tariffs and granted tariff autonomy to China, in return for the mutual grant of most-favored-nation treatment. These provisions were to become effective on January 1, 1929, the date the Peking Tariff Conference had proposed as the point at which the principle of tariff autonomy might be granted to the Chinese. The treaty marked the beginning of an era of Sino-American understanding, of which Kellogg had long dreamed. The implications of this friendship were not always evident, but it was significant that the United States was the first power to have favorably responded to China's initiative. Perhaps it was the Nationalists' desire for understanding with the United States that led to their ready acceptance of the most-favored-nation clause as a condition for tariff autonomy. The Chinese had long opposed this clause in their negotiations with Japanese. At any rate, the United States considered the signing of the treaty as constituting recognition of the Nationalist government, and the latter's effort to cultivate American goodwill had been amply rewarded. [4]

It cannot be said, of course, that from this point on the United States had a definite policy of bilateral friendship with China. For one thing, the Nationalists were far from being united, once their joint military goal had been achieved. Their disunity became apparent already in early August, when the fifth plenary session of the Kuomintang central executive committee was convened. The conference marked the end of the military period and transition to the "tutelage period" of the Nationalist revolution. The conference adopted the principle of the five-power constitution and created a forty-six-member political council including representatives ranging from extreme right to extreme left. It also resolved that the military command and organization be "absolutely unified," conscription adopted, the military budget held to half the national budget, military education systematized, and surplus troops turned to the cultivation of land. But there was a heated debate on an important issue: abolition of political councils. The Kwangtung faction, comprising the leftists, proposed that these councils be abolished as they had been established only for military purposes during the Northern Expedition. Now that the nation was unified, it was maintained, the central government should rule every province directly. The Kwangsi militarists opposed the suggestion; undoubtedly they wanted to preserve their own position as heads of these councils at Canton and Wuhan. They were finally persuaded to agree to the abolition of the political councils as of December 1928, but the appearance of disunity among the Nationalists was real enough, and it apparently had some effect upon Manchurian leaders' hesitance in coming to the Nationalist fold immediately. Reporting on the conference, the American legation in Peking telegraphed that "the dissensions within the Kuomintang are sufficiently serious to jeopardize the carrying out of any genuine program of reconstruction," and that "Chiang thus far has been but partially successful in his attempts to maintain harmony." [5]

These reports, coupled with the continued occupation of American properties by Nationalist soldiers, cautioned the State Department against assuming that China was completely unified and stable. Still, the United States government was interested in strengthening the ties with the new leaders of China. Even Minister MacMurray, who had been the most vocal critic of the Nationalists, conceded that there were some hopeful signs in the new China. Telegraphing Washington in September, he pointed out that, while instability and selfishness still characterized the Nanking regime, it nevertheless personified "the as yet vague Nationalist aspirations of the people." He hoped that these aspirations would in the end triumph over the economic and political difficulties facing the country. MacMurray concluded by saying,

A considerable proportion of the more important Chinese classes have been shaken out of their lethargy and while at present their energies are too often misdirected, these may in time be diverted into genuinely progressive channels. The small leaven of clear headed and patriotic civilian leaders who although in a hopeless minority remain undiscouraged by the conditions, deserve the greatest sympathy. . . . I still [have hope] in the ultimate emergency [sic] of something good from the intellectual movement that has been begun. [6]

State Department policy at this time was in accord with such a spirit of sympathy. When Sun Fo, son of Sun Yat-sen and an influential member of the Nationalist government, visited the United States to solicit assistance from American businessmen, he was cordially received by the Department. While the Washington government held to the position that loan arrangements with Chinese were "a private and not a government business," from this time on American bankers and corporations became actively interested in doing business in China, particularly in the fields of public utilities and transportation. Within a few months after the completion of the Northern Expedition, over two million dollars were loaned to the Communications Ministry to install telephone facilities at Nanking, Shanghai, and Wuhan; the Radio Corporation of America signed a contract for constructing a wireless station in Shanghai; the Shanghai Power Company, incorporated in the State of Delaware, took over control of the international settlement's power plant; and two American firms supplied airplanes and pilots for China's new aviation industry. Moreover, the Nanking government took advantage of the provisions in the Burlingame treaty of 1868, in which the United States expressed willingness to supply technical advisers and experts to China, and succeeded in procuring a number of American economic advisers, who left for China early in 1929.[7]

The improvement in Sino-American relations was in sharp contrast to a further deterioration of China's relation with Japan. Not that the assassination of Chang Tso-lin had resulted in open hostilities between the two countries. Prime Minister Tanaka, for once, stood resolute against further rash action by the Kwantung Army, which had given a blow to his project of creating a domain of peace and coprosperity through understanding with Chang. In view of the unexpected turn of events, Tanaka counseled caution in dealing with Fengtien leaders. Soon after the incident, he directed the Japanese military and civilian officials in Manchuria to endeavor to ease anti-Japanese tension that might result from Chang Tso-lin's accident and to be particularly cautious not to complicate the situation further by some impetuous action. At the cabinet meeting of June 7, the Minister of War presented two proposals for extending the functions of the Kwantung Army.

He proposed that the Army be authorized to proceed to areas along the Peking-Mukden Railway in order to disarm disorderly troops, and, in case some fighting broke out, to concentrate Japanese residents in Manchuria in centers like Harbin and Kirin. Such an authorization would have given the Japanese army greater freedom of movement and could have led to a gradual extension of its power throughout Manchuria. These proposals were rejected at the cabinet meeting, however, on the ground that circumstances necessitating such action did not seem imminent. Tanaka was unwilling to mobilize a huge number of troops to protect every Japanese community in Manchuria. In the worst case, he thought all Japanese residents could be evacuated to the areas belonging to the South Manchuria Railway.[8]

This decision by the Tokyo government frustrated the hope of those within the Kwantung Army who had expected the assassination of Chang Tso-lin to create such confusion in Manchuria that they would be able to stage a coup and bring about a new order of things. Hoping to find a pretext for military occupation, they staged a few bombing incidents in the commercial port of Mukden, but these acts did not result in any retaliation by Chinese who remained quiet throughout.[9]

The day of reckoning was postponed. But the Japanese government still had to formulate its policy toward Manchuria, now that the supreme warlord was gone. Should Japan continue the policy of solving the Manchurian question in Manchuria, that is, through Chang's successors rather than through the Nanking government? Who should these successors be? What if they decided to reach a compromise with the Nationalists or even join the Nanking government? These were questions which bothered Prime Minister Tanaka, who did not adopt a definite policy until the middle of July.

The Japanese military in China were strong advocates of the view that Manchuria should never come under Kuomintang influence. They would put pressure on the new leaders of Manchuria, such as Chang Hsüeh-liang and Yang Yü-t'ing, to tend to the consolidation of their strength in Manchuria and avoid any compromise with the south. In the middle of June two Japanese officers left Mukden for the front to see Chang Hsüeh-liang and persuade him that he and other leaders should now maintain the *status quo* and not compromise with the south by raising the revolutionary flag. Tatekawa Yoshitsugu, attaché at Peking, suggested on June 25 that Japan notify Manchurian authorities of its views regarding "the issue of changing the flag." He asserted,

I believe it is the most necessary and urgent task for Japan to state explicitly that it will not be pleased to see the Nationalist flag raised in Manchuria and Mongolia, to direct the Manchurian government not to submit to the southern regime, by forceful and threatening measures if necessary, and as soon as possible to have [Manchurian leaders] declare themselves to be independent of the south, under the principle of "maintaining the security of the border and pacifying the people," exterminate dangerous activities internally, and devote themselves solely to the unification and maintenance of order within the Three Eastern Provinces.

He added that foreigners, especially Britishers, insisted that Japan should not miss this chance to solve the Manchurian problem once and for all. On July 6 Tatekawa repeated his plea that Japan take positive action now and have Chang Hsüeh-liang, who had been appointed commander in chief of the Three Eastern Provinces, declare that he would dissociate himself from the south and create a "prosperous utopia" in Manchuria with Japanese assistance.[10]

The views of professional diplomats were radically different. As early as June 20, Consul General Hayashi Kyūjirō, who had succeeded Yoshida at Mukden, had come to the conclusion that Manchuria would inevitably come under the Nationalist flag. Therefore he advised the Tokyo government to study policy alternatives to be followed in such an eventuality. On July 16 he telegraphed Tanaka, "Judging from the conditions today, it seems that we cannot stop the raising of the revolutionary flag unless we were to resort to force to prevent it." Consequently, he continued, "would it not be best for us to ascertain, as much in detail as possible, what Hsüeh-liang's attitude would be toward observing the existing treaties, to proceed further with the negotiation of the railway problem, and, on the basis of these, to decide to support Hsüeh-liang after the changing of the flag?" Minister Yoshizawa expressed his complete agreement with these ideas. Professional diplomats believed that Japan should acquiesce in the political union of Manchuria and China proper and concentrate on the protection of legitimate rights. It was assumed that, in the event of the union, Chang Hsüeh-liang would retain control over Manchuria's foreign affairs.[11]

Prime Minister Tanaka wavered between these two views. He was at first opposed to taking any forceful measures in Manchuria; he and the members of his cabinet agreed that to impose Japan's will with force would make the Manchurians suspicious of its "true intentions" and might even drive them to the south as a measure of self-defense. At the same time Tanaka and his government continued to hold the view that Manchuria was all-important for Japan and that it should not again be involved in shifting military alignments and political machinations south of the Wall. They hoped that the Three Eastern Provinces would walk their own path, without being influenced by developments in the south. In reply to Consul General Hayashi's warning that Manchuria might accept the southern flag at any moment, Tanaka telegraphed on June 25, "It would be disadvantageous from various points of view for the Three Eastern Provinces to take hastily a welcoming attitude toward the south. It will be necessary for the Three Eastern Provinces themselves and desirable for us that they maintain the *status quo* for the time being and observe the trend of events under the principle of maintaining the security of the border and pacifying the people." This was a policy of patient watchfulness, neither endorsing nor openly and forcefully opposing Manchuria's joining China proper.[12]

Such an attitude was perhaps the most realistic response to the situation in China. The Nationalists had often intimated that they would fully respect Japanese rights in China and Manchuria. Chang Hsüeh-liang had also stated that, even if he might subscribe to the "three people's principles" in the future, he would never unilaterally abrogate the treaties with Japan. Moreover, Chang was far from contemplating a total submission of the Three Eastern Provinces to Kuomintang rule. What he was seeking was an alliance with the Nationalists on the basis of his retention of control over Manchuria in return for its acceptance of the revolutionary flag. Under the circumstances, Tanaka's policy of waiting was calculated to serve Japan's interests without causing undue friction between the two countries.[13]

Then came the July 7 manifesto by the Nationalists, abrogating all unequal treaties. It was this strong assertion of China's diplomatic initiative which caused Tanaka to modify his policy. As the attempts for revision of the Sino-Japanese treaty of 1896 had all failed, the Tokyo government had expected that the Nanking government would unilaterally terminate the treaty on July 20 when it was to expire. The anticipated happened. On July 19 the Nationalists communicated a note to the Japanese minister at Peking, abrogating the treaties of 1896 and 1903. The obvious implications were that the same fate would eventually meet the treaties of 1905, 1915, and other years guaranteeing Japanese rights in Manchuria.[14]

On July 18 Tanaka made up his mind. Reports from diplomatic and military officials in Manchuria indicated the imminence of a north-south *rapprochement*. Tanaka was not persuaded by the argument of civilian officials that Japan should acquiesce in the union of north and south and concentrate its effort on securing the protection of existing treaty rights. In view of the Nationalist abrogation of the treaties, these rights would not long withstand their attack once they extended influence to Manchuria. Consequently, Tanaka instructed Consul General Hayashi at Mukden to warn Chang Hsüeh-liang against joining the south. At the same time, Hayashi was to promise that, if Chang should persist in a policy of neutrality, Japan would "consider sympathetically measures to strengthen his position" and to prevent the military invasion of Manchuria by Nationalists or armed uprisings within Manchuria.[15]

To make sure that Chang got the message, Tanaka further entrusted Baron Hayashi Gonsuke, who was leaving for Mukden to attend the funeral of Chang Tso-lin, with the task of repeating his warning. On July 31 the Prime Minister saw Baron Hayashi and expounded his views on Manchuria. He reiterated that he had no intention of making Manchuria a Japanese colony or protectorate but only wanted to make it safe for foreign and Japanese business activities, according to the principles of the open door and equal opportunity. In this revealing conversation the Prime Minister said,

I still hope that China will be fundamentally unified and I will do what I can to see the ideal achieved. But there is positively no need for us to sacrifice our ideas regarding Manchuria for the sake of promoting the unification. It is because I thought we would automatically come to the control of Manchuria that I helped the cause of China's unification for a long time. . . . There are those who say that the adoption of the "three people's principles" and the revolutionary flag means little. I am convinced, however, that "a fallen leaf will suggest the coming of autumn," and that Japan's intentions can never be carried out unless the infiltration of southern forces [to Manchuria] can be prevented.

Tanaka asked Hayashi to promise Chang Hsüeh-liang that Japan would give him financial and other assistance if he would accept the principle of Manchurian autonomy. Japan could also give up extraterritoriality if its residents were granted freedom of residing and engaging in business in Manchuria. Nowhere in this talk did Tanaka intimate that he was willing to put military pressure upon the Young Marshal to prevent his union with the Nationalists. The Prime Minister still believed that he could sufficiently influence Chang by verbal suasion.[16]

It is difficult to determine Chang Hsüeh-liang's precise attitude at this time. His peace terms had been accepted almost totally by the Nationalists, and Chiang Kai-shek had warned him against succumbing to Japan. At the same time, it seems likely that Chang thought he could still play on Japan's fear of his union with Nanking and use it to his own advantage. Practically every commentator on this subject has written that the Young Marshal, who already knew who had killed his father, was burning with revengeful thought and determined to dislodge Japanese completely from Manchuria. If these were his ideas, he did not show them at this time. Actually it seems more correct to say that as a realistic politician he could not entirely disregard Japan's offer of assistance, given the intricate power struggle both in Manchuria and in China proper. There is evidence, for example, that Chang was disturbed by the activities of Kuomintang agents in Manchuria and hoped the Japanese authorities might suppress them. He liked to call his policy one of "autonomy and compromise."[17]

This does not mean that Tanaka's policy of moral suasion was a success. To the warnings of both Consul General Hayashi and Baron Hayashi the Young Marshal demurred and agreed only to a temporary suspension of peace talks with Nanking. Being in a good bargaining position, he could play with time, hoping thereby to obtain the best possible terms of compromise with the Nationalists. That is to say, Tanaka's policy was utterly fruitless, and it was simply utilized by Chang Hsüeh-liang for his own advantage and probably even accelerated his union with the Nationalists.[18]

JAPAN'S RETREAT

Given the two divergent policies pursued in China by the United States and Japan, it is not surprising that these two powers should have developed mutual suspicions. American officials were well aware of Japanese designs on Manchuria in the summer of 1928. Immediately after the mysterious explosion of Chang Tso-lin's train on June 4, the State Department received a report that the Chinese in Mukden unanimously believed that Japanese were implicated. Consul General Myers thought it would "apparently require very convincing evidence to overcome the opinion which the Chinese have formed as to the origin of this incident." He reported that "the strongest suspicion will rest on the Japanese military until evidence of a very conclusive nature is disclosed exonerating them, which under the circumstances seems doubtful." The consul general believed that the Japanese plot was evidence of the Tanaka government's determination to assert Japan's special prerogatives in Manchuria. "It would seem," Myers concluded on June 13, "that unless the Nationalist Government recognizes this special position and also comes to an agreement with the Japanese over certain important issues . . . an independent government under Japanese protection will very likely be the outcome."[19]

Toward the end of July, when Consul General Myers learned that his Japanese colleague had warned Chang Hsüeh-liang not to join the south hastily, he reported that the Japanese "were endeavoring to perpetuate the existing condition of factional control" in Manchuria as they objected "to the extension of National-

ist authority to Manchuria until, at least, Japan's position and interests are fully recognized by the Nationalist Government."
Japan seemed to continue its policy of upholding its position and
of protecting its interests in Manchuria, Myers continued. Consequently, as the existence of Manchuria as an autonomous state
to ensure these ends was not possible except under the hegemony
of Japan, Japan faced a crisis. On July 31 Myers advised Minister
MacMurray that the Japanese had implied a military threat in
their warning to Chang Hsüeh-liang, their real desire being "obviously [the] creation of an autonomous state under Japanese influence." The Japanese were "extremely anxious to force provo-
cations, and consequently further demands [are] not impossible." [20]

It is extremely unlikely that the State Department was overly
alarmed by these reports or that its policy of friendship toward
the Nationalists resulted in a stiffer attitude toward Japan. Washington's policies toward China and Japan were still very much
uncoordinated, and the Sino-Japanese crisis had no apparent impact on the professed policy of understanding both with China
and Japan. A good example of this is the State Department's decision not to object to the floating by the Morgan and Company
of a twenty-million-dollar bond issue in the United States, to
refinance previous loans to the South Manchuria Railway. The
United States was also solicitous of Japan's adherence to the
Kellogg-Briand Pact. When Japan, for domestic constitutional
reasons, raised an objection to the phraseology in the pact, stating
that the signatories made the declaration "in the names of their
respective peoples," Kellogg was willing to make an exception
and accept the Japanese interpretation of the phrase.[21]

Some Japanese officials nevertheless believed that the United
States, by its concessions to Nanking, was making it very difficult
for Japan to patch up differences with China. The consul at Nanking commented that the Sino-American agreement of July 25 at
once strengthened the stature of C. T. Wang and other American-
educated officials, often identified as the "pro-American faction,"
within the Nationalist government, and made the solution of
Sino-Japanese disputes harder than ever. Minister Yoshizawa in
Peking was obviously irritated by the "popularity courting policy"

of the United States. He believed that by unilaterally concluding the new tariff agreement the United States had repudiated the Washington customs treaty. Such an act of irresponsibility, cabled the Japanese minister, should serve as a precedent for Japan, when, in the future, it decided not to abide by the Washington treaties. Finally, Arita, chief of the Asian affairs bureau, was dissuaded from going to Nanking to discuss the Manchurian question, because the Sino-American agreement was signed just before his departure and he realized that the Nanking government would not be satisfied with anything less than diplomatic recognition and the restoration of tariff autonomy, which the United States had already granted.[22]

Subsequent American professions of sympathy for the Nanking government tended to intensify the image of close ties between the United States and China. Contemporary observers in Japan particularly recognized a positive policy on the part of the American government to come to the aid of the Chinese, to the detriment of Japanese interests.[23]

Given the picture of Sino-American *rapprochement,* Japan had to decide on a new course of action. It could either retract its strong stand in China and seek friendly relations with the Nationalists, bring about renewed understanding with the United States and other powers in order to solve the China question within the framework of international cooperation, or pursue the policy of consolidating its interests in Manchuria regardless of the attitudes of Nanking and Washington. In the summer and early fall of 1928 all these policies were tried simultaneously, further complicating Japanese-American relations.

The third alternative, continuation of strong and independent policy in Manchuria, was naturally most strongly advocated by the military. In August the General Staff proposed that in the event Chang Hsüeh-liang refused to accept the Japanese warning against joining the Nanking regime, Japan should sever connections with him, observe the trend of events, and, in case Japanese treaty rights were violated, take military action for self-defense. In this eventuality, Japan was to seek the establishment of a pro-Japanese regime in Manchuria by expelling the members of the "new faction" like Chang and Yang Yü-t'ing. The Tanaka cabinet was opposed to such forceful measures and continued to rely on moral suasion to prevent the political union of Manchuria and China. At the same time, the Tokyo government was determined to promote Japan's economic interests in Manchuria even before the political issue was settled. Tanaka instructed Consul General Hayashi to carry on negotiations for the opening of Manchuria to Japanese residence and business, and he authorized the South Manchuria Railway to push its construction program according to the Chang-Yamamoto agreement of the preceding May. At this time Japan was willing to make certain concessions in order to consolidate its rights and interests in Manchuria before Nationalist authority extended to that region. The Foreign Ministry decided in late September that, in return for the Manchurian authorities' promise to open up Manchuria completely to foreigners, Japan would declare its intention of giving up extraterritoriality after a certain period. On the railway issue, too, President Yamamoto of the South Manchuria Railway was willing to consider favorably certain conditions which the Manchurian government was imposing in return for the putting into effect of the Chang-Yamamoto agreement.[24]

This was one approach to the Chinese situation. While thus continuing its independent policy in Manchuria, the Japanese government also pursued the second alternative, namely *rapprochement* with the Nationalists. This course of action was strongly advocated by professional diplomats. Minister Yoshizawa more than once had criticized Tanaka's "rough approach" toward Manchuria. Having specifically in mind the implications of such a policy in Sino-Japanese relations, he argued, in mid-August 1928, that "if we further incite the Nanking government we will either be giving a chance to the Kuomintang leftists and communists to gain power, or driving [the Nationalists] to reliance on Britain and the United States. Or else we will be encouraging the Nationalists once again to approach Soviet Russia." Japan should therefore come to some compromise with the Nanking leaders on outstanding issues with a view to "guiding" them. Specifically, Japan should agree to commence negotiations on treaty revision, reserving its position on the validity of the existing treaties. Yoshizawa repeated his plea that Japan be tolerant of such abstractions as the revolutionary flag and the "three people's principles" in Manchuria and rather be firm on promoting Japan's concrete economic interests there.[25]

Such ideas were eventually accepted by the Tanaka cabinet, which decided to effect *rapprochement* with Nanking. This was best revealed in Tanaka's handling of the treaty revision question. He had at first taken a rigid stand after receiving the Chinese note of July 19, denouncing the 1896 and 1903 treaties. A note of protest, delivered to Nanking on July 31, stated that Japan could never consent to open negotiation on treaty revision so long as the Chinese persisted in their position and that necessary measures would be taken to protect Japanese rights in case the Chinese arbitrarily applied the "interim regulations." Japan would be willing to negotiate "proper revisions" of the existing treaties only if the Chinese would recognize that the treaties were still in effect. While a deadlock was reached on this point, the new Nationalist policy on tariffs eased the tension and led to Japan's conciliatory attitude. Instead of drafting a wholly new tariff schedule under the principle of tariff autonomy, the Nationalists had decided to adopt the graded schedule which the delegates at the Peking Tariff Conference had worked out. It had never been formally ratified, but, as mentioned in Chapter II, all delegates had provisionally agreed to it as an interim schedule before China obtained full tariff autonomy. The rates ranged from 2.5 percent to 22.5 percent, to be levied in addition to the existing 5 percent duties on all imports, and most Japanese goods went into lower rates while luxury items of Western origin were charged higher rates. Believing that this schedule would be acceptable to all countries concerned as an interim measure, the Nationalist Finance Minister, T. V. Soong, pressed for Japanese approval of this idea as early as the end of August.[26]

Tokyo was ready to accept such a proposal. However, it did not forget to impose conditions which had become fixed in Japanese policy since Shidehara's time; the acceptance of the additional taxes was to be conditional upon China's guaranteeing the consolidation of its unsecured foreign debts on the basis of increased customs revenues, and upon the abolition of inland transit dues simultaneously with the imposition of the new duties. It remained to be seen whether Nanking would accept these conditions.[27]

A believer in personal diplomacy, Tanaka decided to express his conciliatory attitude toward the Nationalists by sending private messages to Chiang Kai-shek. On September 12, when it was reported that Chiang would be appointed president of the Executive Yuan in the reorganized Nationalist government, he sent a personal congratulatory message, expressing the hope that the new president would strive for the improvement of Sino-Japanese relations. Later Tanaka sent a longer letter which was to be communicated to Chiang Kai-shek when he formally became president of the Executive Yuan. After stating the hope that Chiang would carry out moderate policies and endeavor to improve relations between the two countries, the message suggested that Chiang immediately dispatch a special envoy to Japan to talk over various outstanding issues. Though Chiang Kai-shek did not in fact become president of the Executive Yuan, he sent Chang Ch'ün as his personal emissary to Tokyo. Chang expressed China's willingness to resume discussion on several issues which had arisen between the two countries. While he was in Tokyo, Tanaka told him that Japan would give as much assistance as possible to the Nationalists, now that they seemed "to be entering a constructive phase of their revolution." [28]

Meanwhile Tanaka did not ignore the third alternative open to Japan. This was to come to some understanding with the powers, especially the United States and Great Britain. To take this alternative was really a confession of Japan's failure to work out a system of stability and coprosperity in the Far East regardless of the attitudes of the powers. In view of the American success in effecting *rapprochement* with China and similar efforts being made by other powers, however, it was believed essential for Japan to avoid isolation. Thus, at the height of the Sino-Japanese crisis the Japanese government willingly gave up the tactic of independent action in China. All of a sudden Japan became solicitous of understanding on the part of the powers.

The task of restoring cooperation with the powers was entrusted to Count Uchida Yasuya, one-time foreign minister, who attended the signing of the Kellogg-Briand Pact in Paris in August. Uchida was instructed to communicate to officials in Paris, Berlin, Rome, London, and Washington the Japanese government's real intentions in China and Manchuria and solicit their sympathetic understanding.[29]

Such an entreaty did not produce concrete results. Neither Britain nor the United States was willing to forego the advantages they were gaining in China for the sake of solidarity with a power which had initially taken unilateral steps and now complained of isolation. The Foreign Ministry in Tokyo had especially sought cooperation with Britain, and Uchida had been instructed to suggest to the Foreign Office that Japanese and British officials confer from time to time in London, Peking, or Tokyo to evolve common policies on such questions as recognition of the Nanking government, tariff, and the salt and customs administrations. London officials were not impressed, as they knew that on many issues, in particular tariff and debt consolidation, the interests of the two countries considerably differed and therefore that no full cooperation was possible or even desirable. China and Britain had just arrived at a settlement of the Nanking incident, and the latter was considering recognizing the Nanking government. Under the circumstances, all London would do for Japan was to agree in principle to constant exchange of views of each other's policies in China. But this simply sanctioned what was already practiced and did not result in collaboration on any specific problems.[30]

An even cooler reception awaited Uchida in Washington. When he saw Kellogg on September 29, not one reference was made by the Secretary to Manchuria, on which the Tokyo government had wanted some understanding. He confined his remarks to treaty revision and the Nationalists, saying, "the present Nationalist Government appeared to be making every effort to build a stable and ordered government in China." This expressed Kellogg's optimism concerning the achievement of stability in the Far East through support of the Nationalists. There was no thought of standing together with Japan; American policy toward Japan was still distinguishable from that toward China.[31]

Japan's belated effort to reach understanding with the major

powers was a miserable failure. This could not have been otherwise. Japan was pursuing its objectives unilaterally in Manchuria,
and its desire for cooperation with Britain and the United States
was merely an expression of its fear of isolation. Nevertheless, it is
significant that for the first time after mid-1925 Japan was acutely
feeling the need for understanding with the West in China. This
reorientation took place under Tanaka, not Shidehara.

THE NATIONALIST UNIFICATION OF CHINA

October 1928 marked the beginning of the "tutelage period"
of the Nationalist revolution. The state council was organized,
composed of sixteen members; it was to act as the highest authority during the tutelage period. Chiang Kai-shek headed the
list as president of the National government, the new name given
to the Kuomintang regime. Five months later the third national
congress of the party was convened. The national congress was
the highest organ of the party, and it now confirmed Chiang in
the position of leadership. Though there remained serious internal
dissensions, the congress was an important symbol of the Nationalist unification of China, and the delegates went home
pledged to realize the "independence and freedom of the Chinese
people." [32]

By this time Manchuria had become formally unified with the
rest of China. The inclusion of Chang Hsüeh-liang in the state
council of the National government had signified that the political
union of Manchuria and China proper was near. Chiang Kai-shek
had also extended his promise that in case a Fengtien-Kuomin-
tang accord was reached Chang would be made chairman of the
Manchurian government council which was to be organized to
administer the Three Eastern Provinces. Between October and
December 1928, Manchurian delegates shuttled back and forth
between Peking and Mukden to negotiate the final terms of compromise. By the end of the year, Chang was ready to accept the
revolutionary flag, and Manchuria was reunified with China on
December 29, 1928.[33]

This reunification was essentially an alliance between Chang
and Chiang, and at first there was no likelihood of a total military

and political union of the two. According to the terms of the compromise, all members of the Manchurian government council, as well as the top officials of the Three Eastern Provinces, were to be appointed in Manchuria rather than in Nanking. Local Kuomintang branches were to be opened only after a group of Manchurian observers went to Nanking to study party affairs. Chang Hsüeh-liang would thus remain a potential threat to Nanking, and Manchuria an *imperium in imperio*. Still, the nominal union could be utilized by Manchurian officials to avoid facing difficult diplomatic problems, especially with Japan, by saying that all diplomatic matters must be referred to Nanking.[34]

The Nationalists' successes were in sharp contrast to the Tanaka cabinet's troubles at home. In carrying out his policy he had often relied on extradiplomatic personnel and had been influenced particularly by the views of Seiyukai politicians and army spokesmen. At a time when China was bent on regaining complete national sovereignty, it was essential for Japan to redefine its basic strategy and clarify its line of command. Tanaka was well aware of such a need, but in this task he was frustrated because of circumstances which were beyond his control. There arose the delicate question of punishing the officers responsible for the assassination of Chang Tso-lin. Briefly speaking, the General Staff was strongly opposed to publicly acknowledging the truth about the incident, though it had become common knowledge in government circles by the end of 1928. The Minseito Party began attacking Tanaka's China policy, and the Emperor wanted him to deal severely with the culprits. Thus, during the first half of 1929, the Prime Minister had to labor to maintain his government's strength in the Diet, while at the same time trying to obtain the army's approval for trying Colonel Kōmoto and others before courts martial. The army, however, stood adamant; feeling that its prestige was at stake, it tried successfully to work through the Seiyukai and isolate Tanaka even from his own party. In the end he resigned, unable to find support among influential army and Seiyukai leaders for his stand, and accused of indecision by the Emperor and Minseito politicians.[35]

Tanaka's China policy was conducted in the middle of such a crisis. It is perhaps to his credit that he was now determined to effect understanding with China, albeit on the best possible terms for Japan. The fact remains, however, that his policy in this period was basically a negative one of beating the least ungraceful retreat, and that, by the time of his resignation in early July 1929, Japan had not recovered the lost ground.

Of the various problems which had to be cleared before the two countries could effect *rapprochement,* the union of Manchuria and China no longer posed a serious issue for Japan. The latter had reconciled itself to this eventuality and realized the futility of preserving Japanese interests in Manchuria by preventing such a union. Consequently, when the revolutionary flag was raised in Manchuria, Japan made no protest. Tanaka simply warned that, should Japanese treaty rights be ignored and order disrupted in Manchuria, Japan would be forced to take "resolute action." Edwin Neville, American chargé in Tokyo, correctly gauged the situation when he reported to Washington, "Judging from the slight interest which the raising of the flag has apparently created in Japan, it would seem that the Japanese had come to regard it as inevitable. If they do not regard it as not necessarily inimical to their interests, at least they seem to realize that further opposition in this direction would only increase antagonism without advantage to Japan, at a time when promotion of negotiations with the Nanking Government is urgently desired." [36]

There were other, more difficult, problems to solve. One was the tariff question. Tokyo had presented conditions for accepting the interim tariff schedule. In late September, T. V. Soong expressed his intention of putting into effect the graduated tariff schedule without further delay. On October 8 he said he would agree to the Japanese demand for the exemption of goods which had already paid increased duties from further inland transit dues. However, he said the stipulation regarding the consolidation of debts, if clearly stated in an official document, would arouse strong opposition in China. He would agree to holding a conference to discuss the unpaid debts and claims, but he would like to have the Japanese agree in writing that the calling of such a conference would not be a precondition for acceptance of the tariff schedule. [37]

Agreement on debt consolidation was a *sine qua non* from

Japan's point of view. It pressed Soong to accept the idea of a creditors' conference in writing in order to discuss modes of consolidating debts on the basis of customs surplus. Soong decided to accept the condition in order to expedite the settlement of the tariff matter. On November 16 he showed to the Japanese negotiator, Consul General Yada, a draft agreement on this issue which represented his last endeavor to reach an understanding with Japan. The draft read, "The Chinese Government will set aside the sum of five million dollars annually from the increased tariff for the purpose of consolidating loans inadequately secured and unsecured. Further arrangement will be discussed at the Conference which the Chinese Government intends to call at an early date." This draft had been presented to and approved by the Nanking government. Though the sum of five million Chinese dollars constituted only 5 percent of the total amount of unsecured debts, the Japanese government would have been satisfied with this recognition of an important principle. Before accord could be reached on this basis, however, Soong announced that he could no longer consent to the second condition put forth by Japan, namely that goods paying the new duties would be exempted from further inland transit dues. He explained that no adequate preparations had been made regarding the abolition of likin, and to abolish it immediately in the provinces of Kiangsu and Chekiang, where the revenue from likin was sent to Nanking, would create a serious financial problem for the central government. The Japanese government could not accept Soong's formula, fearing that Japanese imports to China would then be subjected to increases in duties without any compensation.[38]

Nevertheless, Soong and Yada continued to negotiate. The Japanese government presently offered to accept a graduated inland tax schedule ranging from 1.25 percent to 2.5 percent. Soong expressed his willingness to accept Japan's conditions in return for retaining the transit duties. At length, on December 8, 1928, Soong and Yada agreed upon draft notes to be exchanged between Tokyo and Nanking. One related to the new tariff schedule to be put into effect on February 1, 1929; one to the consolidation of unsecured debts; a third was a secret agreement on the abolition of likin and other matters. This last document recorded the

Chinese government's intention of abolishing likin within two years after the promulgation of the new tariff. It was also stated that the new schedule would be mostly identical with that drafted during the Peking Tariff Conference.[39]

For nearly two months, Chinese and Japanese negotiators worked to hammer out minor points of difference in phraseology. As the Nationalists would start imposing the new tariffs on February 1, 1929, the Tokyo government proceeded to draft the final phraseology of its notes. These were approved by the Chinese government, and on January 30 the two governments formally reached agreement, Japan expressing approval of the new tariff schedule, and China promising to set aside five million dollars annually for debt consolidation and to abolish likin within two years. This was as good a solution of the crucial tariff question as could be obtained by Japan under the existing circumstances.[40]

The second difficult issue to be cleared up between Nanking and Tokyo was the Tsinan incident. In June 1928, Generals Chang Ch'ün and Matsui Iwane, the principal negotiators, had failed to settle the matter, and the incident had remained one of the sorest issues in Sino-Japanese relations. For one thing, the Japanese had not resolved the differences between two different approaches, civilian and military, to the problem. The divergent views still existed when the Tokyo government set about solving the incident.

The civilian approach was represented by Consul General Yada at Shanghai. In October he opened talks with C. T. Wang, and they agreed on a compromise settlement. Japan would state in a note its willingness to withdraw troops from Shantung in specified stages and within a specific time, with the understanding that details would be arranged by the Chinese and Japanese commanders at Tsinan. In return, the Chinese would promise protection of Japanese lives and property, after the withdrawal of the troops, and strict control over antiforeign activities. Furthermore, the Chinese government would issue a statement guaranteeing the free use of the Tsinan-Kiaochow Railway. This was a reasonable agreement which might have been accepted by the Chinese government. Encouraged, Yada suggested to Tanaka on October 23 that Japan might express regrets for the deaths of innocent Chinese during the Tsinan affair, although they were caused by an act of self-defense on the part of the Japanese. If this was done, Yada telegraphed Tanaka, the Chinese were likely to agree to an apology.[41]

This suggestion came in direct conflict with the military's approach. They argued strongly against pulling out troops in return for what they considered a piece of paper carrying Chinese promises. Under their pressure Prime Minister Tanaka instructed Yada to take back all agreements he had been able to arrive at with C. T. Wang. By this time, however, voices of moderation began to make themselves heard within the Japanese government. While Minister Yoshizawa was back in Japan in the fall of 1928, attending the coronation ceremony of the Emperor, he seems to have urged a quick solution of the Tsinan issue by consenting to the withdrawal of troops in return for some tangible concessions on the part of the Chinese, especially with regard to Manchuria. Overriding the military's reluctance, Tanaka decided to accept Yoshizawa's advice and offer several concessions to China on the Tsinan incident if the Nationalists would discuss the opening of Manchuria to Japanese residence and business. The concessions included Japan's readiness to express its regrets over the affair, to be accompanied by a Chinese apology, and to set up a joint Sino-Japanese committee of investigation to study damages and examine guilty officers. The Nationalists, however, would be asked to promise in writing to protect Japanese lives and property in Shantung and to issue such instructions to the local authorities. When all these terms were met, the Japanese government would declare its intention of withdrawing troops within two months.[42]

Minister Yoshizawa's new negotiations with C. T. Wang were filled with obstacles. Nanking flatly refused to trade the opening of Manchuria for a solution of the Tsinan incident, and the Japanese soon gave up efforts to link the two problems directly. Moreover, knowing Tanaka's difficulties at home, Wang at times employed a delaying tactic, hoping to obtain better terms of settlement from another cabinet. By late January 1929, however, Wang decided to resume negotiations, seeing the defeat of a Minseito resolution attacking the Tanaka cabinet. In Tokyo, on the other hand, the army insisted on China's explicit apology.

It was only through Yoshizawa's and Tanaka's strong determination that the army opposition was finally silenced and the Tsinan issue solved. In early March, the negotiators bent their final efforts to come to a final agreement. They agreed not to mention apology in the final documents, make a joint declaration expressing regrets over the incident but determination to wipe it out of memory, and to adopt a conference record setting forth agreements on a joint committee of investigation, future protection of Japanese lives, suppression of anti-Japanese activities, and safe operation of the Tsinan-Kiaochow Railway. The committee was to be composed of an equal number of delegates from both countries. In the course of these final negotiations, Wang admitted that the institution of the joint committee of investigation would buttress the position of his government and that it did not matter whether the committee proved of real substance or not. On March 4, Yoshizawa relayed these agreements to Tokyo and said that they were the best and final product of his efforts which the Japanese government should accept in entirety.[43]

During the following three weeks, a few revisions in phraseology were made. Tanaka attempted, unsuccessfully, to add a clause in China's note explicitly guaranteeing the protection of Japanese lives after the withdrawal of the troops. On March 24, however, the negotiators initialed final drafts, and the documents were signed and exchanged four days later. The sorest issue between China and Japan was solved, and the terms of settlement revealed Japan's retreat from the haughty position it had taken in mid-1928.[44]

The Tsinan settlement was followed by solutions of other incidents, thus paving the way for Japan's recognition of the Nanking government. But Manchurian matters were still negotiated with Fengtien officials, indicating the continued inconsistency in Japanese policy. Although the Tokyo government had decided to make concessions on the Tsinan issue in order to promote a satisfactory solution of outstanding questions in Manchuria through talks with Nanking, no steps were taken in this direction during the remainder of Tanaka's tenure of office.

It will not be necessary to discuss in detail other agreements reached between Nanking and Tokyo in early 1929. On May 2,

Yoshizawa and Wang approved and signed agreements on the Nanking and the Hankow incidents of 1927, which had been negotiated by subordinate officials. The letters exchanged on the Nanking incident were almost identical with those signed by China and the United States over a year before. Similar notes, referring to communist instigation and expressing Chinese willingness to compensate for loss or damage to Japanese lives and property, were exchanged regarding the Hankow incident. Finally, there remained the question of recognition of the new Chinese government. The Japanese government had been unwilling to grant recognition to a government which had unilaterally repudiated the treaty of commerce between the two countries. The impasse could be broken only by some face-saving device by which both sides would agree to resume discussion on treaty revision, shelving for the time being the legal question of the validity of the existing treaties. This could be done by an exchange of notes between Nanking and Tokyo. In the middle of April, following the solution of the Tsinan incident, talks were held on this point between Yoshizawa and Wang. They came to a quick agreement, and on April 18 initialed memoranda expressing their mutual willingness to revise the treaties on the understanding that the interim provisions the Chinese had promulgated to replace the existing treaties would not be applied till the conclusion of a new treaty. The memoranda were published on May 1. This paved the way for Japan's recognition of the National government, which came on June 3.[45]

All these settlements did not contribute to the solution of Manchurian problems. Japanese officials were still interested in protecting treaty rights in Manchuria through Chang Hsüeh-liang, but they made no progress. The firm stand of Chang Hsüeh-liang reflected his growing confidence in his own power. On January 19, 1929, he personally shot to death Yang Yü-t'ing and Ch'ang Yin-huai on the charge of having attempted to prevent the union of north and south. In reality both of these men had opposed Japan and advocated joining the south throughout 1928, and it was Chang Hsüeh-liang who was at first opposed to their ideas. The murder of these two prominent leaders was justified only in terms of aggravating Chang's own power.[46] Its net effect was to augment his strength from the Japanese point of view. Before the excitement over the assassination passed, some Japanese officials began recommending the use of force to solve the railway question. Consul General Hayashi at Mukden, for example, suggested that Japan force the issue of railway construction, which had been agreed to by Chang Tso-lin but which Chang Hsüeh-liang had been reluctant to put into effect, by a forceful occupation of the commercial leaseholds which had been created but not opened to Japanese occupancy. Furthermore, Hayashi urged that Japan be prepared to withdraw advisers from the Fengtien army, stop military transportation on the South Manchuria Railway, cut off the cross point between the Peking-Mukden and the South Manchuria railways, and organize a band of railway surveyors with a view to laying out the proposed railways. The consul general concluded that in order to carry out these measures the police force would at first suffice but that it might become eventually necessary to employ armed forces. In April, officials of the Mukden consulate general, the South Manchuria Railway, and the Kwantung Army discussed and worked out a plan for surveying and building the projected railways. In a telegram of April 4, forwarding the plan, Consul General Morishima Morito insisted that "if we casually abandon our rights in Manchuria which are evidently legal, it will only encourage the rights recovery movement and the Chinese will come to despise us. Then not only will the solution of other issues be rendered more difficult, but they will even talk about recovering Port Arthur, Dairen, and the South Manchuria Railway." [47]

There was thus a basic identity of views between civilian and military officials in Manchuria on the need to carry out the railway scheme. Civilian officials in Tokyo and China proper, however, were unwilling to jeopardize the reviving atmosphere of goodwill between Nanking and Tokyo by drastic action in Manchuria. While they approved of talks with Chang Hsüeh-liang, they wanted to stop short of resorting to forceful measures. Moreover, they did not think the time was opportune for commencing serious negotiation with Nanking on the railway and related issues in Manchuria. All these considerations served to stiffen Chang Hsüeh-liang's position, for he could simply ignore Japanese threats and refer the dispute to Nanking. In the middle of February, he dispatched delegates to Nanking to discuss the railway question with Nationalist officials. C. T. Wang, Sun Fo, and the Manchurian delegates debated the matter and decided to transfer the problem to the Nanking government and so to notify the Japanese. While this decision was not always adhered to by Fengtien authorities, it gave them an excuse for not carrying out the Chang-Yamamoto agreement. Since Tokyo failed to expedite the settlement of the railway question in conjunction with the solution of the Tsinan, Nanking, and other matters, the Manchurian problem remained as deadlocked as ever when Tanaka resigned on July 1.[48]

By the middle of 1929 the Nationalists had successfully resumed the initiative in directing China's diplomacy and imposing their own image of a new order in the Far East. The National government had been recognized and tariff autonomy had been restored in principle by most countries. These achievements could not have been accomplished so easily and quickly if the major powers had coordinated their action and adopted common strategy toward the Chinese initiative. But the time for international action had long passed. The powers responded to China's bid for a new order by creating a framework of bilateral rather than multinational relations between China and the powers.

Such an independent approach was initially Japan's. Ironically, the initiator of this method ended up by retreating step by step from its position of force and even reconsidering the usefulness of international cooperation. As of mid-1929, however, the Japanese government had not sufficiently reoriented its foreign policy. It had tried various approaches, and most recently its basic concern was with restoring relations with China. That was a far cry from the lofty ideal of coprosperity so vigorously pursued by Shidehara and Tanaka before the latter stumbled on the rock of Japanese militarism. Clearly, the time was ripe for a radical overhaul of Japanese foreign policy.

VIII · THE COST OF SOVEREIGNTY,
1929–1930

Like many "developing" countries today, National China displayed a marked dualism between political instability at home and a strong foreign policy. The country was still plagued by former warlords' private armies, and the Nanking government could not claim the land taxes collected in the provinces. Manchuria under Chang Hsüeh-liang enjoyed fiscal autonomy. Feng Yü-hsiang and Chang Fa-k'uei openly revolted in the fall of 1929, and in the summer of 1930 a rebel government was set up in Peking. However, this disunity promoted, rather than prevented, a strong stand on foreign affairs by all Chinese factions. A successful revision of the treaties would enhance Nanking's prestige, and its failure to regain complete sovereignty would be taken advantage of by its opponents for political reasons. Some, like Chiang Kai-shek, understood the danger of thus mixing foreign and domestic affairs and wanted first of all to concentrate on political unification and fiscal reform at home. But even they could not tolerate the *status quo* in relation to tariffs, extraterritoriality, foreign leases and concessions, and foreigners' right to station troops and navigate rivers in the interior of the country. Their tactics might differ from those calling for an immediate and unilateral abolition of all foreign privileges, but all groups were united on the ultimate objectives of foreign policy.

Confronted with such a trend in Chinese policy, the powers showed a moderate interest in cooperation. The Japanese, in particular, were acutely aware of the need for an over-all policy, embracing not only the Far East but also Europe and America. Serious thought was given to reorienting Japanese foreign policy and discarding the practice of pursuing one policy in China and another elsewhere. In the end, this search for a new approach resulted in further alienating the military from the civilian government in Tokyo.

TOWARD COMPLETE SOVEREIGNTY

The changes in Japanese, and to a degree in British and American, attitudes were due primarily to growing pressure from China for abolishing unequal treaties. The basic Chinese program for national independence was outlined at the second plenary conference of the Kuomintang central executive and central advisory committees, which took place in the middle of May 1929. Here it was decided to step up preparations for promulgation of civil, criminal, and commercial laws to replace the extraterritorial system. Gradualism in treaty revision was to be opposed and extraterritoriality explicitly repudiated in all new treaties. Demands were to be made for the retrocession of Weihaiwei, Dairen, Port Arthur, and other leases and settlements. From the Chinese point of view, the years after 1929 were to be those of the final struggle for complete sovereignty.[1]

The leaders of the Nanking government and the Kuomintang wanted to pursue these objectives under their own direction and avoid outbursts of mass hysteria and antiforeignism; these could not only complicate their own effort for treaty revision but also revive the strength of communists and radicals. The freedom of the press and of association was restricted, and popular movements for national freedom were closely supervised. It was hoped that treaty revision could be brought about "from above." Such a policy did not work outside Nanking's immediate areas of control. In Manchuria, in particular, where foreign rights were most notable and the local leaders paid only nominal allegiance to Nanking, foreign relations could take a more radical and less orderly form than intended by the central Chinese government. Manchurian officials were ordering eviction of Korean immigrants from their tenanted farms, negotiating with German and Dutch firms for construction of more railways and a port at Hulutao to compete with Dairen, and planning the seizure of the Chinese Eastern Railway. Communist and noncommunist agitators were meanwhile active throughout Manchuria, helping to keep alive the strong current of anti-Japanese sentiment.[2]

Faced with these developments, the powers from time to time

tried cooperative action, but they failed to evolve any mechanism through which the desire for cooperation could lead to constructive policy. The best examples of this failure in 1929 are the extraterritoriality negotiations and the Chinese Eastern Railway episode.

In April 1929 the Chinese government had addressed an identic note to Britain, the United States, and France, expressing "the desire of China to have the restrictions on her jurisdictional sovereignty removed at the earliest possible date." The note requested an early reply "so that steps may be taken to enable China, now unified and with a strong Central Government, to rightfully assume jurisdiction over all nationals within her domain." Chinese officials hoped, though they did not state explicitly, that extraterritoriality could be abolished on January 1, 1930, and new arrangements could be promulgated governing the activity of foreigners. Britain, while interested in promoting the *rapprochement* that had started in 1928, was not willing to give up all its jurisdictional rights in China immediately. As Foreign Secretary Chamberlain remarked, only "a gradual and progressive solution of the problem" would be to the advantage both of China and Great Britain. Arthur Henderson, who replaced Chamberlain as foreign secretary as the Conservative cabinet gave way to the Labour government headed by Ramsay MacDonald in June, held to a similar position. Though after taking office Henderson expressed the "friendliest feelings" toward China, he regarded as impracticable an immediate and total abolition of extraterritoriality.[3]

Though Britain had tended to act independently in China, the Foreign Office now felt that the powers should present a joint front, lest some of them should make more concessions than it was willing to offer, thereby putting Britain at a disadvantage. Though the replies of France, Britain, and the United States to the Chinese note of April were not identical, London took the initiative in coordinating its views with those of Washington, and it even consulted Tokyo, although the note had not been addressed to Japan. In effect the American and British replies invited China to put forward concrete proposals for the modification of the extraterritorial system.[4]

China was not satisfied with these replies. On September 5 it again communicated identic notes to the powers requesting them "to enter into immediate discussions with the authorized representative of the Chinese Government for making the necessary arrangements whereby extraterritoriality in China will be abolished to the mutual satisfaction of both Governments." [5]

Britain maintained its interest in working together with other governments to meet this continued pressure from China. In late 1929, however, this effort was frustrated as the Nanking government adopted the tactic of dealing individually with the powers. The British Foreign Office discouraged any such move, reasoning that this was merely a device to play off one power against another. In late November, when Nanking made another attempt to deal singly with Britain and put forth some drastic proposals for abolition of extraterritoriality as of January 1, 1930, Under Secretary Wellesley bluntly told Minister Sze that such proceedings were "manifestly insincere." He continued, "if the Chinese Government wish to poison the atmosphere and to undo all the good which had been done in the last two years to create a friendly and sympathetic attitude towards Chinese aspirations they could have thought of no better way than the course which they now propose to take." Britain was not unwilling to negotiate, but would do so only in cooperation with other powers under the principle of a united front. [6]

The desire for cooperation was not at this time reciprocated by the United States, and the Nanking government seemed determined to proclaim abolition of extraterritoriality on January 1, 1930. This led the London officials to conclude that Britain should not long delay starting negotiations but should begin talks on the subject in Nanking before January 1, independent of other powers if necessary, in order to forestall any rash action by the Chinese. Accordingly, on December 20, Secretary Henderson handed an *aide-mémoire* to Minister Sze in order "to induce the Chinese to issue the threatened unilateral denunciation of extraterritoriality in an innocuous form." Henderson expressed the willingness of his government to enter into detailed negotiations as soon as practicable. Nanking welcomed this approach and, after consulting London, issued its expected mandate on December 28. It declared that, beginning January 1, 1930, foreign nationals in China should "abide by the laws, ordinances, and regulations duly promulgated by the Central and Local Governments of China." C. T. Wang made it clear to the British consul at Nanking, however, that the mandate simply called for abolition of extraterritoriality in principle and left the way open for a settlement of the question on the basis of gradualism. No immediate steps were taken to force foreigners to comply with Chinese jurisdiction.[7]

The United States government had stuck to its position of independent action in China. Henry L. Stimson, to whom the conduct of American foreign policy had been entrusted by President Herbert Hoover, continued Kellogg's approach to the China question. He was if anything more outspoken in his friendship toward the Chinese, since he had studied Far Eastern problems at close hand as governor general of the Philippines. Though his study of Chinese history had induced him to view China's "progress" with some skepticism, he believed that the Nationalist movement was "the beginning of a permanent change in the Chinese Government and character" and lauded Kellogg's "wise and high-minded" policy. Stimson had stated publicly that his country was "taking the lead in China in the enunciation and support of the principle of fair play." [8]

Stimson's assumption of office coincided with the arrival in China of the Kemmerer commission, a group of American advisers led by Edwin W. Kemmerer, a noted financial expert. Specialists in the fields of taxation, tariff, railroad, and other economic subjects, they were to study and recommend measures for the rehabilitation of China. Foreign Minister Wang had them in mind when he telegraphed Stimson, congratulating him on the new appointment: "Throughout the history of Sino-American intercourse, we are happy to say that it has always been marked with the most cordial and friendly feelings. . . . In this feeling of trust and friendship is to be found the reason for China turning to America for advice and help in the form of appointment of advisors for the solution of economic problems as well as those of reconstruction." Stimson was happy to note the lead Americans were taking in helping the new leaders of China. In his reply to Wang, he stated the hope that, "with the advice and help which

America has always been glad to offer, the people of China may reach a triumphant solution of their difficult problems and may obtain a constantly increasing measure of happiness and prosperity." [9]

With such a perception of Sino-American relations, it was natural that the new Secretary would consider favorably the problem of restoring judicial autonomy to China. To be sure he was not prepared to surrender extraterritoriality immediately and unconditionally, especially as his advisers in the State Department held to a cautious position. But Stimson saw no need for the United States to coordinate action with other powers, and was irritated when Minister MacMurray suggested that the powers concerned might issue a warning to China that they would not tolerate unilateral abolition of extraterritoriality. The United States should develop its own policy, thought Stimson, in line with Kellogg's approach. After receiving the Chinese note of September 5, Stimson was further convinced of the need to act alone. Brushing aside the British suggestion for joint action, he authorized his staff to continue talks with Minister C. C. Wu irrespective of the attitudes of other powers. [10]

The absence of cooperation is all the more noticeable because throughout 1929 British and American officials held talks in preparation for a forthcoming naval conference. The Geneva naval conference of 1927 had failed, and the two governments were determined to make another serious effort to postpone, if not put an end to, a dangerous naval race which could arise in view of the rise in importance of auxiliary craft — destroyers, cruisers, and submarines — which had not been included in the Washington Conference naval ratios. In 1929 Prime Minister MacDonald and President Hoover personally interested themselves in the question and succeeded in arriving at a tentative agreement. [11] The fact that such cooperation was not reflected in the China question revealed the continued isolation of the latter from other questions in the powers' policies. They dealt with China, not as a part of their over-all global policies, but as a separate question. There was as yet no realization that the Far Eastern question had to be integrated into the over-all question of world politics.

Such observations apply equally well to Japanese policy. It was

suggested above that Japan's policy of dealing with China unilaterally had been a failure, and that Prime Minister Tanaka had
begun to realize the need for once again seeking understanding
among the powers regarding the China question. Before he could
seriously devise a new strategy, however, his cabinet fell and he
was succeeded as prime minister by Hamaguchi Osachi and as
foreign minister by Shidehara Kijūrō.

The new cabinet inherited the acute awareness of the need
for a comprehensive foreign policy. The Minseito Party had for
some time advocated a radical financial reform, to put the national economy back on a normal course after the panic of 1927.
Now that the party had come to power, it decided to lift the gold
embargo which had been imposed during World War I. The
United States and Britain had taken similar measures to protect
their gold reserves during the war, but they had since returned
to the gold standard. It was believed imperative for Japan to do
likewise, but the action had been postponed because of the great
earthquake and the difference of views as to the exchange ratio
at which the yen would be linked to gold. The new cabinet believed that the time was long overdue to restore the price of the
yen by removing the ban on the export of gold. The existing exchange rate of fifty cents to one yen was to be adopted; this would
mean a reduction in Japanese exports in the immediate future,
but imports from abroad would be cheaper. Fundamentally, the
step would result in the restoration of confidence in Japanese finance, easier borrowing from abroad, and the rationalization of
industries by eliminating inefficient enterprises unable to meet
foreign competition.[12]

What such a policy meant in terms of foreign relations is not
difficult to see. The Japanese economy would be linked more
closely with the Western economies, whose assistance would in
turn be needed if Japan were to make the transition successfully.
While the importance of China for the Japanese economy had by
no means diminished, Sino-Japanese coprosperity alone would
no longer be the basic desideratum for Japan. Economic relations
with China would need to be fitted into Japan's over-all economic
policy. The time was foreseen, moreover, when the Chinese economy, too, would be integrated more fully into international trade;

the regaining of tariff autonomy and the adoption of a gold standard, being discussed by Nanking officials and American advisers,
were bound to make Sino-foreign economic relations less paro-
chial than in the past. All these factors rendered it imperative
for Japan, if it were to persist in its "economic diplomacy," to
seek understanding with the Western powers not only on matters
peripheral to the Far East but also on the China question.

The fundamental irony of this shift in Japanese policy, in the
light of subsequent events, is obvious. Just as Japan returned to
the gold standard at the existing exchange rate the Western economy plunged into its crisis, thus nullifying the efforts of the
Hamaguchi cabinet. This, however, would not become evident
until after 1930. What is equally tragic is that, just as Shidehara
gave up his earlier tactic of independent action and considered
solving the China question within the framework of international
cooperation, the army began seriously considering recourse to
unilateral steps in China because of its own estimate of the world
situation.

Recent research has uncovered the existence of various study
groups organized by middle-grade army officers at this time, as
well as their concrete plans for action. Ishihara's world-views and
the policies he advocated have already been mentioned. There
is reason to believe that his ideas were generally accepted by others in Tokyo and Port Arthur. These were mostly graduates of the
Military Academy between the Russo-Japanese War and the
World War, and it can easily be imagined that they should have
craved some drastic action in which they could have leading
roles. Their basic premise, strikingly enough, was the same as that
which Shidehara was to adopt — that Japan needed a comprehensive global strategy. Whereas the latter conceived of this
in terms of obtaining the cooperation of the West to solve the
Far Eastern question, the army officers advocated strong action
in China as an integral part of Japan's fundamental goal, preparation for the next war. This war was expected to be truly global,
necessitating the mobilization of the total resources of the nation.
Japanese unilateral action in China, therefore, was for them to
be merely a first step, in the direction of creating a self-sufficient
empire capable of waging such warfare.[13]

The year 1929 saw definite beginnings of efforts by Ishihara's group to impose its ideas on Japanese military policy. In Tokyo, Koiso Kuniaki, Nagata Tetsuzan, Tōjō Hideki, Tatekawa Yoshit-sugu, and younger men in their thirties pledged themselves to push with vigor their own program for a new order in the Far East, while in Manchuria, Ishihara and Itagaki Seishirō took charge. These latter led Kwantung Army staff officers in a con-crete study of military mobilization in Manchuria and govern-ment of the would-be occupied areas. "We must take resolute steps to gain control over the Manchurian government in prepa-ration for war with the United States," confided Ishihara to the staff officers who accompanied him on a tour of Manchuria in July 1929.[14]

In this way the Tokyo government's program for a compre-hensive foreign policy was confronted with a potential menace from the military. But the clash between these two approaches was not yet openly recognized because Shidehara's new orienta-tion of policy was evolving only slowly. Moreover, in 1929 there was too much unfinished business between Japan and China to be cleared up before the former could start a new course of action. This is why at this time outwardly there was no visible departure in the way Japan handled its relations with China. The Japanese government had extended recognition to the Nanking govern-ment just before Tanaka's fall from power. This still left many problems unsolved, above all the question of Chinese tariff au-tonomy and Japanese rights in Manchuria. It became Shidehara's task to clear up these matters as best he could before he could launch on a more positive program. His basic strategy, after his assumption of office, was to put aside the Manchurian question for the time being and concentrate on the conclusion of a formal tariff treaty, restoring tariff autonomy to China.

Such an approach had much to recommend it. The Manchurian issue could not easily be solved until Nanking-Mukden relations were further clarified and until the National government's real intentions were ascertained. The tariff question was more urgent, as the United States and Britain had already granted tariff auton-omy to China, whereas the Sino-Japanese agreement of the pre-vious January had only been a temporary measure. On this issue

Shidehara's ideas had not visibly changed; he still adhered to the position that Japan would grant tariff autonomy to China only if the latter agreed to a tariff arrangement whereby most Japanese exports would be exempted from high duties and part of the increased revenue employed for the purpose of consolidating the existing debts. He entrusted the task of obtaining a tariff agreement along these lines to Saburi Sadao, new minister to China. Saburi had been a popular figure among the Nationalists ever since he visited them in Wuhan during the first stage of the Northern Expedition and reported his good impressions of them to the Tokyo government.[15] Perhaps for this reason his mission was a success initially. As soon as he arrived at Nanking in early October he and Chiang Kai-shek agreed to "improve the general atmosphere" between the two countries. Finance Minister Soong remarked that China was prepared to pay the existing foreign debts as much as its resources could allow in order to establish credit for the country and procure new loans for reconstruction.[16]

Shidehara might well have felt that his policy was proving a success. But no further agreement on the tariff matter was reached at this time because of Saburi's mysterious death in a Hakone hotel, while he was temporarily back in Japan in late November. His death was officially judged as a suicide, but many, including Shidehara, suspected murder.[17] Losing his trusted aide, the Foreign Minister turned to Obata Yūkichi as Saburi's successor. Obata had long served in China and was counselor of the legation during the Twenty-one Demands episode. Though he himself had strenuously opposed more militant aspects of the demands in 1915, this fact was unknown and the Chinese government refused to accord him *agrément*. China would not retract its opposition, and Japan had to be content with appointing Consul General Shigemitsu Mamoru at Shanghai chargé d'affaires. By the end of the year Shidehara had not been able to resume talks on a tariff agreement.[18]

Thus, although Japan had begun to reformulate its China policy within the framework of cooperation with the West, the accumulation of unfinished business prevented it from taking actual steps to implement the new approach. When an opportunity presented itself in the summer of 1929 to promote Japanese-American cooperation, the Japanese government failed to grasp it.

THE SINO-SOVIET CONFLICT OF 1929

The Sino-Soviet conflict of 1929 was another outcome of China's diplomatic initiative, but it also had the effect of extending Nanking's control over Manchuria. The incident itself can be briefly summarized. Despite the Sino-Soviet agreement of 1924 providing for joint management of the Chinese Eastern Railway, Manchurian and Soviet officials had engaged in bitter dispute over such questions as Soviet political propaganda and trade union activities on the railway. In the spring and summer of 1929, as Feng Yü-hsiang defected from the National government and openly proclaimed hostility, Chiang Kai-shek became more than ever sensitive about Russian infiltration in Manchuria and Inner Mongolia. In late May the search of the Soviet consulate general in Harbin resulted in the seizure of secret documents purporting to show subversive activities of Russians in support of the Chinese communists and Feng Yü-hsiang. Chinese authorities, in Manchuria as well as at Nanking, now decided to force an issue. Troops were dispatched along the Chinese Eastern Railway on the night of July 9–10, and on July 10 they arbitrarily took over control of the telegraphic department of the railway. An order was issued for the closing of various Soviet commercial organs in Manchuria and the expulsion of important Russian officers of the railway. The following day Chinese officials were named to replace the Russians. Moscow countered by giving China three days in which to cancel "all arbitrary orders" which had been issued. Nanking refused to yield, and whatever diplomatic relations there had been between the two countries were now totally severed. Soviet troops were mobilized along the Manchurian-Siberian border.[19]

The responses of the powers to this incident revealed the divergence of their respective national goals. For the United States the incident gave a unique opportunity to test the Kellogg-Briand Pact, which formally went into effect on July 24. On the following day Stimson proposed "a full and impartial investigation of the facts" by a neutral commission of conciliation. Such an approach was in line with America's policy of taking the lead in re-establishing peace and stability in the Far East.[20]

Unfortunately for Stimson, France was the only power that agreed with his proposal. There was a good reason why Japan should not agree to the idea. Ambassador Debuchi in Washington urged his home government not to endorse the American suggestion as intervention by third powers in Manchurian affairs would surely complicate the situation for Japan. In other words, just when Japan was leaving things alone in Manchuria, it was undesirable to complicate the issue by drawing the attention of other powers to that region.[21]

As for Britain, there is evidence to suggest that the Sino-Soviet conflict gave the Foreign Office a breathing space in the extraterritoriality negotiation. When Dr. Wang Ch'ung-hui, president of the Judicial Yuan, visited the Foreign Office late in October to urge an early settlement of the extraterritoriality problem, he was told that the "experience of the Russians in Manchuria was a grave warning of the disastrous results of the hasty abolition of extraterritoriality before adequate arrangements had been thought out for meeting the situation. Any repetition of such a fiasco in so important an international centre as Shanghai, for example, might have the gravest political consequences for China herself."[22]

The Nanking government was alarmed by the impact its action caused abroad and by the reports of Russian troop movements in the Manchurian frontier. Although Feng Yü-hsiang had retired, after his unsuccessful anti-Chiang Kai-shek bid in late May, his forces in northwest China posed a latent threat to the central government. For China to undertake an armed conflict with the Soviet Union was, therefore, out of the question. Instead, the Nanking government decided to seek a peaceful solution of the dispute by negotiating directly with Russia. It was hoped that direct talks between Nanking and Moscow would prevent a third power's intervention and serve to assert formally Nanking's control over Manchuria's foreign affairs. Preliminary discussions were held at Manchuli between the Soviet consul general and the Chinese commissioner of foreign affairs, both stationed at Harbin, in late July and early August.[23]

Nanking's optimism proved premature. Not only would the Soviet Union not agree to the settlement of the issue on Chinese terms but other powers continued to voice their concern. The Narkomindel would not accept a formal conference unless the preconflict status were restored and Russians reinstated as director and assistant director of the Chinese Eastern Railway. Soviet military activities intensified at the Siberian-Manchurian border, and on August 17 Russian troops started bombarding Manchuli. Meanwhile, France was proposing to the Washington Conference powers that they call China's attention to their interests in the railway as specified in a resolution of the conference. On August 26 Secretary Stimson again sought British cooperation in a new scheme by which China might be persuaded to appoint new Russian officials "who are not under suspicion" to replace the dismissed officials. The replies of the United States, Britain, and France to the Chinese note of previous April calling for abolition of extraterritoriality, which were communicated to Nanking on August 12, were certainly not very encouraging.[24]

By the end of August the Nanking government realized that its position was becoming untenable. It decided to seek Germany's advice for a quick settlement of the dispute. The Chinese were now willing to reappoint the Russian director and assistant director of the railway, but they insisted that these officers be under the control of a Chinese assistant director. These terms were unacceptable to Moscow, and Germany refused to champion China's cause. Deadlock ensued, and in November the Soviet Union renewed its armed offensive. On November 17 there was a serious clash around Chalainor between Russian and Chinese troops. Within China, generals supporting Feng Yü-hsiang openly declared their opposition to Chiang Kai-shek, and civil war flared up in the northwest. The Kwangsi army under Chang Fa-k'uei also attacked Kwangtung.[25]

Pressure mounted for a prompt settlement of the Soviet dispute. Manchurian officials desired to take the matter in their own hands and avert a further conflict with Russians by negotiating with them directly. Nanking finally consented, albeit half-heartedly, and in the middle of November talks were reopened between Soviet and Fengtien representatives.[26]

Meanwhile, in Washington, Secretary Stimson once again tried to invoke the Kellogg-Briand Pact. In late November he issued, and urged other powers to issue, a note to the two combatants reminding them of their obligations under the pact. Again Japan objected. Shidehara felt that such a note would irritate both parties and would serve no practical end. He simply gave an informal warning to the Soviet ambassador in Tokyo and reminded him of the serious effects which a Russian invasion of Manchuria might have on Japanese-Soviet relations.[27]

In early December the Soviet and Manchurian negotiators came to a settlement of the dispute and on the 22nd signed the Khabarovsk protocol, restoring the *status quo* which had existed before July 10. Formal negotiations on details were to be postponed till a Sino-Soviet conference was held in Moscow. The Nanking government immediately declared that the protocol was invalid, having been negotiated without approval of Nanking. Normal relations between China and the Soviet Union were not to be restored until late 1932.[28]

The incident was a sobering experience for the National government. No major power sympathized with its arbitrary action and it was powerless to carry out its strong foreign policy because of internal disunion, persisting suspicions between Chiang Kai-shek and Chang Hsüeh-liang, and unpreparedness to start a foreign war. This experience perhaps induced caution as Nanking negotiated the extraterritoriality matter. As a result, China in effect gave up its attempt to put an end to extraterritoriality from January 1, 1930 onward.

The Sino-Soviet dispute also revealed the strain in Japanese policy. On the one hand it refused to cooperate with the United States; Shidehara was wary of unnecessarily irritating Chinese and Russian sensibilities and getting involved in a dispute concerning Manchuria. On the other hand, Japan did not take advantage of the Sino-Soviet conflict to effect a Sino-Japanese *rapprochement*. The Nationalists were reportedly suppressing anti-Japanese activities and concentrating on anti-Russian policy.

This could have been an opportune moment for Japan to support China's cause actively and cement ties between the two countries. The fact that Shidehara did not think so is suggestive. For one thing he interpreted the rupture of Sino-Soviet relations as a test case of China's observance of treaty stipulations. He frankly stated his impression to the Chinese minister that the Chinese authorities were guilty of hasty action in expelling Soviet officials from the Chinese Eastern Railway without first making efforts to protest through regular diplomatic channels.[29] More fundamentally, Shidehara's inaction reflected the subtle changes taking place in Japanese policy. Close bonds between China and Japan were no longer the cardinal objective of Japanese policy in the Far East. Shidehara was now definitely seeking an over-all strategy that would encompass both China and the West. The search was continuing, and that is why Japan neither cooperated with the United States nor encouraged Sino-Japanese ties.

THE YEAR OF TRIAL

The year 1930 saw Japan making some progress in implementing the policy of cooperative action and developing a global foreign policy. Shidehara's task was somewhat facilitated by another outbreak of civil strife in China, which compelled the powers to act together to protect their nationals and also stalled negotiations on treaty revision.

The year was a critical one in the history of National China. The Nanking government was faced with a serious threat of rebellion. The more it succeeded in diplomacy and the more its international status was enhanced, the more alienated became those opposed to Chiang Kai-shek and excluded from positions of power at the center. First of all there were warlords such as Feng Yü-hsiang, Yen Hsi-shan, and Li Tsung-jen, who belonged to different factions but drew together in their common opposition to Chiang. Then there were politicians who did not approve of the way the Nanking government and the Kuomintang were conducting affairs. These malcontents ranged from the former Wuhan leftists to the rightist Western Hills faction. Wang Ching-wei lent his prestige to this anti-Chiang coalition. Finally there were bandits in perpetual revolt against authority, at this time the local Kuomintang branches. These rural areas provided fertile ground for communist activities. Communists had survived their ordeal in the darkest days of 1927–1928, and they had bent their efforts to create red armies and soviets. Following the formation of the fourth army in April 1928, under the leadership of Chu Teh and Mao Tse-tung, at least eleven more armies had been organized by the middle of 1930, comprising at least sixty thousand men. The number of the soviets grew so numerous that in May their representatives held a conference in Shanghai to coordinate their action with one another and with labor unions and red armies. Though the communists had nothing in common with anti-Chiang warlords and politicians, except their opposition to Nanking, their latent military strength and mass support could be of strategic significance when warlords and generals fell upon one another.[30]

Things began to move rapidly when, in April, Yen Hsi-shan, whose influence had recently extended beyond his long-controlled domain of Shansi Province, was persuaded by anti-Chiang generals to declare himself commander in chief of the Chinese army, navy, and air force. Feng Yü-hsiang and Li Tsung-jen were made vice commanders. Chiang Kai-shek immediately issued an order for crushing the rebels. Yen, with his power in north China, decided to organize a rival government in Peking. In this scheme he succeeded not only in obtaining active support of Wang Ching-wei but many Kuomintang politicians who had become alienated from Chiang Kai-shek. On July 13 these politicians issued a declaration, attacking Chiang's "dictatorship" and accusing him of violating basic freedoms of the people. On August 7, at a formal meeting of the rebel leaders, new committee members of the Kuomintang were named. The rebels then proceeded to organize their own government in Peking, and on September 1 seven members of the government council were nominated — Yen Hsi-shan, Wang Ching-wei, Feng Yü-hsiang, Chang Hsüeh-liang, Li Tsung-jen, T'ang Shao-yi, and Hsieh Ch'ih. In central China, in the meantime, the communists decided to take advantage of the power struggle in the north and start their own revolutionary war, under the guidance of Li Li-san. Thirty thousand red troops marched toward Changsha in July, attacked Chinese and foreign residents and buildings, and occupied the city on the 28th. Though the "Changsha commune" lasted for only ten days, the incident served to illustrate the mass support which the communists could command.[31]

The rebel government at Peking lasted only for a month. As was evident from the membership in the government council, Chang Hsüeh-liang's position was of crucial importance for the success of the experiment. Both sides courted him and his Manchurian army. Peking offered recognition of Mukden's political and military autonomy in return for his support, while Nanking extended monetary inducements and promised Chang control over the area north of the Yellow River. Chang Hsüeh-liang, with 250,000 troops under his command, at first remained neutral, weighing the advantages and disadvantages of decisive action. But when, in September, the civil war turned in favor of the Chiang Kai-shek forces, Chang decided to back Nanking and in so doing to entrench Fengtien force in the metropolitan area. Chiang paid his price and consented to Chang's appointment as vice commander in chief of the National army, navy, and air force, a position second only to Chiang Kai-shek's.[32]

By the middle of October, Chiang Kai-shek could claim victory for Nanking. On November 12, the fourth plenum of the central executive and central advisory committees of the Kuomintang was convened, and the delegates declared that "every reactionary element has been eliminated and the foundation has been built for permanent peace and unification of China." Chiang Kai-shek was confirmed as president of the National government and was appointed president of the Executive Yuan. As he was also commander in chief and the conference gave him control over all armies in China, Chiang's power was now unchallenged. Authority over armed forces in Manchuria, however, was delegated to Chang Hsüeh-liang. A series of talks between Chiang and Chang resulted in a decision to unify China's diplomacy at Nanking and to establish provincial branches of the Kuomintang in Manchuria. As if to emphasize the accomplishment of national reunification, the Nanking government under Chiang Kai-shek resolved to convene a national convention, an essential step in the

Nationalist revolution which Sun Yat-sen had long advocated but which had not been carried out. Toward the end of the year Hu Han-min and Tai Chi-t'ao were busily engaged in drafting an election law for this purpose.[33]

The revived civil war had important implications for China's foreign relations. In Changsha the communist attackers wantonly killed foreigners and set fire to their houses, while at Tientsin the Peking government seized the Maritime Customs and installed its own appointee as inspector. These events impressed foreign governments as evidence of China's inability to put its own house in order and speak with one voice on matters of diplomacy. It was symbolic of the drift in foreign opinion of China that Nelson T. Johnson, who had done much to bring about Sino-American *rapprochement* and who had succeeded MacMurray as minister to China early in the year, should have soon lost his confidence in the Nanking government. Writing to a friend in late August, he said,

I cannot see any hope in any of the self appointed leaders that are drifting about over the land at the head of odd bands of troops. They can unite on one thing only and that is lip service to the great slogan, "down and out with the foreigner." . . . When a leader is licked, his men desert with their weapons and munitions and join groups already preying upon the peasantry in the name of reform, communism and the dawn of a new era.

Johnson saw no real difference between the Nanking and Peking factions. He wrote Washington that if "the Nationalist Government wins in this present conflict it will be because it has more money and arms than the northern faction and not because it has ideals that are inspiring the people."[34]

These revaluations of China coincided with certain manifestations of Anglo-American-Japanese solidarity. One obstacle to such cooperation, Japan's unfinished business with Nanking, was partially removed as the two governments successfully negotiated a new tariff treaty in early 1930. Negotiations on this matter, which had been suspended following Minister Saburi's death, were resumed in January 1930, between C. T. Wang and Shigemitsu in Shanghai. After some hard bargaining on both sides, they succeeded in reaching a compromise, in mid-March, by which Japan recognized China's tariff autonomy and the latter agreed to set aside over 40 percent of Japanese export items and impose on them the tariff schedule of 1929. This schedule was similar to the graduated schedule composed at the Peking Tariff Conference and favorable to Japanese merchandise. This temporary arrangement was to last for three years. China also promised that steps had been taken and would continue to be taken for consolidation of unsecured and inadequately secured obligations and that likin would be abolished by October 1930. The tariff treaty and accompanying documents were formally ratified in May, thus putting an end to China's long struggle for tariff autonomy. While neither side was completely satisfied with the results, China was at last granted tariff autonomy by all treaty powers, and Japan managed to postpone its full effects till 1933.[35]

By the spring of 1930, then, Shidehara could feel that the way was cleared for undertaking constructive steps in the Far East with the understanding of the powers. The Japanese government, determined to make a serious effort to put an end to postwar abnormalities in the country's economic life, lifted the gold embargo in January 1930. Trusting in the essential soundness of the Western economies, the Hamaguchi cabinet had taken a fatal step, hoping thereby to attract more foreign capital and accelerate rationalization of home industries.[36]

Britain and the United States had also shown signs of coordinating their China policies. The United States previously had tended to decline cooperation, pursuing its own policy vis-à-vis the extraterritoriality question. This trend was observable in early 1930. In January the British minister in China traveled to Nanking and commenced talks on extraterritoriality with Foreign Minister Wang. The latter presented a draft agreement at once, stipulating Chinese jurisdiction over civil and criminal cases involving British subjects. They were to be tried, however, in "special chambers" in Canton, Hankow, Shanghai, Tientsin, and Harbin, to which foreign legal advisers, not judges, would be attached. Minister Lampson countered with a British draft which insisted on confinement of Chinese jurisdiction to civil cases, appointment of foreign cojudges, and the right of evocation in case justice was suspected of having been denied by Chinese courts.

The United States and China, meanwhile, started negotiation on the same subject in Washington. The American proposal was more detailed and milder than the British, suggesting employment of foreign counselors, not judges, and surrender of civil and criminal jurisdiction without a prior examination of Chinese codes. The difference between the British and American proposals was obvious, and Foreign Secretary Henderson foresaw a "spectacular defeat" of his government unless it coordinated action with Japan to keep the adverse effects of the American proposition to a minimum.[37]

Such alarm proved premature, as London and Washington soon found ways of working more closely together in China. Nelson T. Johnson, the new American minister to China, had as assistant secretary of state supervised Sino-American negotiations on extraterritoriality in Washington. Britain could hope that Johnson's presence in Peking would make it possible to work out a common strategy toward the problem. During the latter part of February and early March plans matured among British officials in London and Peking for a concrete draft agreement to be presented to China. They were now ready to surrender criminal jurisdiction to Chinese courts in return for retention of foreign cojudges. In addition, it was decided to insist upon exclusion of Shanghai, Tientsin, and several other concessions and settlements from Chinese jurisdiction for a certain period of time. In Washington, too, officials were willing to take back some of the steps which were objectionable to Britain, and Hornbeck decided to insist on foreign cojudges and reservation of criminal jurisdiction in return for the relinquishment of extraterritoriality, although he was certain China would reject these demands. In this way the stage was set for American and British cooperation through their ministers in Peking. After March 20 Johnson and Lampson conferred with each other frequently in order to prepare a draft agreement on extraterritoriality acceptable to their respective governments. For a good deal of the spring and summer of 1930 British and American officials in London, Washington, and Peking spent their time attempting to agree on a common stand. As a tactic, they decided to begin by asking much more than they really wanted. The United States government demanded not

only the employment of foreign cojudges and the right of evocation which Britain had asked, but also restriction of Chinese jurisdiction at first to civil cases. On June 4 the United States drafted
a new proposed agreement outlining these positions, on the basis
of the Johnson-Lampson conversations.[38]

Thus the trends in British and American policies in China were
such that the Japanese government's hope for greater cooperation
among these three had a better chance of fulfillment than in 1929
or 1928. Nowhere was this more vividly illustrated than during
the London Naval Conference, which met between January and
April 1930. The conference served a useful purpose for Japan by
showing the solidarity of the United States, Britain, and itself,
with the implication that in the Far East they could cooperate.

The story of the naval conference, its difficulties and eventual
success at arriving at a new ratio for auxiliary craft, does not be-
long here. It is sufficient to note that the so-called "Reed-Matsudaira compromise" broke the deadlock created by Japan's insistence on a 10:7 ratio between Japanese and American auxiliary
crafts. According to the compromise the ratio was reduced to
10:6.975, but each country was allotted an identical submarine
tonnage. There is ample evidence to show that a number of Japanese, American, and British navalists were dissatisfied with the
result but that their responsible superiors accepted it as adequate
for national defense. Once again economic policy triumphed over
military policy; civilian governments held to the basic assumption in peace among the three countries and wanted to confine
foreign policy to economic matters.[39]

For Foreign Minister Shidehara the London Naval Conference
was a test of his new approach. The success of the conference was
absolutely necessary to re-establish the principle of cooperation
among Japan, Britain, and the United States. Quite opportunely,
the intensification of civil strife in China tended to encourage
such hope for cooperation, now that the powers' attention was
again turned to the protection of nationals in China. Negotiations
on treaty revision temporarily stalled, thereby giving Japan an
opportunity to catch up with Britain and the United States. In
mid-August the American minister in Peking advised the State
Department that formal negotiations for treaty revision should

be suspended until "conditions are more conducive to confidence in the ability of the Government at Nanking to speak for more than three or four provinces." The State Department agreed and suggested to London the advisability of postponing extraterritoriality negotiations with China.[40]

In Great Britain the official estimate of the situation was similar to that in the United States. In a Foreign Office memorandum written in mid-July it was argued that there was little prospect of the establishment of a stable central government in China primarily because that country had not had that political experience. With respect to the anti-Nanking uprising, Sir John Pratt's view prevailed that it was unwise to give more than moral support to the Chiang Kai-shek regime, not only because intervention was impracticable but also because it was difficult to see precisely if Chiang was definitely superior to and would win over Yen Hsi-shan. Concerning the extraterritoriality issue, however, Foreign Secretary Henderson strongly felt that Britain should honor its promise to negotiate, thinking it would be better tactics "to present proposals and leave Dr. Wang to discover that [the] state of China is such as to prevent him entering into any engagement on behalf of China as a whole." Accordingly, Minister Lampson was instructed to travel southward and present the draft agreement to the Nanking government on September 11. The proposal was based on the American draft of June 4. The United States followed suit, in order not to be left behind, and presented its own proposal, a slightly modified version of the June 4 draft, on October 28.[41]

To Japan, trying to settle the China question with the understanding of the powers, the delay in Britain's and America's negotiations for treaty revision gave a chance to catch up with them and develop a new framework of cooperative action in the Far East. Here the basic strategy was to act together with Britain and the United States in China wherever practicable and in turn to solicit their support of reasonable Japanese interests. There was a basic vision of a cooperative economic order in the Far East, based on solid understanding and harmony of interests among Japan, China, Britain, and the United States.[42]

There was some progress in the summer and fall of 1930 in

implementing such an ideal. Reversing his earlier stand on the use of force in China, Shidehara enthusiastically supported joint naval action by Japan, the United States, Britain, and Italy in July and August, when their gunboats, anchoring at Changsha, were requested by Hunan officials to bombard the city which had temporarily been captured by communist forces under P'eng Te-huai.[43] In October, Foreign Ministry officials began a study of the extraterritoriality problem and agreed to coordinate action wherever possible with London and Washington. It was also agreed that Japan might give up most of its concessions in China. This was all in line with the strategy of encouraging the emergence of a stable and moderate government in China which could cooperate with Japan and the powers.[44]

These modest beginnings were destined to be short-lived. The more the Tokyo government tried to implement its new ideas, the wider the gap grew between foreign policy and military thinking. For the year 1930 marked a definite turning point in the military's movement for independent action, which became much more specifically defined than earlier. Within the Kwantung Army an over-all blueprint for war and conquest of Manchuria was drawn up, specifying each step in the military occupation of the area. In Tokyo the War Ministry drafted a three-stage plan for the solution of the Manchurian question, as a step toward achieving military preparedness against a Western power. The first stage was to put pressure on Mukden officials to respect Japanese rights and interests in Manchuria. Should this prove ineffective, the second alternative was to be adopted, which was to establish a pro-Japanese regime. The third and final alternative would be military conquest of Manchuria. This three-alternative plan was to remain a basic guideline for the army headquarters in Tokyo. Colonel Nagata of the General Staff went to Manchuria in November and conferred with Ishihara and Itagaki. All three undoubtedly came to a basic agreement as to the general line of approach.[45]

While Shidehara and his staff were interested in seeking understanding with the Western powers to bring about a new order in the Far East, the military advocated Japan's unilateral action in Manchuria precisely because they felt it was hopeless to seek such understanding. Japan was destined to fight a Western power, most probably the United States. Such a gap between Japan's foreign policy and military thinking had existed throughout the 1920's. What was striking in 1930 was that the military not only could no longer be silenced but even began to appear more and more in the right, for the world economic crisis was nullifying Shidehara's efforts and everywhere undermining the basic principles of "economic diplomacy."

National China's diplomatic aspirations had been only partially fulfilled by the end of 1930. Though tariff agreements had been signed with the major powers and negotiations started on extra-territoriality, China was denied complete freedom in exercising tariff and jurisdictional autonomy. The continued political instability invited the powers' joint intervention. There were still foreign enclaves on Chinese soil. Relations with the Soviet Union had not been restored. The cost of sovereignty was prohibitive.

The powers, on their part, never succeeded either in coordinating action with a view to supervising China's growth as a unified nation, or in actively supporting Nanking in the hope of developing particularly close ties with China. For most countries the Far East was still an isolated problem. Japan, which had begun to seek a new comprehensive policy, suffered from the growing rift between the civilian and the military conceptions of that policy. Only some tangible evidence of the workability of the civilian approach could have prevented a crisis in Sino-Japanese relations. Such an outcome was also dependent on the willingness of other powers to work together with the Japanese government in the Far East. Lacking such support, Japanese policy was in danger of complete isolation both abroad and at home.

IX · THE FAILURE OF ECONOMIC
DIPLOMACY, 1930–1931

Throughout the 1920's, foreign policies of the powers in the Far East had been primarily economic policies; each power pursued economic objectives such as increases in trade and investment, nondiscrimination, and economic stability in China. The postwar new order visualized by the powers had been one of coprosperity. Although their economic policies in China took different forms and often clashed with one another, the primacy of economic over political and military considerations had been conducive to creating an atmosphere of good feeling among the major powers. At the same time, their navies and armies had continued to make plans based on considerations of national security and suppositions of future conflict in the Pacific, thus contributing to bifurcation between foreign policy and military policy.

The primacy of economic policy was challenged after 1930, as the impact of the world economic crisis made itself felt in the Far East. Trade patterns were radically transformed, and economic nationalism threatened to revive political rivalry. Cooperative action by the powers was harder than ever before to achieve. In Japan, the basic foundation of Shidehara's foreign policy collapsed, and an atmosphere favoring any alternative to his economic policy prevailed.

THE GREAT DEPRESSION IN THE FAR EAST

The most visible and immediate change brought about by the world depression was a transformation of trade patterns. The radical decline in America's purchasing power and commodity prices resulted in contraction of the American market for Japanese goods. The price of silk, by far the most important item of import from Japan, fell to one-fourth of what it was before the crash, reducing Japanese exports to the United States by over 40 percent between 1929 and 1930. For the first time since 1920, America's share in Japan's export trade fell below 40 percent. The Smoot-Hawley tariff, enacted in June 1930, added a further blow. Although the tariff had been in consideration from before the great crash in the New York stock exchange, its effects were the same; it raised import duties on Japanese goods by an average of 23 percent, seriously affecting Japanese export of chinaware, canned foods, and cultured pearls. At the same time, American exports to Japan declined by over 30 percent between 1929 and 1930, and by another 20 percent between 1930 and 1931. Significantly, however, America's share in total Japanese imports remained stable at about 30 percent, narrowing America's trade deficit vis-à-vis Japan.[1]

China's foreign trade was also affected. The volume of trade remained stable between 1929 and 1930, and even increased by over 20 percent between 1930 and 1931. However, the falling prices of silver nullified this increase in the volume of trade; in terms of the dollar value there was a contraction of the China market for the goods of all countries whose currencies were based on gold. Between 1929 and 1931 American exports to China declined by 30 percent, and Japanese exports by 50 percent. As these figures imply, Japanese export trade suffered a greater decline, and in 1931 Japan was replaced by the United States as the biggest supplier of goods to China.[2]

Japan's failure to hold on to its preeminent place in Chinese trade and in American trade was in part attributable to the adoption of the gold standard in January 1930. Japanese exports would have fallen without the lifting of the gold embargo, owing to the decline in purchasing power abroad; but the removal of the ban on the export of gold, coupled with the retention of the existing exchange rate, resulted in the appreciation of the yen and higher prices of Japanese exports. Domestically, prices of commodities fell because of the decline in export trade. The contraction of the American silk market severely affected agricultural incomes.[3]

The world depression likewise affected the Chinese economy.

China's volume of trade had remained stable and even increased after 1929, but a 50 percent decline in the price of silver more than offset such an increase. China's purchasing power fell, while foreign debts increased correspondingly. The new tariffs put into effect in 1929 had more than doubled customs receipts, and there was a real increase in governmental revenue from trade because, beginning February 1930, the Nanking government ordered that customs duties be collected in gold instead of silver. But foreign and domestic debts had accumulated over the years, and the government had to divert over 25 percent of its income to the repayment of these loans. The need for foreign credit had, if anything, increased, now that the new Chinese government was intent upon undertaking currency reform and other tasks of reconstruction. But foreign bankers and governments were in no position to offer loans to China; they had their own financial problems and would view the situation in China through considerations of their own economic interests.[4]

These radical transformations in the economic picture provided the setting for international relations in the Far East. Already in 1930 some of the implications of these changes were becoming obvious; the powers found it extremely difficult to coordinate action, and Japanese officials became less and less confident of rationalizing their economic diplomacy. The debt consolidation episode is a good example of the first phenomenon. There was some agreement between Japanese officials on this problem in 1930. From the Japanese government's point of view, the unpaid foreign debts of China were still the basic obstacle to the growth of China's foreign trade. Chinese officials, too, were coming to realize that no foreign loans could be obtained until some substantial progress was made toward liquidating the outstanding debts. In the middle of September a Chinese governmental commission on the debt problem agreed upon the basic principle of "a comprehensive settlement of its duly contracted obligations that are now in arrears." The resolution was adopted "to set aside from the customs revenue certain annuities the amount of which would be gradually increased" for consolidation purposes. Informal negotiations were started between Japanese and Chinese officials according to these principles.[5]

Meanwhile Chinese officials made preparations for convening a creditors' conference, as stipulated in the tariff agreement with Japan. The conference met in November, attended by C. T. Wang, T. V. Soong, and Wang Ch'ung-hui for China and diplomatic or consular officials for the creditor nations. There the Chinese delegation expressed willingness to deal sympathetically with "duly contracted obligations." It was resolved that China should first negotiate separately with each country and hold plenary sessions when necessary. As could be seen from the phrase, "duly contracted obligations," political loans such as the Nishihara loans were the thorniest issue in the way of a satisfactory settlement of the debt question. Some prominent Chinese officials, notably Hu Han-min and influential officers of the Kuomintang, advocated a total repudiation of these loans. Others, such as Chiang Kai-shek and T. V. Soong, were willing to consider redeeming some portion of them. Foreign Ministry and Finance Ministry officials in Tokyo agreed on the impracticability of insisting on repayment of the principal and interest of all the Nishihara loans and advocated that a portion of them be paid after a passage of ten years. This portion could eventually be given up in entirety. Another alternative was to relinquish all interest payments which arose after the Peking Tariff Conference. Chinese and Japanese negotiators explored various other possibilities in the winter of 1930–1931. In this way there was some willingness on both sides to seek an amicable settlement of the problem.[6]

While they negotiated with the Chinese, the Japanese officials desired to obtain the cooperation of Britain and America, just as they had cooperated with these nations on naval disarmament and protection of nationals in China. Here they were doomed to disappointment. Britain, as earlier in the decade, was opposed to treating all foreign loans to China together, and considered that any scheme such as the one being discussed between China and Japan would be injurious to British creditors. Most of these creditors held adequately secured railway bonds, and the Foreign Office did not wish them to be considered together with political loans. The London government took little interest in the creditors' conference of mid-November, invitations to which were not issued till later October, believing that the entire question needed much longer time for preparation. The British delegate at the conference simply suggested that China start conferring with each country individually and that a neutral commission might be organized to investigate political loans. All these moves were disappointing to Japan, and Foreign Minister Shidehara decided to plead directly with the Foreign Office. In late November he instructed the ambassador in London to impress upon the British government the seriousness of the debt question for the stabilization of Chinese politics along realistic, moderate lines. Wary of appearing to sponsor the Japanese claims to the Nishihara loans, Britain gave a noncommittal reply to Shidehara's pleas. For its part, Britain sent an economic mission to the Far East to explore prospects for increasing trade with China and Japan. Until the Foreign Office had studied the mission's findings, it would not discuss any joint program with Japan, either for debt consolidation or for new loans to Nanking.[7]

The United States did not so openly refuse to cooperate with Japan, but there is evidence to show that joint action by the two countries was frustrated by the silver interests in the United States. Concerned over the world-wide decline in the price of the metal, they began to propose its sale to China. These interests were represented in Congress by a silver bloc, of whom Senator Key Pittman of Nevada was most prominent. He had succeeded William E. Borah as chairman of the foreign relations committee and like his predecessor was actively interested in the China question. Under his initiative the committee established a subcommittee on commercial relations with China with a view to suggesting action by the United States government to restore the purchasing power of China. Through some reasoning, Pittman and his supporters concluded that China's peaceful and industrial progress could be aided by making available a large quantity of silver for that country. Presumably the metal could be used by the Chinese government to finance the building of roads, the re-establishment of industry, and other needs. It would also mean a wider and more equitable distribution of the silver currency throughout the country and enhance the purchasing power of the people. This in turn would result in a greater demand for foreign imports. After a series of subcommittee hearings conducted in Washington, San

Francisco, Los Angeles, and Seattle, Pittman confidently asserted that, as a result of the proposed supply of silver to China, "our commerce with restored China would be increased tenfold, and [the Chinese] would almost immediately consume all our surplus wheat, greatly reduce our surplus production of automobiles, lumber and manufactured articles, and furnish a demand for more silver, taken with the present demand, than the mines of the world could supply." [8]

Neither American officials nor businessmen as a whole were impressed by these arguments. They felt that the restoration of China's credit by somehow strengthening the central government and stabilizing the finance was essential before large-scale investments or loans could take place. As Minister Johnson wrote, "Give China five years of peace, suppress banditry, disband most of the armies and give her three years of good rains and I feel certain that the country would be very prosperous." These, rather than a silver loan, were the best remedy for China's economic problems. The Chinese government, too, was opposed to the influx of silver and in fact imposed an embargo on the import of the metal. To some Chinese, however, the prospect of an American silver loan appeared to offer an opportunity to rehabilitate the country without first settling the issue of debts. The American-initiated move served to delay Sino-Japanese talks on debt consolidation by offering an apparently attractive alternative. [9]

Just as the Japanese officials' plea for cooperation met with no success abroad, their ideas and policies were severely attacked at home. The collapse of the American market, the decline in trade with China, and the failure to achieve any degree of constructive cooperation with the powers in China, all meant the removal of the basic rationale for Japan's economic diplomacy. Exponents of this policy could show no tangible fruit of their strategy. By the middle of 1930 the effects of the Minseito cabinet's retrenchment policy had become apparent. The removal of the gold embargo and the decline in foreign trade had only accelerated the trend toward social and economic inequalities which had grown after the panic of 1927. There had been created a reservoir of malcontents — those suffering from falling incomes and from unemployment — who could menace the government when occasion arose.

The year 1930 saw an alliance between these malcontents and the military critics of civilian foreign policy. Perhaps this is the most crucial factor in the history of pre-1931 Japanese militarism. While the military strategists had envisaged direct action in Manchuria, they had also felt the need for mass support. For them it would be most desirable to "educate" the public and obtain its backing for their points of view. This was because they were firm believers in "total war," which would be fought not by soldiers alone but to which the national economy, politics, and public opinion would have to be geared. And such mass support was readily available in 1930, as the political upheaval following the London Naval Conference demonstrated. The new naval treaty gave antigovernment forces a golden opportunity to attack the ruling classes of Japan. There is evidence to show that the majority of those agitating against the ratification of the treaty, and attacking the government, were ignorant of the technical details of the new naval ratio. It was enough that the navy appeared to be opposed to it. The opposition party, Seiyukai, seized the opportunity to accuse the government of violating the "right of supreme command," presumably because it had disregarded the navy's opinion in accepting the Reed-Matsudaira compromise. Those economically and socially dissatisfied could easily join the uproar, believing that here was an opportunity to express openly their disgust with the rule of the elites — the well-educated, the wealthy, and the privileged — who were blamed for the general economic stagnation of the 1920's. The upshot was an attempted assassination of Prime Minister Hamaguchi on November 4, causing his death half a year later.[10]

Here were signs that the proponents of strong policy in China could draw support from those psychologically alienated from the government. Professional diplomats, epitomized by Shidehara, seemed to represent wealth, power, and education and to have failed to attend to the needs of the people. The military, who opposed the civilian bureaucrats for different reasons, could readily join forces with this revolt of public opinion. It was no coincidence that the military insurgents should have begun to advocate a "national renovation" — such a slogan was calculated to appeal to the discontented masses. The Cherry-blossom Society, organized by section chiefs and division staff of the War Ministry and the General Staff in October, clearly called for "national reorganization," accusing the leaders of Japan of "forgetting the nation's long-range plans." It was at this time that right-wing groups, centering around Kita Ikki, Ōkawa Shūmei, and Nishida Zei, made contact with Colonel Kōmoto and other military planners and began to become increasingly important as financial sources for the latter's activities.[11]

Shidehara's new policy was thus undermined at two levels. The military opposed him because he chose to have confidence in friendship with Britain and the United States, while the economically dissatisfied masses attacked him for the class he represented. Under the circumstances, his policy could have succeeded only if the Hamaguchi cabinet's economic policy brought relief to the masses and/or its China policy were successful. This latter would depend not only on the Nanking government's moderation but also on the willingness of the Western powers to assist Japan. By 1930 it was obvious that none of these conditions could be fulfilled. The year 1931 was to show decisively how untenable had become the foundation on which Shidehara rested his hope for a solution of Japan's diplomatic problems.

THE SUMMER OF CRISIS

Having weathered the turmoil of the civil war, the Nanking government greeted the new year with renewed confidence. Stiff terms had been presented by Britain and the United States for restoration of judicial autonomy to China. The Chinese naturally could not agree on the proposed conditions for the relinquishment of extraterritoriality: reservation of criminal jurisdiction, employment of foreign cojudges, the right of evocation, and reservation of Shanghai and other ports. In early December 1930, it handed its own draft agreements to London and Washington. Here it was asserted that British and American subjects in China would be subject to its own jurisdiction in civil and criminal cases, beginning retroactively in January 1930. In the middle of the month the Waichiaopu followed this up with further memoranda urging the principal powers concerned to expedite the settlement of the extraterritoriality issue by February 1931, beyond which date China would be obliged to proceed with its own program for abolishing consular jurisdiction.[12]

In the new year the National government decided to terminate extraterritoriality within a year. As political quiet had temporarily returned to China, the powers were willing to expedite negotiation on this problem. While it is beyond the scope of this study to trace the very interesting round of negotiations in the spring of 1931, it may be pointed out that both Washington and London were willing, after receiving Chinese counterproposals of previous December, to offer substantial concessions. As Foreign Secretary Henderson stated, the criterion now for abolishing extraterritoriality was "not whether the Chinese are fit to assume jurisdiction over foreigners, but whether the Chinese are politically sufficiently stabilized to give effect to their determination to put an end to the extraterritorial system." Guided by such a liberal restatement of policy, Minister Lampson resumed his talks with Foreign Minister Wang in March, while the other powers watched with intense interest to see how far the oldest treaty power would surrender its rights. By the end of the month Lampson had given up insisting on the right of evocation and employment of foreign cojudges as conditions for surrendering extraterritoriality. Of the remaining two conditions on which Britain as well as the United States had insisted — the exclusion of Chinese criminal jurisdiction and the reservation of certain concessions from the Chinese legal system — Lampson now offered to bargain away the former condition in return for reservation of Shanghai, Tientsin, Hankow, and Canton. C. T. Wang was not willing to accept even such minimum terms, only offering to acquiesce in the exclusion of the Shanghai international settlement for a period of three years. By early May the deadlock had not been broken. Nanking's stiff stand was such that the British minister concluded that the Nationalist regime must be staking its very existence on a satisfactory solution of the extraterritoriality question and that consequently C. T. Wang had an "extraterritoriality complex." [13]

Meanwhile Japan, too, had become a party to extraterritoriality negotiations. In view of the improvement in Sino-Japanese relations generally, following the signing of the tariff agreement,

Nanking officials wanted to reach quick understanding with Japan so that Britain and the United States could be induced to fall in line. Though Japan wanted at first to observe how Britain fared in its negotiations, in March, Shidehara authorized Shigemitsu to start informal talks. From the Chinese point of view here was a golden opportunity for Japan to show positive goodwill toward its neighbor and practice the principle of friendship and coprosperity. Shidehara and his staff fully agreed, but there were certain aspects of the problem which they were not prepared to yield. In view of the "subtle and complex" relations between the two countries, Shidehara told his representative in China, Japan had to proceed very cautiously and with much deliberation in the abrogation of the extraterritorial system. Basically, Japan demanded two things in return for relinquishing consular jurisdiction. The first condition was similar to that put forth by Britain and the United States; Japan would demand that the South Manchuria Railway zone and preferably all of its settlements and concession areas be excluded from Chinese jurisdiction. The second condition, the opening up of the interior of the country for foreign residence, travel, and trade, had been consistently sought by Japan since 1915. These stipulations were rejected outright by C. T. Wang.[14]

Deadlock had thus been created in China's extraterritoriality negotiations in the spring of 1931. Already on April 20, C. T. Wang and Chiang Kai-shek had conferred and agreed that unless an agreement was reached before May 5, when the national convention was to open, the National government should make a unilateral declaration abolishing extraterritoriality. On May 4, accordingly, a mandate was issued terminating all negotiations with Britain, the United States, France, and Japan which had not surrendered extraterritoriality and promulgating regulations for the administration of foreigners in China. The regulations were to become effective on January 1, 1932. The mandate refused to recognize exclusion of special areas, and there was no mention of the opening of the interior.[15]

The national convention met in Nanking between May 8 and 17. On the 13th the delegates resolved to declare the unilateral abrogation of all unequal treaties. Three days later a lengthy declaration was adopted, dealing with China's internal and external problems. It defined anew the "three people's principles" as the supreme principle of the Chinese revolution and stated that unequal treaties were the greatest obstacle in the path of the revolution.[16]

Confronted with this outburst of nationalism, London, Washington, and Tokyo were obliged to consider further concessions on the matter of extraterritoriality. In Peking the British minister slowly receded from his position on four reserved areas and, as authorized by his government, was ready to give up Canton and Hankow. A month of hard bargaining followed, and Lampson was successful in extracting from C. T. Wang reciprocal concessions. The Chinese Foreign Minister finally agreed to the exclusion of greater Shanghai and Tientsin from Chinese jurisdiction for a period of ten years. Lampson chose to be satisfied with this compromise, and on June 6 the texts of a draft treaty, based on all these agreements, were exchanged between the two negotiators. A similar draft was prepared by the State Department in Washington in July.[17]

While significant strides had been taken toward the solution of the extraterritoriality question by China, Britain, and the United States, final agreement was left in abeyance while the three governments took time to examine the draft agreements. They had to take into account not only their intrinsic merits and demerits but also the reaction of the public, especially foreign residents in China, to the proposed measures.[18] This was most unfortunate, as the settlement of the question was destined to be postponed till 1943 as a result of the failure of the governments concerned to expedite the approval of the draft treaties. But China's political conditions were again partly to blame for this delay.

By his recent successes Chiang Kai-shek had again antagonized many of his supporters and erstwhile comrades of the Kuomintang. They were opposed to the national convention, which they thought only served Chiang's ambitions; just before it met some members of the party had openly declared their defiance in Canton. Shortly afterward a rebel government was organized in the city, embracing such politicians as Wang Ching-wei, Sun Fo, Eugene Ch'en, and T'ang Shao-yi. The revolt could not easily be crushed, and the diplomatic unity of the country was again gone. Because of this turn of events, it was perhaps unavoidable that the extraterritoriality negotiations should have been allowed to lapse in their final stage.[19]

Meanwhile Japan, too, had been reconsidering the extraterritoriality question with a view to making concessions. In Tokyo, Hamaguchi resigned as prime minister in April; he could not carry on his duties due to the injury caused by an assassin's bullet the preceding November. He was succeeded by Wakatsuki Reijirō as head of the Minseito and as prime minister. Toward the end of the month the Foreign Ministry took up the question of extraterritoriality and decided that Japan might give up insisting on reserved areas except the South Manchuria Railway zone. Also, Japan might abandon its position on the opening up of the China interior if the Chinese would agree to abolish extraterritoriality only in China proper. Japan might restore concessions and settlements to China in return for the opening up of the interior, if the Chinese preferred this alternative.[20]

The delay in the settlement of the extraterritoriality question between China on the one hand and Britain and the United States on the other had provided another opportunity for Japan to smooth out differences with China and prevent the latter from concentrating its revolutionary diplomacy on Japan. In May, C. T. Wang and Shigemitsu started talks on specific aspects of the extraterritoriality issue, and both showed eagerness to settle it to the satisfaction of their countries. Meanwhile, with regard to the foreign debt question, the Chinese debt commission had tentatively decided to redeem the Nishihara loans as far as their principal was concerned.[21]

These were hopeful signs. Unfortunately for the success of Sino-Japanese negotiations, neither Tokyo nor Nanking could avoid touching on the most sensitive issue of Manchuria. An ultimate solution of the Manchurian question was an essential goal of Chinese and Japanese diplomacy, and all other issues were ultimately bound up with it.

The Manchurian question had become a test case of civilian bureaucratic supremacy within Japan. Because Shidehara was determined to bring about a new order in the Far East through peaceful means, it was essential for him to justify his policy as well as his control over foreign policy by showing some concrete results of this approach. Lacking such evidence, he could be attacked as ineffective and weak.

In order to satisfy his critics that he was taking steps to solve the question, the Foreign Minister decided to resume negotiation on the thorny railway problem in Manchuria. Unfortunately there was no single authority in China with whom to deal. Tanaka had tried to negotiate with Chang Tso-lin and, after his death, with Chang Hsüeh-liang, but the latter had procrastinated, saying that Japan would have to negotiate at Nanking. The truth was that no final decision had been reached as to whether Nanking or Mukden ought to handle Manchuria's foreign issues. Talks with Russia were still being conducted by Manchurian officials, in the aftermath of the Chinese Eastern Railway dispute, while neither Mukden nor Nanking wanted to discuss the Manchurian railway question with Japan. The result, from the Japanese point of view, was delay and frustration. Though Foreign Minister Shidehara was willing to acquiesce in Chinese construction of certain railways parallel to the South Manchuria Railway and to postpone for the time being Japanese construction of the railways to which Chang Tso-lin had given his consent, these concessions did not impress the Chinese. They noted that Japan was still absolutely opposed to Chinese construction of several other railways which, if completed, were expected to deal a severe blow to the South Manchuria Railway. Moreover, the Chinese interpreted Shidehara's terms as mere inducements for Japan's retention of the Kwantung leasehold and the South Manchuria Railway.[22]

To make the matter worse, certain incidents occurred in the late spring and summer of 1931 which all but wrecked any attempt at agreement on Manchuria. These were the famous Wanpaoshan and Captain Nakamura incidents.

Wanpaoshan, situated several miles west of Changchun, was the location of a Korean community engaged in rice cultivation. About four hundred Korean immigrants had recently leased land from a native landlord and developed rice paddies. The Chinese resented their presence and especially objected to their construction of an irrigation canal which could cause an inundation of the area. In late May the Chinese police suddenly arrested ten Koreans, and Japanese police were sent to the scene. On July 1 the quarrel came to a head as armed Chinese peasants proceeded to destroy the ditches the Koreans had dug and clashed with Japanese police. There were no casualties, but Korean-Chinese antagonism, probably abetted by Japanese propagandists, spread to Korea itself. There several hundred Chinese residents were attacked, killed, and injured.[23] The Nakamura incident occurred simultaneously. Captain Nakamura Shintarō, an intelligence officer attached to the General Staff, had set out on a secret mission in the interior of Manchuria in early June. From north Manchuria he visited the Taonan-Solun region where he mysteriously disappeared. Investigations conducted by the Kwantung Army and by consular officials produced evidence purporting to show that Nakamura was arrested on June 27 by Chinese troops at a place east of Solun and was soon thereafter shot to death. Though the evidence was mostly hearsay, the Japanese government and army were satisfied with the investigations.[24]

Nanking and Tokyo officials at first did their best to minimize the serious repercussions of these incidents on the deteriorating relations between the two countries. Regarding the massacre of Chinese in Korea, Foreign Minister Shidehara immediately expressed his regrets to the Chinese minister and promised solatia to the victims. Tokyo wished to treat the Wanpaoshan farm incident locally, through negotiation at Mukden, and Shidehara considered suggesting the establishment of a joint committee of conciliation to settle similar incidents in the future according to the principle of "coexistence and coprosperity." He ordered the withdrawal of Japanese police from Wanpaoshan as soon as practicable. On the Nakamura incident, too, the Foreign and War ministries rejected proposals for determined reprisal, and Shidehara instructed the consular officials in Mukden to approach Manchurian officials and urge a quick settlement of the affair to prevent a crisis.[25]

The attitude of the Nanking government was at first moderate. While it could not agree to the local negotiation of the Wanpaoshan case, especially as it was desirous of affirming its control over Manchuria's foreign relations, it decided not to dramatize the massacre of Chinese in Korea. Instead the Chinese minister in

Tokyo was instructed to visit Korea to make an inquiry. The Nationalist authorities in Nanking did not encourage but on the contrary apparently tried to suppress the anti-Japanese boycott which was started in Shanghai largely under the initiative of merchants and industrialists. Chiang Kai-shek could not afford a foreign crisis when he was just starting his third extermination campaign against the communists and preparing for a showdown with the rebel government in Kwangtung.[26]

Despite such efforts on both sides, Sino-Japanese relations never recovered from the crisis of mid-1931. Actually, the Japanese military strategists were not unhappy about this turn of events. They could exploit Shidehara's failure to solve the Manchurian problem to their advantage and work to implement their own program. In Manchuria, Ishihara and Itagaki continued to sharpen their ideas and began communicating them to a few staff officers of the Kwantung Army. Their trip to north Manchuria in July is said to have led to a final formulation of their detailed plans for action in the near future. In Tokyo, meanwhile, their compatriots, such as Nagata, Tatekawa, and Koiso, worked to convince their superiors of the need for bold action.[27]

Two immediate questions had to be settled by these men. First, they had to agree on timing. Second, they had to decide whether they would match their action in Manchuria with a *coup d'état* at home, in order to establish a government which would more readily approve of their policy and cooperate with them in mobilizing national resources for war. They never reached a final agreement on either point. On the question of timing, Ishihara and Itagaki had tentatively set a date for September 1931. The Tokyo group, however, decided on the spring or summer of 1932. The idea there was that that much time would be needed to prepare public opinion at home and abroad; its support was considered essential for a speedy success of the contemplated action in Manchuria. The result of this divergence of views on timing was far-reaching, as the Mukden incident gave the impression of unilateral action by the Kwantung Army.[28]

On the second problem there was a serious division of opinion between those who advocated dual action and those who emphasized one or the other of the two uprisings, one in Manchuria and the other in Japan. The so-called March incident revealed this split. Some of the men in responsible positions of the War Ministry and the General Staff, including members of the Cherry-blossom Society, had conspired with the ultranationalist thinker, Ōkawa Shūmei, and begun plotting a *coup d'état* in the winter of 1930–1931. Their plan was to choose a day when the cabinet members would be assembled in the Diet, hold a mass rally near the building, call out a regiment presumably to control the situation, and force the cabinet members' resignation. No large-scale violence was premeditated, the only weapons to be used being pseudo-bombs which would be thrown at the Minseito and Seiyukai headquarters and the Prime Minister's official residence. A military dictatorship was to be established under the then War Minister Ugaki. The plot was to have been assisted by a mob of ten thousand demonstrators whom ultranationalist groups were to supply. The date was set for March 20. The plan collapsed because the "Manchuria first" group, led by Nagata, worked assiduously to dissuade the top conspirators from carrying it out. Not discouraged, some of them would continue to harbor similar plans. Men such as Nagata and Ishihara, however, were averse to seeing their plans for Manchuria frustrated because of premature plots at home. They believed that eventually the Minseito cabinet would go out of office and a favorable opportunity would present itself when strong action could be taken in Manchuria without resorting to a *coup d'état* at home. This split within the conspirators has had profound impact on historical writing, providing various theories of "Japanese fascism." While historians have exaggerated the importance of the March incident, there is no question that the problem of "internal reconstruction" had to be faced sooner or later since the military were agreed that the governmental policy of reliance on the West was bankrupt and the Japanese civilian leaders were imbued with unwarranted trust in the goodness of Western countries.[29]

THE MANCHURIAN INCIDENT

Events began to move rapidly in August 1931. On August 1 the Japanese army announced its annual shift of important personnel. The most notable changes were the promotion of Lieutenant General Honjō Shigeru, once military attaché at Peking, as commander of the Kwantung Army, and the transfer of Major General Tatekawa Yoshitsugu, also formerly attaché and an accomplice in the assassination of Chang Tso-lin, from chief of the second (intelligence) division of the General Staff to that of its first (operations) division. This division had direct control over the military operations of the Kwantung Army. Radical young officers such as Colonel Shigetō Chiaki, Lieutenant Colonels Nemoto Hiroshi and Hashimoto Kingorō, who together with Tatekawa had had a hand in the March incident, remained in their respective positions in the second division. For the conspirators in Manchuria it augured well that one of their most trusted men should head the crucial operations division and that the Kwantung Army should now be commanded by a man of General Honjō's caliber and experience.[30]

A less noticed but equally significant assignment was the appointment of Colonel Imamura Hitoshi, hitherto chief of the personnel section of the War Ministry, as chief of the operations section of the General Staff, subordinate to the operations division. Thus Imamura became the counterpart in the General Staff of the War Ministry's Colonel Nagata, chief of the military administration section. The latter was privy to the plans being formulated by Ishihara and others in Manchuria and was himself engaged in formulating a program for determined national action to solve the China question. It now became the task of Nagata and Imamura to work out the details for implementing such a program. The basic idea was to prepare Japan for action in 1932. By early September they had completed their assignment, and Imamura presented the result of his study on operational problems to his chief, General Tatekawa.[31]

It was also in the month of August that a final exchange of views was made between Japanese strategists in Tokyo and Manchuria. A conference of the divisional commanders of the army, held in Tokyo on August 3–4, provided an opportunity to Colonel Itagaki to accompany the commander of the Kwantung Army and meet afresh with officers of the supreme headquarters. To the latter Itagaki reaffirmed the Kwantung Army's determination to take action. Toward the end of the month, another member of the Port Arthur group, Major Hanaya Tadashi, was sent to Tokyo to ascertain the supreme command's attitude on the Captain Nakamura incident. He conferred with Tatekawa, Nagata, Hashimoto, and others, and discussed the plot being worked out in Manchuria. Here again they failed to agree on timing; some advised delay, thinking they should wait till the Wakatsuki cabinet fell, but Hanaya persisted in saying that the decision had been made.[32]

The two neighbors in the Far East were fast approaching a crisis. An open conflict could have been avoided only if there had been strong leadership in both Japan and China capable of imposing their determination to maintain peace on the respective populations. A strong government in Japan might have restrained army action in Manchuria and postponed a showdown with China on the basis of some compromise settlement on the issue of Japanese treaty rights. But the government in Tokyo was too weak and too unwilling to risk its existence by a strong stand. War Minister Minami Jirō openly criticized the government's inaction in China and Manchuria, and the Seiyukai Party prepared a nation-wide campaign against Shidehara's policy. Influential newspapers, which ordinarily supported the government in power, were full of articles and reports about the situation in China. Now more than ever before, the Tokyo government could not retreat in China unless it was willing to risk a cabinet downfall.[33]

On the Chinese side, Chiang Kai-shek would have had to be much stronger than he was if conflict with Japan was to be avoided or even postponed. In the north Chang Hsüeh-liang and Yen Hsi-shan vied with each other for hegemony in north China; in the south the Canton rebel regime was supported by Kwangtung and Kwangsi generals; in Anhwei, Shih Yu-san revolted against Nanking; and in central China the communist armies, which had survived the fierce extermination campaign of July, continued their harassment of governmental troops. Some, like Chang Hsüeh-liang, were calling for an end to internal strife to present a united front against Japan; others, such as Yen Hsi-shan and Shih Yu-san, sought Japanese assistance against Chiang Kai-shek; and the Canton government defied Nanking by sending Eugene Ch'en on a diplomatic mission to Tokyo. The Chinese government's existence as the center of power depended on an understanding with Chang Hsüeh-liang, and this in turn necessitated a joint and strong stand against Japan.[34]

Under these circumstances, no solution of the Wanpaoshan and the Nakamura incidents, not to speak of more fundamental problems, could be expected. The Nanking government repeatedly presented protests blaming Japanese officials for the anti-Chinese riots in Korea. Japan responded by explicitly relating the Korean riots to the Wanpaoshan incident and asserting that the Japanese government had absolutely no legal obligation to make compensation to Chinese. Concerning the Captain Nakamura incident, the Japanese military were advocating punitive action, such as occupying the Taonan-Solun area pending a satisfactory solution of the case. To forestall any such rash action, the civilian government in Tokyo had to act speedily. Although the evidence which had been gathered was not completely convincing, the Japanese government chose to be satisfied with it and to press the Chinese to assume responsibility for the incident. Mukden authorities sent investigators on their own initiative, and Chang Hsüeh-liang expressed willingness to act on the findings of an impartial survey. The Nanking government, however, was highly skeptical of the Japanese presentation of the case and some leading officials gave out statements to the effect that Nakamura was still alive and that the entire "murder" was manufactured by the Japanese for the sake of ulterior ends. The Chinese had not admitted their responsibility when, on September 4, Japan presented demands for apology, compensation, future guarantee, and punishment of the guilty soldiers.[35]

Responsible officials in China and Japan realized the extreme seriousness of the situation. They made a desperate, last-minute effort to stem the tide and restore sanity in Sino-Japanese relations. But more than soothing words and reassurances of goodwill were needed, and nothing short of the miraculous could prevent a clash in Manchuria. In the middle of August, Count Uchida Yasuya, the new president of the South Manchuria Railway, confided to a Manchurian official that he was worried lest an unexpected clash should occur. He pledged his and Foreign Minister

Shidehara's determined devotion to the cause of peace and expressed hope that truly friendly and cooperative relations would be established between Japan and China through fair and just means. Negotiations over the Nakamura incident made some progress in the middle of September when a Manchurian investigating team came to the conclusion that the Japanese officer had in fact been shot and burnt.[36]

These were modest but hopeful beginnings. On September 12, when Minister Shigemitsu, appointed to the post early in August, conferred with T. V. Soong on the Nakamura incident, the latter said, "we are facing a crisis in Sino-Japanese relations, and it is imperative for us to be very cautious and devote ourselves to the cause of peace between the two countries." A few days later Shigemitsu saw Chiang Kai-shek. The Japanese minister expressed his belief that, though there were many difficult and complicated problems plaguing the two countries, "ultimately our countries are destined to be tied closely together, and it will serve both the two nations' happiness and the cause of world peace to develop this close relationship smoothly." He concluded by saying that he hoped Chiang Kai-shek would assist both nations in this task. Chiang expressed his hearty agreement. Responsible officials on both sides were so worried about the existing situation in Manchuria that they decided to have a conference of Shigemitsu, Uchida, and Soong to discuss a basic settlement of the whole complex of Manchurian issues. Soong was first to visit Peking to confer with Chang Hsüeh-liang, who had entered the city on June 1, and then proceed to Dairen. There he would be joined by Shigemitsu and Uchida, and the three were to study the situation in Manchuria at first hand and draw up recommendations for a fundamental solution. Soong and Shigemitsu decided to leave Shanghai together by sea on September 20. Berths were reserved and preparations made.[37]

They might have made some progress toward averting a showdown if the Kwantung Army plotters had carried out their project on the date they had originally set, September 28. But they had made a last-minute change and decided to execute their scheme on the 18th. Their plot had been prepared in secret, and even the commander and the chief of staff of the Kwantung Army had not been informed of its details. But the whole scheme had involved movements of arms and materiel which could not fail to attract the attention of discerning eyes. Consul General Hayashi at Mukden, for example, telegraphed the Foreign Ministry on September 15 that the Kwantung Army seemed to be preparing for action in the near future, as there were signs of its troop movements and transportations of arms and munitions. General Miyake Mitsuharu, chief of staff of the Kwantung Army, felt the need to confer with the supreme command. He had been informed of Tokyo's careful plans for action in 1932 and wanted to ascertain its views now that Sino-Japanese relations in Manchuria seemed to be heading for a crisis. On September 14 Miyake requested that Tatekawa and Koiso be sent to Manchuria to observe the situation at first hand. Pressing matters kept Koiso in Tokyo, and the supreme command dispatched Tatekawa on September 15. Though he was privy to the plot of Ishihara's group in Port Arthur, General Tatekawa was in a responsible position to work out the long-range plan aimed at action in 1932. Before his departure, he was instructed by the War Minister and the Chief of Staff to urge caution on the Kwantung Army and induce Ishihara and others to wait till there was greater hope for unity among government officials. Just before he left Tokyo, Tatekawa took the crucial step of informing his former staff in the intelligence division of his mission. These men became worried lest the plan by the compatriots should be frustrated by his mission. No time could be lost, and the premeditated scheme had to be executed before the emissary conveyed his message, which presumably represented the will of the Emperor. The Tokyo group telegraphed Itagaki, warning him of Tatekawa's coming.[38]

Receiving the information, the conspirators in Manchuria immediately called a conference at Mukden. After a heated debate on whether to carry out their project before General Tatekawa showed up or to wait and decide on action afterward, they determined to execute the premeditated plan on the 18th, the day the emissary was to arrive in Manchuria.[39]

Shortly after half-past ten on the evening of the 18th, before Tatekawa, who had just arrived at Mukden, had time to convey the Tokyo headquarters' message, an officer of the Kwantang Army ignited an explosive along the South Manchuria Railway a few miles north of Mukden. With a blast five feet of a rail blew up. Within a few hours all of Mukden was in Japanese hands.[40]

CONCLUSION

The Manchurian crisis was much more than the machination of a few Japanese army insurgents; Kwantung Army officers had always kept in close touch with high officials of the War Ministry and the General Staff. It cannot be said, however, that the crisis marked an abrupt break in international relations in the Far East. In the context of China's diplomatic initiative, military action in Manchuria was Japan's negative response to the Chinese idea of a new order. It was, to be sure, not the only response imaginable. The Japanese government had tried to meet the challenge by working out its own conception of a new order, based on Sino-Japanese understanding and within the framework of cooperation with the Western countries. Such a search, however, was based on an unrealistic evaluation of Chinese diplomacy as well as of the policies of the powers.

Much depended for the success of Japanese strategy on the attitudes of the United States and Britain. There had been a degree of cooperation between the two, as well as between them and Japan, in 1930 and 1931, on such matters as naval disarmament, extraterritoriality, and protection of foreigners in places of danger in China. But neither Britain nor the United States was really interested in assisting Japan to develop its conception of a Far Eastern order. During the spring and summer of 1931 both Secretary of State Stimson and Foreign Secretary Henderson traveled back and forth in order to cope with the financial crisis of the West, and if anything their governments tended to view the Far East in terms of its relevance to their domestic economies.

William J. Castle, under secretary of state in Washington, was perhaps the only Western official who correctly understood the basic needs of Japanese policy at that time. He wrote,

without any kind of alliance, without any kind of recognition of a Monroe Doctrine of the Far East . . . we ought to be willing to play pretty closely with Japan. It seems to me that, if Japan can feel that we are whole heartedly her friend, she will be much more likely to play the kind of game we want played in China than if the Japanese can feel that we are friendly only with big reservations. . . . I am convinced that selfish interests make it imperative that we have Japan as a friend in the western Pacific, so long at least as Japan maintains an ethical code which we can recognize.[1]

This was exactly what Shidehara and Foreign Ministry officials had in mind when they visualized a new cooperative order in the Far East. Time was against them, however. It would be another twenty years before such a conception would be seriously entertained by the United States.

Did the unrealistic approach of Shidehara doom his foreign policy? The army certainly believed that it was achieving something concrete, while the civilian bureaucrats had simply procrastinated. This view had begun to prevail even outside of the army and explains the overwhelming support given the Kwantung Army immediately after the Mukden incident.

The problem is further complicated by the fact that in the middle twenties Shidehara and the Foreign Ministry did try to bring about a new order in the Far East without relying on the cooperation of the West. Japan then resorted to an independent course of action in order to realize an era of Sino-Japanese "coexistence and coprosperity." The efforts failed, not so much because the idea was unrealistic (witness its bold and initially successful execution in the 1930's), as because the "economic diplomacy" which inspired it gave rise to untenable assumptions. It was believed that the nation's economic interests should and could be promoted in all directions, that problems of noneconomic nature could be handled individually, and consequently that there was no need to develop a comprehensive foreign policy. Independent action in China, understanding with the West outside of China, indifference to the military implications of Soviet and Chinese radicalism, unwillingness to relate the naval rivalry with the United States to the question of overall Japanese-American relations — all were expressions of this policy. It was only after it failed to produce the expected results that Japan again turned to the idea of cooperative action with the

West in the Far East. It cannot be doubted that Japan's difficulties after 1928 were due to a great extent to its unilateral action before then.

The general civilian approach in the middle 1920's was consistently criticized by the military. They argued that Japan should have a comprehensive foreign policy encompassing not only China but other countries as well. For them such a comprehensive policy would entail strong action in China in order to make it serve Japan's needs as a war power in preparation for future warfare. But the military were not the only critics. In 1924, Gotō Shimpei, representing the antithesis of Shidehara's approach, condemned those "who hope to solve American problems with the United States alone, and Chinese problems only with China" as ignorant of international politics. He predicted the failure of this approach.[2] Despite such criticisms the civilian government refused to integrate its China policy with its policies with respect to other countries. By doing so, and by failing to bridge the widening gap between the economic diplomacy and the military's thinking, the civilian leaders were unconsciously paving the way for their troubles in the late 1920's and early 1930's.

This is the crux of the problem. To ask why the Japanese government adopted such an attitude is to raise a basic question about the nature of Far Eastern diplomacy after the Washington Conference. Japan was not the only power which began to pursue an independent course of action in China. Others were doing so after the middle of the decade. Nor was Japan alone in developing a bifurcation between foreign policy and military thinking as they related to the Far East. The same phenomenon was visible in the United States. All this attested to the confused framework of international relations in the Far East and the isolation of this region in world politics. Nations dealt with each event as it arose, without relating it to other problems or examining it as part of a general foreign policy. In the meantime China was trying to define and impose an international order of its own choice. As a consequence, even the treaties, old and new, could no longer serve as a provider of stability.

In the final analysis, the failure of the major powers to develop a recognizable framework of international relations, after they had destroyed the old system of imperialist diplomacy, provided the setting for the Far Eastern crisis. Japanese policy in the 1920's was a striking testimony to that failure as well as a revelation of its own role in inhibiting the evolution of a new system. Subsequent events in the Far East were to show how potent was the drive for an ever newer order, whether undertaken by Japan, the United States, the Soviet Union, or China.

NOTES

ABBREVIATIONS

BGD   British Government Documents
CFMA   Chinese Foreign Ministry Archives
DBFP   *Documents on British Foreign Policy*
DVP   *Dokumenty vneshnei politiki SSSR*
FRUS   *Papers Relating to the Foreign Relations of the United States*
GFMA   German Foreign Ministry Archives
JFMA   Japanese Foreign Ministry Archives
JMA   Japanese Military Archives
LC   Library of Congress
KMWH   *Ko-ming wen-hsien*
NGN   *Nihon gaikō nenpyō narabi shuyō bunsho*
SDA   State Department Archives

INTRODUCTION: THE AMERICAN INITIATIVE

1. The best treatment of the treaty system, its origin and development, is John K. Fairbank, *Trade and Diplomacy on the China Coast: The Opening of the Treaty Ports, 1842–1854* (Cambridge, Mass., 1964). See also Hosea Ballou Morse, *The International Relations of the Chinese Empire,* 3 vols. (Shanghai, 1910–1918); Immanuel C. Y. Hsü, *China's Entrance into the Family of Nations: The Diplomatic Phase, 1858–1880* (Cambridge, Mass., 1960).

2. There exists no comprehensive study of the diplomacy of imperialism in the Far East. Factually the most reliable are William L. Langer, *The Diplomacy of Imperialism, 1890–1902,* 2nd ed. (New York, 1951); Nakayama Jiichi, *Nichi-Ro sensō igo: Higashi Asia o meguru teikokushugi no kokusaikankei* (After the Russo-Japanese War: International relations of imperialism in East Asia; Osaka, 1957). Interpretations of imperialism in Asia are attempted by such works as Alfred Vagts, *Deutschland und die Vereinigten Staaten in der Weltpolitik,* 2 vols. (New York, 1935); E. M. Zhukov, ed., *Mezhdunarodnie otnosheniia na Dal'nem Vostoke,* 2nd ed. (Moscow, 1956). The most satisfactory analysis of the term "imperialism" is Richard Koebner and Helmut Dan Schmidt, *Imperialism: The Story and Significance of a Political Word, 1840–1960* (Cambridge, 1964).

3. On the "realism" of Meiji diplomacy, see Hilary Conroy, *The Japanese Seizure of Korea, 1868–1910: A Study of Realism and Idealism in Inter-*

national Relations (Philadelphia, 1960). Earlier manifestations of Japan's pan-Asian sentiment are treated in Marius B. Jansen, *The Japanese and Sun Yat-sen* (Cambridge, Mass., 1954); Oka Yoshitake, "Kokuminteki dokuritsu to kokka risei" (National independence and the reason of state), *Kindai Nihon shisō-shi kōza* (Studies in modern Japanese intellectual history), VIII, 9–79 (Tokyo, 1961).

4. *Obata Yūkichi*, ed. Ujita Naoyoshi (Tokyo, 1957), Chap. 5; *Shidehara Kijūrō*, ed. Ujita Naoyoshi (Tokyo, 1955), Chap. 5.

5. James W. Morley, *The Japanese Thrust into Siberia 1918* (New York, 1957); Hosoya Chihiro, *Siberia shuppei no shiteki kenkyū* (A historical study of the Siberian expedition; Tokyo, 1955).

6. Yale C. Maxon, *Control of Japanese Foreign Policy: A Study of Civil-Military Rivalry, 1930–1945* (Berkeley and Los Angeles, 1957), Chap. 3; Kurihara Ken, "Dai-ichiji, dai-niji Man-Mō dokuritsu undō" (The first and second attempts at Manchurian and Mongolian independence), *Kokusai seiji* (International relations), No. 6:52–65 (Sept. 1958). Concerning naval thinking during the war, the best source of information is a manuscript appendix to the official war history, entitled "Taishō yonen naishi kunen sen'eki kaigun senshi furoku dai-roppen kimitsu hoshū" (Appendix to the naval war history of 1915–1920, series 6: Secret supplementary material). This document is in the War History Division of Japan's Defense Agency.

7. *Nichi-Bei bunka kōshō-shi* (History of Japanese-American cultural relations), Vol. 2: *Tsūshō sangyō hen* (Trade and industry), ed. Ohara Keishi (Tokyo, 1954), Chap. 1. For a fuller discussion of Hara's foreign policy, see Mitani Taichirō, "Tenkanki (1918–1921) no gaikō shidō" (Direction of diplomacy in the transition period, 1918–1921), in Shinohara Hajime and Mitani Taichirō, eds., *Kindai Nihon no seiji shidō* (Political leadership in modern Japan; Tokyo, 1965), pp. 293–374.

8. Good examples of the plea for "people's diplomacy" can be found in *Tai-Bei kokusakuron-shū* (Essays on our policy toward the United States), ed. Kuzuu Yoshihisa (Tokyo, 1924).

9. American policy in the Far East before World War I is documented in A. Whitney Griswold, *The Far Eastern Policy of the United States* (New York, 1938), Chaps. 1–4; Edward H. Zabriskie, *American-Russian Rivalry in the Far East: A Study in Diplomacy and Power Politics, 1895–1914* (Philadelphia, 1946); Charles Vevier, *The United States and China 1906–1913: A Study of Finance and Diplomacy* (New Brunswick, N.J., 1955); William R. Braisted, *The United States Navy in the Pacific, 1897–1909* (Austin, Tex., 1958).

10. Roy Watson Curry, *Woodrow Wilson and Far Eastern Policy* (New York, 1957); Arthur S. Link, *Wilson: The Struggle for Neutrality, 1914–1915* (Princeton, 1960), Chap. 9. The quotation is from Wilson's annual message to Congress, Dec. 7, 1915 (*Congressional Record*, 64th Congress, 1st Session, Vol. 53, Pt. 1, pp. 95–100).

11. Conrad Brandt, *Stalin's Failure in China, 1924–1927* (Cambridge, Mass., 1958), Chap 1; Allen S. Whiting, *Soviet Policies in China, 1917–1924* (New York, 1954), pp. 33, 148–150; I. F. Kurdiukov, V. N. Nikiforov, and A. S. Perevertailo, eds., *Sovetsko-Kitaiskie otnosheniia 1917–1957: Sbornik dokumentov* (Moscow, 1959), pp. 43–45, 51–53.

12. Chow Tse-tsung, *The May Fourth Movement: Intellectual Revolution in Modern China* (Cambridge, Mass., 1960), Chaps. 2–7.

13. German Foreign Ministry Archives (Büro des Reichsministers, China) contain various memoranda touching on the subject of new treaty arrangements with China.

14. During the war the value of American exports to Japan and China increased by over 500 percent and 150 percent, respectively. America's share in total Japanese trade in 1918 amounted to 32 percent, and in Chinese trade 13 percent. Turning a net exporter of capital for the first time in its history, the United States began financing Japanese industrialization and China's commercial and transportation developments. See *Nichi-Bei bunka kōshō-shi*, Vol. 2, Chap. 6; C. F. Remer, *Foreign Investments in China* (New York, 1933), Chap. 15.

15. Memo by MacMurray, April 21, 1921, SDA 811.30/131; Hosoya Chihiro, "Siberia shuppei o meguru Nichi-Bei kankei" (Japanese-American relations during the Siberian expedition episode), *Kokusai seiji*, No. 17: 73–90 (Dec. 1961); *NGN*, I, 510, 525–527.

16. Curry, Chap. 7.

17. Memo by MacMurray, Apr. 28, 1920, SDA 741.9411/26; memo by MacMurray, Apr. 21, 1921, SDA 811.30/131; Foreign Ministry memos, Feb. 2, Mar. 12 and 15, 1921, JFMA PVM 19; a draft treaty of Apr. 14, 1921, *ibid.* Code numbers of these and other Japanese Foreign Ministry documents cited are those adopted by Cecil Uyehara, *Checklist of Archives in the Japanese Ministry of Foreign Affairs* (Washington, 1954).

18. Memo by Komura, Oct. 15, 1920, JFMA PVM 19; Alston to Curzon, Aug. 22, 1919, *DBFP*, 1st ser., VI, 686–687 (London, 1956); Alston to Tilley, Dec. 11 and 30, 1919, *ibid.*, VI, 762, 913; Alston to Curzon, Jan. 1, 1920, *ibid.*, VI, 858; Tilley to Alston, Dec. 11, 1919, *ibid.*, VI, 880; Foreign Office to Admiralty, Jan. 21, 1920, *ibid.*, VI, 1053–54; Foreign Office memo, Feb. 28, 1920, *ibid.*, VI, 1016–22; memo of conversation between Hughes and Balfour, Nov. 11, 1921, *FRUS 1922* (Washington, 1938), I, 1–3.

19. *NGN*, I, 529–530; *Shidehara*, pp. 227–232; *FRUS 1922*, I, 4.

20. *Shidehara*, pp. 231–232; memo by Hughes presented to the State Department on Mar. 8, 1934, Hughes Papers (LC). See also John Chalmers Vinson, "The Imperial Conference of 1921 and the Anglo-Japanese Alliance," *Pacific Historical Review*, 31.3:257–266 (Aug. 1962).

21. Various drafts are found in Hughes memo of Mar. 8, 1934, Hughes Papers; the final text in *FRUS 1922*, I, 33–36; diary of Chandler P. Anderson, Nov. 20, 1921, Chandler P. Anderson Papers (LC).

22. *FRUS 1922*, I, 276–281. The quotation is from the Hughes memo of Mar. 8, 1934, Hughes Papers.

23. Asada Sadao, "Japan's 'Special Interests' and the Washington Conference 1921–1922," *American Historical Review*, 67.1:62–70 (Oct. 1961).

24. Arai Tatsuo, *Katō Tomosaburō* (Tokyo, 1958), pp. 77–78; Shidehara Kijūrō, *Gaikō gojū-nen* (Fifty years of diplomacy; Tokyo, 1951), p. 59.

25 *FRUS 1922*, I, 356–363, 934ff, 363–371, 373–375.

26. Robert T. Pollard, *China's Foreign Relations 1917–1931* (New York, 1933), pp. 207–209; Sun Yat-sen, *San Min Chu I*, tr. Frank W. Price, ed. L. T. Chen (Shanghai, 1927), *passim*

27. *FRUS 1922,* I, 282–287, 289–291.

28. *Ibid.,* I, 353, 376; memo by MacMurray, Apr. 21, 1921, SDA 811.30/131.

I. THE LOST OPPORTUNITY, 1922–1925

1. Memo by MacMurray, Jan. 31, 1924, Hughes Papers.

2. *Nichi-Bei bunka kōshō-shi,* Vol. 2, Chaps. 1, 6.

3. *Shina kindai no seiji keizai* (Modern China's politics and economy), ed. Nikka jitsugyō kyōkai (Sino-Japanʌse Business Association) (Tokyo, 1931), pp. 198–225.

4. Li Chien-nung, *The Political History of China 1840–1928,* tr. Teng Ssu-yu and Jeremy Ingalls (New York, 1956), Chap. 13; Hu Hua, *Chung-kuo hsin-min-chu-chu-i ko-ming-shih* (A history of China's new democratic revolution; Peking, 1950), Chap. 2.

5. *NGN,* II, 22–23, 25–26; Uchida to consuls in Manchuria, May 18, 1922, JFMA MT 1.6.1.4.1.3; memos by the War ministry, May 27 and 28, 1922, *ibid;* Takao to Shidehara, Oct. 24, 1925, JFMA PVM 12–55. Cf. Ugaki Kazushige, *Ugaki nikki* (Ugaki diary; Tokyo, 1954), pp. 41–42, 48; Caffrey to Hughes, Sept. 15, 29, Oct. 30, and 31, 1924, SDA 893.00/5524, 5576, 5692, and 5698; Ikei Masaru, "Dai-ichiji Feng-Chih sensō to Nihon" (The first Fengtien-Chihli war and Japan), in *Gaikōshi oyobi kokusai seiji no shomondai* (Problems in diplomatic history and international politics; Tokyo, 1962), pp. 349–378; Ikei Masaru, "Dai-niji Feng-Chih sensō to Nihon" (The second Fengtien-Chihli war and Japan), *Hōgaku kenkyū* (Journal of law, politics, and sociology), 37.3:48–75 (Mar. 1964).

6. MacMurray to Sterling, Nov. 6, 1924, SDA 500A4e/190.

7. Hughes to Schurman, Dec. 23, 1922, *FRUS 1923* (Washington, 1938), I, 713–714; Hughes to Chilton, July 9, 1923, *ibid.,* I, 675–677.

8. *Ibid.,* I, 620–631; *FRUS 1924* (Washington, 1939), I, 521–523.

9. Schurman to Hughes, July 10, 1922, *FRUS 1922,* I, 779–780.

10. The American group to Hughes, Aug. 4, 1922, *ibid.,* I, 783–785; the American Chamber of Commerce of China to Schurman, Aug. 7, 1922, SDA 500A4e/104; Schurman to Hughes, Dec. 8, 1922, SDA 893.51/4152.

11. Hughes to Schurman, Oct. 17, 1922, *FRUS 1922,* I, 787–788.

12. Schurman to Hughes, July 25, 1922, *ibid.,* I, 780–781; Geddes to Hughes, Nov. 2, 1922, *ibid.,* I, 793–794; State Department to the Japanese embassy, Nov 23, 1922, *ibid.* I, 794–796.

13. Japanese embassy to State Department, Oct. 19 and Dec. 28, 1922, *ibid.,* I, 788–790, 797–801.

14. *NGN,* II, 27–28; Wilson to MacMurray, Feb. 8, 1923, SDA 893.51/4198; *FRUS 1923,* I, 525–532.

15. Memo by MacMurray for Kellogg, Mar. 19, 1925, SDA 500A4e/199; Kellogg to Hughes, Jan. 28, 1925, SDA 500A4e/223; memo by Wellesley, Jan. 8, 1923, SDA 500A4e1/12; Sterling to MacMurray, Aug. 8, 1924, SDA 500A4e/190; MacMurray to Sterling, Nov. 6, 1924, *ibid.*

16. Pollard, pp. 259–261; Schurman to Hughes, Jan. 4, 1923, *FRUS 1923,* I, 592; Koo to Schurman, Dec. 26, 1923, *ibid.,* I, 600–605; Schurman to Hughes, Apr. 27, 1923, *ibid.,* I, 594; Jusserand to Hughes, Dec. 10, 1924,

FRUS 1924, I, 440–441; Fu Ch'i-hsüeh, *Chung-kuo wai-chiao-shih* (A diplomatic history of China; Taipei, 1957), pp. 309–314.

17. Schurman to Hughes, Dec. 8, 1923, *FRUS 1923*, I, 596–597; Chilton to Hughes, Dec. 15, 1923, *ibid.*, I, 597; Hughes to Schurman, Dec. 24, 1923, *ibid.*, I, 598.

18. MacMurray to Hughes, Nov. 17, 1925, Hughes Papers.

19. Memo by MacMurray, Jan. 31, 1924, *ibid.;* Hughes to Lodge, Apr. 17, 1924, *ibid.*

20. Memo of conversation between MacMurray and Saburi, Jan. 9, 1923, *ibid.; Shidehara*, pp. 264–267.

21. *Taiheiyō sensō e no michi: Kaisen gaikō-shi* (The road to the Pacific War: Diplomatic history of the opening of the war), ed. Kokusai seiji gakkai (Japan Association of International Relations; Tokyo, 1962–1963), I, 31–32. The date 1917 is inferred from the document mentioned in note 6 to Introduction.

22. *Ibid.*, p. 47; Louis Morton, *Strategy and Command: The First Two Years* (Washington, 1962), pp. 26–34.

23. V. P. Savvin, *Vzaimootnosheniia Tsarskoi Rosii i SSSR s Kitaem* (Moscow, 1930), pp. 104–105; Whiting, p. 195; Peter S. H. Tang, *Russian and Soviet Policy in Manchuria and Outer Mongolia 1911–1931* (Durham, 1959), pp. 141–142.

24. Brandt, *Stalin's Failure*, pp. 20ff; Hua Kang, *Chung-kuo ta-ko-ming-shih* (History of China's great revolution; Shanghai, 1932), Chaps. 2, 3; Robert C. North and Xenia J. Eudin, *M. N. Roy's Mission to China: The Communist-Kuomintang Split of 1927* (Berkeley and Los Angeles, 1963), pp. 12–19.

25. Chicherin to Sun, Feb. 7, 1922, *DVP* (Moscow, 1961), V, 83–84; Price to Hughes, May 7, 1921, *FRUS 1921* (Washington, 1936), I, 332–335; Schurman to Hughes, Oct. 9, 1922, SDA 893.51/4052; Shao Chuan Leng and Norman D. Palmer, *Sun Yat-sen and Communism* (New York, 1960), pp. 78, 88.

26. C. Martin Wilbur and Julie Lien-ying How, *Documents on Communism, Nationalism, and Soviet Advisers in China 1918–1927* (New York, 1956), pp. 140–142.

27. Conrad Brandt, Benjamin I. Schwartz, and John K. Fairbank, eds., *A Documentary History of Chinese Communism* (Cambridge, Mass., 1952), pp. 70–71.

28. Schurman to Hughes, Sept. 22, 1923, *FRUS 1923*, I, 552–555.

29. Schurman to Hughes, Dec. 1, 11, 22, and 27, 1923, *ibid.*, I, 557–559, 567, 576, 578; Hughes to Coolidge, Dec. 13, 1923, *ibid.*, I, 569–570.

30. See Chiang Kai-shek's diary during his tour of Russia, printed in *Min-kuo shih-wu-nien i-ch'ien chih Chiang Chieh-shih hsien-sheng* (Chiang Kai-shek before 1926), ed. Mao Szu-ch'eng (n.p., n.d.), V, 48–70.

31. Wilbur and How, pp. 144–145; Li Chien-nung, pp. 450–458.

32. Whiting, pp. 221–223. In September 1924, representatives of the Soviet Union and the Fengtien government signed a similar agreement on the Chinese Eastern Railway.

33. *Chiang Chieh-shih hsien-sheng*, diary entries of Mar. 14 and Oct. 9, 1924; Wilbur and How, pp. 245–247.

34. *Chiang Chieh-shih hsien-sheng*, diary entries of Nov. 18 and Sept. 18, 1924; Li Chien-nung, pp. 462ff.

35. Wilbur and How, p. 319; Mayer to Hughes, Nov. 7 and 11 [12?], 1924, *FRUS 1924*, I, 391, 393–395.

36. Yoshizawa to Shidehara, Dec. 4, 1924, JFMA PVM 12–54; Mayer to Hughes, Dec. 4 and 9, 1924, *FRUS 1924*, I, 431–433, 439–440; Schurman to Hughes, Jan. 5, 1925, *ibid.*, I, 442–443.

37. Mayer to Hughes, Dec. 3, 1924, *ibid.*, I, 403–407.

38. Yoshizawa to Shidehara, Dec. 3, 1924, Jan. 13, 15, 17, and 18, 1925, JFMA PVM 12–51; Caffrey to Hughes, July 11, 1924, *FRUS 1924*, I, 468; Hughes to Mayer, Dec. 3, 1924, *ibid.*, I, 407; Bancroft to Hughes, Nov. 24 and Dec. 15, 1924, SDA 893.51/4737 and 893.01/156; memo by Perkins, Feb. 18, 1925, SDA 893.01/182; Howard to Kellogg, May 16, 1925, SDA 893.01/192.

39. Crane to Hughes, Feb. 28 and Mar. 16, 1921, SDA 893.00/3817 and 3815; Price to Hughes, Jan. 11, 1921, SDA 893.00/3736; Price to Hughes, May 7, 1921, *FRUS 1921*, I, 332–335; Price to Crane, Apr. 26, 1921, SDA 893.00/3896; Bergholz to Hughes, Aug. 17, 1921, SDA 893.00/4039; Tenney to Crane, Aug. 12, 1922, SDA 893.00/4656; Hughes to Bergholz, June 25, 1921, *FRUS 1921*, I, 339–340.

40. Jenkins to Hughes, Oct. 27, 1923, and Mar. 12, 1924, SDA 893.00/5291 and 5416; Johnson to MacMurray, Mar. 16, 1925, Nelson T. Johnson Papers (LC); Schurman to Coolidge, Apr. 8, 1924, Jacob Gould Schurman Papers (Cornell University).

41. Hughes to Mayer, Dec. 3, 1924, *FRUS 1924*, I, 407; MacMurray to Mayer, n.d., SDA 500A4e/190.

42. For the seamen's strike, see Nym Wales, *The Chinese Labor Movement* (New York, 1945), Chaps. 1–3.

43. Johnson to MacMurray, Mar. 4 and 15, 1923, Johnson Papers; Schurman to Hughes, Mar. 20, 1923, SDA 893.00/4924; *Chiang Chieh-shih hsien-sheng*, diary entry of Sept. 9, 1924.

44. Boyé to Schubert, Aug. 8, 1924, GFMA Container No. 1520; Maltzu to Boyé, Aug. 22 and 25, 1924, *ibid.*; Franoux to Maltzau, Aug. 20, 1924, *ibid.*; Li Chien-nung, pp. 464–466; *Chiang Chieh-shih hsien-sheng*, diary entries of Sept. 25, Oct. 9 and 11, 1924; *Sun Chung-shan hsüan-chi* (Collected works of Sun Yat-sen; Peking: Jen-min ch'u-pan-she, 1956), II, 870–872; Hsü Sung-ling, "I-chiu-erh-ssu-nien Sun Chung-shan te pei-fa yü Kwang-chou shang-t'uan shih-pien" (Sun Yatsen's Northern Expedition of 1924 and the Canton Merchants Association incident), *Li-shih yen-chiu* (Historical studies), Mar. 1956, pp. 59–69.

45. *Saikin Shina kankei shomondai tekiyō* (Summary of recent problems concerning China), edited annually by the Gaimushō (Foreign Ministry) for confidential use of Diet members, Vol. 1 for 1924; Mayer to Hughes, Dec. 3, 1924, *FRUS 1924*, I, 405–407.

46. Amō to Shidehara, Aug. 30, Dec. 16 and 22, 1924, JFMA PVM 12–53; memo of conversation between Bancroft and Shidehara, Dec. 3, 1924, Edgar A. Bancroft Papers (Cambridge, Mass.). See also Yoshizawa to Shidehara, Dec. 7, 1924, JFMA PVM 12–51; Yoshida to Shidehara, Dec. 19, 1924, JFMA PVM 12–54.

47. *Ugaki nikki,* pp. 48–49.

48. *Taiheiyō sensō,* I, 199–204, 216–218; *Gotō Shimpei,* ed. Tsurumi Yūsuke (Tokyo, 1937–1938), Vol. 4, Chap. 4; Gotō's memo entitled "Nichi-Ro-Shi kankei no konpongi" (Basic principles of Japanese-Russian-Chinese relations), dated 1924, Gotō Shimpei Papers (Tokyo Institute for Municipal Research).

49. *Taiheiyō sensō,* I, 226–235; *NGN,* II, 36–57.

50. While Joffe was in Japan, the Chinese government requested the abrogation of the Sino-Japanese treaties of 1915. The demand was aimed at terminating the lease of Kwantung Territory; the original Russian lease would have expired in 1923. The Japanese government immediately responded, saying it could not even discuss such a matter, since the 1915 treaties were still valid, extending the lease for another ninety-nine years.

51. *Taiheiyō sensō,* I, 238–243.

52. See the various documents in JFMA PVM 14. The final agreements are printed in *NGN,* II, 63–68.

53. Ōta to Shidehara, July 14, 1924, JFMA PVM 12–51.

II. COLLAPSE OF THE WASHINGTON SYSTEM, 1925–1926

1. Lo Chia-lun, ed., *Kuo-fu nien-p'u* (A chronicle of the father of the nation; Taipei, 1958), II, 715–716, 721–722.

2. *Saikin Shina* (1925), Vol. 1, *passim;* Kuomintang central executive committee to the central executive committee of the Communist Party of the USSR, Mar. 12, 1925, *DVP,* VIII (1963), 188.

3. Wilbur and How, pp. 88, 148, 72; Hua Kang, Chaps. 2, 3; JFMA MT 5.3.2.155, *passim.*

4. Remer, *Foreign Investments,* pp. 495–499; *Shina kindai,* pp. 425–432; Horiuchi's report, Sept. 1925, JFMA MT 5.3.2.155.

5. Hua Kang, Chap. 3.

6. Yada to Shidehara, Feb. 14, 1925, JFMA PVM 12-56; Horiuchi to Shidehara, Apr. 20, 1925, *ibid.;* Shidehara to Yoshizawa, May 7, 1925, JFMA MT 5.3.2.155; memo of conference of Kimura, Saburi, and representatives of Japanese spinning industry, May 28, 1925, *ibid.*

7. Shidehara to Horiuchi, May 27, 1925, *ibid.*

8. Horiuchi's report, Sept. 1925, *ibid.*

9. A graphic account of the May 30th incident is given in *China Year Book 1926,* pp. 919ff.

10. Pollard, p. 267; *Chiang Chieh-shih hsien-sheng,* diary entries of July 1 and 7, 1925.

11. Yoshizawa to Shidehara, June 9, 1925, JFMA MT 5.3.2.155.

12. Yoshizawa to Shidehara, June 3 and 10, 1925, JFMA PVM 12–56; Yoshizawa to Shidehara, July 10, 1925, JFMA MT 5.3.2.155.

13. Mayer to Kellogg, June 24, 1925, *FRUS 1925* (Washington, 1940), I, 763–765.

14. Perkins to Kellogg, July 29, 1925, SDA 500A4e/297.

15. Memo of conversation between Shidehara and Eliot, July 9, 1925, JFMA MT 5.3.2.155.

16. Perkins to Kellogg, July 29, 1925, SDA 500A4e/297.

17. Kellogg to Strawn, Sept. 11, 1925, SDA 500A4e/323.

18. Cunningham to Kellogg, May 31 and June 3, 1925, *FRUS 1925*, I, 647, 649–650; Cunningham to Kellogg, June 1, 1925, SDA 893.5045/103; Mayer to Kellogg, June 6 and 12, 1925, *FRUS 1925*, I, 659, 664–666; Mayer to Kellogg, July 1, 1925, SDA 893.5045/153; Mayer to Kellogg, July 10, 1925, *FRUS 1925*, I, 778–779.

19. Kellogg to Mayer, July 1, 1925, *ibid.*, I, 767–768.

20. *Saikin Shina* (1925), Vol. 1.

21. *Ugaki nikki*, June 13 and 15, 1925; a General Staff report on Soviet influence in China, Nov. 1, 1925, JFMA PVM 12–51.

22. Yada to Shidehara, June 25, 1925, JFMA PVM 12–56.

23. Memo of conference between Kimura and Nikka jitsugyō kyōkai representatives, June 10, 1925, JFMA MT 5.3.2.155.

24. Shidehara to Morioka, June 10, 1925, *ibid.*; Shidehara to Karai, June 27, 1925, *ibid.*; memo of conversation between Shidehara and Eliot, July 9, 1925, *ibid.*

25. Murakami to Shidehara, June 30, 1925, JFMA PVM 12–56; Murakami to Shidehara, July 8, 1925, JFMA MT 5.3.2.155; Shidehara to Murakami, July 22, 1925, *ibid.*; a draft cabinet decision of July 25, 1925, *ibid.*

26. Chilton to Grew, July 7, 1925, *FRUS 1925*, I, 776–777; Kellogg to Chilton, July 23, 1925, *ibid.*, I, 793–797; Shidehara to Yoshizawa, July 3, 1925, JFMA PVM 12–57.

27. Kellogg to MacMurray, July 30, 1925, *FRUS 1925*, I, 804–805; Chilton to Kellogg, Aug. 19, 1925, *ibid.*, I, 820–821; Sze to Kellogg, Aug. 19, 1925, *ibid.*, I, 839–840.

28. Yoshizawa to Shidehara, Aug. 18, 1925, JFMA PVM 12–57; Shidehara to Yoshizawa, Aug. 20, 1925, *ibid.*; Grew to Chilton, Aug. 22, 1925, *FRUS 1925*, I, 821–822.

29. Boyé to Schubert, Oct. 24 and Aug. 22, 1925, GFMA, Container No. 1520; Schubert to Boyé, Jan. 5, 1926, *ibid.*; memo of conversation between Shidehara and Solf, Oct. 12, 1925, JFMA PVM 12–57; Schurman to Kellogg, Dec. 3, 1925, *FRUS 1926* (Washington, 1941), I, 1001-02.

30. Wilbur and How, pp. 92, 164–165.

31. Honjō to Tsuno, Jan. 24, 1926, JFMA PVM 12–55; Wilbur and How, pp. 321–330.

32. MacMurray to Johnson, Nov. 13, 1925, SDA 893.00/8052.

33. *Shina kindai*, pp. 517–518

34. Foreign Ministry memo on Chinese strategy, Sept. 8, 1925, JFMA PVM 12–57; Yoshizawa to Shidehara, Oct. 19, 1925, *ibid.*

35. Chilton to Kellogg, Sept. 18, 1925, *FRUS 1925*, I, 850; Perkins to Kellogg, July 29, 1925, SDA 500A4e/297; Sterling to MacMurray, Aug. 8, 1925, SDA 500A4e/190; *The Special Tariff Conference on the Chinese Customs Tariff (October 1925–April 1926)* (Peking, 1928), pp. 43–44.

36. Kellogg to the American delegation, Sept. 9, 1925, *FRUS 1925*, I, 842–847.

37. Kellogg to MacMurray, Oct. 5 and 23, 1925, *ibid.*, I, 854–856, 859–860; Kellogg to Borah, Aug. 20, 1925, William E. Borah Papers (LC).

38. Shidehara to Matsudaira, Oct. 20, 1925, JFMA PVM 12–57.

39. *Special Tariff Conference*, p. 197.

40. *Ibid.*, pp. 241–250; American delegation to Kellogg, Dec. 2, 1925, *FRUS 1925*, I, 883.

41. *Special Tariff Conference*, pp. 116–117.

42. *Ibid.*, p. 130

43. Stanley F. Wright, *China's Struggle for Tariff Autonomy 1843–1938* (Shanghai, 1938), pp. 519, 526–529.

44. A draft cabinet decision, Nov. 20, 1925, JFMA PVM 12–57; Shidehara to Japanese delegation, Jan. 9, 1926, *ibid.*

45. Chinese delegation to Foreign Ministry, Jan. 12, 1926, CFMA, "Chung-Jih hu-hui-an" (Sino-Japanese Reciprocal Treaty); Yoshizawa to Wang, Jan. 19, 1926, *ibid.*; Wang to Yoshizawa, Jan. 27, 1926, *ibid.*; Taxation Bureau to Foreign Ministry, Feb. 9, 1926, *ibid.*; Chinese legation in Tokyo to Foreign Ministry, Jan. 1, 1926, *ibid.*

46. Li Chien-nung, pp. 488–493.

47. MacMurray to Kellogg, Dec. 7, 9, 11, and 23, 1925, *FRUS 1925*, I, 620–622, 623–624.

48. A chronicle of the Chinese civil war prepared by the General Staff, Dec. 1925, JMA T 627. Code numbers in this and other documents in Japanese military archives are those adopted by John Young, *Checklist of Microfilm Reproductions of Selected Archives of Japanese Army, Navy, and Other Government Agencies* (Washington, 1959). See also Yoshida to Shidehara, rec. Nov. 27 and Dec. 1, 1925, JFMA PVM 12–54; Kodama to Shidehara, rec. Nov. 28, 1925, *ibid.*; Arita to Shidehara, rec. Nov. 30, 1925, *ibid.*; Yoshizawa to Shidehara, rec. Nov. 29, 1925, *ibid.*; Kwantung Army memo, Mar. 1926, JMA T 632; Yada to Shidehara, rec. Dec. 19, 1925, JFMA PVM 12–57; Yoshizawa to Shidehara, Jan. 13, 1926, *ibid.*

49. Chinese Foreign Ministry to MacMurray, Jan. 16, 1926, *FRUS 1926*, I, 1004–05; Kellogg to Sze, Mar. 1, 1926, *ibid.*, I, 1018–22; Boyé to Schubert, Jan. 10, 1926, GFMA Container No. 1520; Stresemann to Boyé, Jan. 12, 1926, *ibid.*; Wallroth to Rantzau, Feb. 5, 1926, *ibid.*; Schubert to Rantzau, Feb. 8, 1926, *ibid.*; Stresemann to Rantzau, Feb. 19, 1926, *ibid.*

50. MacMurray to Kellogg, Mar. 9, 12, 13, 15, and 16, 1926, *FRUS 1926*, I, 595–596, 598–602; Wilbur and How, p. 329.

51. Wright, p. 537.

52. Shidehara to Japanese delegation, Feb. 28, 1926, JFMA PVM 12–57.

53. Wright, pp. 544, 571–572, 574ff.

54. Japanese delegation to Shidehara, May 8 and July 1, 1926, JFMA PVM 12–57; memo of conversation between Johnson and Peel, June 18, 1926, SDA 500A4e/612; Strawn to Kellogg, May 12, 1926, SDA 500A4e/706; C. F. Remer, *A Study of Chinese Boycotts* (Baltimore, 1933), p. 108.

55. Strawn to Kellogg, Sept. 16, 1926, SDA 500A4e/652 1/2; Japanese delegation to Shidehara, June 5, 1926, JFMA PVM 12–57; MacMurray to Kellogg, July 7 and Aug. 30, 1926, SDA 893.00/7504 and 7713; MacMurray to Kellogg, Aug. 14, 1926, SDA 893.01/223 and 225.

56. Johnson to MacMurray, June 24, 1926, Johnson Papers; memo by Johnson for Kellogg, Aug. 20, 1926, SDA 893.01/228; Kellogg to MacMurray, Aug. 24, 1926, *FRUS 1926*, I, 682.

57. Shidehara to Japanese delegation, May 17 and June 1, 1926, JFMA PVM 12–57; Japanese delegation to Shidehara, June 20, 1926, *ibid.*

58. Japanese delegation to Shidehara, May 26 and June 5, 1926, *ibid.;* a Foreign Ministry memo, n.d., *ibid.;* Shidehara to Japanese delegation, June 15, 1926, *ibid.*
59. Wright, pp. 720–747.
60. Wesley R. Fishel, *The End of Extraterritoriality in China* (Berkeley and Los Angeles, 1952), Chap. 6.
61. For a summary of Japanese attitude toward the League of Nations, see Roy Hidemichi Akagi, *Japan's Foreign Relations 1542–1936: A Short History* (Tokyo, 1936), Chap. 19.

III. DIPLOMACY OF THE NORTHERN EXPEDITION, 1926–1927

1. The best source on the military campaigns of the Nationalists is *KMWH*. For some accounts of warlord betrayals, see such first-hand reports as Ch'en Kung-po, *Tzu-chuan* (Autobiography; Hongkong, 1957), pp. 59ff; Kuo Mo-jo, "Pei-fa t'u-tz'u" (The Northern Expedition), in his *Ko-ming ch'un-ch'iu* (History of the revolution; Shanghai, 1951), II, 289–415.
2. Hollington K. Tong, *Chiang Kai-shek: Soldier and Statesman* (Shanghai, 1937), I, 107–122.
3. Wilbur and How, pp. 220, 222, 228–231, 245, 248–253; Brandt, *Stalin's Failure*, pp. 86–87.
4. Wilbur and How, pp. 372ff, 413–421; Ch'en Kung-po, pp. 98–133; Sasaki Tōitsu, *Wuhan ka Nanking ka* (Wuhan or Nanking?; Tokyo, 1927), *passim.*
5. Kayanuma Hiro, *Chūgoku kakumei yonjū-nen* (Forty years of the Chinese revolution; Tokyo, 1954), p. 125; *Chiang Chieh-shih hsien-sheng,* diary entry of Aug. 20, 1926.
6. *Mori Kaku,* ed. Yamaura Kan'ichi (Tokyo, 1940), pp. 535–539; *Yamamoto Jōtarō denki* (Biography of Yamamoto Jōtarō; Tokyo, 1942), pp. 507–508.
7. Wilbur and How, p. 383; Lockhart to MacMurray, Jan. 20, 1927, SDA 893.00/8342; *Chiang Chieh-shih hsien-sheng,* diary entries of Apr. 3, July 24, and Aug. 31, 1926; Satō Shunzō, *Shina no kokunai tōsō* (The internal struggle in China; Tokyo, 1941), pp. 130–140.
8. *KMWH*, XII, 1825–28.
9. Sasaki, *Wuhan,* pp. 17–18, 143; Ch'en Kung-po, pp. 66–72. A graphic account of the taking of the Hankow British concession is given in Sasaki, *Wuhan,* pp. 35–46.
10. *Ch'ing-tang shih-lu* (True records of the purification of the party; n.p., 1928), pp. 258–260.
11. *Chiang Chieh-shih hsien-sheng,* diary entries of Apr. 3, 26, July 9 and 26, 1926.
12. *KMWH*, XII, 1952–54; *ibid.,* XIII, 2003; Shao Ting-hsün, "Chung-kuo ti-i-tz'u ko-ming chan-cheng shih-ch'i ti Mei-Jih kou-chieh" (American and Japanese imperialistic collaboration in China during China's first revolutionary war), *Li-shih yen-chiu* (Aug. 1958), p. 22.
13. *Chiang Chieh-shih hsien-sheng yen-shuo chi* (Collected speeches of Chiang Kai-shek; Canton, 1927), pp. 641–648, 664.

14. Adams to MacMurray, Sept. 16, 1926, SDA 893.00/7899; Lockhart to MacMurray, Sept. 15, 1926, SDA 893.00/7782.

15. Taxation Bureau to Foreign Ministry, Apr. 10, 27, and June 16, 1926, CFMA, "Hsiu-kai shui-tse-an" (Tariff revision); Foreign Ministry to Taxation Bureau, Apr. 18, 1926, *ibid.*; American delegation to Kellogg, Aug. 7, 1926, *FRUS 1928* (Washington, 1943), II, 370–371.

16. A typical example was a letter from representatives of the "Shanghai association for maintaining Chinese goods," the "Shanghai association of citizens proposing the use of national goods," and the Shanghai Chamber of Commerce. They argued, first, that the Sino-Japanese treaty of 1896 was legally up for revision in 1926. Second, the Sino-Soviet treaty of 1924 had indicated the framework of a bilateral treaty according to the principle of equality. Third, revision was overdue under the terms of the Nine-Power Treaty. "Unless the treaty with Japan is abrogated," asked the memorialists, "what good is there to talk about the friendship between the two nations of the same race?" (Sun Ch'uan-fang to Foreign Ministry, Aug. 30, 1926, CFMA, "Chung-Jih hsiu-yüeh-an" [Sino-Japanese treaty revision]).

17. Yoshizawa to Shidehara, Oct. 17, 1926, JFMA PVM 62; *FRUS 1926*, I, 984–1001; *Peking shūhō* (Peking weekly; Dec. 5, 1926), pp. 10–12.

18. Mayer to Kellogg, Jan. 25, 1927, *FRUS 1927* (Washington, 1942), II, 349; Wright, pp. 616–619.

19. *KMWH*, XII, 1839–42; Vincent to MacMurray, July 19, 1926, SDA 893.00/7579.

20. Remer, *Chinese Boycotts*, p. 108; *Chiang Chieh-shih hsien-sheng*, diary entries of Apr. 14 and June 5, 1926; *Kuang-chou Wu-han shih-ch'i ko-ming wai-chiao wen-hsien* (Documents of revolutionary diplomacy during the Canton and Wuhan periods; Shanghai, 1933), English section, pp. 1–29; Wright, pp. 602–616; Mayer to Kellogg, Oct. 20, 26, 29, and Nov. 3, 1926, *FRUS 1926*, I, 883–885, 888–889, 892–893, 896–897.

21. Dorothy Borg, *American Policy and the Chinese Revolution 1925–1928* (New York, 1947), p. 228; Evan Luard, *Britain and China* (London, 1962), p. 38.

22. *FRUS 1926*, I, 923–929.

23. *Peking shūhō* (Jan. 16, 1927), pp. 18–20; Ch'en to Kellogg, Dec. 31, 1926, *FRUS 1926*, I, 935.

24. Wilbur and How, p. 384.

25. Hung Chün-p'ei, *Kuo-min cheng-fu wai-chiao-shih* (Diplomatic history of the National government; Shanghai, 1930), I, 88–89; Pollard, pp. 301–302.

26. Howard to Kellogg, Jan. 19, 1927, *FRUS 1927*, II, 344–345.

27. Morioka to Shidehara, Jan. 31, 1927, JFMA S.1.6.1.5.4; Yada to Shidehara, Feb. 1, 1927; *ibid.*; Shidehara to Matsudaira, Feb. 2, 1927, *ibid.*; Pollard, pp. 302–303.

28. Chamberlain's statement in the House of Commons, Feb. 10, 1927, BGD: *Parliamentary Debates, Commons*, 5th ser., 202:317–327; Takao to Shidehara, rec. Feb. 13, 1927, JFMA S.1.6.1.5.4; BGD: *Papers Relating to the Agreements Relative to the British Concessions at Hankow and Kiukiang* (London, 1927).

29. Kellogg to Mayer, Nov. 1, Oct. 5, 16, and 25, 1926, *FRUS 1926*, I, 895–896, 871, 880, 887; Kellogg to MacMurray, Dec. 4, 1926, *ibid.*, I, 907; Mayer to Kellogg, Oct. 3, 1926, *ibid.*, I, 869; Kellogg to Mayer, Oct. 22, 1926, *ibid.*, I, 885. The decision against the use of force to maintain treaty rights was partially owing to the State Department's view of American public opinion. Some, though not all, American missionaries in China, particularly educators in the northern cities, had urged the relinquishment of part of the existing treaties. In the United States there were various groups, including missionary boards, peace organizations, and *ad hoc* committees which were actively interested in upholding the cause of Chinese nationalism. Although State Department officials were privately critical of these groups' stereotyped pictures of China, they judged that the American public was overwhelmingly opposed to the use of force to preserve the treaty status. Cf. Paul A. Varg, *Missionaries, Chinese, and Diplomats: The American Protestant Missionary Movement in China, 1890–1952* (Princeton, 1958), Chap. 9; Borg, Chap. 5; MacMurray to Kellogg, Nov. 29, 1926, SDA 893.00/7767; Luce to Kellogg, Sept. 9, 1926, SDA 893.00/7625; Ward to Kellogg, Sept. 21, 1926, SDA 893.00/7666; Johnson to N. Roosevelt, Nov. 15, 1926, Johnson Papers; Johnson to Gauss, Feb. 15, 1927, *ibid.*

30. Memo by Johnson, Jan. 19, 1927, *ibid.;* Williams to office of naval operations, Jan. 13, 1927, SDA 893.00/8063.

31. Kellogg to MacMurray, Jan. 11, 1927, *FRUS 1927*, II, 45; MacMurray to Kellogg, Jan. 15 and 18, 1927, *ibid.*, II, 47, 49, 51; memo by Johnson, Jan. 19, 1927, Johnson Papers; memo of conversation between Kellogg and Sze, Jan. 24, 1927, *FRUS 1927*, II, 53; memo by Kellogg, Jan. 27, 1927, *ibid.*, II, 59; Kellogg to MacMurray, Jan. 28 and 31, 1927, *ibid.*, II, 61, 65–66; Kellogg to Mayer, Jan. 25, 1927, *ibid.*, II, 56; British embassy to Kellogg, Jan. 26, 1927, *ibid.*, II, 56–58; Kellogg to MacMurray, Jan. 28, 31, and Feb. 1, 1927, *ibid.*, II, 59–61, 65–66, 68. The State Department avoided the term "neutrality" so as not to give the impression of interfering with China's internal affairs, and it also insisted that the French settlement at Shanghai was not included in the proposal. (Kellogg to MacMurray, Feb. 11, 1927, *ibid.*, II, 72–73.)

32. MacMurray to Kellogg, Feb. 5 and 19, 1927, *FRUS 1927*, II, 69–70, 74; Takao to Shidehara, rec. Feb. 8 and 13, 1927, JFMA S.1.6.1.5.6; Yada to Shidehara, Feb. 10, 1927, *ibid.*

33. Memos of conversations between Kellogg and Sze, Dec. 7, 1926 and Jan. 6, 1927, SDA 711.93/105 and 112.

34. British embassy to State Department, Sept. 17, 1926, *FRUS 1926*, I, 854–855; State Department to British embassy, Oct. 5, 1926, *ibid.*, I, 855.

35. Warnshuis to Johnson, Dec. 27, 1926, SDA 711.93/106; House Concurrent Resolution 46, 69th Congress, 2nd Session.

36. Memo by Johnson for Kellogg, Jan. 19, 1927, Johnson Papers; Mayer to Kellogg, Jan. 25, 1927, SDA 711.93/116; *FRUS 1927*, II, 350–353.

37. Gauss to Kellogg, Jan. 31, 1927, SDA 711.93/125; Borg, pp. 246, 251–252; Abbott to Johnson, rec. Feb. 1, 1927, SDA 711.93/134; Lewis to Wright, Jan. 27, 1927, SDA 711.93/126.

38. Memo of conversation between Kellogg and Sze, Jan. 27, 1927, *FRUS 1927*, II, 353–354; memo of conversation between Peck and Sze, Jan. 27,

1927, SDA 711.93/124; *Peking shūhō* (Feb. 20, 1927), p. 21; *ibid.* (Jan. 30, 1927), p. 29; Davis to MacMurray, Feb. 5, 1927, SDA 893.00/8368; Gauss to MacMurray, Feb. 4, 1927, SDA 893.00/8381; MacMurray to Kellogg, Feb 10 and 15, 1927, *FRUS 1927*, II, 360–361, 362.

39. Memo by Johnson for Kellogg, Oct. 26, 1927, Johnson Papers.

40. Kellogg to MacMurray, Feb. 15, 1927, *FRUS 1927*, II, 383; Johnson to Hornbeck, Mar. 10, 1927, Johnson Papers; Johnson to MacMurray, Sept. 29, 1927, *ibid.*

41. *NGN*, II, 88–91.

42. *Ibid.*, II, 83–88. See also Shinobu Junpei, *Man-Mō tokushu ken'ekiron* (A study of Japan's special rights and interests in Manchuria and Mongolia; Tokyo, 1932).

43. Foreign Ministry memo, n.d. [Jan. 1927], JFMA PVM 32. See also Yanaibara Tadao, *Manshū mondai* (The Manchurian question; Tokyo, 1934), 78–85.

44. Memo by Matsui, Aug. 2, 1926, JFMA S.1.6.1.5.3.

45. Hata to Matsui, Aug. 19, 1926, JMA T 641.

46. Shidehara to Yoshida, Aug. 24, 1926, *ibid.*; Foreign Ministry memo, Nov. 26, 1926, JFMA S.1.6.1.5.3; Foreign Ministry memo, n.d. [late 1926], *ibid.*

47. *Ibid.*

48. *NGN*, II, 91–92.

49. Japanese legation to Foreign Ministry, Oct. 14, 1926, CFMA, "Hsiukai shui-tse-an"; Chinese delegation to Foreign Ministry, Oct. 19, 1926, *ibid.*; Arnold to MacMurray, Dec. 7, 1926, *FRUS 1926*, I, 373.

50. Yoshizawa to Shidehara, Oct. 25 and 29, 1926, JFMA PVM 62; memos of conversations between Shidehara and Wang, Oct. 21 and 28, 1926, *ibid.*; *Saikin Shina* (1926), III, 100–105.

51. A draft imperial decision, Jan. 19, 1927 (original date, Jan. 8), JFMA PVM 59.

52. Foreign Ministry memo, Feb. 5, 1927, *ibid.*; Yoshizawa to Shidehara, rec. Jan. 23, 1927, *ibid.*; Shidehara to Yoshizawa, Jan. 25, 1927, *ibid.*

53. Foreign Ministry memo and various drafts for a new treaty, Jan. 1927, CFMA, "Chung-Jih hsiu-yüeh-an."

54. The Japanese draft of Mar. 22, 1927, *ibid.*

55. See *Saikin Shina* (1927), III, 84ff.

56. Memo of conversation between Shidehara and Wang, Nov. 4, 1926, JFMA S.1.6.1.5.3.

57. Shidehara to Matsui, Feb. 4, 1927, *ibid.*; Takao to Shidehara, Jan. 21, 1927, *ibid.*

58. MacVeagh to Kellogg, Sept. 10, 13, and 21, 1926, SDA 893.00/7620, 7628, and 7711; Shidehara to Takao, Jan. 12, 1927, JFMA S.1.6.1.5.3; *Saikin Shina* (1927), II, 171–172, 172–173, 174, 178–179; Matsudaira to Shidehara, Jan. 31, 1927, JFMA S.1.6.1.5.6.

59. Kellogg to Mayer, Jan. 24, 1927, *FRUS 1927*, II, 377; Foreign Ministry memo, n.d. [Jan. 1927], JFMA PVM 32.

60. Kimura's marginal comment on Matsui's memo of Aug. 2, 1926, JFMA S.1.6.1.5.3; Murakami to Shidehara, rec. Jan. 8, 1927, JFMA PVM 59; Takao to Shidehara, Jan. 2, 1927, JFMA S.1.6.1.5.3; Horiuchi Kanjō, *Chūgoku no*

arashi no naka de (Amid the storms of China; Tokyo, 1950), pp. 62–63; Mayer to Kellogg, Jan. 25, 1927, *FRUS 1927*, II, 349; *Saikin Shina* (1927), II, 223.

61. Yada to Shidehara, Dec. 26, 1926, and Jan. 9, 1927, JFMA S.1.6.1.5.3; Yoshizawa to Shidehara, rec. Dec. 18, 1926, *ibid.;* Wilbur and How, p. 528.

IV. REVOLUTION AND COUNTERREVOLUTION, 1927

1. Gauss to Kellogg, Mar. 21 and 22, 1927, *FRUS 1927*, II, 89–90; Brandt, *Stalin's Failure*, p. 113; Gauss to Kellogg, Mar. 23, 1927, *FRUS 1927*, II, 90.

2. *Saikin Shina* (1927), IV, 220–222. Graphic accounts of the episode by eyewitnesses are given by Alice Tindale Hobart, *Within the Walls of Nanking* (London, 1927); Pearl Buck, *My Several Worlds* (New York, 1954), Pt. III.

3. Li to Ch'en and Teng, Mar. 25, 1927, *KMWH*, XIV, 2378–79; Ch'eng to Ch'en, Mar. 25, 1927, *ibid.*, 2379–80; MacMurray to Kellogg, Mar. 27, 1927, *FRUS 1927*, II, 164–165. Cf. Harold Isaacs, *Tragedy of the Chinese Revolution*, 2nd rev. ed. (Stanford, 1961), p. 145.

4. Davis to Kellogg, Mar. 28, 1927, *FRUS 1927*, II, 151–163.

5. *Ibid.*

6. Barton to Chamberlain, Mar. 29, 1927, BGD: *Papers Relating to the Nanking Incident of March 24 and 25, 1927* (London, 1927); Giles to Chamberlain, Apr. 9 and 19, 1927, *ibid.*

7. *Saikin Shina* (1927), IV, 224–234.

8. *Ibid.*, IV, 238, 240–241, 244–245; Morioka to Shidehara, Mar. 25, 1927, JFMA PVM 26.

9. Yada to Shidehara, rec. Mar. 29, 1927, *ibid.*

10. *Saikin Shina* (1927), IV, 241; Fujimura to Shidehara, Mar. 25, 1927, JFMA PVM 26; Morioka to Shidehara, Mar. 25, 1927, *ibid.*

11. Li to Ch'en and Teng, Mar. 25, 1927, *KMWH*, XIV, 2378–79; Ch'eng to Ch'en, Mar. 25, 1927, *ibid.*, pp. 2379–80; Davis to Kellogg, Mar. 28, 1927, *FRUS 1927*, II, 161, 162; Williams to office of naval operations, Mar. 27, 1927, SDA 893.00/8480; *Shidehara*, pp. 317–322.

12. Memo by Matsui, Mar. 28, 1927, JFMA PVM 32; memo by Ugaki, Apr. 8, 1927, *NGN*, II, 92–95.

13. Shidehara to Yada, Mar. 26, 1927, JFMA PVM 27; *Saikin Shina* (1927), IV, 298–299; MacVeagh to Kellogg, Mar. 28, 1927, *FRUS 1927*, II, 164.

14. MacMurray to Kellogg, Mar. 29, 1927, *ibid.*, II, 165–166; *Saikin Shina* (1927), IV, 264–266.

15. *Ibid.*, IV, 299.

16. Shidehara to Yoshizawa, Mar. 30, 1927, JFMA PVM 27.

17. Yada to Shidehara, Mar. 29, 1927, *ibid.;* Shidehara to Yada, Mar. 31, 1927, *ibid.;* Yada to Shidehara, Apr. 2 and 3, 1927, *ibid.*

18. Isaacs, pp. 152, 162, 166, 165; Chiang to Li, etc., Apr. 3, 1927, *KMWH*, XVI, 2797–98; memo by Wu Ching-heng, Apr. 1927, frontispiece in *ibid.*

19. Wilbur and How, pp. 9, 11, 408.

20. Isaacs, Chap. 11; John B. Powell, *My Twenty-five Years in China* (New York, 1945), pp. 152–160.

21. *KMWH*, XVI, 2810–20; *Chiang yen-shuo chi*, pp. 677–686.

22. Kellogg to MacMurray, Apr. 2, 1927, *FRUS 1927*, II, 175–177; MacMurray to Kellogg, Apr. 1, 1927, *ibid.*, II, 172–173; Yada to Shidehara, Apr. 2, 1927, JFMA PVM 27.

23. *Saikin Shina* (1927), IV, 304–305, 270–271; MacMurray to Kellogg, Apr. 5, 1927, *FRUS 1927*, II, 181–182.

24. Hung Chün-p'ei, pp. 105–106; *Saikin Shina* (1927), IV, 271.

25. Howard to Kellogg, Apr. 5, 1927, *FRUS 1927*, II, 179–181; Kellogg to MacMurray, Apr. 5, 1927, *ibid.*, II, 181; memos of conversations between Kellogg and British chargé, and between Kellogg and Matsudaira, Apr. 6, 1927, *ibid.*, II, 181–182, 183–184; Kellogg to Howard, Apr. 7, 1927, *ibid.*, II, 184–185; MacMurray to Kellogg, Apr. 9, 1927, *ibid.*, II, 186–187; memo of conversation between Shidehara and Eliot, Apr. 2, 1927, JFMA PVM 27; *Saikin Shina* (1927), IV, 275.

26. Yada to Shidehara, Apr. 13, 1927, JFMA PVM 27.

27. Lockhart to Kellogg, Apr. 14 and 15, 1927, *FRUS 1927*, II, 192–194, 195–196.

28. MacMurray to Kellogg, Apr. 15, 1927, *ibid.*, II, 197–198; Yoshizawa to Shidehara, Apr. 15, 1927, JFMA PVM 27.

29. MacMurray to Kellogg, Mar. 29, 1927, *FRUS 1927*, II, 166–168; MacMurray to Kellogg, Apr. 9 and 23, 1927, SDA 893.00/8633 and 8757.

30. Jenkins to Kellogg, Apr. 17, 1927, SDA 893.00/8699.

31. Memos of conversations between Kellogg and British, Italian, and Spanish ambassadors, Apr. 14, 1927, SDA 893.00/8678, 8679, and 8680; Kellogg to MacMurray, Apr. 20 and May 9, 1927, *FRUS 1927*, II, 203–204, 219–220.

32. MacMurray to Kellogg, May 28, 1927, *ibid.*, II, 222–223; Johnson to Schurman, May 17, 1927, Johnson Papers; Johnson to Monroe, May 16, 1927, *ibid.*

33. Howard to Kellogg, May 3, 1927, *FRUS 1927*, II, 216–217; Locker-Lampson's statements in the House of Commons, Apr. 26, May 10 and 16, 1927, BGD: *Parliamentary Debates, Commons*, 1927, 5th ser., 205:662–663 and 206:203, 898–899; Chamberlain's speech in *ibid.*, 206:19–23; Newton to Ch'en, May 17, 1927, BGD: *Papers Relating to the Nanking Incident*, pp. 30–31.

34. Yada to Shidehara, Apr. 2 and 3, 1927, JFMA PVM 27.

35. *Saikin Shina* (1927), IV, 319.

36. *Mori*, pp. 527–529; Shidehara, *Gojū-nen*, pp. 257–260.

37. *Tanaka Giichi Denki* (Biography of Tanaka Giichi), Vol. 1 (Tokyo, 1958), pp. 324–330; Ishigami Ryōhei, *Hara Kei botsugo* (After Hara Kei's death; Tokyo, 1960), pp. 286–298, 303–317; *Yamamoto*, pp. 508–510.

38. *Tanaka*, Vol. 2 (Tokyo, 1960), pp. 566–569.

39. Tanaka to Yoshizawa, Apr. 23, 1927, JFMA PVM 27; *FRUS 1927*, II, 212; *Saikin Shina* (1927), IV, 368, and II, 238–240.

40. *Ibid.*, II, 225–226, 236.

41. *Ibid.*, II, 233, 236.

42. Tanaka to Yoshizawa, May 20, 1927, JFMA PVM 41.

43. Kamata to division of information, Feb. 8, 1928, JFMA S.1.6.1.5.30.
44. *FRUS 1927*, II, 108–115; *Saikin Shina* (1927), II, 250.
45. *Tanaka*, II, 620–621, 628. See also Baba Akira, "Dai-ichiji Shantung shuppei to Tanaka gaikō" (The first Shantung expedition and the Tanaka diplomacy), *Aziya kenkyū* (Asiatic studies), 10.3:50–77 (Oct. 1963).
46. *Tanaka*, II, 621–623; Kellogg to MacMurray, May 28, 1927, *FRUS 1927*, II, 123–124.
47. *Kuo-wen chou-pao* (Kuowen weekly), May 15 and June 5 and 26, 1927.
48. Wilbur and How, pp. 11–13; Isaacs, pp. 172, 184–194, 212–216; Hatano Kan'ichi, *Chūgoku kyōsantō-shi* (A history of the Chinese Communist Party; Tokyo, 1961), I, 187–200; Brandt, *Stalin's Failure*, pp. 132ff; Wang's report, Nov. 5, 1927, *KMWH*, XVI, 2851–65; Feng Yü-hsiang, *Wo te sheng-huo* (My life; Shanghai, n.d.), Chap. 37.
49. Arnold J. Toynbee, ed., *Survey of International Affairs 1927* (London, 1929), pp. 329–330; Hollington Tong, I, 164ff; *KMWH*, XVII, 310ff.
50. Chamberlain's statements in the House of Commons, July 28 and Nov. 8, 1927, BGD: *Parliamentary Debates, Commons*, 1927, 5th ser., 209: 1528–30, and 210:24–26.
51. Kellogg to MacMurray, July 12, 1927, *FRUS 1927*, II, 398; Mayer to Kellogg, Aug. 17 and Oct. 27, 1927, SDA 893.00/9320 and 9540; attaché's reports, Aug. 18 and Sept. 2, 1927, SDA 893.00/9459 and 9523; Johnson to Lamont, Aug. 19, 1927, Johnson Papers.
52. Kellogg to Wilbur, Sept. 13, 1927, SDA 893.00/9401; memo of conversation between Johnson and Wei, Sept. 13, 1927, Johnson Papers.
53. Memo by MacMurray, Oct. 20, 1927, *FRUS 1927*, II, 363–365; memos of conversations between Johnson and Wei, Sept. 13, and between Johnson and Lee, Dec. 13 and 15, 1927, Johnson Papers; memo of conversation between Kellogg, Johnson, and Sze, Dec. 15, 1927, *ibid.*; Kellogg to MacMurray, Dec. 18, 1927, *FRUS 1927*, II, 366–367; MacMurray to Kellogg, Dec. 28, 1927, *ibid.*, II, 368–370.
54. Foreign Ministry memo, n.d., JFMA PVM 41.
55. Minutes of the meetings are found in JFMA PVM 41.
56. *Tanaka*, II, 631–634, 638–639; Baba, pp. 73ff.
57. *Tanaka*, II, 654–658.
58. *Ibid.*, II, 739.
59. *Ibid.*, II, 740. The Japanese faith in Chiang Kai-shek was noted by the American consul general at Shanghai, who reported that only the Japanese and pro-Japanese Chinese took Chiang seriously whereas the latter was in fact "doomed to obscurity." (Cunningham to Kellogg, Sept. 14, 1927, SDA 893.00/9512.)
60. *Tokyo Asahi shimbun*, Oct. 3 (evening), 13, and 24, 1927; Hollington Tong, I, 187–188; memo of conversation between Tanaka and Chiang, *NGN*, II, 102–106.

V. COPROSPERITY IN MANCHURIA, 1927

1. Kodama to Tanaka, Apr. 23, 1927, JFMA S.1.6.1.5.3; Yoshida to Kimura, Apr. 21, 1927, JFMA PVM 23.

2. Memo by Saitō, June 1, 1927, JMA T 635.
3. *Tanaka*, I, 547ff; Ishigami, pp. 289–290, 365.
4. *Mori*, pp. 115–117, 417ff.
5. *Yamamoto*, pp. 85ff, 530–532.
6. Tanaka to Yoshizawa, May 20, 1927, JFMA PVM 41.
7. Tanaka to Yoshizawa and Yoshida, June 2, 1927, *ibid.*
8. Yoshizawa to Tanaka, rec. June 10, 1927, *ibid.*
9. Yoshida to Tanaka, June 8 and 9, 1927, *ibid.*
10. Memo by Kimura, June 1927, NGN, II, 97–101.
11. See JFMA PVM 41 for minutes of the conference.
12. *Tanaka*, II, 654–658.
13. Usui Katsumi, "Shōwa shoki no Chū-Nichi kankei: Hokubatsu e no kanshō" (Sino-Japanese relations during the early Showa period: The intervention in the Northern Expedition), in *Kokushiron-shū* (Essays in Japanese history; Kyoto, 1959), II, 1664–65; Takehiko Yoshihashi, *Conspiracy at Mukden: The Rise of the Japanese Military* (New Haven, 1963), pp. 23–26; Sadako N. Ogata, *Defiance in Manchuria: The Making of Japanese Foreign Policy, 1931–1932* (Berkeley and Los Angeles, 1964), pp. 10–11.
14. For a probable origin of a document which was drafted around this time and later developed into the forged "Tanaka memorandum," see Inou Dentarō, " 'Tanaka Jōsōbun' o meguru nisan no mondai" (Problems of the "Tanaka memorandum"), *Kokusai seiji*, No. 26:72–87 (July 1964).
15. Tanaka to Yoshida, July 20, 1927, JFMA PVM 23.
16. Yoshida to Tanaka, July 23, Aug. 1 and 2, 1927, *ibid.; Saikin Shina* (1927), IV, 64.
17. Yamazaki to Kimura, Aug. 17, 1927, JFMA PVM 23.
18. Honjō to Minami, July 30, 1927, *ibid.;* Yoshida to Tanaka, Aug. 3, 1927, *ibid.*
19. Tanaka to Yoshida, Aug. 5, 1927, *ibid.*
20. Yoshida to Tanaka, Aug. 4, 1927, *ibid.;* Yamazaki to Kimura, Aug. 17, 1927, *ibid.;* Yoshida to Tanaka, Aug. 5, 1927, *ibid.*
21. Yoshida to Tanaka, Aug. 5, 1927, *ibid.;* Yamazaki to Kimura, Aug. 17, 1927, *ibid.*
22. Yoshida to Tanaka, Aug. 6, 1927, *ibid.; Saikin Shina* (1927), IV, 79–80.
23. *Yamamoto*, pp. 561–562.
24. *Ibid.*, pp. 559–560, 563–564.
25. Memo of conversation between Tanaka, Debuchi, and Yamamoto, Aug. 12, 1927, JFMA PVM 23.
26. *Saikin Shina* (1927), IV, 92–94.
27. Tanaka to Yoshizawa, Sept. 6, 1927, JFMA PVM 23; Mori to Yoshizawa, Sept. 6, 1927, *ibid.; Saikin Shina* (1927), IV, 97–101.
28. *Ibid.*, IV, 103–104; Tanaka to Yoshida, Sept. 10, 1927, JFMA PVM 23; Tanaka to Yoshizawa, Sept. 9, 1927, *ibid.;* Yoshizawa to Tanaka, Sept. 10, 1927, *ibid.*
29. *Yamamoto*, pp. 539–542, 564, 567–568.
30. *Ibid.*, pp. 564, 569–575, 578.
31. *Ibid.*, pp. 578–580; *Saikin Shina* (1927), IV, 129ff.

32. The texts of the two documents are in JFMA PVM 24; Yoshizawa to Tanaka, Oct. 16, 1927, *ibid.*

33. Yoshizawa to Tanaka, Oct. 12 and 13, 1927, *ibid.*; Honjō to Hata, Oct. 13, 1927, *ibid.*; Yamamoto to Saitō, Oct. 14, 1927, *ibid.*; Tanaka to Yoshizawa, n.d., *ibid.*

34. Yoshizawa to Tanaka, Oct. 16 and 26, 1927, *ibid.*; Tanaka to Yamamoto, Oct. 18 and 21, 1927, *ibid.*; Yoshida to Tanaka, Oct. 20, 1927, *ibid.*; *Yamamoto*, p. 583; Arita Hachirō, *Bakahachi to hito wa yū* (They call me Foolish Hachi; Tokyo, 1959), pp. 49–50; memo of conversations between Debuchi and Yamamoto, Oct. 28, 1927, and between Arita, Mori, and Yamamoto, Oct. 29, 1927, JFMA PVM 24; Yoshizawa to Tanaka, Oct. 20, 1927, *ibid.*; Tanaka to Yoshizawa, Nov. 7, 1927, *ibid.*

35. Yoshizawa to Tanaka, Nov. 14, 1927, *ibid.*; Kamata to Yamamoto, Nov. 14, 30, and Dec. 5, 1927, *ibid.*; Tanaka to Yoshizawa, Nov. 26 and Dec. 2, 1927, *ibid.*; Honjō to Minami, Dec. 4, 1927, *ibid.*

36. *Survey of International Affairs 1927*, pp. 374–379; memo by Foreign Ministry, Jan. 25, 1928, GFMA Container No. 1520; memo of conversations between Tanaka and Dougalevsky, May 24, June 16, and July 1, 1927, JFMA PVM 22; *Tanaka*, II, 748–749.

37. *Nichi-Bei bunka kōshō-shi*, II, 27–37.

38. Herbert Feis, *The Diplomacy of the Dollar: First Era, 1919–1932* (Baltimore, 1950), pp. 34, 36; memo by Harrison, Mar. 25, 1927, Leland Harrison Papers (LC).

39. Myers to MacMurray, June 7 and Nov. 23, 1927, SDA 893.00/9170 and 793.94/1638; Myers to Kellogg, July 29, 1927, SDA 793.94/1617.

40. Memo by Chapin, Nov. 3, 1927, SDA 793.94/1641; Sturgeon to Kellogg, Sept. 2, 1927, SDA 793.94/1622; memo by Johnson for Lamont, Aug. 29, 1927, Johnson Papers.

41. *Saikin Shina* (1927), IV, 204–205; Council on Foreign Relations, ed., *Survey of American Foreign Relations 1930* (New Haven, 1930), pp. 241–242.

42. Myers to MacMurray, Nov. 23, 1927, SDA 793.94/1638; Mayer to Kellogg, Sept. 13, 1927, SDA 893.00/9409; Mayer to Kellogg, Nov. 22, 1927, SDA 894.51So 8/4; MacVeagh to Kellogg, Nov. 21, 1927, *FRUS 1927*, II, 484–486; memo of conversation between Tanaka and MacVeagh, Nov. 30, 1927, JFMA PVM 22.

43. Memo by Johnson, Nov. 1, 1927, SDA 894.51So 8/–; Lamont to Olds, Nov. 11, 1927, SDA 894.51So 8/48.

44. Memo by Olds, Nov. 21, 1927, SDA 894.51So 8/50; Johnson to MacMurray, Feb. 6, 1928, Johnson Papers; memo of conversations between Johnson and Sze, Nov. 22, Johnson and Lee, Nov. 30, and Johnson and Matsudaira, Dec. 1, 1927, Johnson Papers and SDA 894.51So 8/7; memo of press conference, Nov. 25, 1927, Johnson Papers; *New York Times*, Nov. 30, 1927.

45. *Survey of American Foreign Relations 1930*, p. 242; *New York Times*, Nov. 30, 1927; memos of press conferences, Nov. 26, and Dec. 2, 1927, Johnson Papers; Kellogg to MacVeagh, Dec. 3, 1927, *FRUS 1927*, II, 489–490; *Saikin Shina* (1927), IV, 207; MacVeagh to Kellogg, Jan. 4, 1928, SDA 894.51So 8/44.

46. Gerald E. Wheeler, *Prelude to Pearl Harbor: The United States Navy and the Far East 1921–1931* (Columbia, Mo., 1963), Chaps. 3, 6.

47. Yada to Yoshizawa, Oct. 5, 1927, JFMA PVM 23.

VI. MILITARY INSUBORDINATION, 1928

1. Hollington Tong, I, 196–202.

2. *Shina kindai*, pp. 570–571.

3. Isaacs, pp. 282–290.

4. Hollington Tong, I, 203–204; *KMWH*, XVIII, 3199–3201, 3203; Pollard, p. 339.

5. *KMWH*, XVIII, 3191–94; Hollington Tong, I, 213.

6. *Tanaka*, II, 862–863; War Ministry memo, Mar. 5, 1930, JMA T 859; *Minami Jirō*, ed. Mitarai Tatsuo (Tokyo, 1957), pp. 150–155.

7. *Tanaka*, II, 863–864.

8. *Ibid.*, II, 864–866.

9. *Ibid.*, II, 866; Hollington Tong, I, 213.

10. MacVeagh to Kellogg, Apr. 9, 1928, SDA 793.94/1659; *Tanaka*, II, 826–828; Chin to Yada, Apr. 18, 1928, JFMA PVM 55; Arai to Hata, Apr. 18, 1928, JFMA S.1.6.1.5.30; *Mori*, pp. 610–611, 617–619; Itō Masanori, *Gunbatsu kōbōshi* (The rise and fall of the military cliques; Tokyo, 1958), II, 134.

11. *FRUS 1928*, II, 136–137; *Taiheiyō sensō*, I, 300.

12. Suzuki to Arai, Apr. 19, 1928, JMA T 859; Minami to Arai, Apr. 19, 1928, *ibid.*

13. Matsubara Kazuo, *Kokusai kankei tsūkan, 1928–1929* (Foreign relations yearbook, 1928–1929; Tokyo, 1929), pp. 37–39; *KMWH*, XIX, 3544–45; *Tanaka*, II, 849–855.

14. *Taiheiyō sensō*, I, 300.

15. Resumé of the Tsinan incident, JFMA PVM 55.

16. *Ibid.*; report by the protocol force, Mar. 5, 1930, JMA T 859.

17. *KMWH*, XIX, 3629; résumé of the incident in JFMA PVM 55.

18. Colonel Katsuki's report, May 28, 1928, JMA T 863; résumé in JFMA PVM 55.

19. *KMWH*, XIX, 3558; *Survey of International Affairs 1928* (London, 1929), pp. 407–409.

20. Katsuki's report, JMA T 863; Lo Chia-lun's report, June 14, 1928, *KMWH*, XIX, 3597–3609; Chiang's report, May 3, 1929, *ibid.*, pp. 3636–39.

21. *Ibid.*, pp. 3545, 3563.

22. *Ibid.*, pp. 3546–47, 3633, 3600; Katsuki's report, JMA T 863. Cf. Chang Ch'i-yün, *Tang-shih kai-yao* (An outline history of the party), 5 vols. (Taipei, 1959), II, 575–576; Usui, "Shōwa shoki," p. 1667.

23. Kuroda's report, JMA T 852; *KMWH*, XIX, 3632–33; Usui, "Shōwa shoki," p. 1666.

24. *Taiheiyō sensō*, I, 301–302.

25. Katsuki's report, JMA T 863; Kuroda's report, JMA T 852.

26. *Ibid.*; résumé in JFMA PVM 55.

27. *KMWH*, XIX, 3601–04.

28. *Ibid.*, XIX, 3604–05.

29. *Ibid.*, XIX, 3606, 3569, 3570–75.

30. *Tanaka*, II, 855, 861; Okamoto to Tanaka, May 10, 1928, JFMA S.1.6.1.5.30; *Minami*, pp. 162–163; Suzuki to Fukuda, May 15, 1928, JFMA PVM 25; Hata to Fukuda, May 15, 1928, JMA T 843; Okamoto to Tanaka, June 1, 1928, JFMA PVM 25. For Japanese civilian views of the crisis, see Yoshizawa to Tanaka, May 8 and 21, 1928, JFMA PVM 25 and JMA T 866; Usui, "Shōwa shoki," p. 1667.

31. *KMWH*, XIX, 3548–52.

32. Okamoto to Tanaka, May 9 and 10, 1928, JFMA S.1.6.1.5.30; *KMWH*, XIX, 3550.

33. *Taiheiyō sensō*, I, 353–362.

34. Arita's memo, Apr. 1928, JFMA PVM 32; Sakonji to Arita, May 19, 1928, JFMA S.1.6.1.5.31.

35. Foreign Ministry memo, Mar. 10, 1928, JFMA PVM 23; Yoshida's memo, Apr. 27, 1928, *ibid.*

36. *Yamamoto*, pp. 606–612.

37. *Taiheiyō sensō*, I, 298; Foreign Ministry memo, Apr. 1928, JFMA S.1.6.1.5.31.

38. Foreign Ministry memo, Apr. 28, 1928, *ibid.*

39. Takao to Tanaka, Apr. 22 and 26, 1928, JFMA S.1.6.1.5.30; Yoshizawa to Tanaka, rec. May 8, 1928, *ibid.*

40. Yoshizawa to Tanaka, May 6 and rec. May 10, 1928, *ibid.*; *FRUS 1928*, II, 140.

41. Foreign Ministry memo, May 16, 1928, JFMA S.1.6.1.5.31. See also Sakonji to Arita, May 19, 1928, JFMA S.1.6.1.5.32; Hayashi to Tanaka, rec. May 1, 1928, JFMA S.1.6.1.5.3.

42. Cabinet decision of May 16, 1928, JFMA S.1.6.1.5.31.

43. Okamoto to Tanaka, May 10, 1928, JFMA S.1.6.1.5.30.

44. Tanaka to Yoshizawa, May 16 and 17, 1928, JFMA S.1.6.1.5.31; Tanaka to Yada, May 16 and 17, 1928, *ibid.*; cabinet decision of May 18, 1928, *ibid.*; Shirakawa to commanders of Japanese armies in Manchuria, Korea, Taiwan, and China, May 18, 1928, JMA T 851; *Tanaka*, II, 943–944.

45. Yoshizawa to Tanaka, rec. May 19, 1928, JFMA S.1.6.1.5.31.

46. Yoshizawa to Tanaka, rec. May 19, 1928, JFMA S.1.6.1.5.31; Yada to Tanaka, May 18, 1928, *ibid.*

47. Shigetō to Hata, May 23, 1928, *ibid.*; Okamoto to Tanaka, May 27, 1928, *ibid.*; Yoshizawa to Tanaka, rec. May 30, 1928, *ibid.*; Yada to Tanaka, May 29, 1928, *ibid.*

48. Yoshizawa to Tanaka, June 5, 1928, JFMA S.1.6.1.5.32.

49. Yoshizawa to Tanaka, rec. June 2, 1928, JFMA S.1.6.1.5.30; *Tanaka*, II, 948; Hata to Tatekawa, May 31, 1928, JMA T 854; Ueda to Debuchi, May 30, 1928, JFMA S.1.6.1.5.31.

50. *Taiheiyō sensō*, I, 303–306; Usui Katsumi, "Chang Tso-lin bakushi no shinsō" (The truth about Chang Tso-lin's accidental death), in *Himerareta Shōwa-shi* (Inside stories of the Showa period; Tokyo, 1956), p. 31.

51. Arita, pp. 44–46; *Taiheiyō sensō*, I, 306–308.

52. Usui, "Chang Tso-lin," pp. 32–34; Kōmoto Daisaku, "Watakushi ga Chang Tso-lin o koroshita" (I killed Chang Tso-lin), *Bungei shunjū* (Liter-

ary miscellany), 32.12:194–201 (Dec. 1954). According to Sasaki Tōitsu, who had accompanied the Northern Expedition, he had also played a part in the assassination of Chang Tso-lin, but for a somewhat different reason. Sasaki felt that Japan could best protect its rights in Manchuria by letting the Nationalists and their sympathizers rule north of the Wall. The idea was that if these persisted in their violent attack on foreign rights, Japanese would be awakened from their complacency and feel justified in resorting to radical measures in Manchuria. Sasaki writes that it was he who had first broached the idea to Kōmoto. See his *Aru gunjin no jiden* (Autobiography of a soldier; Tokyo, 1963), pp. 191–193.

53. *Taiheiyō sensō*, I, 308–309.

54. Chamberlain's statements in the House of Commons, Feb. 8, Mar. 19 and 28, 1928, BGD: *Parliamentary Debates, Commons*, 5th ser., 213: 115–118, and 215: 12, 1146.

55. *Ibid.*, 217: 1853–54, 2062, and 220: 1835.

56. MacMurray to Kellogg, Feb. 14, 1928, SDA 893.00/9808.

57. Borg, pp. 382–384.

58. MacMurray to Kellogg, Apr. 7, 1928, SDA 893.00/9859.

59. *Ibid.*; MacMurray to Kellogg, Apr. 14, 1928, SDA 893.00/9864.

60. Johnson to Lewis, Mar. 8, 1928, Johnson Papers; Johnson to Bristol, Mar. 10, 1928, *ibid.*; Johnson to Wishart, Feb. 20, 1928, SDA 893.00/9751; MacMurray to Kellogg, Jan. 8, 1928, SDA 893.0146/25; MacMurray to Stanton, Jan. 7, 1928, *FRUS 1928*, II, 255; Hornbeck to Hiller, Mar. 3, 1928, *ibid.*, II, 215; Bristol to Wilbur, Mar. 10, 1928, SDA 893.00/9803; MacMurray to Kellogg, Mar. 12, 1928, SDA 893.0146/29; Mayer to Kellogg, Mar. 5, 1928, *FRUS 1928*, II, 308–309; memos by Hornbeck, Mar. 5 and 13, 1928, SDA 893.00/9789 and 893.0146/29; Hornbeck to Johnson, Mar. 14, 1928, SDA 893.00/9803; Kellogg to Wilbur, Mar. 20, 1928, SDA 893.0146/29.

61. MacMurray to Kellogg, Jan. 9 and Feb. 14, 1928, SDA 893.00/9768 and 9808; Dorsey to MacMurray, Apr. 26, 1928, SDA 893.0146/52; MacMurray to Kellogg, May 11, 1928, SDA 893.00Tsinan/44; Price to MacMurray, May 18, 1928, SDA 893.00Tsinan/86.

62. Memos of conversations between Kellogg, Johnson, and Sze, May 17; between Hornbeck and Lee, June 1, 1928; and between Johnson and the Swedish minister, June 13, 1928, Johnson Papers and SDA 893.00Tsinan/75.

63. MacMurray to Kellogg, May 17, 1928, *FRUS 1928*, II, 223–224; memo by Butler, Dec. 31, 1928, Mark L. Bristol Papers (LC).

64. MacMurray to Kellogg, June 1, 1928, SDA 893.00/10020; memo by Hornbeck, May 17, 1928, SDA 893.00/9970.

65. MacVeagh to Kellogg, May 17, 1928, *FRUS 1928*, II, 224; Kellogg to MacMurray, May 18, 1928, *ibid.*, II, 226; memos of conversations between Kellogg and Matsudaira, May 22 and 24, 1928, *ibid.*, II., 227, 231.

66. MacVeagh to Kellogg, May 24, 1928, SDA 893.00/10076; Johnson to Dawson, June 6, 1928, Johnson Papers.

67. Morton, *Strategy*, p. 34.

VII. CHINA BECOMES A POWER, 1928–1929

1. Chinese legation to State Department, July 13, 1928, *FRUS 1928*, II, 416.

2. Johnson to Morley, June 4, 1928, Johnson Papers; Kellogg to Mac-Murray, July 11, 1928, *FRUS 1928*, II, 453–454.

3. Memo of conversation between Johnson and Sawada, July 14, 1928, Johnson Papers.

4. *FRUS 1928*, II, 475–477; MacMurray to Kellogg, July 28, 1928, *ibid.*, II, 479.

5. *KMWH*, XXI, 4098–99; Perkins to Kellogg, Aug. 14, 1928, SDA 893.00/10181.

6. MacMurray to Kellogg, Oct. 1, 1928, SDA 893.00/10225.

7. Memos of conversations between Johnson and Lee, July 23, between Johnson, Hornbeck, and Lee, Aug. 3, and between Johnson and Sun, Aug. 13, 1928, Johnson Papers; Remer, *Foreign Investments*, pp. 274ff; *Beikoku tai-Shi keizai seiryoku no zenbō* (America's economic influence in China), ed. Gaimushō (Tokyo, 1940), Chaps. 2, 4, 6.

8. *Yamamoto*, pp. 615, 617; Shirakawa to Muraoka, June 6, 1928, JMA T 844; Usui, "Chang Tso-lin," p. 36; *Tanaka*, II, 957–958.

9. Saitō to Hata, June 10, 1928, JMA T 844; Usui, "Chang Tso-lin," p. 37.

10. Saitō to Hata, June 7, 1928, JMA T 861; Yoshizawa to Tanaka, June 18, 1928, JFMA PVM 53; Tatekawa to Hata, June 25 and July 6, 1928, JMA T 864, T 845.

11. Hayashi to Tanaka, June 20 and July 16, 1928, JFMA PVM 53; Yoshizawa to Tanaka, July 17, 1928, *ibid.*

12. Hata to Saitō, July 4, 1928, JMA T 845; Tanaka to Hayashi, June 25, 1928, JFMA PVM 53.

13. Yoshizawa to Tanaka, June 18, 1928, JFMA PVM 52; Hayashi to Tanaka, July 16, 1928, JFMA PVM 53; Iriye Akira, "Chang Hsüeh-liang and the Japanese," *Journal of Asian Studies*, 20.1:34–37 (Nov. 1960).

14. *Asahi* (July 17–20, 1928).

15. Tanaka to Hayashi, July 18, 1928, JFMA PVM 53; Neville to Kellogg, July 25, 1928, SDA 793.94Manchuria/20.

16. Yoshida to Hayashi, July 31, 1928, JFMA PVM 53.

17. Hayashi to Tanaka, July 19, 1928, ibid.; *Kuo-wen chou-pao*, July 29, 1928; *Asahi* (July 19 and 20, 1928); Hayashi to Tanaka, July 20, 1928, JFMA PVM 53; Muraoka to Suzuki, July 21, 1928, *ibid.*; Hayashi to Tanaka, July 21 and 23, 1928, *ibid.*

18. Hayashi to Tanaka, July 25, 1928, *ibid.*; *KMWH*, XXI, 4088–90; Washizawa Yoshiji, "Shina o mokugeki shite" (Witnessing China), *Peking shūhō* (Sept. 23, 1928); Hayashi to Tanaka, Aug. 9, 10, and 11, 1928; JFMA PVM 53; Tanaka to Hayashi, Aug. 13, 1928, *ibid.*

19. Myers to Kellogg, June 5, 8, and 13, 1928, SDA 893.00/10133, 10134, and 10135.

20. Myers to Kellogg, Aug. 7, 1928, SDA 893.00PR Mukden/12; Mac-Murray to Kellogg, July 31, 1928, SDA 793.94Manchuria/21.

21. Wheeler, *Prelude*, p. 43; *Tanaka*, II, 894–895.
22. Okamoto to Tanaka, rec. July 28, 1928, JFMA PVM 59; Yoshizawa to Tanaka, rec. July 29, 1928, *ibid.; Taiheiyō sensō*, I, 312.
23. *Mori*, pp. 626–628.
24. General Staff memo, Aug. 7, 1928, JFMA PVM 53; Hayashi to Tanaka, July 20, 1928, JFMA PVM 23; Yoshizawa to Tanaka, Aug. 8, 1928, *ibid.;* Tanaka to Hayashi, Sept. 24, 1928, *ibid.; NGN*, II, 123–124; *Yamamoto*, pp. 621–624.
25. Yoshizawa to Tanaka, Aug. 10, 1928, JFMA PVM 53; Yoshizawa to Tanaka, Aug. 17, 28, and 30, 1928, JFMA PVM 59.
26. Tanaka to Yoshizawa, July 21, 1928, *ibid.;* memo of conversation between Arita and Wang, July 25, 1928, *ibid.;* Okamoto to Tanaka, rec. July 30 and Aug. 4, 1928, *ibid.;* Yoshizawa to Tanaka, rec. July 31 and Aug. 3, 1928, JFMA PVM 64 and PVM 59.
27. Memo by Foreign Ministry, Aug. 17, 28, 31, and Sept. 10, 1928; JFMA PVM 62; Tanaka to Yoshizawa, Sept. 19, 1928, JFMA PVM 64. Shidehara had never attached much importance to the abolition of likin, regarding it as impractical. But he had insisted on an imposition of excise taxes on Chinese products as a condition for higher import duties. Tanaka had apparently given up this idea and decided to insist on the former condition.
28. Tanaka to Yada, Sept. 10 and 12, 1928, JFMA PVM 64; *NGN*, II, 122–123; *Asahi* (Oct. 13, 1928); MacVeagh to Kellogg, Oct. 20, 1928, SDA 793.94Manchuria/41; Tanaka to Yada, Oct. 4, 1928, JFMA PVM 59.
29. Foreign Ministry memo, July 20, 1928, JFMA PVM 29; Tanaka to Adachi and Sawada, Aug. 13, 1928, *ibid.; NGN*, II, 117–119.
30. Tanaka to Nagaoka, Sept. 1, 1928, JFMA PVM 29; Uchida to Tanaka, rec. Sept. 10, 1928, *ibid.;* Saburi to Tanaka, rec. Sept. 17, 20, and 22, 1928, *ibid.;* Yoshizawa to Tanaka, Sept. 27, 1928, *ibid.;* Hori to Tanaka, rec. Oct. 29, Nov. 2 and 5, and Dec. 28, 1928, *ibid.;* Okamoto to Tanaka, Dec. 18 and 20, 1928, *ibid.* Uchida fared somewhat better in Paris. There Raymond Poincaré and Aristide Briand assured him that they well understood Japan's peculiar position in China as well as the need for international cooperation. (Adachi to Tanaka, rec. Aug. 26, 27, and 29, 1928, *ibid.*)
31. Japanese embassy to State Department, n.d., *FRUS 1928*, II, 425–427; memo of conversation between Kellogg and Uchida, Sept. 29, 1928, *ibid.*, 427–430.
32. *Shina kindai*, pp. 587–592.
33. South Manchuria Railway, president's office to Tokyo office, Oct. 18 and 19, 1928, JFMA PVM 52.
34. Hayashi to Tanaka, Dec. 8, 1928, *ibid.;* Okamoto to Tanaka, Dec. 19, 1928, *ibid.;* Myers to Kellogg, Jan. 7, 1929, SDA 793.94Manchuria/48; *Asahi* (Dec. 17, 1928); *Kuo-wen chou-pao* (Oct. 17 and Nov. 18, 1928); Kawagoe to Tanaka, Dec. 4, 1928, JFMA S.1.6.1.5.32; Hayashi to Tanaka, Dec. 14, 1928, JFMA S.1.6.1.2.3.
35. *Tanaka*, II, 1028–39; Oka Yoshitake and Hayashi Shigeru, ed., *Taishō democracy ki no seiji: Matsumoto Gōkichi seiji nisshi* (Politics of the Taisho democracy: Matsumoto Gōkichi political diary; Tokyo, 1959), pp. 605–608.
36. Hayashi to Tanaka, Dec. 29 and 31, 1928, JFMA PVM 53; Tanaka

to Hayashi, Dec. 30, 1928, *ibid.;* Neville to Kellogg, Jan. 12, 1929, SDA 793.94Manchuria/49.

37. Yada to Tanaka, Sept. 23 and Oct. 8, 1928, JFMA PVM 23.

38. Tanaka to Yada, Oct. 11, 1928, *ibid.;* Yada to Tanaka, Oct. 12, Nov. 9, 16, 22, and 26, 1928, *ibid.;* Kadono to Tanaka, Dec. 1, 1928, *ibid.*

39. Tanaka to Yada, Nov. 30, 1928, *ibid.;* Yada to Tanaka, Dec. 7 and 8, 1928, *ibid.*

40. Tanaka to Hori, Jan. 25, 1929, *ibid.; NGN,* II, 124–125.

41. Okamoto to Tanaka, Oct. 23 and 24, 1928, JFMA PVM 25; Yada to Tanaka, Oct. 23 and 24, 1928, *ibid.*

42. Tanaka to Yada, Oct. 23 and Nov. 24, 1928, *ibid.;* Fujita to Tanaka, Oct. 23, 1928, *ibid.;* commander, third division, to Suzuki, Oct. 26, 1928, *ibid.;* Yada to Tanaka, Nov. 22 and 23, 1928, *ibid.;* Foreign Ministry memo entitled, "Items agreed upon with Minister Yoshizawa on his return to Shanghai and Nanking," n.d., *ibid.;* Cabinet decision of Jan. 13, 1929, *ibid.;* memo of conversation between Yoshizawa and Minami, Jan. 15, 1929, *ibid.*

43. Yoshizawa to Tanaka, Jan. 27 and 30, Feb. 5 and 11, and Mar. 4, 1929, *ibid.;* Tanaka to Yoshizawa, Feb. 2, 5, 9, 14, and 16, 1929, *ibid.;* War Ministry memo, Feb. 2, 1929, *ibid.;* War Ministry memo, Feb. 13, 1929, *ibid.* Tanaka had told Chang Ch'ün the previous September that the Tsinan incident would be easily settled if the Manchurian question was solved. (Yoshizawa to Tanaka, Jan. 26, 1929, *ibid.*)

44. Tanaka to Yoshizawa, Mar. 8, 19, and 21, 1929, *ibid.;* Yoshizawa to Tanaka, Mar. 13, 19, and 23, 1929, *ibid.*

45. *NGN,* II, 131–134; Shigemitsu to Tanaka, Apr. 13, 18, 19, and May 5, 1929, JFMA PVM 59; Tanaka to Shigemitsu, Apr. 19, 1929, *ibid.;* Tanaka to Yoshizawa, May 24, 1929, *ibid.*

46. Morishima Morito, *Inbō ansatsu guntō* (Conspiracies, assassinations, swords; Tokyo, 1950), pp. 30–32; Earl A. Selle, *Donald of China* (London, 1948), pp. 257–259.

47. Usui Katsumi, "Tanaka gaikō ni tsuite no oboegaki" (A memorandum on the Tanaka diplomacy), *Kokusai seiji,* No. 11:32 (Jan. 1960); Hayashi to Tanaka, Jan. 22, 25, and 27, and rec. Feb. 1, 1929, JFMA PVM 23; Tanaka to Hayashi, Jan. 31, 1929, *ibid.;* Morishima to Tanaka, Apr. 4, 1929, *NGN,* II, 128–130; Hayashi's memo, Apr. 1929, JFMA PVM 23.

48. *Yamamoto,* p. 644; Usui, "Tanaka," p. 33; Shigemitsu to Tanaka, Apr. 3, 1929, JFMA S.1.1.1.0–20.

VIII. THE COST OF SOVEREIGNTY, 1929–1930

1. *Shina kindai,* pp. 592–595. Britain had offered to retrocede Weihaiwei to China at the Washington Conference, but negotiations had dragged on without settlement.

2. *Taiheiyō sensō,* II, 230–239 (Tokyo, 1962).

3. *FRUS 1929* (Washington, 1943), II, 559–561; Lampson to Chamberlain, May 31, 1929, *DBFP,* 2nd ser., VIII, 57–59 (London, 1960); Lampson to Chamberlain, May 15, 1929, *ibid.,* VIII, 35–41; Chamberlain to Lampson, May 14, 1929, *ibid.,* VIII, 33–34; Henderson to Giles, June 13,

1929, *ibid.*, VIII, 87; Henderson to Ingram, June 27, 1929, *ibid.*, VIII, 96–98.

4. Chamberlain to Ingram, May 16, 1929, *ibid.*, VIII, 45–48; Ingram to Lampson, May 23, 1929, *ibid.*, VIII, 54–55; Henderson to Ingram, June 27, 1929, *ibid.*, VIII, 96–98; the British reply in *ibid.*, VIII, 130–133; Stimson to MacMurray Aug. 1, 1929, *FRUS 1929*, II, 596–599; the French reply in *ibid.*, II, 580–581.

5. MacMurray to Stimson, Sept. 10, 1929, *ibid.*, *II*, 604–606.

6. Memos of conversations between Wellesley and Sze, Oct. 31, Nov. 11 and 25, 1929, *DBFP*, 2nd ser., VIII, 180–181, 194–196, 208–209; Henderson to Howard Nov. 14, 1929, *ibid.*, VIII, 199–200; memo by Pratt, Oct. 22, 1929, *ibid.*, VIII, 173–175; Henderson to Lampson, Nov. 2, 1929, *ibid.*, VIII, 185–188.

7. Campbell to Henderson, Nov. 19 and Dec. 3, 1929, *ibid.*, VIII, 204, 225–226; Henderson to Lampson, Dec. 2, 4, and 20, 1929, *ibid.*, VIII, 222, 227–228, 245; Lampson to Henderson, Dec. 30 and 31, 1929, *ibid.*, VIII, 252–253, 255–257.

8. Stimson to Cooley, Jan. 7, 1929, Henry L. Stimson Papers (Yale University); Stimson's farewell address before the Philippine Senate, Feb. 11, 1929, *ibid.*; Stimson to Bristol, Sept. 14, 1928, Bristol Papers.

9. Wang to Stimson, Feb. 3 [?], 1929, Stimson Papers; Stimson to Kwong, Feb. 19, 1929, *ibid.*; Stimson diary, Feb. 27 and 28, 1929, *ibid.* On the appointment and work of the Kemmerer Commission see *New York Times* (Jan. 13, 1929); Frank Tamagna, *Banking and Finance in China* (New York, 1942), pp. 220–222; *Shina kindai*, pp. 161–172, 182–193. In September 1929, there were sixty-odd foreign advisers to the Nanking government. Of these at least thirty-two were American, Britain supplying fifteen (mostly in the navy), Germany seven, France four, and Japan two. (MacMurray to Stimson, Sept. 24, 1929, SDA 893.01A/84.)

10. Fishel, pp. 154–157, 160–163; MacMurray to Stimson, July 15, 1929, *FRUS 1929*, II, 578–580; Stimson to MacMurray, July 9, 1929, *ibid.*, II, 581–582; Stimson to MacMurray, Oct. 22 and 28, 1929, *ibid.*, II, 611–612, 614–615.

11. Robert H. Ferrell, *American Diplomacy in the Great Depression: Hoover-Stimson Foreign Policy 1919–1933* (New Haven, 1957), Chap. 5.

12. William W. Lockwood, *The Economic Development of Japan: Growth and Structural Change 1868–1938* (Princeton, 1954), pp. 62–64.

13. *Taiheiyō sensō*, I, 364–370.

14. *Ibid.*, I, 366–367.

15. See Chapter III.

16. Shigemitsu to Shidehara, rec. Oct. 20, and Oct. 22, 1929, JFMA PVM 59 and PVM 64.

17. Shidehara, *Gojū-nen*, p. 94.

18. *Obata*, Chaps. 5, 11.

19. Lampson to Chamberlain, June 4, 1929, *DBFP*, 2nd ser., VIII, 63–64; Karakhan to Hsia, May 31, 1929, *Sovetsko-Kitaiskie otnosheniia*, pp. 123–126; Karakhan to Hsia, July 13, 1929, *ibid.*, pp. 126–130; Foreign Ministry to Hsia, July 16, 1929, *ibid.*, p. 130; Hsia to Karakhan, July 17, 1929,

ibid., pp. 130–132; Karakhan to Hsia, July 17, 1929, *ibid.*, pp. 132–133; Dirksen to Trautmann, July 20, 1929, GFMA Container No. 1520.

20. Stimson to MacMurray, July 19 and 24, 1929, *FRUS 1929*, II, 215–217, 234–236; memo of conversation between Stimson and Wu, July 19, 1929, Stimson Papers; Stimson to Claudel, July 25, 1929, *FRUS 1929*, II, 242–244.

21. Debuchi to Shidehara, rec. July 28, 1929, JFMA PVM 72.

22. Henderson to Lampson, Oct. 29, 1929, *DBFP*, 2nd ser., VIII, 179–180.

23. *Shina kindai*, pp. 803ff; Lampson to Henderson, July 2, 1930, *DBFP*, 2nd ser., VIII, 1016.

24. Peter Tang, pp. 243–244; MacMurray to Stimson, Aug. 18, 1929, *FRUS 1929*, II, 285; Lampson to Henderson, July 2, 1930, *DBFP*, 2nd ser., VIII, 1022; Howard to Henderson, Aug. 26, 1929, *FRUS 1929*, II, 305.

25. Trautmann to Voretzsch, Sept. 26, 1929, GFMA Container No. 1520; Trautmann to Dirksen, Nov. 15, 1929, *ibid.*; MacMurray to Kellogg, Nov. 19, 1929, *FRUS 1929*, II, 344.

26. Peter Tang, p. 252

27. Stimson to Neville, Nov. 26, 1929, *FRUS 1929*, II, 350–352; Neville to Stimson, Nov. 27, 1929, *ibid.*, II, 355–356; *Shidehara*, pp. 386–387.

28. Peter Tang, pp. 256–265; memo of conversation between Johnson and Young, Oct. 21, 1930, Johnson Papers; Chang Hsüeh-liang to C. T. Wang, Oct. 27, 1930, JFMA S.1.6.1.0.2; Wang Chia-chen to Chang Tso-hsiang, Nov. 30 and Dec. 3, 1930, *ibid.*

29. Memos of conversations between Shidehara and Wang, and between Shidehara and Troianovsky, July 19, 1929, JFMA PVM 72.

30. Pratt's memo, May, 1930, *DBFP*, 2nd ser., VIII, 370–373; Foreign Office memo, July 19, 1930, *ibid.*, VIII, 384–388; Benjamin I. Schwartz, *Chinese Communism and the Rise of Mao* (Cambridge, Mass., 1961), Chap. 9.

31. *Shina kindai*, pp. 600–605; Hatano, I, 489–513.

32. *Man-Mō jijō* (Manchurian and Mongolian affairs), ed. South Manchuria Railway Research Bureau, No. 106:15–19 (July 1930), and No. 109:5 (Oct. 1930). For an account of the role played by Donald, an Australian adviser to Chang Hsüeh-liang, in this episode, see Selle, pp. 263–266.

33. *Shina kindai*, pp. 605–615.

34. *FRUS 1930* (Washington, 1945), II, 150ff, 226ff; Johnson to Norton, Aug. 28, 1930, Johnson Papers; Johnson to Hornbeck, Aug. 9, 1930, *ibid.*

35. Imai Seiichi, "Shidehara gaikō ni okeru seisaku kettei" (Decision-making in the Shidehara diplomacy), *Nenpō seijigaku* (Annals of the Japanese Political Science Association), 1959, pp. 98–100; NGN, II, 161–168.

36. Akashi Teruo and Suzuki Norihisa, *Nihon kin'yū-shi* (A financial history of Japan), II, 240ff (Tokyo, 1958); Sakurauchi Yukio, *Jiden* (Autobiography; Tokyo, 1952), pp. 254–259.

37. Lampson to Henderson, Jan. 10 and 18, 1930, *DBFP*, 2nd ser., VIII, 265, 274–275; Henderson to Lampson, Jan. 20, 1930, *ibid.*, VIII, 276–277; Henderson to Hewlett, Feb. 8, 1930, *ibid.*, VIII, 284; Wellesley to Atherton, Feb. 15, 1930, *ibid.*, VIII, 293–294; the American proposal in *FRUS 1930*, II, 363–367.

38. Howard to Henderson, Jan. 10, 1930, *DBFP*, 2nd ser., VIII, 266–268; Lampson to Henderson, Feb. 16, Mar. 6, 10, 21, and 28, 1930, *ibid.*, VIII, 295–296, 309–310, 310–315, 329–330, 332–335; Henderson to Lampson, Feb. 26, 1930, *ibid.*, VIII, 303–305; Campbell to Henderson, Mar. 18, 1930, *ibid.*, VIII, 327–328; Lindsay to Henderson, Apr. 23, 1930, *ibid.*, VIII, 355–356; Hornbeck to Campbell, Mar. 17, 1930, *FRUS 1930*, II, 408; American draft agreement, n.d., *ibid.*, II, 426–434; White to Johnson, June 9, 1930, *ibid.*, II, 446–448.

39. Ferrell, *Great Depression*, Chap. 6; Wheeler, *Prelude*, Chap. 7; *Okada Keisuke* (Tokyo, 1956), Part 1.

40. Johnson to Stimson, Aug. 14, 1930, quoted in Fishel, p. 286; Castle to Atherton, Aug. 21, 1930, *FRUS 1930*, II, 457–458.

41. Memo of July 19, 1930, *DBFP*, 2nd ser., VIII, 384–388; Pratt's memo, May, 1930, *ibid.*, VIII, 369–373; Henderson to Lampson, Aug. 23, 1930, *ibid.*, VIII, 397–398; Lampson to Wellesley, Aug. 31, 1930, *ibid.*, VIII, 399; the text of the British proposal is in *ibid.*, VIII, 412–420, and that of the American proposal in *FRUS 1930*, II, 472–480.

42. See *Taiheiyō sensō*, I, 335.

43. *Ibid.*, I, 338–339.

44. *Ibid.*, I, 342–343.

45. *Ibid.*, I, 371–379.

IX. THE FAILURE OF ECONOMIC DIPLOMACY, 1930–1931

1. *Nichi-Bei bunka kōshō-shi*, II, 38–50.

2. *Shina kindai*, pp. 207–211; *Beikoku tai-Shi*, pp. 64–68.

3. Lockwood, p. 64.

4. *Shina kindai*, pp. 174–180.

5. Shigemitsu to Shidehara, Nov. 10, June 1 and 4, 1930, JFMA PVM 70; Shidehara to Shigemitsu, June 18, 1930, *ibid.*; Arita to Shigemitsu, July 12, 1930, *ibid.*; Horiuchi to Tani, June 30, 1930, *ibid.*; Shigemitsu to Arita, Aug. 1, 1930, *ibid.*; Shidehara to Shigemitsu, Aug. 26, 1930, *ibid.*; Shigemitsu to Shidehara, Nov. 14, 1930, *ibid.*

6. *Shina kindai*, pp. 94–95; Shigemitsu to Shidehara, rec. Dec. 5, 1930, JFMA PVM 70; Shidehara to Shigemitsu, Dec. 17, 1930, and Jan. 20, 1931, *ibid.*

7. Shigemitsu to Shidehara, Oct. 22, Nov. 22, and Dec. 6, 1930, *ibid.*; Matsudaira to Shidehara, Dec. 3 and 12, 1930, *ibid.*; Shidehara to Matsudaira, Nov. 29, 1930, *ibid.*; Henderson to Snow, Dec. 19, 1930, *DBFP*, 2nd ser., VIII, 449–450; Tilley to Henderson, Sept. 20, 1930, *ibid.* VIII, 421–423; *China Year Book 1932*, pp. 189–193.

8. Pittman's speech of Oct. 8, 1930, location not noted, Key Pittman Papers (LC); Hornbeck to Johnson, June 26, 1930, Johnson Papers.

9. Johnson to Hornbeck, Aug. 26, 1930, *ibid.*; Johnson to Norton, Aug. 28, 1930, *ibid.*; Yano to Shidehara, Dec. 3, 1930, JFMA PVM 71; Shigemitsu to Shidehara, Dec. 4, 1930, *ibid.*; memo by South Manchuria Railway's Tokyo office, Dec. 8, 1930, *ibid.*; Satō to Sugiyama, Jan. 12, 1931, *ibid.*; Shigemitsu to Shidehara, Feb. 5, 1931, *ibid.*

10. *Taiheiyō sensō*, I, 100ff.

11. Ōtani Keijirō, *Rakujitsu no joshō: Shōwa rikugun-shi* (Prelude to the setting sun: History of the army during the showa era), I, 28–30 (Tokyo, 1959); Hata Ikuhiko, "Sakurakai shuisho" (A statement of intentions of the Cherry-blossom Society), *Rekishi kyōiku* (Historical education), 6.2:81–89 (Feb. 1958).

12. Lampson to Henderson, Sept. 19, 1930, *DBFP*, 2nd ser., VIII, 420–421; the texts to the British and the American governments are in *ibid.*, VIII, 432–436, and *FRUS 1930*, II, 485–489; Chinese legation to State Department, Dec. 19, 1930, *ibid.*, II, 497; Johnson to Stimson, Dec. 18, 20, and 21, 1930, *ibid.*, II, 495–496, 498, 499.

13. Henderson to Lindsay, Mar. 7, 1931, *DBFP*, 2nd ser., VIII, 476–478; Lampson to Henderson, June 8, 1931, *ibid.*, VIII, 559–601.

14. *Shina kindai*, p. 899; Shigemitsu to Shidehara, May, 8, 1931, JFMA PVM 65; Shidehara to Shigemitsu, Apr. 4, 1931, *ibid.*; various Foreign Ministry memos in *ibid.*

15. *Shina kindai*, pp. 897–899.

16. *Ibid.*, pp. 616–627.

17. Lampson to Henderson, June 6, 1931, *DBFP*, 2nd ser., VIII, 545–559; a draft treaty between China and the United States, revised as of July 14, 1931, *FRUS 1930*, II, 893–908.

18. Fishel, pp. 185–187.

19. *Shina kindai*, pp. 633–637.

20. Foreign Ministry memos, Apr. 26, 1931, and without dates, JFMA PVM 65.

21. *Taiheiyō sensō*, I, 348–352; Shigemitsu to Shidehara, Mar. 19, 1931, JFMA PVM 70.

22. Pao Wen-yüeh to Chang Tso-hsiang, Nov. 15, 1930, JFMA S.1.6.1.0.1; Wang Chia-chen to Jung Chen, Nov. 24, 1930, *ibid.*; Wang Shu-han to Ts'ang Shih-i, Nov. 21, 1930, *ibid.*; Hayashi to Shidehara, Jan. 6, 1931, JFMA PVM 53; Foreign Ministry memo, Apr. 16, 1931, *ibid.*; Shidehara to Shigemitsu, Nov. 14, 1930, JFMA S.1.1.1.0–20; Shidehara to Hayashi, Jan. 17, 1930, *ibid.*; *NGN*, II, 168–171; National government to Chang Hsüeh-liang, Feb. 13, 1931, JFMA S.1.6.1.0.1; Chang to National government, Feb. 14, 1931, *ibid.* See also *Taiheiyō sensō*, II, 245–258.

23. Tashiro to Shidehara, June 3, 12, July 1 and 2, 1931, JFMA S.1.1.1.0–18; Shigemitsu to Shidehara, July 8, 1931, *ibid.*

24. Kwantung Army memo, Aug. 1, 1931, JFMA S.4.2.6.0.2; Shidehara to Hayashi, Aug. 10, 1931, *ibid.*

25. Shidehara to Shigemitsu, July 8 and 11, 1931, JFMA S.1.1.1.0–18; Shidehara to Hayashi, July 16, 1931, *ibid.*; Shidehara to Ishii, July 28, 1931, *ibid.*; Tashiro to Shidehara, Aug. 6, 1931, *ibid.*; Sugiyama to Miyake, Aug. 8, 1931, JFMA S.4.2.6.0.2; *Shidehara*, p. 465.

26. Lindley to Henderson, July 16 and 24, 1931, *DBFP*, 2nd ser., VIII, 634–635, 645–646; Ōta to Shidehara, July 9, 1931, JFMA S.1.1.1.0–18; Chiang to Chang, July 11, 1931, *ibid.*

27. *Taiheiyō sensō*, I, 398–399, 422–426.

28. Imamura Hitoshi, "Manshū hi o fuku koro" (When Manchuria was on fire), *Himerareta Shōwa-shi*, pp. 60–62.

29. Ōtani, I, 33–40; *Taiheiyō sensō*, I, 379–381. See also Seki Haruhiko,

"Tairiku gaikō no kiki to sangatsu jiken" (The March incident and the crisis of diplomacy toward the continent), in Shinohara and Mitani, pp. 433–490.

30. *Minami*, pp. 214–216.

31. Imamura, "Manshū," pp. 60–62

32. *Taiheiyō sensō*, I, 398–399, 406–408.

33. *Ibid.*, I, 401–403, 409–413.

34. *Ibid.*, II, 268–273.

35. Shigemitsu to Shidehara, July 23 and Sept. 18, 1931, JFMA S.1.1.1.0–18; Kamimura to Shidehara, Aug. 24, 1931, *ibid.*; Shidehara to Shigemitsu, Aug. 4 and 13, 1931, *ibid.*; Shidehara to Hayashi, Aug. 11, 1931, JFMA S.4.2.6.0.2; Minami to Honjō, Aug. 10, 1931, *ibid.*; Hayashi to Shidehara, Aug. 17, 19, 21, and Sept. 4, 1931, *ibid.*; War Ministry memo, Aug. 28, 1931, *ibid.*; Yano to Shidehara, Sept. 5, 1931, *ibid.*; Shidehara to Hayashi, Sept. 4, 1931, *ibid.*; *Shidehara*, pp. 464–465.

36. Uchida to Shidehara, Aug. 17, 1931, JFMA PVM 30; Hayashi to Shidehara, Sept. 14, 1931, JFMA S.4.2.6.0.2.

37. Shigemitsu to Shidehara, Sept. 12 and 15, 1931, JFMA PVM 30; Shigemitsu Mamoru, *Gaikō kaisōroku* (Diplomatic memoirs; Tokyo, 1953), pp. 101–102.

38. *Shidehara*, p. 466; *Minami*, pp. 255–257; Hanaya Tadashi, "Manshū jihen wa kōshite keikaku sareta" (Thus was plotted the Manchurian incident), *Himerareta Shōwa-shi*, pp. 45–46; *Taiheiyō sensō*, I, 418.

39. *Ibid.*, I, 434–437.

40. *Ibid.*, I, 438–439.

CONCLUSION

1. Castle to Johnson, Oct. 13, 1930, Johnson Papers.

2. "Basic principles of Japanese-Russian-Chinese relations," spring 1924, Gotō Papers.

BIBLIOGRAPHY

GLOSSARY

INDEX

BIBLIOGRAPHY

The following list includes all the primary sources consulted and those secondary works which are directly relevant to this study. Among the latter, those by Dorothy Borg, Usui Katsumi, and the contributors to Taiheiyō sensō e no michi (The road to the Pacific War) stand out. These writers have been pioneers in gathering data. Yet it is amazing that the 1920's have not been subjected to the kind of close analysis which characterizes the study of certain areas of Far Eastern international relations in the decades immediately preceding and following.

As for the published primary sources, only the Papers Relating to the Foreign Relations of the United States covers the entire decade. At present Documents on British Foreign Policy has nothing for the middle twenties, and the Soviet publication Dokumenty vneshnei politiki SSSR has only reached 1926. The latter has but a few documents on China and Japan not available elsewhere. For China, Japan, and Germany one has to turn to unpublished sources. The Academia Sinica (Nankang, Taiwan) has not made available for research the Nanking government's diplomatic papers, but it has a valuable collection of documents for the pre-1927 period which are available. Most Japanese and German official documents which survived World War II have been microfilmed. Of these the Japanese Foreign Ministry papers are of immense value. Because of their richness, one must exercise restraint lest he be carried away and neglect the task of correlating them with sources from other countries.

Since this book is concerned with the way in which the officials of various countries perceived changes in the international environment, their personal papers and published biographies are of great value. Especially illuminating have been the papers of Nelson T. Johnson, Charles Evans Hughes, and Gotō Shimpei, the published writings of Chiang Kai-shek, and the biographies of Shidehara, Tanaka, Kellogg (by Ferrell), and Stimson (by Morison).

MANUSCRIPT SOURCES

Chandler P. Anderson Papers. Library of Congress.

Edgar A. Bancroft Papers. In the possession of Miss Catharine W. Pierce, Cambridge, Mass.

William E. Borah Papers. Library of Congress.

Mark L. Bristol Papers. Library of Congress.

CFMA: Chinese Foreign Ministry Archives. Academia Sinica, Taiwan.

Norman Davis Papers. Library of Congress.

W. Cameron Forbes Papers. Houghton Library, Harvard University.

GFMA: German Foreign Ministry Archives. Microfilmed; Library of Congress.

Gotō Shimpei Papers. Tokyo Institute for Municipal Research.

Joseph C. Grew Papers. Houghton Library, Harvard University.

Leland Harrison Papers. Library of Congress.

Charles Evans Hughes Papers. Library of Congress.

Japan, Defense Agency, War History Division, Archives.

JFMA: Japanese Foreign Ministry Archives. Microfilmed; Library of Congress.

JMA: Japanese Military Archives. Microfilmed; Library of Congress.

Nelson T. Johnson Papers. Library of Congress.

Key Pittman Papers. Library of Congress.

Jacob Gould Schurman Papers. Cornell University.

SDA: United States, State Department Archives. National Archives, Washington.

Henry L. Stimson Papers. Yale University.

United States, Department of Commerce Archives. National Archives, Washington.

D. Curtis Wilbur Papers. Library of Congress.

PUBLISHED WORKS

Abend, Hallett.   My Life in China, 1926-1941. New York, 1943.

Adler, Selig.   The Isolationist Impulse: Its Twentieth Century Reaction. New York, 1957,

Akagi, Roy Hidemichi.   Japan's Foreign Relations, 1542-1936: A Short History. Tokyo, 1959.

Arai Tatsuo 新井達夫. Katō Tomosaburō 加藤友三郎 . Tokyo, 1958.

Arita, Hachirō 有田八郎 . Bakahachi to hito wa yū 馬鹿八と人はいう (They call me Foolish Hachi). Tokyo, 1959.

Asada Sadao.   "Japan's 'Special Interests' and the Washington Conference, 1921-1922," American Historical Review, 67.1:62-70 (Oct. 1961).

Ashida Hitoshi 芦田均.   Dainiji sekai taisen gaikō-shi 第二次世界大戦外交史 (A diplomatic history of World War II). Tokyo, 1959.

Baba Akira 馬場明. "Dai-ichiji Shantung shuppei to Tanaka gaikō" 第一次山東出兵と田中外交 (The first Shantung expedition and the Tanaka diplomacy); Aziya kenkyū アジア研究 (Asiatic studies), 10.3:50-77 (Oct. 1963).

Banno Masataka 坂野正高 . "Dai-ichiji taisen kara go-sanjū made: Kokken kaifuku undō shi oboegaki" 第一次大戦から五・卅まで国権回復運動史覚書 (From World War I to the May 30th incident: A study of the rights recovery movement); in Ueda Toshio 植田捷雄, ed. , Gendai Chūgoku o meguru sekai no gaikō 現代中国を繞る世界の外交 (World diplomacy and China), pp. 1-67. Tokyo, 1951.

Beikoku tai-Shi keizai seiryoku no zenbō 米国対支経済勢力の全貌 (America's economic influence in China), ed. Gaimushō 外務省 (Foreign Ministry). Tokyo, 1940.

339

BGD: British Government Documents, published

Papers Relating to the Agreements Relative to the British Concessions at Hankow and Kiukiang, ed. Foreign Office. London, 1927.

Papers Relating to the Nanking Incident of March 24 and 25, 1927, ed. Foreign Office. London, 1927.

Papers Relating to the Solution of the Nanking Incident of March 24 and 25, 1927, ed. Foreign Office, London, 1928.

Parliamentary Debates: Commons. London.

Bloch, Kurt. German Interests and Policies in the Far East. New York, 1939.

Borg, Dorothy. American Policy and the Chinese Revolution, 1925-1928. New York, 1947.

Brandt, Conrad. Stalin's Failure in China, 1924-1927. Cambridge, Mass., 1958.

------, Benjamin I. Schwartz, and John K. Fairbank. A Documentary History of Chinese Communism. Cambridge, Mass., 1952.

British government documents, see BGD.

Brown, Delmer M. Nationalism in Japan. Berkeley and Los Angeles, 1955.

Bryn-Jones, David. Frank B. Kellogg: A Biography. New York, 1937.

Buck, Pearl. My Several Worlds. New York, 1954.

Chang Kia-ngau. China's Struggle for Railroad Development. New York, 1943.

Chang Po-chao 張伯昭, Ting Shuo-ho 丁守和 , and Yin Hsü-i 殷敘彝. "Shih-yüeh ko-ming tui Chung-kuo ko-ming te ying-hsiang" 十月革命对中国革命的影響 (The influence of the October revolution on the Chinese revolution); Li-shih yen-chiu 歷史研究 (Historical studies; Oct. 1957), pp. 7-26.

Ch'en Kung-po 陳公博. Tzu-ch'uan 自傳 (Autobiography). Hongkong, 1957.

Chiang Chieh-shih hsien-sheng yen-shuo chi 蔣介石先生演說集 (Collected speeches of Chiang Kai-shek). Canton, 1927.

Chiang Kung-sheng 蔣恭晟. Chung-Mei kuan-hsi chi-yao 中美關係 紀要 (A memorandum on Sino-American relations). Shanghai, 1930.

Ch'ien Tuan-sheng. The Government and Politics of China. Cambridge, Mass., 1950.

Chin-tai-shih tzu-liao 近代史資料 (Documents of modern history), ed. Chung-kuo k'o-hsüeh-yüan 中國科學院 (China academy of science). Peking, 1954 -.

China Weekly Review. Shanghai, 1921-1931.

China Year Book. London and Tientsin, 1921-1931.

Chou Keng-sheng 周鯁生. Chieh-fang shih-ch'i chih wai-chiao wen-t'i 解放時期之外交問題 (Diplomatic problems during the period of liberation). N. p., 1927.

Chow Tse-tsung. The May Fourth Movement: Intellectual Revolution in Modern China. Cambridge, Mass., 1960.

Christopher, James W. Conflict in the Far East, 1928-1933. Leyden, 1950.

Clyde, Paul H. The Far East. 3rd ed.; Englewood Cliffs, N. J., 1958.

Crane, Katharine. Mr. Carr of State: Forty-Seven Years in the Department of State. New York, 1960.

Current, Richard N. Secretary Stimson. New York, 1956.

Dallin, David. The Rise of Russia in Asia. New Haven, 1949.

Daniels, Roger. The Politics of Prejudice: The Anti-Japanese Movement in California and the Struggle for Japanese Exclusion. Berkeley, 1962.

341

DBFP: Documents on British Foreign Policy, ed. E. L. Woodward, Rohan Butler, and J. P. T. Bury; 1st ser. , Vol. 6 (London, 1956); 2nd ser. , Vol. 8 (London, 1960).

Documents on British Foreign Policy, see DBFP.

Dokumenty vneshnei politiki SSSR, see DVP.

Dull, Paul S. "The Assassination of Chang Tso-lin, " Far Eastern Quarterly, 11.4:453-463 (Aug. 1952).

Dulles, Foster Rhea. Forty Years of American-Japanese Relations. New York, 1937.

DVP: Dokumenty vneshnei politiki SSSR. Moscow, 1957-.

Ellis, L. Ethan. Frank B. Kellogg and American Foreign Relations, 1925-1929. New Brunswick, N. J. , 1961.

Etō Shinkichi 衛藤瀋吉. "Nanking jiken to Nichi-Bei" 南京事件と 日・米 (The Nanking incident, Japan, and the United States); in Saitō Makoto 斉藤真 , ed. , Gendai America no naisei to gaikō 現代アメリカ の 内政と外交 (Politics and foreign policy of contemporary America), pp. 299-324. Tokyo, 1959.

Feis, Herbert. The Diplomacy of the Dollar: The First Era, 1919-1932. Baltimore, 1950.

Feng Yü-hsiang 馮玉祥. Wo-te sheng-huo 我的生活 (My life). 3 vols.; Chungking, 1944.

Ferrell, Robert H. American Diplomacy in the Great Depression: Hoover-Stimson Foreign Policy, 1929-1933. New Haven, 1957.

------Frank B. Kellogg; Henry L. Stimson (Vol. 11 of The American Secretaries of State and Their Diplomacy, ed. R. H. Ferrell). New York, 1963.

Field, Frederick V. American Participation in the Chinese Consortiums. Chicago, 1931.

Fischer, Louis. Soviets in World Affairs. 2 vols.; New York, 1930.

Fishel, Wesley R. The End of Extraterritoriality in China. Berkeley and Los Angeles, 1952.

FRUS: Papers Relating to the Foreign Relations of the United States. Washington, D.C.

Fu Ch'i-hsüeh 傅啟學. Chung-kuo wai-chiao-shih 中國外交史 (A diplomatic history of China). Taipei, 1957.

Funazu Shin'ichirō 船津辰一郎. Tokyo, 1958.

Gendai-shi shiryō 現代史資料 (Documents of modern history), Vol. 7: Manshū jihen 満洲事変 (The Manchurian incident), ed. Kobayashi Tatsuo 小林竜夫 and Shimada Toshihiko 島田俊彦. Tokyo, 1964.

Gensui Uehara Yūsaku den 元帥上原勇作傳 (Biography of Marshal Uehara). 2 vols.; Tokyo, 1937.

Gotō Shimpei 後藤新平, ed. Tsurumi Yūsuke 鶴見祐輔. 4 vols.; Tokyo, 1937-1938.

Graebner, Norman A. An Uncertain Tradition: American Secretaries of State in the Twentieth Century. New York, 1961.

Grew, Joseph C. Turbulent Era: A Diplomatic Record of Forty Years, 1904-1945. 2 vols.; Boston, 1952.

Griswold, A. Whitney. The Far Eastern Policy of the United States. New York, 1938.

Hanabusa Nagamichi 英修道. Manshūkoku to monko kaihō mondai 満洲国と門戸開放問題 (Manchukuo and the Open Door question). Tokyo, 1934.

Hanaya Tadashi 花谷正. "Manshū jihen wa kōshite keikaku sareta" 満洲事変はこうして計画された (Thus was plotted the Manchurian incident); in Himerareta Shōwa-shi 秘められた昭和史

(Inside stories of the Showa period; a special issue of Chisei 知
性 [Intellect]), pp. 40-50. Tokyo, 1956.

Hara Kei nikki 原敬日記 (Hara Kei diary), ed. Hara Keiichirо 原奎一
郎. 9 vols.; Tokyo, 1950-1951.

Harada Kumao 原田熊男. Saionji kō to seikyoku 西園寺公と政局 (Prince
Saionji and politics). 8 vols.; Tokyo, 1952.

Hashimoto taisa no shuki 橋本大佐の手記 (Memoir of Colonel Hashimoto),
ed. Nakano Masao 中野雅夫. Tokyo, 1963.

Hata Ikuhiko 秦郁彦. Gun fascism undō-shi 軍ファシズム運動史 (A history
of the military fascist movement). Tokyo, 1962.

Hatano Kan'ichi 波多野乾一. Chūgoku kyōsantō-shi 中国共産党史
(A history of the Chinese Communist party). 10 vols.; Tokyo,
1961.

Hayashi Gonsuke 林権助. Waga nanajū-nen o kataru 我が七十年を語る
(Reminiscences of my seventy years). Tokyo, 1935.

Hewlett, Sir Meyrick. Forty Years in China. London, 1943.

Hirano Reiji 平野零兒. Manshū no inbōsha: Kōmoto Daisaku no
unmeiteki na ashiato 満洲の陰謀者：河本大作の運命的な足あと
(A conspirator in Manchuria: Fateful steps of Kōmoto Daisaku).
Tokyo, 1959.

Hobart, Alice Tindale. Within the Walls of Nanking. London, 1928.

Hoover, Herbert C. The Cabinet and the Presidency, 1920-1933
(Vol. 1 of his Memoirs). New York, 1952.

Horiuchi Kanjō 堀内干城. Chūgoku no arashi no naka de 中国の嵐の中
で (Amid the storms of China). Tokyo, 1950.

Hornbeck, Stanley K. The United States and the Far East. Boston,
1942.

Howard, Sir Esme. Theatre of Life. 2 vols.; Boston, 1935-1936.

Hsü Sung-ling 徐嵩齡. "I-chiu-erh-ssu-nien Sun Chung-shan te pei-fa
yü Kwang-chou shang-t'uan shih-pien" 一九四二年孫中山的

北伐與廣州商團事變 (Sun Yat-sen's Northern Expedition of 1924 and the Canton Merchants Association incident); Li-shih yen-chiu (Mar. 1956), pp. 59-69.

Hu Hua 胡華. Chung-kuo hsin-min-chu-chu-i ko-ming-shih 中國新民主主義革命史 (A history of China's new democratic revolution). Peking, 1950.

Hua Kang 華崗. Chung-kuo ta-ko-ming-shih 中國大革命史 (A history of China's great revolution). Shanghai, 1932.

Hung Chün-p'ei 洪鈞培. Kuo-min cheng-fu wai-chiao-shih 國民政府外交史 (Diplomatic history of the National government). Shanghai, 1930.

Ichihashi Yamato. Japanese in the United States. Stanford, 1932.

Ikei Masaru 池井優. "Dai-ichiji Feng-Chih sensō to Nihon" 第一次奉直戰爭と日本 (The first Fengtien-Chihli war and Japan); in Gaikōshi oyobi kokusai seiji no shomondai 外交史及び國際政治の諸問題 (Problems in diplomatic history and international politics), pp. 349-378. Tokyo, 1962.

------"Dai-niji Feng-Chih sensō to Nihon" 第二次奉直戰爭と日本 (The second Fengtien-Chihli war and Japan); Hōgaku kenkyū 法學研究 (Journal of law, politics, and sociology), 37.3:48-75 (Mar. 1964).

Imai Seiichi 今井清一. "Shidehara gaikō ni okeru seisaku kettei" 幣原外交における政策決定 (Decision-making in the Shidehara diplomacy); Nenpō seijigaku 年報政治学 (Annals of the Japanese Political Science Association; 1959), pp. 92-112.

Imamura Hitoshi 今村均. "Manshū hi o fuku koro" 満洲火を噴く頃 (When Manchuria was on fire); in Himerareta Shōwa-shi, pp. 60-71.

345

------Kōzoku to kashikan 皇族と下士官 (Imperial families and non-commissioned officers). Vol. 2 of his Kaisōroku 回想録 (Memoirs); Tokyo, 1960.

Inou Dentarō 稲生典太郎. "'Tanaka jōsōbun' o meguru nisan no mondai" 「田中上奏文」をめぐる二三の問題 (Problems of the "Tanaka memorandum"); Kokusai seiji 国際政治 (International relations), No. 26:72-87 (July 1964).

Inukai Ken 犬養健. Yōsukō wa imamo nagarete iru 揚子江は今も流れている(Still flows the Yangtze River). Tokyo, 1960.

Iriye Akira. "Chang Hsüeh-liang and the Japanese," Journal of Asian Studies, 20.1:33-43 (Nov. 1960).

Isaacs, Harold. The Tragedy of the Chinese Revolution. 2nd rev. ed.; Stanford, 1961.

Ishigami Ryōhei 石上良平. Hara Kei botsugo 原敬没後 (After Hara Kei's death). Tokyo, 1960.

Ishii Itarō 石井射太郎. Gaikōkan no isshō 外交官の一生 (The life of a diplomat). Tokyo, 1950.

Israel, Fred L. Nevada's Key Pittman. Lincoln, 1963.

Itō Masanori 伊藤正徳. Gunbatsu kōbōshi 軍閥興亡史 (The rise and fall of the military cliques). 3 vols.; Tokyo, 1958.

Itō Takeo 伊藤武雄. Kōryū to tōfū 黄龍と東風 (The yellow dragon and the east wind). Tokyo, 1964.

Jansen, Marius B. The Japanese and Sun Yat-sen. Cambridge, Mass., 1954.

Jessup, Philip C. Elihu Root. 2 vols.; New York, 1938.

Johnson, Claudius O. Borah of Idaho. New York, 1936.

Kajima Morinosuke 鹿島守之助. Nichi-Bei gaikō-shi 日米外交史 (Diplomatic relations between Japan and the United States). Tokyo, 1958.

Katō Kanji taishō den 加藤寛治大將傳 (The life of Admiral Katō Kanji). Tokyo, 1941.

Kayanuma Hiro 萱沼洋. Chūgoku kakumei yonjū-nen 中國革命四十年 (Forty years of the Chinese revolution). Tokyo, 1954.

Kazama Takashi 風間阜. Kinsei Chūgoku-shi 近世中國史 (Recent Chinese history). Tokyo, 1937.

Kikkawa Gaku 橘川學. Arashi to tatakau tesshō Araki 嵐と闘う哲將荒木 (General Araki fights against a storm). Tokyo, 1955.

KMWH: Ko-ming wen-hsien 革命文献 (Documents of the revolution), ed. Lo Chia-lun 羅家倫. Taipei, 1953-.

Ko-ming wen-hsien, see KMWH.

Kobayashi Yukio 小林幸男. "Nis-So kokkō chōsei no ichi danmen" 日ソ國交調整の一斷面 (An aspect of the normalization of Japanese-Soviet diplomatic relations); Kokusai seiji, No. 6:130-142 (Sept. 1958).

Kodama Yoshio 兒玉譽士夫. Ware yaburetari 我れ敗れたり (I was defeated). Tokyo, 1950.

------Jūsei ransei akusei 銃声乱世悪政 (Rifle shots, confused times, corrupt government). Tokyo, 1961.

Komai Tokuzō 駒井德三. Tairiku shōshi 大陸小志 (Small ambitions on the big continent). Tokyo, 1944.

Kōmoto Daisaku 河本大作. "Watakushi ga Chang Tso-lin o koroshita" 私が張作霖を殺した (I killed Chang Tso-lin); Bungei shunjū 文芸春秋 (Literary miscellany), 32.12:194-201 (Dec. 1954).

Koo Hui-lan. An Autobiography. New York, 1943.

Kuang-chou Wu-han shih-ch'i ko-ming wai-chiao wen-hsien 廣州武漢時期革命外交文献 (Documents of revolutionary diplomacy during the Canton and Wuhan periods), ed. Kao Ch'eng-yüan 高承元. Shanghai, 1933.

347

Kuo-fu nien-p'u 國父年譜 (Chronicle of the father of the nation),
    ed. Lo Chia-lun.   2 vols.; Taipei, 1958.

Kuo Mo-jo 郭沫若.   "Pei-fa t'u-tz'u" 北伐途次 (The Northern
    Expedition); in his Ko-ming ch'un-ch'iu 革命春秋 (History
    of the revolution), Vol. 2.   Shanghai, 1951.

Kuo-wen chou-pao 國聞週報 (Kuowen weekly).   Peking.

Kurihara Ken 栗原健.   Tennō: Shōwa-shi oboegaki 天皇：昭和史覚書
    (The emperor: A memorandum on Showa history).   Tokyo, 1955.

Kutakov, L. N.   Istoriia Sovetsko-Iaponskikh diplomaticheskikh
    otnoshenii.   Moscow, 1962.

Lamont, Thomas W.   Across World Frontiers.   New York, 1950.

Lay, A. C. Hyde.   Four Generations in China, Japan, and Korea.
    Edinburgh and London, 1952.

Leng Shao Chuan and Norman D. Palmer.   Sun Yat-sen and Communism.
    New York, 1960.

Levi, Werner.   Modern China's Foreign Policy.   Minneapolis, 1953.

Li Chien-nung.   The Political History of China, 1840-1928, tr.
    Teng Ssu-yu and Jeremy Ingalls.   New York, 1956.

Liu, F. F.   Military History of Modern China, 1924-1949.
    Princeton, 1956.

Lockwood, William W.   Economic Development of Japan: Growth and
    Structural Change, 1868-1938.   Princeton, 1954.

MacNair, H. F. and Donald F. Lach.   Modern Far Eastern International
    Relations.   2nd ed.; New York, 1955.

Man-Mō jijō 満蒙事情 (Manchurian and Mongolian affairs), ed.
    South Manchuria Railway Research Bureau.   Dairen.

Mantetsu chōsa shiryō 満鉄調査資料 (South Manchuria Railway
    documents).   Dairen.

Matsubara Kazuo 松原一雄. Kokusai kankei tsūkan 國際關係通鑑 (International affairs yearbook). Tokyo, 1928, 1929.

Maxon, Yale C. Control of Japanese Foreign Policy: A Study of Civil-Military Rivalry, 1930-1945. Berkeley and Los Angeles, 1957.

McKenna, Marian C. Borah. Ann Arbor, 1961.

Min-kuo shih-wu-nien i-ch'ien chih Chiang Chieh-shih hsien-sheng 民國十五年以前之蔣介石先生 (Chiang Kai-shek before 1926), ed. Mao Szu-ch'eng 毛思誠. 20 vols.; n.p., n.d.

Minami Jirō 南次郎, ed. Mitarai Tatsuo 御手洗辰雄. Tokyo, 1957.

Mori Kaku 森恪, ed. Yamaura Kan'ichi 山浦貫一. Tokyo, 1940.

Morin, Relman. East Wind Rising: A Long View of the Pacific Crisis. New York, 1960.

Morishima Morito 森島守人. Inbō ansatsu guntō 陰謀暗殺軍刀 (Conspiracies, assassinations, swords). Tokyo, 1950.

Morison, Elting E. Turmoil and Tradition: A Study of the Life and Times of Henry L. Stimson. Boston, 1960.

Morton, Louis. "War Plan 'Orange': Evolution of a Strategy," World Politics, 11.2:221-250 (Jan. 1959).

------Strategy and Command: The First Two Years. Washington, 1963.

Moulton, Harold S. Japan: An Economic and Financial Appraisal. Washington, 1931.

Naitō Juntarō 內藤順太郎. Zai-Shina bōseki sōgi 在支那紡績爭議 (Strikes at cotton mills in China). Tokyo, 1925.

Nakamura Takahide 中村隆英. "Go-sanjū jiken to zaikabō" 五卅事件と在華紡 (The May 30th incident and the cotton spinning industry in China); in Kindai Chūgoku kenkyū 近代中國研究 (Studies in modern China), 6:99-169 (Tokyo, 1964).

349

Nashimoto Yūhei 梨本祐平. Chūgoku no naka no Nihonjin 中國の中の日本人 (Japanese in China). 2 vols.; Tokyo, 1958.

Neumann, William L. "Ambiguity and Ambivalence in Ideas of National Interest in Asia," in Alexander De Conde, ed., Isolation and Security, pp. 133-158. Durham, N.C., 1957.

------America Encounters Japan: From Perry to MacArthur. Baltimore, 1963.

NGN: Nihon gaikō nenpyō narabi shuyō bunsho 日本外交年表並主要文書 (Chronology and main documents of Japanese foreign policy), ed. Gaimushō. 2 vols.; Tokyo, 1955.

Nichi-Bei bunka kōshō-shi 日米文化交渉史 (History of Japanese-American cultural relations), Vol. 2: Tsūshō sangyō hen 通商産業編 (Trade and industry), ed. Ohara Keishi 小原敬士. Tokyo, 1954.

Nihon gaikō nenpyō narabi shuyō bunsho, see NGN.

North China Herald. Shanghai.

North, Robert C. and Xenia J. Eudin. M.N. Roy's Mission to China: The Communist-Kuomintang Split of 1927. Berkeley and Los Angeles, 1963.

Obata Yūkichi 小幡酉吉, ed. Ujita Naoyoshi 宇治田直義. Tokyo, 1957.

Ogata, Sadako N. Defiance in Manchuria: The Making of Japanese Foreign Policy, 1931-1932. Berkeley and Los Angeles, 1964.

Ōhata Tokushirō 大畑篤四郎. "Washington kaigi kaisai to Nichi-Bei kankei" ワシントン会議と日米関係 (The convening of the Washington Conference and Japanese-American relations); Kokusai seiji, No. 17:91-106 (Dec. 1961).

------"Washington kaigi Nihon seifu kunrei ni tsuite no kōsatsu" ワシントン会議日本政府訓令についての考察 (A study of the Japanese government's instructions to the delegates at the Washington Conference); in Gaikōshi oyobi kokusai seiji no shomondai, pp. 255-274.

Okada Keisuke 岡田啟介. Tokyo, 1956.

Okano Masujirō 岡野増次郎. Wu P'ei-fu 吳佩孚. Tokyo, 1937.

Osgood, Robert E. Ideals and Self-Interest in America's Foreign Relations: The Great Transformation of the Twentieth Century. Chicago, 1953.

Ōtani Keijirō 大谷敬二郎. Rakujitsu no joshō: Shōwa. rikugun-shi 落日の序章：昭和陸軍史 (Prelude to the setting sun: History of the army during the Showa era), Vol. 1. Tokyo, 1959.

Paauw, Douglas. "The Kuomintang and Economic Stagnation, 1928-1937," Journal of Asian Studies, 16.2:213-220 (Feb. 1957).

Pan Shū-lan. The Trade of the United States with China. New York, 1924.

Papers Relating to the Foreign Relations of the United States, see FRUS.

Peking shūhō 北京週報 (Peking weekly). 1921-1931.

Perkins, Dexter. "The Department of State and American Public Opinion," in Gordon A. Craig and Felix Gilbert, eds., The Diplomats, 1919-1939, pp. 282-308. Princeton, 1953.

Piggott, Francis S. G. Broken Thread. Hampshire, England, 1950.

Pollard, Robert T. China's Foreign Relations, 1917-1931. New York, 1933.

Powell, John B. My Twenty-Five Years in China. New York, 1945.

Pratt, Sir John. War and Politics in China. London, 1943.

Preliminary 50 Biographies, ed. Howard L. Boorman. New York, 1960.

Pusey, Merlo J. Charles Evans Hughes. 2 vols.; New York, 1952.

Remer, Charles F. Foreign Investments in China. New York, 1933.

------A Study of Chinese Boycotts. Baltimore, 1935.

Renouvin, Pierre. La Question d'Extrême-Orient, 1840-1940.
Paris, 1947.

------Histoire des relations internationales, Vols. 7 and 8.
Paris, 1957, 1958.

Rōyama Masamichi 蝋山政道 . "Manshū mondai o meguru Nichi-
Bei gaikō no sōten" 満洲問題をめぐる日米外交の争点
(Points of conflict between Japan and the United States concerning
Manchuria); in Ueda Toshio, ed., Kindai Nihon gaikō-shi no
kenkyū 近代日本外交史の研究 (Studies in modern Japanese
diplomatic history), pp. 541-562. Tokyo, 1956.

Saikin Shina kankei shomondai tekiyō 最近支那関係諸問題摘要
(Summaries of recent problems relating to China), ed. Gaimushō.
Tokyo.

Saitō Yoshie 斉藤良衛 . Azamukareta rekishi: Matsuoka to sangoku
dōmei no rimen 欺れた歴史：松岡と三國同盟の裏面
(The betrayal of history: Inside stories of Matsuoka and the
Axis alliance). Tokyo, 1955.

Sakurauchi Yukio 櫻内幸雄 . Jiden 自傳 (Autobiography).
Tokyo, 1952.

Sasaki Tōitsu 佐々木到一. Wuhan ka Nanking ka 武漢乎南京乎
(Wuhan or Nanking ?). Tokyo, 1927.

------Aru gunjin no jiden 或る軍人の自傳 (Autobiography of a soldier).
Tokyo, 1963.

Satō Kenryō 佐藤賢了 . Tōjō Hideki to Taiheiyō sensō 東條英機
と太平洋戦争 (Tōjō Hideki and the Pacific War). Tokyo, 1960.

Satō Shunzō 佐藤俊三 . Shina no kokunai tōsō 支那の國内闘争
(The internal struggle in China). Tokyo, 1941.

Savvin, V. P. Vzaimootnosheniia Tsarskoi Rosii i SSSR s Kitaem.
Moscow, 1930.

Scalapino, Robert A.　Democracy and the Party Government in Prewar
　　Japan: The Failure of the First Attempt.　Berkeley and Los
　　Angeles, 1953.

Schwartz, Benjamin I.　Chinese Communism and the Rise of Mao.
　　Cambridge, Mass., 1952.

Segawa Yoshinobu 瀨川善信 .　"1924-nen Beikoku imin-hō to Nihon
　　gaikō" 1924 年米國移民法ヒ日本外交 (The American
　　immigration act of 1924 and Japanese diplomacy); Kokusai seiji,
　　No. 26:55-71 (July 1964).

Shao Ting-hsün 邵鼎勛 .　"Chung-kuo ti-i-tz'u ko-ming chan-cheng
　　shih-ch'i ti Mei-Jih kou-chieh" 中國第一次革命戰爭時期
　　的美日勾結　(American and Japanese imperialistic collaboration
　　in China during China's first revolutionary war); Li-shih yen-chiu
　　(Aug. 1958), pp. 11-30.

Shidehara Kijūrō 幣原喜重郎 .　Gaikō gojū-nen 外交五十年 (Fifty
　　years of diplomacy).　Tokyo, 1951.

Shidehara Kijūrō, ed. Ujita Naoyoshi 宇治田直義 .　Tokyo, 1955.

Shigemitsu Mamoru 重光葵 .　Shōwa no dōran 昭和の動乱 (Tribulations
　　of the Showa era).　2 vols.; Tokyo, 1952.

------Gaikō kaisōroku 外交回想錄 (Diplomatic memoirs).　Tokyo,
　　1953.

Shina kindai no seiji keizai 支那近代の政治経済　(Modern China's
　　politics and economy), ed. Nikka jitsugyō kyōkai 日華実業協
　　会 (Sino-Japanese Business Association).　Tokyo, 1931.

Shinobu Junpei 信夫淳平 .　Taishō gaikō jūgo-nen 大正外交五十年
　　(Diplomatic history of the fifteen years of the Taisho era).
　　Tokyo, 1927.

------Man-Mō tokushu ken'eki-ron 満蒙特殊権益論　(A study
　　of Japan's special rights and interests in Manchuria and
　　Mongolia).　Tokyo, 1932.

353

Shinobu Seizaburō 信夫清三郎．Taishō democracy-shi 大正デモクラシー 史 (History of the Taisho democracy). 3 vols.; Tokyo, 1954-1959.

Shinohara Hajime 篠原一 and Mitani Taichirō 三谷太一郎, eds. Kindai Nihon no seiji shidō 近代日本の政治指導 (Political leadership in modern Japan). Tokyo, 1965.

Sokolsky, George E. The Tinder Box of Asia. New York, 1932.

Sonoda Ikki 園田一亀 . Kaiketsu Chang Tso-lin 快傑張作霖 (Chang Tso-lin, the hero). Tokyo, 1922.

Special Tariff Conference on the Chinese Customs Treaty (October 1925-April 1926), The, ed. Chinese Foreign Ministry. Peking, 1928.

Sprout, Harold and Margaret. Toward a New Order of Sea Power: American Naval Policy and the World Scene, 1918-1922. Princeton, 1940.

Stanton, Edwin F. Brief Authority: Excursions of a Common Man in an Uncommon World. New York, 1956.

Stimson, Henry L. and McGeorge Bundy. On Active Service in Peace and War. New York, 1948.

Stuart, John L. Fifty Years in China. New York, 1954.

Suematsu Taihei 末松太平．Watakushi no Shōwa-shi 私の昭和史 (My story of the Showa era). Tokyo, 1963.

Suma Yakichirō 須磨彌吉郎 . Gaikō hiroku 外交秘録 (Confidential diplomatic reminiscences). Tokyo, 1956.

Sun Chung-shan hsüan-chi 孫中山選集 (Collected works of Sun Yat-sen). 2 vols.; Peking: Jen-min ch'u-pan she 人民出版社 , 1956.

Survey of International Affairs, ed. Arnold J. Toynbee. London.

Tai-Shi kaikoroku 対支回顧録 (Biographies of men active in China), ed. Tai-Shi kōrōsha denki hensankai 対支功労者傳記編纂会 (Biographical commission on activities in China). 4 vols.; Tokyo, 1936.

354

Taiheiyō sensō e no michi: Kaisen gaikō-shi 太平洋戦争への道: 開戦外交史 (The road to the Pacific War: Diplomatic history of the opening of the war), ed. Kokusai seiji gakkai 國際政治学会 (Japan Association of International Relations). 8 vols.; Tokyo, 1962-1963.

Taishō democracy ki no seiji: Matsumoto Gōkichi seiji nisshi 大正デモクラシー期の政治:松本剛吉政治日誌、 (Politics of the Taisho democracy: Matsumoto Gōkichi political diary), ed. Oka Yoshitake 岡義武 and Hayashi Shigeru 杯茂. Tokyo, 1959.

Takagi Seiju 高木清壽. Tōa no chichi Ishihara Kanji 東亜の父石原莞爾 (Ishihara Kanji, the father of East Asia). Tokyo, 1954.

Takeuchi, S. Tatsuji. War and Diplomacy in the Japanese Empire. Chicago, 1935.

Tanaka Giichi denki 田中義一傳記 (Biography of Tanaka Giichi). 2 vols.; Tokyo, 1958, 1960.

Tang, Peter S. H. Russian and Soviet Policy in Manchuria and Outer Mongolia, 1911-1931. Durham, N. C., 1959.

Thompkins, Pauline. American-Russian Relations in the Far East. New York, 1949.

Tilley, Sir John. London to Tokyo. London, 1942.

Tokonami Takejiro 麻次竹二郎. Tokyo, 1939.

Tokyo Asahi shimbun 東京朝日新聞.

Tong, Hollington K. Chiang Kai-shek: Soldier and Statesman. 2 vols.; Shanghai, 1937.

Tōyama Shigeki 遠山茂樹, Imai Seiichi 今井清一, and Fujiwara Akira 藤原彰. Shōwa-shi 昭和史 (History of the Showa era). Rev. ed.; Tokyo, 1959.

Tupper, Eleanor and George E. McReynolds. Japan in American Public Opinion. New York, 1937.

Ugaki Kazushige 宇垣一成 . Ugaki nikki 宇垣日記 (Ugaki diary).
Tokyo, 1954.

Usui Katsumi 臼井勝美 . "Chang Tso-lin bakushi no shinsō"
張作霖爆死の真相 (The truth about Chang Tso-lin's
accidental death); in Himerareta Shōwa-shi, pp. 26-28.

------"Go-sanjū jiken to Nihon" 五卅事件と日本 (The May 30th incident
and Japan); Aziya kenkyū, 4.2:43-64 (Oct. 1957).

------"Shidehara gaikō oboegaki" 幣原外交覚書 (A memorandum
on the Shidehara diplomacy); Nihon rekishi 日本歴史 (Japanese
history), No. 126:62-68 (Dec. 1958).

------"Shōwa shoki no Chū-Nichi kankei: Hokubatsu e no kanshō"
昭和初期の中日関係：北伐への干渉 (Sino-Japanese
relations during the early Showa period: The intervention in the
Northern Expedition); in Kokushiron-shū 國史論集 (Essays in
Japanese history), 2 vols. (Kyoto, 1959), II, 1657-72.

------"Tanaka gaikō ni tsuite no oboegaki" 田中外交についての覚書
(A memorandum on the Tanaka diplomacy); Kokusai seiji,
No. 11:26-35 (Jan. 1960).

Varg, Paul A.   Missionaries, Chinese, and Diplomats: The American
Protestant Missionary Movement in China, 1890-1952.
Princeton, 1958.

Vespa, Amleto.   Secret Agent of Japan: A Handbook to Japanese
Imperialism. London, 1938.

Vinacke, Harold H.   A History of the Far East in Modern Times.
6th ed.; New York, 1959.

Vinson, John Chalmers.   The Parchment Peace: The United States
Senate and the Washington Conference, 1921-1922. Athens, Ga.,
1955.

------William E. Borah and the Outlawry of War. Athens, Ga., 1957.

------"The Imperial Conference of 1921 and the Anglo-Japanese Alliance," Pacific Historical Review, 31.3:257-266 (Aug. 1962).

Wheeler, Gerald E. "Isolated Japan: Anglo-American Diplomatic Cooperation, 1927-1936," Pacific Historical Review, 30.2:165-178 (May 1961).

------Prelude to Pearl Harbor: The United States Navy and the Far East, 1921-1931. Columbia, Mo., 1963.

Whiting, Allen S. Soviet Policies in China, 1917-1924. New York, 1954.

Wilbur, C. Martin and Julie Lien-ying How. Documents on Communism, Nationalism, and Soviet Advisers in China, 1918-1927. New York, 1956.

Willert, Arthur. The Empire in the World. Oxford, 1937.

Williams, William A. "China and Japan: A Challenge and a Choice of the 1920's," Pacific Historical Review, 26.3:259-279 (Aug. 1957).

Wilson, Hugh R. Diplomat between Wars. New York, 1941.

Wright, Stanley F. China's Struggle for Tariff Autonomy, 1843-1938. Shanghai, 1938.

Wu-sa t'ung-shih 五卅痛史 (A lamentable story about the May 30th incident), ed. Ch'en-pao 晨報 editorial staff and the Tsinghua Student Association. Peking, 1925.

Yamamoto Jōtarō denki 山本条太郎傳記 (Biography of Yamamoto Jōtarō). Tokyo, 1942.

Yanaga Chitoshi. Japan since Perry. New York, 1949.

Yanaibara Tadao 矢内原忠雄 . Manshū mondai 満洲問題 (The Manchurian question). Tokyo, 1934.

Yoshihashi Takehiko. Conspiracy at Mukden: The Rise of the Japanese Military. New Haven, 1963.

357

Yoshizawa Kenkichi 芳沢謙吉 . Gaikō rokujū-nen 外交六十年
  (Sixty years of diplomacy). Tokyo, 1958.

Young, Arthur N.   China and the Helping Hand, 1937-1945. Cambridge,
  Mass., 1963.

Zhukov, E. M.   Mezdunarodnye otnosheniia na Dal'nem Vostoke
  1840-1949. Moscow, 1956.

Akashi Teruo　明石照男

Anganki　昂昂溪

Ankuochun　安國軍

Arita Hachirō　有田八郎

Chang Chi　張継

Chang Ch'i-yün　張其昀

Chang Ch'ün　張群

Chang Fa-k'uei　張發奎

Chang Hsüeh-liang　張學良

Chang Tso-lin　張作霖

Chang Tsung-ch'ang　張宗昌

Ch'ang Yin-huai　常蔭槐

Changchun　長春

Changsha　長沙

Chekiang　浙江

Ch'en Chiung-ming　陳炯明

Ch'en Kung-po　陳公博

Ch'en Tu-hsiu　陳獨秀

Ch'en Yu-jen　陳友仁

Ch'eng Ch'ien　程潛

Chiang Kai-shek　蔣介石

Chihli　直隸

Ch'ing-tang shih-lu　清黨實錄

Chu Teh　朱德

Chungking　重慶

"Dai-ichiji dai-niji Man-Mō dokuritsu undō"　第一次第二次満蒙独立運動

Dairen　大連

Debuchi Katsuji　出淵勝次

Etō Toyoji　江藤豊二

Fang Sheng-t'ou　方聲濤

feng p'iao　奉票

Feng Yü-hsiang　馮玉祥

Fengtien　奉天

Fukuda Hikosuke　福田彦助

genrō　元老

Gotō Shimpei　後藤新平

Hailin　海林

Hailung　海龍

Hakone　箱根

Hamaguchi Osachi　浜口雄幸

Hanaya Tadashi　花谷正

Hangchow　杭州

Hankow　漢口

Hanyang　漢陽

Hara Kei　原敬

Harbin　哈爾濱

Hashimoto Kingorō　橋本欣五郎

Hata Ikuhiko	秦郁彦	Kawakami Toshitsune	川上俊彦
Hayashi Gonsuke	林権助	Kenseikai	憲政會
Hayashi Kyūjirō	林久治郎	Kiangsu	江蘇
Ho Yao-tsu	賀耀祖	Kiaochow	膠州
Ho Ying-ch'in	何應欽	Kimura Eiichi	木村鋭市
Honjō Shigeru	本庄繁	Kirin	吉林
Hori Yoshiatsu	堀義貴	Kita Ikki	北一輝
Hosoya Chihiro	細谷千博	Kiukiang	九江
Hsiakwan	下関	Kiyoura Keigo	清浦奎吾
Hsieh Ch'ih	謝持	Kobe	神戸
Hsinchiu	新邱	Koiso Kuniaki	小磯國秋
Hsinho	新河	"Kokuminteki dokuritsu to kokka risei"	國民的独立と國家理性
Hsuchow	徐州		
Hsü Ch'ien	徐謙	Kōmoto Daisaku	河本大作
Hu Han-min	胡漢民	Kumamoto	熊本
Huang Fu	黄郛	Kunchow	袞州
Hulutao	葫蘆島	Kuo Sung-ling	郭松齢
Hunan	湖南	Kuominchun	國民軍
		Kuzuu Yoshihisa	葛生能久
Ichang	宜昌	Kwangsi	廣西
Imamura Hitoshi	今村均	Kwangtung	廣東
Inoue Junnosuke	井上準之助	Kwantung	関東
Ishihara Kanji	石原莞爾		
Ishii Kikujirō	石井菊次郎	Li Chi-shen	李済琛
Itagaki Seishirō	板垣征四郎	Li Li-san	李立三
		Li Shih-tseng	李石曽
Kaifeng	開封	Li Tsung-jen	李宗仁
Kailu	開魯	Li Yüan-hung	黎元洪
Kainei	會寧	Liao Chung-k'ai	廖仲愷
Katō Takaaki	加藤高明		

Lincheng 臨城
Liu Hsiang 劉湘
Liuli 琉璃
Lushan 廬山

Machino Takema 町野武馬
Manchuli 満洲里
Mao Tse-tung 毛澤東
Matsui Iwane 松井石根
Minami Jirō 南次郎
Minseitō 民政党
Miyake Mitsuharu 三宅光春
Mo Te-hui 莫德惠
Mori Kaku 森恪
Morioka Shōhei 森岡正平
Morishima Morito 森島守人
Muraoka Chōtarō 村岡長太郎

Nagata Tetsuzan 永田鉄山
Nakamura Shintarō 中村震太郎
Nakayama Jiichi 中山治一
Nanchang 南昌
Nemoto Hiroshi 根本博
Nichi-Ro sensō igo 日露戦争以後
Nihon kin'yū-shi 日本金融史
Nishida Kōichi 西田畊一
Nishida Zei 西田税
Nishihara 西原

Obata Yūkichi 小幡酉吉
Oka Yoshitake 岡義武

Ōkawa Shūmei 大川周明

Pai Ch'ung-hsi 白崇禧
P'eng Te-huai 彭德懐

Saburi Sadao 佐分利貞夫
Saitō Tsune 斉藤恆
Sakonji Seizō 左近司政三
"Sakurakai shuisho" 桜会趣意書
Seiyūkai 政友会
Shameen 沙面
Shanghai 上海
Shanhaikwan 山海関
Shantung 山東
Shidehara Kijūrō 幣原喜重郎
Shigemitsu Mamoru 重光葵
Shigetō Chiaki 重藤千秋
Shih Yu-san 石友三
"Shina o mokugeki shite" 支那を
　目撃して

Siberia shuppei no shiteki kenkyū
　シベリヤ出兵の史的研究
"Siberia shuppei o meguru Nichi-Bei
　kankei" シベリヤ出兵をめぐる
　日米関係
Solun 索倫
Soong, T. V. (Sung Tzu-wen) 宋子文
Sun Ch'uan-fang 孫傳芳
Sun Fo 孫科
Sun Yat-sen 孫逸仙
Sung Mei-ling 宋美齢

Suzuki Norihisa 鈴木憲久	Uchida Yasuya 内田康哉
Sze, Alfred (Shih Chao-chi) 施肇基	Ugaki Kazushige 宇垣一成
Tahushan 打虎山	Wakatsuki Reijirō 若槻禮次郎
Tai-Bei kokusakuron-shū 対米國策論集	Wang, C.T. (Wang Cheng-t'ing) 王正廷
Tai Chi-t'ao 戴季陶	Wang Ching-wei 汪精衛
Taian 泰安	Wang Ch'ung-hui 王寵惠
Takao Tōru 高尾享	Wang Yung-chiang 王永江
Taku 大沽	Wanhsien 萬縣
Talai 大賚	Wanpaoshan 萬寶山
Tanaka Giichi 田中義一	Washizawa Yoshiji 鷲澤与四二
Tangchiachuang 黨家莊	Weihaiwei 威海衛
Tangku 塘沽	Whampoa 黃埔
Tang-shih kai-yao 黨史概要	Wu, C.C. (Wu Ch'ao-shu) 伍朝樞
T'ang Shao-yi 唐紹儀	Wu Chih-hui 吳稚暉
T'ang Sheng-chih 唐生智	Wu P'ei-fu 吳佩孚
Taonan 洮南	Wuchang 五常
Tatekawa Yoshitsugu 建川美次	Wuchang 武昌
Tientsin 天津	Wuhan 武漢
Tōjō Hideki 東條英機	Wuhu 蕪湖
Tsinan 済南	
Tsingtao 青島	Yada Shichitarō 矢田七太郎
Tsining 済寧	Yamagata Aritomo 山縣有朋
Tsitsihar 齊齊哈爾	Yamamoto Gombei 山本權兵衛
Tu Hsi-kuei 杜錫珪	Yamamoto Jōtarō 山本条太郎
Tuan Ch'i-jui 段琪瑞	Yang Chieh 楊杰
Tumen 圖們	Yang Sen 楊森
Tungliao 通遼	Yang Yü-t'ing 楊宇霆
Tunhwa 敦化	Yangtsun 楊村
	Yen Hsi-shan 閻錫山

Yenki 延吉
Yingkow 營口
Yoshida Shigeru 吉田茂
Yoshizawa Kenkichi 芳澤謙吉
Yüan Shih-k'ai 袁世凱

INDEX